SHAKESPEARE SURVEY

SHAKESPEARE SURVEY

AN ANNUAL SURVEY OF SHAKESPEARIAN STUDY AND PRODUCTION

23

EDITED BY
KENNETH MUIR

CAMBRIDGE
AT THE UNIVERSITY PRESS
1970

Published by the Syndics of the Cambridge University Press
Bentley House, 200 Euston Road, London N.W.1
American Branch: 32 East 57th Street, New York, N.Y.10022

Library of Congress Catalogue Card Number: 49-1639

Standard Book Number: 521 07903 9

Shakespeare Survey was first published in 1948. For the first eighteen volumes it was edited by Allardyce Nicoll under the sponsorship of the University of Birmingham, the University of Manchester, the Royal Shakespeare Theatre and the Shakespeare Birthplace Trust

Printed in Great Britain
at the University Printing House, Cambridge
(Brooke Crutchley, University Printer)

EDITOR'S NOTE

Four articles in the present volume (by Michel Grivelet, Harold Fisch, Edward Wilson and Kenneth Muir) were written in honour of Geoffrey Bullough on his retirement.

As previously announced, *Shakespeare Survey 24* will include some of the papers from the International Conference—entitled 'Shakespeare: Theatre Poet'—which is to be held at Stratford-upon-Avon in 1970. The central theme of No. 25 will be 'Shakespeare's Problem Plays'. Contributions on that or other subjects, which should not normally exceed 5000 words, should reach the Editor (Department of English Literature, University of Liverpool, P.O. Box 147, Liverpool, L69 3BX) by 1 September 1971.

Since the last issue went to press, three eminent Shakespearians have died. John Dover Wilson and Peter Alexander were members of the original Advisory Board and Peter Ure was a member at the time of his death.

K.M.

CONTRIBUTORS

BRIDGET CUSACK, *Lecturer in English, University of Edinburgh*

GARETH LLOYD EVANS, *Senior Lecturer and Staff Tutor in Literature, Extra-Mural Department, University of Birmingham*

HAROLD FISCH, *Professor of English, Bar-Ilan University, Israel*

R. A. FOAKES, *Professor of English, University of Kent*

HANS WALTER GABLER, *Lecturer in English, University of Munich*

MICHEL GRIVELET, *Professor of English, University of Dijon*

WERNER HABICHT, *Professor of English, University of Heidelberg*

G. R. HIBBARD, *Reader in English, University of Nottingham*

KENNETH HUDSON, *Senior Lecturer, Centre for Adult Studies, Bath University of Technology*

KENNETH MUIR, *Professor of English Literature, University of Liverpool*

RICHARD PROUDFOOT, *Lecturer in English, King's College, University of London*

D. F. ROWAN, *Professor of English, University of New Brunswick*

VIVIAN SALMON, *Reader in English, Bedford College, University of London*

LEAH SCRAGG, *Lecturer in English, University of Manchester*

G. V. SMITHERS, *Professor of English, University of Durham*

EDWARD M. WILSON, *Professor of Spanish, University of Cambridge*

CONTENTS

PLATES

Plates I and II are reproduced by permission of the Provost and Fellows of Worcester College, Oxford; plates III–VII are reproduced by permission of the Governors of the Royal Shakespeare Theatre.

SHAKESPEARE AND THE TUNE OF THE TIME

BRIDGET CUSACK

Linguistic changes do not occur overnight. At any point along the development of English, old and new usages coexist, sometimes as sheer alternatives, sometimes with overtones on the one side or on the other of obsolescence, up-to-dateness, formality or colloquialism fitting them to one register or variety of English rather than to another. Exploitation of the possibilities created by this situation in its late sixteenth and early seventeenth century form is an essential part of Shakespeare's dramatic and poetic technique, and to recognize that in a particular scene, speech or line, or in one character, he is making use of the shifting linguistic conditions of his time is to see more of his skill as a manipulator of language, as well as to understand better the particular incident involved.

In *Romeo and Juliet* for example, just before the Balcony scene, Mercutio has a longish speech in which he mocks Romeo's infatuation with Rosaline by calling after him:

Romeo, Humours, Madman, Passion, Louer,
Appeare thou in the likenesse of a sigh,
Speake but one rime, and I am satisfied:
Cry me but ay me, Pro[nounce] but Loue and d[oue],
Speake to my goship *Venus* one faire word,
One Nickname for her purblind Sonne and her,
Young *Abraham Cupid* he that shot so true,
When King *Cophetua* lou'd the begger Maid,
He heareth not, he stirreth not, he moueth not,
The Ape is dead, I must coniure him,
I coniure thee by *Rosalines* bright eyes,
By her High forehead, and her Scarlet lip,
By her Fine foote, Straight leg, and Quiuering thigh,
And the Demeanes, that there Adiacent lie,
That in thy likenesse thou appeare to vs.
(657a, 1–15; II, i, 7–21)[1]

It is evident that there are two parts to this pseudo-conjuration, the first extending as far as 'the begger Maid', and the second beginning at 'I coniure thee', and in presentation the actor would no doubt assume a special delivery to suit the nature of the burlesque in each part. The problem is, however, the two intervening lines:

He heareth not, he stirreth not, he moueth not,
The Ape is dead, I must coniure him.

Are these also part of the mock-ritual summons? Or are they spoken by Mercutio as an interjected comment in his own normal voice and tone? Are both lines even alike in this?

There is a possible clue for the second line in the use of 'Ape'. As a kind of affectionate-abuse term it is properly suited to Mercutio's normal style. Comparison with other Shakespearian instances confirms that it has no special ranting status. Lady Hotspur, for instance, uses it to her husband:

Cut you mad-headed Ape,
(357b, 11; *1 Hen. IV,* II, iii, 80)

[1] In the line-references (except for the poems and *Pericles*) the first entry in each case gives the 1623 Folio reference, with page-numbering as in the 1955 Yale/Oxford and the 1864 Lionel Booth facsimiles, followed by the column and line-number, and the second entry is by act, scene, and line as in the Globe edition of Shakespeare's *Works*.

and Doll Tearsheet addresses Falstaff by it:

> Ah, you sweet little Rogue, you: alas, poore Ape, how thou sweat'st?
> (385 b, 64–5; *2 Hen. IV*, II, iv, 233–4)

But the evidence on this line can only be rated as non-commital, although it seems likely that it is introductory comment to the section in high-style, rather than part of it.

In the line that precedes it, on the other hand, the grammar is the key; that is, that all three verbs are given an *-eth* inflexion, and that the three negatives follow the pattern verb+*not*. Both syntax and morphology here are according to perfectly acceptable Elizabethan usage, but in each case Shakespeare is employing one of two alternative modes of expression.

The *-eth* inflection for 3rd singular present indicative exists in Shakespeare's time alongside the *-s* inflection we now use. Historically, it is the obsolescent form, the ending prevalent in earlier Southern English, but being replaced by the originally Northern *-s*. That this take-over is only partially complete is indicated by the two verbs *do* and *haue* retaining *doth* and *hath* almost exclusively; the use of the form *has*, in fact, is one of the comic characteristics of the Welshman, Fluellen, in *Henry V*.

In other verbs the old and new inflexions appear together in parallel constructions, and even in the same line, where the alternatives can be of use for purposes of metre, emphasis or mere variety, as in:

> With her, that hateth thee and hates vs all,
> (465 b, 52; *2 Hen. VI*, II, iv, 52)

and:

> He rowseth vp himselfe, and makes a pause.
> (1594 ed. E2r, 2; *Lucrece*, 541)

And yet this apparent interchangeability in usage is confined to verse, and not carried through into Shakespeare's prose, where *-s* is almost invariably used. So that the two inflexions are not equal options, but there is a quality of ordinariness and colloquialism in *-s* which *-eth* does not share, and, conversely, to use *-eth*, as Mercutio does here, is to select the form marked for formality.

The evidence is even clearer in the syntactic characteristics of Mercutio's line, for in writing

> He heareth not, he stirreth not, he moueth not,

Shakespeare is using one of two possible negative constructions, the alternative being the *do*+*not*+verb constructions we use today, and which Shakespeare has in lines such as:

> To her, that is not heere, nor doth not heare.
> (205 a, 41; *A.Y.L.I.*, V, ii, 117)

The verb+*not* method is the older way of expressing negation; the construction with *do* is the newcomer in the process of ousting its predecessor. The stage which this had reached at this period is apparent from a comparison of various Shakespearian instances of the two structures. There are complexities of motivation: selection of verb, for example, can influence the choice of construction, for certain verbs, such as *care*, *doubt* and *fear* appear in the negative without *do* far more often than with it. The selection of accompanying grammatical features can also determine this one, as when *know* used intransitively gives *I know not*, but, with an object:

> I doe not know the French for fer, and ferret, and firke. (423 b, 52–3; *Hen. V*, IV, iv, 32–3)

However, where co-textual considerations such as these do not apply, the relationship between the two negative constructions seems to be the one which subsequent development confirms—that the use of *do* characterizes colloquialism and informality, whereas verb+*not* is a feature of more conservative and formal English. The same can be seen in regard to negative commands, and questions both negative and positive. At the same time, the converse applies to non-negative statements, for there the use of *do* marks formality, except in certain circumstances, such as the very few instances where it is the emphatic *do* of present-day English:

It is no matter, if I do halt, I haue the warres for my colour, and my Pension shall seeme the more reasonable

(380a, 15–16; *2 Hen. IV*, I, ii, 274–6)

or where it is associated, perhaps for emphasis, with verbs such as *confess*, *think* or *believe*:

I doe beleeue the swearer.

(45b, 16; *Merry Wives*, II, ii, 40)

Moreover, there is a close enough association of formality and verse, for verse, if we examine pieces of Shakespearian prose and verse of equal length, almost always to yield higher proportions of those structures which in prose are associated only with special non-colloquial speeches. Thus a very few lines of verse, taken, admittedly, from a royal speech, can provide four examples of the verb + *not* negative, to a single *do not* structure:

I doubt not that, since we are well perswaded
We carry not a heart with vs from hence,
That growes not in a faire consent with ours:
Nor leaue not one behinde, that doth not wish
Successe and Conquest to attend on vs.

(410a, 39–43; *Hen. V*, II, ii, 20–4)

Nevertheless, the difference between the constructions, like the morphological alternatives *-eth* and *-s* is so poised that neither structure is out of place in verse of any type. Thus the lines above include the one *doth not wish*, and in *Romeo and Juliet* Juliet can within a few lines say both:

O sweare not by the Moone,

(658a, 19; *Rom. & Jul.*, II, ii, 109)

and:

Do not sweare at all.

(658a, 23; *Rom. & Jul.*, II, ii, 112)

But again the situation in Shakespearian prose reveals the difference in usage, for outside verse, negatives and questions without *do* are very rare, and non-emphatic statements with *do* are virtually absent.

The way in which this operates can be seen most strikingly where the formal syntactic options rare in prose are used at those points where the situation demands a deliberately assumed mock-heroic style. Thus in *1 Henry IV* the normal question form in prose is exemplified by:

Doest thou heare me, *Hal*?

(359a, 59; II, iv, 233)

But in Falstaff and Hal's play-acting rehearsal of the royal interview, where the medium is still prose, this gives place to the type:

Swearest thou, vngracious Boy?

(361a, 33; II, iv, 490)

Similarly, colloquial negative imperatives in the same play are of the form:

Doe not thou when thou art a King, hang a Theefe.

(351b, 20–1; I, ii, 69–70)

But in Falstaff's burlesque 'King Cambysses' vaine':

Weepe not, sweet Queene, for trickling teares are vaine.

(360b, 44–5; II, iv, 431)

Returning to Mercutio's line, we thus have two definite clues, even disregarding the rhetorical triple repetition of pattern, and both morphology and syntax stamp

He heareth not, he stirreth not, he moueth not

as part of Mercutio's mock-formal, mock-conjuration style.

Shakespearian examples of these same features exploited to similar ends are numerous. There are characters whose speech constantly operates in direct contrast to surrounding colloquialism, particularly Pistol, introduced in *Henry V* by the entrance line:

Base Tyke, cal'st thou mee Hoste?

(409a, 55; II, i, 31)

and assigned this kind of distinctive language throughout, as in:

the Duke of Exeter doth loue thee well

(416b, 15–16; III, vi, 23)

and:

Trayl'st thou the puissant Pyke?
(419b, 48; IV, i, 40)

Several of the linguistic features characterizing Armado in *Love's Labour's Lost* are of similar kind.

Shakespeare also uses the non-colloquial flavour of certain structures in writing plays-within-plays such as *Pyramus and Thisbe* and *The Murder of Gonzago*, where he achieves much of his effect by putting increased emphasis on those features in the language associated with verse, creating a sort of hyper-poetry as a result:

This man, with Lanthorne, dog, and bush of thorne,
Presenteth moone-shine. For if you will know,
By moone-shine did these Louers thinke no scorne
To meet at *Ninus* toombe, there, there to wooe:
This grizy beast (which Lyon hight by name)
The trusty *Thisby*, comming first by night,
Did scarre away, or rather did affright:
And as she fled, her mantle she did fall;
Which Lyon vile with bloody mouth did staine.
(160a, 61–b, 5; *M.N.D.*, v, i, 136–44)

The resources of Early Modern English grammar are not the only linguistic opportunity exploited here. Just as Shakespeare was able to catch English morphology and syntax as they changed, so too the changing vocabulary of English at this period provided him with equally fruitful material.

Vocabulary alters in various ways: words drop out of use, new words are introduced, certain terms become fashionable 'in' words, and shifts of meaning take place. As with grammatical changes, old and new possibilities often exist side by side, but are rarely completely interchangeable.

Where a word goes out of use, for instance, it does so by a process of gradual withdrawal from up-to-date usage, from colloquial varieties, and from spoken English. It goes through the stages of old-fashioned—archaic—understood but not used—obsolete—incomprehensible. Similarly a new word will at first be used in certain registers only, such as up-to-date slang or some technical variety of English, before it is completely assimilated. Thus very many words as part of their total 'meaning' will have a particular status, which will type the user. Often there will be a number of different ways of saying the same thing, all with different overtones of this sort.

Thus, when a Shakespearian character needs to say '(be) called', this can be expressed in terms we still use:

Know sir, that I am cal'd *Hortensio*,
(222b, 19; *T. Shrew*, IV, ii, 21)
a daughter, cal'd *Katerina*,
(215a, 26–7; *T. Shrew*, II, i, 42–3)
my name is *Broome*.
(46a, 62; *Merry Wives*, II, ii, 167)

And there is also the expression, less current nowadays:

a Seruant nam'd *Lucilius*.
(677a, 47; *Timon*, I, i, 111)

These formulae are apparently interchangeable in Early Modern English.

In addition a more complex form was available:

My name is call'd *Vincentio*,
(226a, 51; *T. Shrew*, IV, v, 55)
Is not your name sir call'd *Antipholus*?
(99a, 6; *Com. Errors*, v, i, 286)

Although at first sight this seems a further mere alternative, its occurrence is comparatively rare, and the characters who use it are usually old men: the two instances quoted above are spoken by Lucentio's father in *The Taming of the Shrew*, who is

a man old, wrinckled, faded, withered,
(226a, 39; IV, v, 43)

and whose venerability is his essential characteristic when at Petruchio's instigation Katherine greets him as a 'faire louely Maide', and by the old father of the two Antipholus twins in *The Comedy of Errors*. So when in *Henry V* Pistol announces himself by saying

My name is *Pistol* call'd
(420a, 5; IV, i, 62)

he is using the phraseology of a generation back, and his linguistic alienation from other characters is brought about by the selection of the vocabulary as well as the inversion in the syntax.

A different sort of lexical point arises with further possibilities for '(be) called', in that Shakespeare can in addition employ two terms with yet a more extreme departure from the norm. First, there is the word *hight*. It became outmoded in the standard language in the late medieval period, but was still sufficiently understood, as part of people's passive vocabulary, for Shakespeare to use it. But where he does, it is specifically *because* it is archaic. Thus in *Pericles* the medieval poet, Gower, is given a pseudo 'olde' English in his capacity as Chorus, saying

this Maid
Hight *Philoten*.
(1609 ed., F1v, 13–14; IV, Prol. 17–18)

The Mechanicals' play in *A Midsummer Night's Dream* is, in the lines already quoted above, marked by the same item as linguistically outmoded and rustic:

This grizy beast (which Lyon hight by name).

The second archaic term which the Early Modern English linguistic situation provided Shakespeare with is the verb *clepe*. That this was not so very old-fashioned is apparent from its straightforward use by both Hamlet and Macbeth, but other instances in the plays show that it did carry overtones of a quaint out-of-dateness. In *Love's Labour's Lost* it is put into the mouth of Holofernes, the schoolmaster, as he inveighs against modern advanced pronunciation:

he clepeth a Calf, Caufe: halfe, haufe
(136a, 8–9; V, i, 24–5)

And in past-participle form, prefixed by an archaic *y-* prefix, it serves a double purpose in *The Pageant of the Nine Worthies* in *Love's Labour's Lost*: it not only types the language, but also acts as starting point for a series of puns from the more sophisticated spectators:

Pedant. Iudas I am, ycliped Machabeus.
Dumaine. Iudas Machabeus clipt, is plaine Iudas.
Berowne. A kissing traitor. (142a, 22–4; V, ii, 602–4)

Moreover, just as some words can be said to have as part of their meaning the fact that they have the implication [+archaic], others are of note because they are marked as [+new]. Sir Nathaniel, the word-hunting curate in *Love's Labour's Lost*, is not content with *called*, but extends it:

I did conuerse this *quondam* day with a companion of the Kings, who is intituled, nominated, or called, *Don Adriano de Armatho.* (135b, 52–4; V, i, 6–9)

His additional synonyms are recorded in other mid- and late-sixteenth-century works, but they are still new enough and polysyllabic enough to stand out as neologisms.

Further frequent similar instances of Shakespeare using [+archaic] or [+new] words in his plays can often fail to strike us now. Words distinctly novel then may now be commonplace, and terms already obsolescent in Early Modern English are all too easily classed with words which are obsolete now, but perfectly normal then. Items obsolescent in Shakespeare's time include *eke* 'also', *targe*, *gore*, *dole* 'sorrow', *perdy* and *wight*, whose occurrence chiefly in plays-within-plays and in the speech of characters such as Pistol is noteworthy. New vocabulary is also associated most closely with particular characters, such as Armado,

A man of fire, new words, fashions owne Knight
(123b, 24; *L. L. Lost*, I, i, 179)

and the various characters who in attempting scholarship achieve only malapropism.

Certain other items of Early Modern English vocabulary may be described as [+fashionable];

humour is one such, used by Nym in practically every speech he utters in *Henry V* and *The Merry Wives of Windsor*, and making Page comment:

The humour of it (quoth'a?) heere's a fellow frights English out of his wits ... I neuer heard such a drawling-affecting rogue.

(44b, 9–12; *Merry Wives*, II, i, 142–6)

It is the over-working of the term which arouses adverse comment, and this applies even more to fashionable adjectives, where items freely used elsewhere are ridiculed when employed indiscriminately and too often. Over-worked *sweet* is of this type, mocked by other characters when used by the romantic lover or the courtier, especially where associated with an inanimate noun, or in reference to a person, but without the underlying close relationship which normal speakers use it to indicate:

Berowne. White handed Mistris, one sweet word with thee.
Princess. Hony, and Milke, and Suger: there is three.

(138b, 57–8; *L. L. Lost*, V, ii, 230–1)

Armado. Annointed, I implore so much expence of thy royall sweet breath, as will vtter a brace of words.
Princess. Doth this man serue God?
Berowne. Why aske you?
Princess. He speak's not like a man of God's making.

(141a, 62–b4; *L. L. Lost*, V, ii, 523–9)

Hector. Goodnight sweet Lord *Menelaus*.
Thersites. Sweet draught: sweet quoth-a? sweet sinke, sweet sure.

(592b, 9–11; *Tr. & Cress.*, V, i, 82–4)

Fair has a similar status and reception. Pandarus (who also shows an addiction to *sweet*) adopts it as greeting to Helen and Paris, as part of a planned 'complementall assault':

Pandarus. Faire be to you my Lord, and to all this faire company: faire desires in all faire measure fairely guide them, especially to you faire Queene, faire thoughts be your faire pillow.
Helen. Deere L[ord] you are full of faire words.

(581b, 17–21; *Tr. & Cress.*, III, i, 46–50)

And presumably a similar standing underlies the vocabulary Mercutio finds fault with Tybalt for using as an all-purpose modifier:

The Pox of such antique lisping affecting phantacies, these new tuners of accent: Iesu a very good blade, a very tall man, a very good whore.

(659b, 50–2; *Rom. & Jul.*, II, iv, 29–32)

As well as coming in and out of use and of fashion, words are constantly changing in another way as they shift their meaning. Again, the alteration involves a period when both old and new senses are in circulation, and so material is provided for a special type of word-play in Shakespeare's plays. Most puns depend on the similarity in sound of two distinct words, but there are others which are based on two meanings of the same item, as in Peto's pun on an angry Falstaff:

he frets like a gum'd Veluet.

(356a, 4; *1 Hen. IV*, II, ii, 2)

Here the sense 'is worn away' is the older meaning, and 'is angry' is the newer figurative sense, which since Shakespeare's time has replaced the other. That *both* were available in Early Modern English produces the joke.

It is, moreover, not infrequent to have word-play where one speaker uses a term in one sense, and is taken up by a second who deliberately switches to another meaning for the same word. Of this type is an exchange in *Two Gentlemen of Verona* using the double 'argument' and 'condition' senses of *circumstance:*

Proteus. So, by your circumstance, you call me foole.
Valentine. So, by your circumstance, I feare you'll proue.

(20a, 39–40; I, i, 36–7)

The most striking instance, however, is in *Romeo and Juliet*. Romeo, in love with Rosaline, is trying to stand out against Benvolio's probing to discover who the lady is.

Benvolio attempts a 'now let's be serious about this' approach:

> Tell me in sadnesse, who is that you loue?
> (652b, 45; I, i, 205)

which Romeo parries by switching to the other, newer, sense of *sad*:

> What shall I grone and tell thee?
> (652b, 46; I, i, 206)

When Benvolio refuses to be fobbed off by a quibble, Romeo is driven to a different linguistic prevarication:

> In sadnesse Cozin, I do loue a woman.
> (652b, 50; I, i, 210)

Syntactic ambiguity of surface structure is similarly exploited elsewhere, even leading to explicit comment after an exchange in *Twelfth Night*:

> *Viola.* Saue thee Friend and thy Musick: dost thou liue by thy Tabor?
> *Clown.* No sir, I liue by the Church.
> *Viola.* Art thou a Churchman?
> *Clown.* No such matter sir, I do liue by the Church: For, I do liue at my house, and my house dooth stand by the Church.
> *Viola.* So thou maist say the Kings lyes by a begger, if a begger dwell neer him: or the Church stands by thy Tabor, if thy Tabor stand by the Church.
> *Clown.* You haue said sir: To see this age: A sentence is but a cheu'rill gloue to a good witte, how quickely the wrong side may be turn'd outward.
> (264b, 40–52; III, i, 1–15)

Often, too, the ambiguities involved are not available today, such as that dependent on the ethic dative pronoun in Petruchio's

> knocke me heere soundly
> (212b, 22; *T. Shrew*, I, ii, 8)

which Grumio deliberately misinterprets as direct object, and the ambiguous interrogative pronoun in

> *Longaville.* . . . what is she in the white?
> *Boyet.* A woman somtimes, if you saw her in the light.
> (127b, 19–20; *L. L. Lost*, II, i, 197–8)

The present-day form, *Who is she?*, in which the question would have to be framed, would give no chance for the punning reply and evasion.

Yet further features of English in the Early Modern period gave scope to a writer who was aware of what was written and spoken around him. In regard to morphology, Shakespeare's use of the *-eth/-s* alternative inflections in the verb has already been discussed above. There were also other instances of two forms being available for the same grammatical item. There was, for example, a choice of plural inflections in a few words which at an earlier stage had had weak forms, but were now taken into the majority strong class in normal use. Thus the plural of *eye* was *eyes*, but where Shakespeare wanted to mark old-fashionedness he could bring in the almost obsolete weak plural form *eyne*. With this status it appears in *Pyramus and Thisbe* (160b, 42; *M.N.D.*, V, i, 178), and, in combination with specially selected vocabulary, in the drinking song in *Antony and Cleopatra*:

> *Plumpie Bacchus, with pinke eyne.*
> (841b, 7; II, vii, 121)

Very much more frequently, however, where alternatives in form are available, Shakespeare, as poet rather than as dramatist, appears to select one instead of the other not in order to mark some special kind of English, but simply to achieve the metre or rhyme needed.

This applies also to options of syntax and vocabulary, but in these two, as has been discussed, much more than verse technique is involved. In other linguistic matters, however, versification provides almost the sole motivation for choice; yet in this, too, Shakespeare is using the fact that he happened to live when he did.

In morphology this most frequently involves

the use of alternative forms of past tenses and past participles. For example, in certain verbs the poet can employ as past participles not only forms like *spoken*, *forgotten*, *chosen*, *arisen*, *fallen*, *mistaken*, but also forms made by analogy with the past tense, that is *spoke*, *forgot*, *chose*, *arose*, *fell*, *mistook*. As all these are shorter by a syllable than the forms to which they are options, they suit certain lines of verse better than the more usual participles, as in:

And thereupon these errors are arose.
(99b, 55; *Com. Errors*, v, i, 388)

In other verbs, under the influence of borrowings from Latin past participles in *-ate*, a stem ending in a dental consonant can stand as past participle without the *-ed* it usually has, again providing an alternative shorter by one syllable. Thus alongside:

I was contracted to them both, all three
Now marry in an instant,
(798b, 21–2; *Lear*, v, iii, 228–9)

we have:

For first he was contract to Lady *Lucie*.
(528b, 1; *Rich. III*, iii, vii, 179)

Arising from the coexistence of old and new as alternatives at this particular point of time are the double pronunciations available for many words, in regard to stress, number of syllables, and even sound-quality.

The stress-pattern in many English words has altered since Shakespeare's time. Today *extreme* is stressed on the second syllable whether it is adjective or noun, but in Early Modern English it had this pattern only when a noun, and carried stress on the first syllable when an adjective. Shakespeare thus assigned to it whichever stress-pattern its grammatical function demanded:

Temp'ring extremities with extreame sweete.
(656b, 56; *Rom. & Jul.*, ii, Prol. 14)

Twixt my extreames and me, this bloody knife
Shall play the vmpeere.
(669a, 33–4; *Rom. & Jul.*, iv, i, 62–3)

Alteration in stress, however, is not confined to the period between Shakespeare and ourselves, and in many cases stress was already shifting in Early Modern English. When this is happening in his own time Shakespeare can therefore employ whichever pattern he wants. Thus there occur in *Richard II* both:

The Reuennew whereof shall furnish vs,
(332a, 15; i, iv, 46)

and:

My Manors, Rents, Reuenues, I forgoe;
(344a, 12; iv, i, 212)

and in *Romeo and Juliet*:

For exile hath more terror in his looke,
(665a, 12; iii, iii, 13)

alongside:

And turn'd it to exile, there art thou happy.
(666a, 21; iii, iii, 140)

Our present-day stressing is there, but so also is the pattern that preceded it.

Exploited as often, but less relevant to the present study in that the same opportunities are in existence today to a large extent, are the possibilities of omitting weakly-stressed syllables in certain words, so as to reduce the overall number of syllables. This is a feature of normal spoken English, especially where colloquial varieties are concerned, but in verse there is the option between a full and a reduced form. Of this type is *(vn)naturall*, appearing in the space of one play both with value given to the optional syllable:

And euery thing that seemes vnnaturall,
(428b, 51; *Hen. V*, v, ii, 62)

and with reduction:

How shall we then behold their naturall teares?
(422a, 18; *Hen. V*, iv, ii, 13)

Sometimes such a choice has a basis in linguistic change of the Early Modern period, and the prime instance of this is where an earlier disyllabic ending was altering in Shakespeare's time to a monosyllabic one.

Affected by this development were endings such as *-ial* and *-ion*, which changed at this period from a pronunciation [iəl] and [iən] to [jəl] and [jən]. Shakespeare's versification normally gives words containing these elements a pattern that demands monosyllabic pronunciation:

> To our Pauillion shal I leade you first,
> (575b, 53; *Tr. & Cress.*, I, iii, 305)
> And of it left his Sonne Imperiall Lord,
> (431b, 21; *Hen. V*, V, Epil. 8)
> Most holie and Religious feare it is.
> (759b, 46; *Hamlet*, III, iii, 8)

But although he is employing here what was the current form in his day, he can also use the earlier pronunciation which made two syllables of the ending:

> Desire them all to my Pauillion,
> (419b, 32; *Hen. V*, IV, i, 27)
> The Sword, the Mase, the Crowne Imperiall,
> (421b, 12; *Hen. V*, IV, i, 278)
> Yet for I know thou art Religious.
> (646a, 55; *Tit. And.*, V, i, 74)

It is noticeable that this is particularly associated with line-endings, as is the use of non-reduced forms of words such as *(vn)naturall* quoted above.

Into this category fall also the very many words ending in sequences such as *-cious*, *-sion* and *-tion*, where as well as the reduction of the ending to a monosyllable, palatalization of the preceding consonant was taking place, with the [jə] subsequently reduced further to [ə] to give our present-day [viʃəs] *vicious*, [viʒən] *vision*, and [kwestʃən] *question*. The endings of this group too have the possibility of disyllabic pronunciation in Shakespeare's verse, though the degree of palatalization in the consonant is debateable. So there are contrasts such as:

> For now sits Expectation in the Ayre,
> (408b, 56; *Hen. V*, II, Prol. 8)
> As were a Warre in expectation,
> (412a, 34; *Hen. V*, II, iv, 20)

and:

> For hee is gracious, if hee be obseru'd,
> (359a, 22; *2 Hen. IV*, IV, iv, 30)
> And neuer shall it more be gracious.
> (114b, 56; *Much Ado*, IV, i, 109)

Development in pronunciation and development in morphology are linked in a further instance of this use of an older pronunciation. The *-ed* in the past forms of weak verbs was, by the Early Modern period, given no vowel except, as nowadays, after the dental stops [t] and [d]. Shakespeare therefore writes lines like:

> the Duke
> Hath banisht moodie discontented fury.
> (442b, 31–2; *1 Hen. VI*, III, i, 122–3)

But when he wishes he can revert to the older pronunciation which gave the ending a weakly stressed vowel, and where the verb has a disyllabic stem with stress on the first syllable this can be used to give a pattern suited to the required metre:

> That banished, that one word banished.
> (664b, 28; *Rom. & Jul.*, III, ii, 113)

In many instances both alternatives are used within a single line:

> Hence banished, is banisht from the world.
> (665a, 18; *Rom. & Jul.*, III, iii, 19)

It has been suggested[1] that the reason that the two forms are juxtaposed in lines such as this is more complex than simply the achievement of metrical regularity, and that what is involved is some kind of differentiated emphasis. Certainly, the recurrence of this same feature many times might suggest some sort of underlying motivation for the pattern, but the examples do not appear to share any common factor other than their surface pattern. What is of interest, though, is that in this matter Shakespeare utilizes almost every kind of linguistic alternative where choice lies between options that differ in length by a

[1] By Abbott, §474 (see note 1 on p. 11).

syllable. Thus it is a choice between monosyllabic and disyllabic pronunciation that produces:

> Was it his spirit, by spirits taught to write,
> (1609 ed. F2v, 28; Sonnet 86)

and the omission or retention of the vowel in an ending which allows:

> To this vnlook'd for vnprepared pompe,
> (312a, 8; *K. John*, II, i, 560)

and:

> Which art my neer'st and dearest Enemie.
> (365b, 11; *1 Hen. IV*, III, ii, 123)

And the existence of *-eth* and *-s* is used in:

> Panting he lies, and breatheth in her face.
> (1593 ed. B2r, 20; *Ven. & Adon.*, 62)

Not only metre, but rhyme too shows exploitation of the existence of alternative pronunciations. For where value was given to a normally omitted syllable, a scheme of stress + weak stress + stress was substituted for the scheme stress + (nothing) + weak stress; and in this case the final syllable on which increased stress was laid reverted to the vowel it had before reduction to [ə] or [i]. Thus already in Early Modern English the stress pattern and the vowel of the final syllable in adjectives such as *temperate* was different from those in verbs and nouns such as *celebrate* and *potentate*. *Temperate* consisted of only two syllables, the second being weakly stressed:

> Shee is not hot, but temperate as the morne.
> (217a, 35; *T. Shrew*, II, i, 296)

There was also, however, an older pronunciation which Shakespeare could use, giving the adjective the stress pattern of *celebrate* in three syllables, and making a rhyme with words having stressed *-ate*:

> Shall I compare thee to a Summers day?
> Thou art more louely and more temperate:
> Rough windes do shake the darling buds of Maie,
> And Sommers lease hath all too short a date.
> (1609 ed. B4v, 13–16; Sonnet 18)

Variation in the number of syllables brought about by omitting or pronouncing the vowel in the *-ed* verb ending has been discussed above. This also provided material for rhymes. For although most Shakespearian rhymes employ past tenses and past participles in their normal reduced form, giving rhymes such as *prest* (pressed) *: rest* (150b, 52–3; *M.N.D.*, II, ii, 64–5), *inclind : finde : mind* (1594 ed. L4v, 2–5; *Lucrece*, 1654–7), *Crown'd : round* (841b, 9–10; *Ant. & Cleo.*, II, vii, 123–4), and *beguil'd : childe* (147a, 34–5; *M.N.D.*, I, i, 238–9), yet there are also rhymes based on a fuller pronunciation of *-ed*, such as *murthered : dead* (349b, 34–5; *Rich. II*, V, vi, 39–40) and *widowed : bed* (664b, 49–50; *Rom. & Jul.*, III, ii, 134–5).

In other cases degree of stress and sound-quality are not both involved in the option, but a choice of sound only. Of this type is the *-y* ending; words with this as their final syllable, such as *misery* can be used at the end of a scene to provide a rhyming couplet not only of the variety:

> Doe not draw backe, for we will mourne with thee:
> Oh could our mourning ease thy misery,
> (638a, 14–15; *Tit. And.*, II, iv, 56–7)

but also:

> But Kings and mightiest Potentates must die,
> For that's the end of humane miserie.
> (444b, 24–5; *1 Hen. VI*, III, ii, 136–7)

Even more notable as a pronunciation-alternative peculiar to the Early Modern period is the varying quality of vowel in words showing two developments from Middle English ę̄, such as *sea*. Shakespeare normally rhymes such words with each other (*Seas : ease*, (1609 ed. C1v, 17–18; *Pericles*, II, Prol. 27–8)), but very occasionally etymology is set aside, and then he rhymes not only with Early Modern English [ii] (M.E. ẹ̄), but with [ee] (M.E. *ai*) as well, writing both:

> Man more diuine, the Master of all these,
> Lord of the wide world, and wilde watry seas,
> (87b, 6–7; *Com. Errors*, II, i, 20–1)

and:

> Euery thing that heard him play,
> Euen the Billowes of the Sea.
> (554a, 13–14; *Hen. VIII*, III, i, 9–10)

The nature of this option involves difficulties of interpretation and explanation as to why the two pronunciations existed, and why one eventually became accepted, but the existence of the alternative in this word at least is evident. It seems not unlikely, too, that the *play:Sea* rhyme carried associations of old-fashionedness about it, for the couplet is from a song written into a play, and this is a kind of writing where archaism is frequently used, and, furthermore, this particular song is also given slight archaism in the past tense *sprung*, and in the monosyllabic pattern placed on *Euen* in the second line quoted above.

In every aspect of the language, then, over which Shakespeare had control (that is, in everything but orthographical and typographical matters), he manipulated Early Modern English[1] to suit his own dramatic and poetic ends by exploiting fully the opportunities of selection, both free and loaded, which were open to him because of the time when he lived. Much work has already been done (particularly by Gladys Willcock), moreover, to show that there was in this period a large-scale concern with linguistic issues, and that Shakespeare himself and the society in which he worked (and which he reflected in his plays) were interested in and eager to talk about their language. The whole basis of *Love's Labour's Lost*, and of parts of other plays, such as *Henry V*, lies in this.

What is abundantly evident from the plays is that his audience was expected to—and presumably, therefore, did—hear and respond to linguistic signals which need pointing out

[1] For discussion of the linguistic alternatives and opportunities in Early Modern English and especially their use by Shakespeare see the following works.

Covering several aspects of the language

E. A. Abbott, *A Shakespearean Grammar* (London, 1869; reprinted 1966). Still useful for examples, though less so in classification and interpretation.

W. Franz, *Die Sprache Shakespeares in Vers und Prosa* (Halle, 1939).

Principally on grammar

Alvar Ellegard, *The Auxiliary Do*, Gothenburg Studies in English, 2 (Stockholm, 1953).

Angus McIntosh, '*As You Like It*: A Grammatical Clue to Character', *Review of English Literature*, IV (1963), 68–81.

Vivian Salmon, 'Sentence Structures in Colloquial Shakespearian English', *Transactions of the Philological Society* (London, 1965), pp. 105–40, and 'Elizabethan Colloquial English in the Falstaff Plays', *Leeds Studies in English*, N.S. I (1967), 37–70.

Principally on vocabulary

George Gordon, *Shakespeare's English*, Society for Pure English, Tract 29 (Oxford, 1928).

Principally on pronunciation

N. Chomsky and M. Halle, *The Sound Pattern of English* (New York, 1968).

B. Danielsson, *Studies in the Accentuation of Polysyllabic Latin, Greek, and Romance Loan-Words in English* (Stockholm, 1948).

E. J. Dobson, *English Pronunciation 1500–1700* (Oxford, 1953).

Helge Kökeritz, *Shakespeare's Pronunciation* (New Haven, 1953), and 'Elizabethan Prosody and Historical Phonology', *Annales Academiae Regiae Scientiarum Upsaliensis* (*Kungl. Vetenskapssamhällets I Uppsala Årsbok*, Upsala, 1961).

The language and its social background

Hilda M. Hulme, 'The Spoken Language and the Dramatic Text: Some Notes on the Interpretation of Shakespeare's Language', *Shakespeare Quarterly*, IX (1958), 379–86.

Arthur H. King, *The Language of Satirized Characters in Poetaster*, Lund Studies in English, 10 (Lund, 1941).

W. Labov, 'The Reflection of Social Processes in Linguistic Structures', *Readings in the Sociology of Language*, ed. J. A. Fishman (The Hague/Paris, 1968), pp. 240–51.

Gladys D. Willcock, 'Shakespeare and Elizabethan English', *A Companion to Shakespeare Studies*, ed. Granville-Barker and Harrison (Cambridge, 1934), pp. 117–36, and *Shakespeare as Critic of Language*, Shakespeare Association Papers, 18 (London, 1934).

today, especially where we tend to class together as interchangeable alternatives items which have since fallen out of use, and which, while they share a common general sense or function, are in fact distinguished in their own period.

When Shakespearian characters meet each other, for instance, they employ a number of different greetings-formulae. Linguistically exotic characters may use

Armado. Men of peace well incountred.
Pedant. Most millitarie sir salutation,
(136a, 21–2; *L. L. Lost*, v, i, 37–8)

but even 'normal' speakers can choose between expressions such as *Good morrow*, (*God*) *saue you* and *How now?* An Elizabethan audience would have been familiar from their own experience with the niceties of which greeting it was appropriate to use to which person, and would be quick to catch points at which the expected linguistic behaviour was departed from. In the two parts of *Henry IV*, particularly, this is crucial, for the knife-edge relationships between Hal and the various members of the Boar's Head Tavern crowd are constantly being stressed and explored, even in the shortest speech. So Poins and the Prince exchange a formal greeting softened by the use of familiar names:

Prince. Good morrow *Ned*.
Poins. Good morrow sweet *Hal*.
(351b, 66–352a, 1; *1 Hen. IV*, I, ii, 123–4)

and their parting in the same scene is even more formal:

Prince. Farewell.
Poins. Farewell, my Lord.
(352b, 10–11; *1 Hen. IV*, I, ii, 216–17)

Peto and Hal are yet more conscious of their social positions:

Prince. . . . and so good morrow *Peto*.
Peto. Good morrow, good my Lord.
(362a, 19–21; *1 Hen. IV*, II, iv, 600–2)

But set against this background is the very different relationship, and therefore very different language, between Falstaff and Hal. At one point this is thrown into even greater emphasis by juxtaposition to an infinitely more formal greeting from Falstaff to the nobleman with the Prince:

Prince. How now blowne *Iack*? how how Quilt?
Falstaff. What *Hal*? How now mad Wag, what a Deuill dost thou in Warwickshire? My good Lord of Westmerland, I cry you mercy, I thought your Honour had already beene at Shrewsbury.
(369a, 51–5; *1 Hen. IV*, IV, ii, 53–9)

It is this kind of speech, characteristically, which Falstaff retains while he struggles to maintain the old footing with Hal after the Prince becomes King:

'Saue thee my sweet Boy.
(401b, 49; *2 Hen. IV*, v, v, 47)

To the audience for which Shakespeare was writing, the very pronouns ('I speake to thee, my heart', 401b, 54; *2 Hen. IV*, v, v, 50) stress Falstaff's demand to have things kept as they have been. The King replies, framing his negative in the non-colloquial mode, returning Falstaff's *thou* pronoun, but as appropriate now from a King to his subject rather than as the pronoun of familiar friendship and equality:

I know thee not, old man: Fall to thy Prayers:
How ill white haires become a Foole, and Iester?
(401b, 55–6; *2 Hen. IV*, v, v, 51–2)

And we know that the old Falstaff–Hal relationship has been shattered. Perhaps only the genius of a great dramatist could achieve this in so few words; certainly at no other period could it be done with such simplicity and such devasting finality.

SOME FUNCTIONS OF SHAKESPEARIAN WORD-FORMATION

VIVIAN SALMON

Many critics of Shakespeare's style have commented on his lexical innovations, but only too often exemplification has consisted of random listing where neologisms such as *bare-faced*, *countless*, *distrustful*, *dog-weary*, *ensconce*, *fancy-free*, *ill-got*, *lack-lustre* and *crop-ear* have been quoted without any analysis of the patterns on which they were formed, the underlying grammatical relationships in the compounds or the purposes for which they were coined.[1] Some scholars have discussed the characteristics of Shakespeare's diction in general, without distinguishing his neologisms;[2] others have concerned themselves with individual methods of word-formation, such as functional conversion,[3] or have investigated the effect of particular neologisms to the neglect of general linguistic considerations.[4] At the other extreme, Franz's grammar lists all the types of word-formation exemplified in Shakespeare's usage, but without providing any guidance, except casually, on the extent of their originality or their purpose,[5] while in another comprehensive work, Jespersen's grammar of post-medieval English, Shakespearian examples are quoted only as incidental items in a general survey.[6] The lack of any reasoned account of the principles directing Shakespeare's lexical creativity has led to the kind of vague, subjective assessment of its nature and purpose which characterizes certain neologisms in *Troilus and Cressida*, including *conflux*, *protractive*, *persistive*, *appertainments*, *soilure* and *embrasures*, as 'strange and shapeless, fashioned for argument rather than delight... They seem endowed with a deliberate harshness to which the frequent ending of *-ive*, as in *persistive* and *-ure* as in *soilure* give emphasis'.[7] Judgements of this nature, with which the linguist cannot concur, suggest that there is room for a study which will investigate the reasons for Shakespeare's neologisms and the types of word-formation which proved most rewarding; but the immensity of the topic precludes anything but a brief survey with the minimum of exemplification. However meagre the results, it is

[1] Cf. G. Gordon, 'Shakespeare's English', in *Shakespearian Comedy* (Oxford, reprint 1945), p. 142.

[2] E.g. B. Groom, *The diction of poetry from Spenser to Bridges* (Toronto, 1955). Cf. also his 'Formation and use of compound epithets in English poetry from 1579', *S.P.E. Tract* XLIX (Oxford, 1937), 300–4.

[3] B. von Lindheim, 'Syntaktische Funktionsverschiebung als Mittel des Barocken Stils bei Shakespeare', *Shakespeare-Jahrbuch*, XC (1954), 229–51; also Y. M. Biese, 'Origin and development of conversions in English', *Annales Academiæ Scientiarum Fennicæ*, Ser. B, XLV, 2 (Helsinki, 1941).

[4] E.g. H. Stahl, 'Schöpferische Wortbildung bei Shakespeare?' *Shakespeare-Jahrbuch*, XC (1954), 252–78. This study makes valuable comments on individual formations e.g. *foxship*, *boggler*.

[5] W. Franz, *Die Sprache Shakespeares in Vers und Prosa* (Halle/Saale, 1939). (On word-formation, cf. pp. 100–53.)

[6] O. Jespersen, *A modern English grammar on historical principles*, Part VI (with P. Christophersen, N. Haislund and K. Schibsbye) (London, 1946). Cf. especially Chapters VI and VII.

[7] B. Ifor Evans, *The language of Shakespeare's plays* (London, 3rd ed. 1964), p. 143.

hoped that they will illustrate one aspect of Shakespeare's craftsmanship as a poet and dramatist—however trivial it may appear by comparison with his achievement as a whole—and assist in a more precise characterization of his style.

Two initial difficulties confront students of Elizabethan word-formation. One, which has been discussed by W. S. Mackie, among others, is the extent to which one can rely on the *N.E.D.*'s attribution of neologisms to Shakespeare.[1] His originality cannot be demonstrated with absolute certainty, but the fact that so many of these formations are nonce-words suggests that they were created for some particular linguistic context, which often reveals itself on inspection. They are at least easier to handle than loan-words, which are excluded from discussion here, partly for reasons of space, and partly because the linguistic acumen required to introduce a borrowed word into English is of a different—and perhaps inferior—order from that which is involved in creating one anew, even if from existing elements. The second difficulty lies in the choice of linguistic method; if this were a study of Elizabethan word-formation as exemplified in Shakespearian drama, it would be undertaken with all the rigour and precision of current linguistic techniques. Since the aim of the investigation is to discover the function of Shakespearian neologisms, as a contribution to the study of his style, and to present the results to readers who are critics rather than linguists, technicalities have been eschewed as far as possible. A few linguistic terms cannot be avoided, the most important of them being 'surface structure' and 'deep structure'.[2] The external form of a compound or derived word, for example, *N+adj.*, is its surface structure; the underlying sentence which clarifies the grammatical relationships between the elements of the compound is the deep structure, identical surface structures often concealing dissimilar deep structures, e.g. *heart-sick*, *ice-cold : he is sick at heart*, *it is as cold as ice*. More familiar terms are those which refer to the three most productive methods of word-formation in Elizabethan English: compounding (the juxtaposition, usually under one strong stress, of two or occasionally more normally independent words or 'free morphemes');[3] derivation (the formation of a new word from the juxtaposition of one or more free morphemes and one or more affixes—'bound morphemes') and functional conversion (derivation by zero-morpheme) in which a word is used in an abnormal grammatical category without change of form. Many other methods of word-formation were available to Shakespeare and his contemporaries, such as 'back-formation' (e.g. *to weather-fend*, formed from *weather-fended* 'protected from the weather'), rhyme (e.g. *pell-mell*, *kicky-wicky*) and ablaut (*skimble-skamble*) but there are too few neologisms based on such patterns in Shakespearian drama to allow useful discussion, and only the major types and their functions will be described here.[4]

Before examining Shakespeare's practice in detail, it might be valuable to distinguish the overall results of word-creation. One result is purely grammatical, when the addition of an affix does not affect the referential meaning of a word, but only its grammatical function. Thus in affixing *-ment* to the existing verb *define*

1 'Shakespeare's English: and how far it can be investigated with the help of the "New English Dictionary"', *Modern Language Review*, XXXI (1936), 1–10.

2 Even these terms are used rather less precisely than would be appropriate in a rigorous linguistic analysis.

3 For a definition of 'compound' cf. H. Marchand, *The categories and types of present-day English word-formation* (Munich, 2nd ed. 1969), esp. pp. 20–4. For further discussion, cf. R. B. Lees, *The grammar of English nominalizations* (The Hague, 1963), Preface.

4 For fuller details of the types productive in Elizabethan English cf. Marchand, *Categories and types*, where the earlier history of twentieth-century types is discussed.

Shakespeare nominalizes a concept which previously was solely verbal. This kind of formation, akin to affixation for case and tense in its demands on originality, is equally characteristic of non-poetic language. A second result of word-formation is semantically and grammatically null; where a grammatical affix is added to an existing word of the same category (e.g. an adjective-forming affix to an existing adjective) the only obvious result is in the phonetic structure of the word. This kind of formation is restricted almost entirely to poetic language, where such formations may be metrically convenient (e.g. *plump*, *plumpy*). The association of such words with metrical form may of course bestow on them the connotation of 'poetic', and they may eventually become an element in traditional poetic diction. Thirdly, some formations may result in the concise expression of lengthier deep structures as a result of syntactic processes present in the language as a whole (not merely in that of the poet); useful as it may be to describe these processes for a general account of the language, all that is of interest in analyzing a poet's practice is the discovery of his reasons for selecting a compound or derived word in preference to the explicit expression of its deep structure. Shakespeare creates words, then, because they are useful to him grammatically, phonetically or syntactically; the exemplification which follows begins with a brief note on some grammatical formations. They are not specific to poetic language, but since a few of this type are sometimes quoted as instances of Shakespeare's lexical creativity they cannot be ignored.

An Elizabethan who wished to nominalize a concept hitherto expressed only as a verb could choose between suffixes of English or Romance origin; most common among the latter were *-ment*, *-ure* and *-ance* (*-ence*), while the native suffix was *-ing*. Shakespeare appears to have been the first to use several in *-ment*, which, introduced in medieval loan-words from French and Latin, had been regularly affixed to English stems since about 1300. It has always been more productive than *-ure*, which is first recorded as a suffix with an English base in 1545, and of which Shakespeare made some original use. (No doubt he should be credited with some formations in *-ance*, but few of these have been noted.) The existence of a choice of verbal-noun suffixes meant the possibility of distinguishing between their grammatical functions; although *-ing*, *-ment* and *-ure* could all denote concrete objects as well as abstract actions (e.g. *building*, *reinforcements*, *jointure*), derivations in *-ment* and *-ure* tended to denote 'particular instance of an action' rather than duration of an action. Thus an aspectival distinction evolved between the native suffix, denoting in most cases continuous and incomplete action, and the foreign suffix denoting completed action, or actions regarded as a whole. Among the formations in *-ment* which the *N.E.D.* attributes to Shakespeare are three with native bases, *bodement*, *fleshment*, *bewitchment* as well as *allayment*, *amazement*, *cloyment*, *condolement*, *appertainment*, *distilment*, *encompassment*, *excitement*, *impartment*, *insultment*, *prevailment*, *recountment*, *reinforcement*, and *subduement*. The usefulness of such formations becomes obvious if one tries replacing them with verbal nouns in *-ing* in examples such as the following:

> Alas! their love may be call'd appetite . . .
> That suffer surfeit, cloyment, and revolt
> (*T. N.*, 984, 986)
>
> The like allayment could I give my grief
> (*Tr. & Cress.*, 2396)
>
> In the fleshment of this dread exploit
> (*Lear*, 1199)
>
> Sweet bodements! good![1] (*Mac.*, 1640)

[1] The quotations are from W. J. Craig's edition (London, reprint 1955), but the through line-numbering of the Norton/Hinman Folio Facsimile has been adopted. For quotations not in the Folio references are to Craig's edition.

That the use of forms in *-ment* is not merely a metrical convenience is obvious from the fact that, in this respect, the *-ing* forms would have been equally acceptable, as is also the case with the following instances in *-ure*:

> Though he hath fallen by prompture of the blood
> (*M. for M.*, 1192)

> That suffer in exposure
> (*Mac.*, 896)

> But, with an angry wafture of your hand
> (*J. C.*, 887)

Other formations in *-ure* attributed to Shakespeare include *enacture*, *impressure*, and *insisture*. He also experimented with another version of *exposure*, in

> More than a wild exposture to each chance
> (*Cor.*, 2475)

by analogy with *posture*, but *exposure*, by analogy with *closure*, no doubt owes its survival to its closer association with the verb base. Shakespeare also tried *annexment* instead of the existing *annexion*, but both were superseded by *annexation* (from 1611).

Once these patterns for the formation of verbal nouns were available in English, any native speaker could—and many others beside poets did—create verbal nouns at will. The actual choice of suffix depended on aspectival and no doubt phonetic considerations, although what the latter were has not yet been explained. In the same way, there was a choice in forming verbal adjectives between native *-ing* and Romance *-ive* (*persisting*, *persistive*) which may have been dependent on aspect. In creating verbal nouns and adjectives Shakespeare therefore displayed no more originality than his contemporaries; unlike his more imaginative poetic compounds, they would have been created by someone else at some time, if not by him.

When Shakespeare's lexical creativity was directed towards genuinely poetic or dramatic ends, they were outside the requirements of normal Elizabethan speech. At the simplest level, his neologisms are invented for metrical reasons, and there are three major functions of word-formation in relation to metrical stress:

1. To avoid the juxtaposition of two heavy stresses.

Shakespeare provides intermediate unstressed syllables by creating nouns and adjectives with unstressed suffixes and verbs with unstressed prefixes. The affixes in question are those which normally have only grammatical function but in this case co-occur with bases whose function they cannot affect but whose phonetic form they can change for metrical reasons. Among such neologisms are:

blastments (substituted for *blasts*)

> Contagious blastments are most imminent
> (*Ham.*, 505)

climatures (for *climates*)

> Unto our climatures and countrymen
> (*Ham.*, I, i, 125)

vasty (for *vast*)

> I can call spirits from the vasty deep
> (*1 Hen. IV*, 1578)

brisky (for *brisk*)

> Most brisky juvenal, and eke most lovely Jew
> (*M. N. D.*, 908)

plumpy (for *plump*)

> Come, thou monarch of the vine,
> Plumpy Bacchus, with pink eyne!
> (*Ant. & Cleo.*, 1466–7)

steepy (for *steep*)

> Bowing his head against the steepy mount
> (*Timon*, 95)

The contexts in which *brisky* and *plumpy* occur —one a parody of old-fashioned poetry and the other a rhymed song including an obvious archaism—suggest that both adjectives have taken on the connotation of 'poetic'. With verbs, the appropriate stress-pattern was achieved by the use of the prefixes *be* and *en*; added to nouns, they did have a grammatical function, and added to certain types of verb they had a semantic one, i.e. they brought about a change of meaning, but more concisely than by the verbalization of a deep structure. *En+rank* n. provides *enrank* v., whereas *en+twist* v. reduces 'twist around' to *entwist* v. In some instances, however, *en* and *be* appear to have no function except a metrical one:

bemeet (=*meet*)

> Our very loving sister, well be-met
> (*Lear*, 2865)

enguard (=*guard*)

> He may enguard his dotage with their powers
> (*Lear*, 847)

endart (=*dart*)

> But no more deep will I endart mine eye
> (*Rom. & Jul.*, 444)

Once again, such formations have acquired a 'poetic' flavour, because of their association with metre.

2. To eliminate superfluous unstressed syllables.

For this purpose Shakespeare adopts two expedients: functional conversion and the compounding of *adj.+adj.* with no medial conjunction. Strangely enough, conversion of verbs to nouns has little genuinely poetic effect, whereas that of nouns to verbs adds dramatic energy to Shakespeare's style. Among examples of the former type of conversion (the other will be discussed later) are:

dispose (Shakespeare's alternative being *disposure*)

> His goods confiscate to the duke's dispose
> (*Com. Errors*, 24)

avouch (alternative *avouchment*)

> The sensible and true avouch/Of mine own eyes
> (*Ham.*, 72–3)

attest (alternative *attestation*)

> That doth invert the attest of eyes and ears
> (*Tr. & Cress.*, 3116)

accuse (alternative *accusation*)

> By false accuse doth level at my life
> (*2 Hen. VI*, 1460)

Shakespeare is also credited with the first nominal use of numerous forms which are both nominal and verbal, e.g. *repair*, *burst*, *bump*, *dawn*, *howl*, *jaunt*, *reprieve*; but unlike the examples just quoted, they were not in competition with polysyllabic forms which would have motivated their creation for metrical reasons. Adjectival compounds of *adj.+adj.* may be presumed to have metrical function when the two elements are semantically compatible, since their close juxtaposition produces no dramatic effect through the tension of contrast. Compounds of the following type have little merit:

> Had bak'd thy blood, and made it *heavy-thick*
> (*K. John*, 1342)

> Be *secret-false*: what need she be acquainted?
> (*Com. Errors*, 801)

> Nor *heady-rash*, provok'd with raging ire
> (*Com. Errors*, 1693)

> As ever I have found thee *honest-true*
> (*Mer. Ven.*, 1772)

> an enterprise/Of *honourable-dangerous* consequence
> (*J. C.*, 565–6)

> If ever I were *wilful-negligent*
> (*W. Tale*, 346)

> That fools should be so *deep-contemplative*
> (*A.Y.L.I.*, 1004)

To the Elizabethans these formations may hardly have seemed compounds at all. When adjectives are modified by adverbs (e.g. *deeply contemplative*) the structure is a normal syntactic group and not a compound. The distinction is clear in contemporary English since most adjectives and their related adverbs differ in form (except e.g. *hard*, as in *He works hard* and *This is hard work*). In Elizabethan English the two forms often coincided for historical reasons, the adverb (e.g. *new*) being derived from the O.E. adjective with adverbial suffix *-e* (*neowe*). When unstressed final vowels disappeared, the adjective and the adverb shared the same form, and often, as with *newly*, the adverbial function was made explicit in the 16th century by the addition of a further suffix, *-ly*. Apparently the Folio compositors were uncertain of the status of these compounds; sometimes they linked the two elements with a hyphen, e.g. *headie-rash*, sometimes they separated them with a comma, e.g. *heauy*, *thicke*, and sometimes they printed them entirely separately, e.g. *secret false*. These variations suggest that the combination of *adj.*+*adj.* was felt in some way to be non-syntactic, and its very frequent occurrence in poetry implies that it was deliberately exploited for metrical purposes, whether the omitted syllable was the adverb suffix *-ly* or the conjunction *and*.

3. To ensure coincidence of metrical and lexical stress.

Many compounds result from Shakespeare's rearrangement of the normal order of clause elements for metrical reasons. Reversal of subject and object, for example, is common in traditional poetic style; compounding occurs when a noun (usually subject or object) is placed after a prepositional or participial phrase which it normally precedes. The Folio compositors sometimes acknowledge these phrases as compound epithets by hyphenation, but by no means invariably: modern editors usually do, e.g.:

Before the always-wind-obeying deep
(*Com. Errors, 66*)

The to-and-fro-conflicting wind and rain
(*Lear,* III, i, II)

A jewel in a ten-times-barr'd-up chest
(*Rich. II,* 188)

Nor no without-book prologue, faintly spoke
(*Rom. & Jul.,* I, iv, 7)

Another common rearrangement which results in a compound verb is that of verb and adverb/preposition. In O.E. verbs were commonly compounded with prefixed adverb/preposition (locative particles such as *over*, *under*, *out*, *up*), but these prefixes were normally separable, as in modern German. By 1500 locative particles normally followed the verb, except for *out*, *under* and *over*. *Out* remained highly productive as the first element of a compound verb, but with the meaning 'out-do, surpass' (as in *out-Herods Herod*); in the literal sense new formations were created as late as the sixteenth century, though Marchand questions whether they were in any but literary use.[1] *Over* is also most productive in the sense 'surpass'; in a literal sense neologisms are now restricted to literary or poetic language and, to judge from the examples quoted by Marchand, have been since the sixteenth century.[2] The normal sense of *under* in compound verbs is 'below a fixed norm'; with a locative meaning its derivative yield has been extremely slight. Thus wherever adverb/prepositions, including *out*, *under* and *over*, occur as first elements—in a locative sense—in verbs attributed to Shakespeare, it seems likely that he is contravening the rules of word-formation for some poetic purpose, and with compounds such as *underpeep*, *over-veil*, *after-eye*, *uphoard* in the following examples he is clearly concerned to equate lexical and metrical stress (*out* does not occur with a literal sense in any Shakespeare finite-verb neologisms):

the flame of the taper
Bows toward her, and would under-peep her lids
(*Cym.*, 926–7)

Thou shouldst have made him
As little as a crow, or less, ere left
To after-eye him (*Cym.*, 281–3)

night is fled
Whose pitchy mantle over-veil'd the earth
(*1 Hen. VI*, 772–3)

Or if thou hast uphoarded in thy life
Extorted treasure (*Ham.*, 133–4)

[1] *Categories and types*, p. 109.
[2] *Ibid.*, p. 98.

Finally, compound nouns with the required stress pattern are created by the rearrangement of adverbs normally following the noun:

> Which often, since my here-remain in England
> (*Mac.*, 1980)

> My people did expect my hence-departure
> (*W. Tale*, 567)

> Till Harry's back-return again to France
> (*Hen. V*, 2891)

> Before thy here-approach
> (*Mac.*, 1961)

Neologisms created for metrical reasons are on the whole, though not exclusively, characteristic of Shakespeare's earlier work; in his mature style he was less concerned to avoid metrical irregularity by such obvious means. Also associated with his early style is rhetorical neologism, for antithesis and pun. Antithesis may be achieved in various ways; new compounds may be created by the juxtaposition of two elements of which one is in semantic opposition to another in an existing compound:

> Once to behold with your sun-beamed eyes ...
> You were best call it 'daughter-beamed eyes'
> (*L. L. Lost*, 2065, 2068)

or compounds may be formed of two contrasted elements:

> This senior-junior, giant-dwarf, Dan Cupid
> (*L. L. Lost*, 946)

Antithetical derivatives may be formed by contrasted affixes, especially *un*/zero:

> Pay her the debt you owe her, and unpay the villany you have done her (*2 Hen. IV*, 717–18)

> A happy gentleman ... By you unhappied
> (*Rich. II*, 1321–2)

> *Falstaff*. What a plague mean ye to colt me thus?
> *Prince*. Thou liest: thou art not colted; thou art uncolted (*1 Hen. IV*, 771–3)

where there is also a pun on *colt* 'cheat' and *colt* 'provide with a horse'. The suffixes *-less* and *-ed* 'possessing' are contrasted in:

> Father'd he is, and yet he's fatherless
> (*Mac.*, 1741–2)

while antithesis may also be realized by contrasted bases with like affixes:

> When that which makes me bend makes the king bow;
> He childed as I father'd (*Lear*, III, vi, 118–19)

A more complex antithesis occurs in:

> Speaking in deeds and deedless in his tongue
> (*Tr. & Cress.*, 2660)

in which 'words' are opposed to 'deeds' while 'positive' (*speaking*) is opposed to 'negative' (*deedless*). Neologism for rhetorical purposes may result in apparent trivialities, but there is always some element of conciseness in these formations which is dramatically effective. *Father'd* and *fatherless* are the surface structures of: *he has a father; he has no father*, two statements which gain emotional impact by their conciseness. In puns, a single formation has two deep structures: *uncolted* is the surface structure of *he has no colt*, *he is not colted*. Much more effective, however, was another rhetorical device—*enallage*, i.e. functional conversion, when it resulted in the production of new verbs. Some examples will be discussed below.

Shakespeare's lexical inventiveness was perhaps more generally employed in the delineation of character and setting, though the relationship between character and language is too large a topic to discuss here in any detail. He himself draws attention to the 'golden words' of Osric, who is satirized for his affectation, but his vocabulary tends to be unusual or old-fashioned rather than original. The 'fire-new words' of another affected courtier, Armado, are mainly loan-words or compounds like *black-oppressing*, *curious-knotted*, drawn from the 'mint of phrases in his brain', and at the other end of the social scale are the malformations of the uneducated, like Dogberry's *dissembly* and Mrs Quickly's *continuantly*. There are also the accidental neologisms of 'foreigners' who, like Parson Evans, 'make fritters of English'. Similarly, the relationship between language and setting can only be touched on here. Critics have discerned a high proportion of neologisms and words of Latin origin in *Troilus and Cressida*, among the former being the formations *protractive*, *persistive* and *immures* 'walls' (by functional conversion) and the loan-words *conflux*, *tortive*, *unplausive*, *abruption* and *deceptious*. But a close analysis would be necessary to prove that the proportion of words of Latin origin, and of new formations from Latin elements, is higher here than in the non-classical tragedies such as *Hamlet* and *King Lear*. It is likely that formal speeches in any of the tragedies will be characterized by a highly Latinate vocabulary. The relationship between characterization, setting and neologism needs fuller investigation, but there is one strictly limited aspect of characterization in which Shakespeare undoubtedly exercises his lexical creativity—comic and abusive nomenclature, for which he uses imperative-clause or *adj.+noun* patterns as personal nouns, by functional conversion. These patterns provide names which characterize their owners by reference to a typical action or attribute, of a nature eliciting contempt or derision. As Marchand notes: 'Personal substantives have at all times had a pejorative tinge . . . A very few combinations only are neutral terms designating the holder of an office, but even then the occupation is always an inferior one'.[1] Among Shakespearian inventions of the imperative-clause type are *Starvelackey*, *Pickbone*, *Patchbreech*, *Tearsheet*, *Martext* and *Keepdown* and one particularly contemptuous nickname bestowed on Claudio when Benedick challenges him to a duel—'my lord Lackbeard'. The emotional impact is all the greater since the term of abuse is combined with the honorific 'lord'. Nominal phrases (*adj.+noun*) occur less commonly as personal names, and although they characterize with reference to an attribute, it is not necessarily pejorative. Shakespearian inventions include *Deepvow* and *Copperspur*, the deep structure being *x has y* ('he has a copper spur') as compared with the deep structure of the imperative type, *x does y* ('he starves lackeys').

Some of the functions of word-formation already described are exemplified comparatively rarely; by contrast, compounding and derivation for the purpose of economy of expression characterize all periods and types of Shakespearian drama. While conciseness is a desirable feature of ordinary language, it is an essential one of dramatic style; in normal speech, there is usually a choice between a simple surface structure and the verbalization of a lengthier deep structure, although of course many compounds have become regularly established (e.g. *able-bodied seaman*, *long-playing record*, to select examples of a pattern of compound epithet frequently occurring in traditional poetic diction). But English poetry has generally shown a preference for compounds, not only because of their conciseness but also because their presence has come to be a hall-mark of poetic language (however artificial). Consequently, it has become a convention to accept without question in poetry many compounds which would be impossible in prose. Shakespeare's *night-shriek*, for example, is formed on a pattern (*noun+noun*) used for sub-classification of concepts, e.g. *soup-*, *dinner-*, *breakfast-*, *tea-plate*, and if occurring in normal language, would imply the existence of other sub-classifications, e.g. *evening-shriek*, *afternoon-shriek*, *morning-shriek*. Accustomed as we are to the frequency of compounds in poetry, we accept *night-shriek* as it stands. But the poet is more often concerned with adjectival compounds, since it is not incumbent on him to find new names for new objects (the major function of neologism in ordinary language) but rather to find new ways of regarding existing objects and concepts, their actions and

[1] *Ibid.*, p. 380. Marchand classifies these types as pseudo-compounds.

attributes. In describing the appearance of living creatures, the poet's range is limited by the number of their physical and mental characteristics; in describing the natural world, his imagination is unrestricted and, not surprisingly, it is in this area that the most genuinely poetic compounds are to be found. In creating such epithets, Shakespeare was imitating a style of diction most notably exploited by Spenser, but derived eventually from the practice of earlier English poets, the precepts of the Pléiade, and the Hellenistic influences on sixteenth-century English culture; from Homer English poets learned such compound epithets as 'rosy-fingered' dawn.[1] The patterns on which they modelled their own lexical creations were those of normal speech, and often the results were not distinguishable from it; it was not the pattern, but its semantic realization, that could produce true poetry. Even for Shakespeare, much of the virtue of the compound epithet lay in its conciseness or its metrical value; the occurrence of the 'simultaneity of apprehension' for which the juxtaposition of two elements in a compound has been praised, is comparatively rare.[2]

The patterns on which Shakespeare modelled his compound epithets, for conciseness of expression and for conformity with the current 'norm' for poetic language, include the following:

1. Epithets based on activity.

Noun + pres. part. + noun = object + verb + subject

heaven-kissing hill
(deep structure 'the hill kisses heaven')
temple-haunting martlet
earth-treading stars
oak-cleaving thunder-bolts

Noun/adj. + pres. part. + noun = complement + verb + subject

summer-seeming lust
(deep structure 'lust befits summer')
little-seeming substance

(Prep.) + noun + pres. part. + noun = prep. phrase + verb + subject

beauty-waning widow
(deep structure 'the widow wanes in beauty)
sky-aspiring thoughts
(deep structure 'thoughts aspire to the sky')
summer-swelling flower
(deep structure 'the flower swells in summer')
night-tripping fairy
(deep structure 'the fairy trips by night')

Adv./adj. + pres. part. + noun = adv. + verb + subject

lazy-pacing clouds
(deep structure 'the clouds pace lazily')
highest-peering hill
fearful-hanging rock

(By) + noun + past part. + noun = agent + verb + subject

star-crossed lovers
(deep structure 'the lovers are crossed by stars')
cloud-capped towers
tempest-tossed body

Adv./adj. + past part. + noun = complement + verb + subject

high-grown field
(deep structure 'the field grows high')
big-swoln face
down-fallen birthdom

(Prep.) + noun + past part. + noun = prep. phrase + verb + subject

fen-sucked fogs
(deep structure 'the fogs are sucked from the fens')

[1] On sixteenth-century poetic diction, cf. V. L. Rubel, *Poetic diction in the English Renaissance from Skelton through Spenser* (New York, 1941). Chapter XIII is devoted to Spenser. Cf. also F. M. Padelford and W. C. Maxwell, 'The compound words in Spenser's poetry', *JEGP*, xxv (1926), 498–516.

[2] Cf. Groom, 'Formation and use of compound epithets' (*S.P.E. Tract*), 296.

belly-pinched wolf
(deep structure 'the wolf is pinched in the belly')
child-changed father
(deep structure 'the father is changed into a child')

Adv./adj.+past part.+noun = adv.+verb+subject

rash-embraced despair
(deep structure 'despair is embraced rashly')
still-vexed Bermoothes

The compounds of greatest complexity are those in which the first element represents a prepositional phrase in the deep structure, since the precise relationship between the two elements—and consequently the choice of preposition—is sometimes obscure. It is not immediately obvious, for example, that *air-drawn* has the deep structure 'it is drawn in the air', interpreted by Schmidt as 'visionary', and the deep structure of *thought-executing* almost defies verbalization (Schmidt interprets 'doing execution in the same moment as it is thought of'). Among many other such compounds are *death-practised duke* (Schmidt, 'threatened with death by stratagems'), *water-flowing tears* (Schmidt, 'tears flowing like water'), *water-standing eye* (Schmidt, 'eye perpetually filled with water').[1]

2. Epithets based on physical or mental attributes.

The surface structure of these compounds is *adj.+noun+-ed*, where *-ed* is not the past participle suffix but means 'possessing'. The second element is usually literal in sense, denoting a part of the body; Shakespearian compounds refer to nearly all external features, and one or two internal organs in a metaphorical sense e.g. *fat-kidneyed.* The second element may also denote the mind e.g. *brain*, *wit*, *spirit.* Epithets based on this pattern have become a commonplace in poetic diction, e.g. *grey-eyed morn*, *sour-eyed disdain*, *lean-looked hunger* (deep structure 'hunger possesses lean looks'); Shakespeare uses many of the traditional ones, but exploits the pattern extremely effectively for original descriptions of nature e.g. *russet-pated choughs*, *tawny-finned fishes*, *nimble-pinioned doves* and for witty characterizations of human beings e.g. *beef-witted*, *waspish-headed.* The second element is occasionally metaphorical, as in *wide-skirted meads*, but metaphor in the first element is more common e.g. *dog-hearted* ('possessing a nature as cruel as that of a dog'). The opportunities for conciseness of expression afforded by such compounds may be illustrated by a comparison of the deep structures of three with identical surface structures: *honey-mouthed* (not actually Shakespeare's coinage), *flap-mouthed* (applied to a dog) and *trumpet-tongued.* Schmidt glosses *flap-mouthed* as 'having broad hanging lips', so that the deep structure would contain several elements, 'the dog has a mouth: the mouth has lips: the lips are like flaps'. *Honey-mouthed*, 'sweet and smooth in speech', is more complex, since *mouthed* 'he possesses a mouth' is a metonymic usage for 'speech'; hence the underlying elements of the compound are 'he utters speech: the speech resembles honey: honey is sweet: honey is smooth'. While *flap-mouthed* depends on a literal visual image, *honey-mouthed* depends on metonymy and synaesthetic imagery. In *trumpet-tongued*, glossed as 'proclaiming loudly as with the voice of a trumpet' there is another metonymic use of *tongue* for 'speech', but the characteristics which suggest the resemblance between *tongue* and *trumpet* ('he possesses a tongue like a trumpet') are neither visual nor dependent on any inherent material quality but refer to the effects produced by the use of both. Several different statements therefore underlie this

[1] References to 'Schmidt' are to the *Shakespeare-Lexicon*, rev. G. Sarrazin (2 vols., Berlin, 5th ed., 1962).

compound, which on the surface is as simple as *flap-mouthed*.

Such epithets have a double function. Not only are they a means of concise, and therefore dramatic, expression—and as such, at their most complex, characteristic of Shakespeare's mature style—but they also mark his language as 'poetic' in the tradition of which Spenser is usually regarded as the founder. Another type of compound adjective shares these functions; this has the structure *adj.+adj.* where the elements are in semantic contrast. Compounds with two semantically compatible elements (*x and y*) are created for metrical reasons; where the deep structure is *x and yet y* the tension between the meanings of *x* and *y* creates a powerful dramatic effect, destroying the 'simultaneity of apprehension' possibly suggested by compounding:

> There lurks a still and dumb-discoursive devil
> (*Tr. & Cress.*, 2481)
>
> When truth kills truth, O devilish-holy fray
> (*M.N.D.*, 1154)
>
> At this odd-even and dull-watch o' the night
> (*Oth.*, 136)

Noun compounds are less characteristic of traditional poetic style, though Shakespeare creates many individual examples of striking effect e.g. *snow-broth* as a description of the blood which runs in the veins of the inhuman Angelo. One pattern, however, recurs as a means of achieving economy of expression; it contains the agent noun in *-er*, on the use of which there were fewer grammatical restrictions in 1600 than at the present day. British English (though not apparently American) no longer tolerates new formations which are 'minimally nominal' which 'because they are minimal are dispensable, that is, they could always be replaced by *One who*, *Those who*, structures ... Their power to attract attention is proportionate to their dispensability'.[1] Shakespearian examples include:

> Thou monstrous injurer of heaven and earth
> (*K. John*, 476)
>
> Be these sad signs confirmers of thy words
> (*K. John*, 945)
>
> Hence shall we see
> If power change purpose, what our seemers be
> (*M. for M.*, 345–6)
>
> The rabble ... The ratifiers and props of every word
> (*Ham.*, 2845)

Such formations were obviously valuable for conciseness, but what we cannot know is whether for the Elizabethans, as for us, they were marks of 'poetic style'; since Shakespeare also uses them in prose, they were probably not: 'The oath of a lover is no stronger than the word of a tapster; they are both the confirmer of false reckonings' (*A.Y.L.I.*, 1738–40). For conciseness of expression, they were even more valuable in compounds with the surface structure [*prep.*]+*noun*+*verb*+*er*, e.g. *shoulder-clapper* 'one who claps shoulders', *night-brawler* 'one who brawls at night' and many others (e.g. *bed-presser*, *purpose-changer*, *bed-swerver*, *horse-back-breaker*).

Another type of noun-compound which results in conciseness of expression is also emotionally effective, for dramatic rather than poetic purposes. This is the type already described as productive of personal names (*Starvelackey* ...) but used, not for characterization of individuals, but for the purposes of abuse. These structures, originating as colloquialisms, seem always to have retained a colloquial connotation, and they are all the more effective when inserted into formal or lyrical contexts. Among Shakespeare's original terms are Puck's description of Lysander as a *lack-love* and a *kill-courtesy*, Berowne's attack

[1] B. M. H. Strang, 'Swift's agent-noun formations in *-er*', in *Wortbildung, Syntax und Morphologie* (Marchand Festschrift), ed. H. E. Brekle and L. Lipka (The Hague, 1968), p. 222. Professor Strang adds (p. 223) 'it seems reasonable to consider that the generation of minimal *-er* forms was so syntactic a process that it hardly felt like word-formation at all'.

on the person who has betrayed his love for Rosaline as 'some mumble-news', and Hotspur's reference to an unreliable friend as a *lack-brain*. Nouns formed on this pattern may also function attributively:

> Brethren and sisters of the hold-door trade
> [prostitution] (*Tr. & Cress.*, 3587)
>
> Looking on it with lack-lustre eye
> (*A.Y.L.I.*, 994)
>
> You poor, base, rascally, cheating, lack-linen mate!
> (*2 Hen. IV*, 1151–2)

The underlying structure is 'he lacks love' 'he kills courtesey' etc. Another pejorative noun-compound type, of colloquial origin, has the surface structure *adj./noun+noun*, and the deep structure *x has y*. Shakespearian neologisms include a contemptuous reference to Othello as a *thick-lips*, Ford's address to the wife whom he suspects of deceitfulness as *brazen-face*, Falstaff's castigation of those who wear 'high shoes' as *whoreson smooth-pates* and Capulet's abuse of Juliet as *tallow-face*. Falstaff himself is called a *fatguts* and *barebone*. Such compounds may also function attributively, as in

> I am thy king, and thou a false-heart traitor
> (*2 Hen. VI*, 3140)
>
> Make curl'd-pate ruffians bald
> (*Timon*, 1776)

The dramatic energy and economy of expression which characterize Shakespeare's mature style are mostly indebted to neologisms of a third grammatical category—verbs, whether resulting from derivation, compounding or functional conversion. All affixes, except those used for purely grammatical or metrical purposes, represent some degree of conciseness of expression, but there are two which, as verbal prefixes, Shakespeare exploits with special success—*dis-* and *un-*. During Shakespeare's lifetime, *dis-*, first introduced as an element in Romance loan-words, was becoming attached without restriction to English bases, though perhaps still with some effect of novelty. It could be prefixed to verbs and, with greater complexity in the deep structure, to verbs derived from nouns by functional conversion:

> you have fed upon my signories,
> Dispark'd my parks (*Rich. II*, 1334–5)

Since the meaning of *dis-* is reversative here, the deep structure is 'You have changed a park. The park is a common', where *park* n. functions as *park* v. 'to make into a park'. This is one of the fairly rare instances from earlier plays; others from later plays include *disbench* 'drive from a bench', *disedge* 'take the edge off one's appetite', *discandy* 'cease to exist in solid form', *disquantity* 'diminish in numbers' and *disorb* 'move from its sphere'. *Un-* also has a reversative function when the base to which it is prefixed is originally verbal i.e. not the result of functional conversion: *uncharge* 'not to charge, acquit of blame', *unshout* 'not to shout, to withdraw one's shouts', *unbuild* 'pull down', *unspeak* 'not to speak, withdraw what one has said'. The effectiveness of these derivatives often depends on the semantic incompatibility of the prefix and base; it is possible to deny one's words, but not to 'unspeak' them, to keep silence, but not to 'unshout' what has been shouted, or to 'unbuild' what has been built. When prefixed to a verb derived from a noun by functional conversion, *un-* means 'remove (an attribute etc.)'; *unhair* 'remove the hair', *unsex* 'remove one's sexuality (i.e. femininity and its associated tenderness)', *unsphere* 'remove from their spheres', *unchild* 'remove one's children', *unwit* 'remove one's intelligence'; the effect here depends partly on our knowledge that, although the structure seems to argue for the existence of the verbs *hair*, *sex*, *sphere*, *child*, *wit* they do not in fact occur in the sense which we are led to expect.

Compound verbs have already been described as arising from the rearrangement of normal order for metrical reasons; a few with a locative first element seem to have been created simply because they imparted a 'poetic' tone to the language (rearrangement makes no stress difference) e.g.

> I must up-fill this osier cage of ours
> (*Rom. & Jul.*, 1012)

> Thou art up-rous'd by some distemperature
> (*Rom. & Jul.*, 1047)

> With love's light wings did I o'erperch these walls
> (*Rom. & Jul.*, 863–4)

but there is one group, with *out* as the first element, which Shakespeare creates for the complexity of the deep structure and its consequent dramatic force. *Out* is used in the sense of 'exceed, surpass', and the verb to which it is prefixed is the product of functional conversion from a noun. *Out-Herod* has become almost a paradigm of this type; it demonstrates perhaps more clearly than any other instance how difficult it is to verbalize the second element. *Herod* v. presumably implies 'to act as Herod' just as *villain* implies 'to act villainously.' *Outparamour*, in

> Wine loved I deeply ... and in women out-paramoured the Turk
> (*Lear*, 1870–2)

seems to depend on a different deep structure. *Paramour* v. must signify 'to have a lover', and *outparamour* 'to exceed in having lovers'. The deep structures of *outvenom* and *outtongue* are reasonably transparent, but in

> I would out-night you did no body come
> (*Mer. Ven.*, 2433)

night v., from *night* n. is to be interpreted from the context as 'to refer to nights'.

The third type of verbal neologism, arising from functional conversion alone, is another factor in the dramatic energy of Shakespeare's mature style. Relatively simple is the conversion of an adjective to a verb (exemplified even in the early style) where the compound avoids the overt expression of the factitive verb *make*:

safe 'make safe'

> I tell you true: best you saf'd the bringer
> Out of the host (*Ant. & Cleo.*, 2607–8)

dumb 'make dumb'

> What I would have spoke
> Was beastly dumb'd by him
> (*Ant. & Cleo.*, 579–80)

There is greater variety in the functioning of nouns as verbs. Sometimes they have no referential meaning, but simply the connotation of anger or impatience, in instances such as the following:

> Master Fer! I'll fer him!
> (*Hen. V*, 2410)

> Grace me no grace, nor uncle me no uncle
> (*Rich. II*, 1198)

More commonly, a concrete noun may function in the place of an abstract verb, particularly in respect of bodily activities which, as a result, are presented to us more vividly:

> To lip a wanton in a secure couch,
> And to suppose her chaste
> (*Oth.*, 2452–3)

The physical immediacy of *lip* for *kiss* increases the effect of horror at the deception of genuine passion by a (supposedly) unworthy object; greater complexity of meaning arises from the metaphorical use of concrete nouns for abstract verbs, as in

> Still virginalling
> Upon his palm! (*W. Tale*, 200–1)

where *virginal* signifies 'touch the palm of the hand with the fingers as though playing upon the virginals'. Other well-known examples include *pageant* 'imitate as though acting in a play', *mountebank* 'treat with deceitfulness', *furnace* 'exhale (sighs) as though from a furnace'.

Another group of nouns functioning as verbs has the deep structure *to turn x into y*, usually with only partly figurative sense, as in *stranger* 'turn into a stranger', *god* 'turn into a god', *coward* 'turn into a coward'—

what read you there
That hath so cowarded and chas'd your blood
(*Hen. V*, 702–3)

while other nouns function as verbs with the deep structure 'to act as (noun)':

Lord Angelo dukes it well
(*M. for M.*, 1583)

my true lip
Hath virgin'd it e'er since
(*Cor.*, 3396–7)

Apart from these obvious groupings, there are numerous instances where nouns function as verbs in highly individual ways, which often defy the ingenuity of editors to explicate, as in *elf* 'tie in the manner of elves'

Blanket my loins, elf all my hair in knots
(*Lear*, 1261)

flap-dragon 'engulf like a morsel floating in liquid'

to see how the sea flap-dragoned it
(*W. Tale*, 1539–40)

Shakespeare's text being finite in extent, it is inevitable that many of the examples quoted will already have been the subject of comment—and more perceptive and detailed comment than is possible here. Nevertheless, it is hoped that a survey of this kind may help to explain Shakespeare's usage in the large number of instances which it has been impossible to quote, but which sometimes cause difficulty in interpretation, and will also add something to our knowledge of Shakespeare's craftsmanship in using the syntactic processes of Elizabethan English to create the words he required for the various purposes of his dramatic art.

GUIDE-LINES FOR INTERPRETING THE USES OF THE SUFFIX '-ED' IN SHAKESPEARE'S ENGLISH

G. V. SMITHERS

Some years ago an eminent and richly experienced editor of Shakespeare revealed in conversation that he had decided to emend the word *becomed* in the following passage in *Romeo and Juliet* (IV, ii, 25–7):

Juliet. I met the youthful lord at Lawrence' cell,
And gave him what *becomed* love I might,
Not stepping o'er the bounds of modesty.

When it was explained to him why he must on no account make away with this form, he at once gave up the idea; and all was well. If this was a startling hint that what was at issue might not be fully clear even to one of the elect, it must be added that in the *O.E.D.* itself (whose editors were in a much stronger position to deal with something that is essentially a philological question, and a simple one for such as them) some of the copious related material in Shakespeare's vocabulary has been inadequately or erroneously classified and thus left unclear, or has occasionally been misunderstood and misinterpreted. It may therefore be useful to state here explicitly, in a compressed but systematic form, the relevant facts of English word-formation and to show by economical illustration how they apply to Shakespeare's usage.[1]

When, through phonetic or other changes, two originally distinct linguistic elements coalesce under one and the same form, some at least of the original differences in their use and their meaning of course commonly persist. But native speakers of the language (including the 'well' or highly educated) are normally unaware that two distinct entities are involved, let alone that the two forms are not identical in all aspects. Given that speech is, roughly speaking, a less than fully conscious activity, this is entirely natural, unavoidable, and proper. In a sense, it does not matter: though, for instance, the mass of native speakers of English may be unaware that the single linguistic form written *-ing* does duty (like the equivalent F. *-ant*) both as a present participle and as a gerund, this has no great bearing on the capacity of them all to use it idiomatically in both functions.

In another sense, however, it matters profoundly: the implicit ambiguity opens the door to changes, whether extensions or restrictions in use, or the introduction of substitutes for the form in some of its uses. In practical terms, the result may be a marked change in the productivity of certain linguistic elements, including such as that under discussion here, which is a suffix. More specifically, it may lead to uses which in a historical view are less precise and may by readers in later times be supposed (erroneously) to be 'errors', but which in fact are sometimes open to explanation, e.g. as products of what is traditionally known as analogical change.

[1] The following discussion is a summary statement of things covered in a systematic study now in hand of Shakespeare's word-formation and other aspects of his usage. In all references to the text the line-numbering of Alexander's edition has been adopted.

The starting-point for clarification of Shakespeare's uses of the element *-ed* is the fact that it represents *two* older elements, which so far as the history of English is concerned must be regarded as distinct things. As the ending of the past participle of weak verbs it represents O.E. *-ed*, *-od*/*-ad*. Its other antecedent is a suffix (O.E. *-ede*), which was used to form adjectives from nouns, and the sense of which was 'provided or endowed with, having, having the quality of': O.E. *hēalede* 'ruptured' beside *hēala* 'rupture', *hoferede* 'hump-backed' beside *hofer* 'hump'. A specially important point here is that there was no cognate verb.

The dual use of the element *-ed* is ancient, and must go back to the Indo-European stage, since it is matched in various other languages of the group.[1] Thus Latin *caudātus*, *cornūtus*, and *pellītus* are all formed on nouns (*cauda* 'tail', *cornu* 'horn', *pellis* 'skin'); in all three the suffix (which is an I.E. * *-to-*) forms an adjective in which it adds to the sense of the noun the notion 'having, provided with'; and, as with the O.E. examples of *-ede* cited above, there are no cognate verbs. The suffix is preceded by a vowel which belongs to the stem, but which, by a process called by Jespersen 'metanalysis', may itself become part of what is felt as a suffix: the sequence *-ā-tus* happened to be adopted into English, and at that stage, at least, it developed into a suffix *-ate* (since it was then sometimes added to base-words which had not had a stem-vowel *-ā-*). Thus the element *-ate*, in its dual role of what was originally a Latin past-participial ending in some of the verbs adopted from that language (e.g. *animate*, *inchoate*, *inviolate*) and of an adjective-forming suffix added to nouns, is in historical terms an equivalent case to *-ed*. And in practice, it is highly germane to Shakespeare's uses of *-ed*, since it even exhibits the same kind of innovation in use, as we shall see below.

So far as Shakespeare's vocabulary is concerned, the use of *-ed* as an ending of the past participle can be left aside for present purposes: the subject of inquiry is its other main type of function as an adjective-forming suffix. Though comparatively rare in extant O.E. documents, this suffix was used in M.E. to make formations that are demonstrably new,[2] and became strikingly prolific in the literature of the sixteenth and seventeenth centuries, partly because of the general licence and inclination to strike out nonce-formations. But it is amply attested in current English, in such words as *cultured* and *moneyed*. In Shakespeare's writings there are copious examples of the type, as so far defined; from this point they will be referred to as 'Group I'.

The simplest Shakespearian words of this class are those that exhibit the original use of the suffix:

What false Italian
—As poisonous-*tongu'd* as *handed*—hath prevail'd
On thy too ready hearing? (*Cym.*, III, ii, 4–6)

That (*poisonous*) *-tongu'd and -handed* in *Cymbeline* III, ii, 5 simply mean 'with (poisonous) tongue and hands' is vouched for by Huloet in 1552: *Handed longe, or longe handes hauynge.*

An undeniable and simple instance of a formation on a noun is *affection'd* in *Twelfth*

[1] See e.g. W. Wilmanns, *Deutsche Grammatik* (2nd ed., Strassburg, 1899), II, §§335–8; F. Kluge, *Nominale Stammbildungslehre der altgermanischen Dialekte* (Halle, 1926), §§225–6; A. Meillet and J. Vendryes, *Traité de grammaire comparée des langues classiques* (2nd ed., Paris, 1948), §§538–40, §575; K. Brugmann and B. Delbrück, *Vergleichende Grammatik der indogermanischen Sprachen* (2nd ed., Strassburg, 1911), II, I, §§292, 299, 303; H. Hirt, *Indogermanische Grammatik*, III (Heidelberg, 1927), §202 and IV (1928), §37; H. Marchand, *The Categories and Types of Present-day English Word-formation* (Wiesbaden, 1960), 4. 22. 1–4. 23. 7.

[2] E.g. *wolden-eiȝed* 'wall-eyed' (*Kyng Alisaunder* 5265) on O.E. *waldenege* (though the pattern with a two-member base, and a second member denoting a physical or other attribute of a human being, was already available in O.E., e.g. *sur-eagede* 'blear-eyed').

Night, II, iii, 139 (*an ~ ass that cons state without book*), interpreted in the *O.E.D.* (s.v. 3) as 'passionate, wilful; self-willed, obstinate'. Another clear case (i.e. since there was no cognate verb available as a model) is a word recorded only once in English, in *The Tempest*, which was evidently struck out by Shakespeare and was a nonce-formation that did not catch on:

My bosky acres and my *unshrubb'd* down,
Rich scarf to my proud earth. (IV, i, 81–2)

Cymbeline offers an equally clear and straightforward one:

Let us
Find out the prettiest *daisied* plot we can.
(IV, i, 400–1)

Again this was clearly coined by Shakespeare: it is the earliest example, and the only other two on record are of the eighteenth and nineteenth centuries.

Even in this group, however, the semantic content of the suffix has (in many words) come to provide shades of meaning distinct from (though manifestly associable with) the notion 'having, provided with'. A similative implication seems probable in *Cymbeline*, II, iii, 22:

His steeds to water at those springs
On *chalic'd* flow'rs that lies.

Not surprisingly, this is the earliest recorded example of *chaliced* in this use (glossed by the *O.E.D.* as 'having a cup-like blossom'), and the only others are two nineteenth-century ones. And since the word is used otherwise only as 'contained in a chalice', again in two nineteenth-century examples, it is clearly of Shakespeare's own making. A somewhat different use of the suffix is illustrated in *Antony and Cleopatra*, II, i, 27:

That sleep and feeding may prorogue his honour
Even till a *Lethe'd* dullness.

Lethe'd is registered in the *O.E.D.* as the sole example of the word, as *lethied*, and of course treated as a formation on *Lethe*, with a cross-reference to *Lethean*, first recorded in 1645 in a similar sense to *Lethe'd*. It is perhaps a slightly vaguer use than *chalic'd*—though this is not because of the suffix, but because the base-word offers more than one point of reference. But the gloss in the *O.E.D.*, implicit in the equation with *Lethean*, meets the case: 'pertaining to or causing oblivion or forgetfulness of the past'.

The numerous instances of Group I (of which the foregoing are a very limited sample) are far from exhausting the Shakespearian words formed with the adjectival suffix *-ed*. This is because Shakespeare's use of the suffix (which, as * *-to-*, was at the Indo-European stage added to verbal roots, or to nouns with no cognate verb) is not restricted to words for which there was originally no cognate verb. In fact, Shakespeare's usage exhibits a significant extension of the morphological basis for adjectival formations in *-ed*: it constitutes a substantial (yet entirely natural) innovation, which has strikingly enlarged the number of words formed with the adjectival *-ed* and has expanded the semantic range of the suffix.

The means of gaining an accurate understanding of the individual Shakespearian words concerned (many of which would otherwise remain puzzling, and have indeed sometimes puzzled learned and acute persons) is to classify them according to the grammatical function or functions of the base-word. The first step towards marking off the next class of adjectival formations in *-ed* (which we shall call Group II) is to recognize that, by the drastic pruning of grammatical endings in M.E., the two members of a noun-verb pair such as present English *love* had come to be identical in the spoken and the written form. This must have happened well before 1400, since the distinction would, in most varieties of M.E., have depended mainly on the survival of final *-n* in verbs (in the infinitive) and—in certain varieties of M.E. with a conservative type of accidence—

on the survival of the suffixal *-i-* in verbs of the old weak Class II. A framework for expanding the number of *-ed* formations by the creation of new ones on individual base-words which existed both as noun and verb was therefore available before 1400. That a very pronounced increase in all classes of adjectives in *-ed* is noticeable in the later sixteenth and the early seventeenth centuries is therefore likely to be due to the general impulse of that time to lavish coining of new words of all kinds. That there are so many nonce-formations among the Shakespearian examples (of all three groups of adjectives in *-ed* that we shall distinguish) supports this notion.

Some Shakespearian uses in this class are fortunately straightforward. There can be no doubt about the force of the *-ed* in the following passage:

> Revenge the jeering and *disdain'd* contempt
> Of this proud king.
> (*1 Hen. IV*, I, iii, 183–4)

The word is the only recorded example of this sense (glossed in the *O.E.D.* as 'characterized by disdain; disdainful, scornful'). But the use of the adverb *disdainedly* twice by Coverdale in 1535 in the sense 'scornfully, disdainfully' shows that the adjective was probably in being before Shakespeare's time (since it is likely to have been the immediate model for Coverdale's word). The *O.E.D.* has recorded the Shakespearian adjective under the same head-word as the sense 'treated with disdain; despised, scorned' (which is clearly past participial), and classified both these parts of the material as 'past participial adjective'. Both aspects of the procedure are the normal practice of the *O.E.D.* in such cases; and the first is a corollary of the second. The definition of Shakespeare's use here (as of the comparable ones elsewhere) as '*ppl.a.*' is not really acceptable. In terms of the English material it is not true; and if it is founded on the view that I.E. * *-to-* was a suffix used to form past participial adjectives, it is true only of one type of material and not of the other (represented in *L. caudātus* etc.), and is therefore misleading. Since the gloss 'characterized by' (which is entirely valid) is palpably another way of putting 'having the quality of', Shakespeare's use is close to one of the chief senses of the suffix at an early stage, and is thus historically orthodox. A general point emerges from consideration of this Shakespearian word: since Shakespeare knew and used the adjective *disdainful* (not less than nine times) in a precisely equivalent sense, the suffix *-ed* was evidently an equivalent of *ful* and therefore adjectival (which is one specific reason, incidentally, for boggling at the *O.E.D.*'s classification of it as '*ppl.*').

This equivalence also applies to our next two examples of Group II words, the first of which is used only once by Shakespeare, in *The Merchant of Venice*:

> Thus ornament is but the *guiled* shore
> To a most dangerous sea. (III, ii, 97–8)

Guiled is a unique example of this use 'full of guile; treacherous', and in the *O.E.D.* is in the usual way registered under the same head-word as the true past participial use 'beguiled; deceived' (recorded only once, in *The Romaunt of the Rose*), and as usual classed along with it as '*ppl.a.*'. Shakespeare knew the synonymous *guileful* and used it (twice). *Beguiled* of *Lucrece* 1544 should also be noted; but it occurs in a context that does not conclusively establish whether it is a formation with the *-ed* suffix or the past participle of the verb, and it should therefore perhaps be left out of account. The *O.E.D.* records, under *beguiled* '*ppl.a.*' (analyzed by it exclusively as a formation on the verb), an illustrative quotation of 1561 which is a probable, if not altogether assured, example of the adjectival formation with the suffix *-ed*. If this suspicion is right, Shakespeare was not first in the field with *beguiled* (though he may well have evolved it independently).

Another fairly clear example under this head is *delighted*, used three times by Shakespeare:

> If virtue no ~ beauty lack
> (*Oth.*, I, iii, 289)
>
> This sensible warm motion to become
> A kneaded clod; and the ~ spirit
> To bathe in fiery floods . . .
> (*M. for M.*, III, i, 121–3)
>
> . . . to make my gift,
> The more delay'd, ~ . . .
> (*Cym.*, V, iv, 101–2)

The *O.E.D.* registers only the first two examples under the separate word *delighted*, and does not mention the third either there or under the verb *delight*. Its gloss for the first two is as usual acceptable—'Endowed or attended with delight; affording delight, delightful'. They are listed as examples of sense 2, for which the only others are three dated 1634, 1667, and 1747; and for the only other sense, 'filled with delight, highly pleased or gratified', only two quotations are given, the first of which (*c.* 1687) is probably past participial, and the second ambiguous as a formation. Thus *delighted* is evidently a Shakespearian coinage in sense 2, which is to be regarded as an adjective formed on the noun. The *O.E.D.* is of course to be understood as implying the latter point, under the usual regrettably unspecific formula 'from DELIGHT verb and substantive + -ED': in the *O.E.D.*'s own terms, the true participial *-ed* is classified in a separate entry as -ED[1], while the suffix *-ed* forming adjectives from nouns is entered as -ED[2].

These examples must suffice for the equivalence of words in this group with adjectives in *-ful*. The signs are that some, at least, were struck out as synonymous variants of the corresponding formations in *-ful*. It is therefore important to note that in the latter class the base-word in formations going back to the O.E. stage was always a noun, except for *deorcful*, which is a rendering of L. *tenebrosus* and plausibly suspected of being an imitation of it. This strengthens the probability that members of Group II in *-ed* were in fact formed on the noun and not the cognate verb—even though, admittedly, adjectives in *-ful* began to be formed in early modern English on individual words that existed both as a noun and as a verb, such as *changeful*.

Bradley, the editor of this volume of the *O.E.D.*, has commented on this latter point (s.v. *-ful* suffix, 1) in terms highly relevant to the character of adjectival formations of Group II with the suffix *-ed*:

> As the sbs. to which *-ful* is appended are often nouns of action or state coincident in form with the stems of related vbs., it happens frequently that *a word really from a sb.* + -ful *is associated in ordinary apprehension rather with the vb. than the sb.* [my italics]

This is in effect the same point as has been made below[1] about Group II formations in *-ed*. Moreover, the essential force of the suffix *-ful* at the O.E. and the M.E. stages respectively, according to Bradley's definition, is 'having, characterized by' (the attributes denoted by the sb.) and 'possessing the qualities of' (e.g. *masterful*, *manful*)—and *-ed* is, in many adjectival formations, to be analyzed as expressing one or other of these.

A Shakespearian example of the second, in fact, is available in *Hamlet*:

> Good Hamlet, cast thy *nighted* colour off.
> (I, ii, 68)

The force of *-ed* in the adjective is 'pertaining to, having the quality of', and would easily and naturally come to be felt as similative—'(a colour) *like* night' i.e. 'dark'. This latter is the specific sense intended by Shakespeare, as in *King Lear*, IV, v, 13:

> Edmund, I think, is gone
> In pity of his misery, to dispatch
> His *nighted* life,

[1] P. 33.

where the adjective can be interpreted as meaning 'night-like', but specifically refers to the darkness of Gloucester's condition after he has been blinded.

A specially instructive example of the same type is the following in *Cymbeline*, IV, ii, 228:

Yea, and *furred* moss besides, when flow'rs are none.

This is not registered in the *O.E.D.*, and does not fit any of the four senses there defined (one of which is 'provided with or having fur'), since it can hardly be anything other than 'resembling fur' or 'having the quality of fur'. In any case, Shakespeare's use is to be regarded as a coinage, again of nonce-formation type. Three points are to be noted: all four recorded senses of *furred* are attested for *furry*; those two that clearly imply formation on the noun are attested for *furred* a hundred and fifty years earlier than for *furry*; one of those recorded in *furry* is defined as 'resembling fur, fur-like, soft' (which is what must be posited for *furred* in our example), and is also applied to moss but is attested only once—and in the later nineteenth century. Moreover, *furry* is not recorded in any sense till *c.* 1674. It is thus clear that *furred* is virtually an equivalent of *furry*, and that it is the older type (though later extensively replaced by *furry*).

A representative of this group of formations that is worth noticing is the following instance in *The Winter's Tale*, I, ii, 172 and *Othello*, I, iii, 270 respectively:

So stands this squire
Offic'd with me

No, when light-wing'd toys
Of feather'd Cupid seel with wanton dullness
My speculative and *offic'd* instruments,
That my disports corrupt and taint my business . . .

The *O.E.D.* does not recognize or record an adj. *officed* formed on the noun: it registers both these forms under the verb *office*. The first is treated as a past participle and as the earliest example of the sense 'to appoint to, or place in, office'. But the only other example (dated 1763) of this alleged sense is syntactically different from Shakespeare's use, since *offic'd* is preceded by *was* and might therefore be the past participle, and is semantically different in meaning more probably '(was) given the task (of explaining)'. Shakespeare's use is unambiguously adjectival, and is most smoothly and naturally analyzed as a formation directly on the noun.

The example in *Othello* is in the *O.E.D.* registered separately under the verb, as a past participial adj. formed on it, and is glossed 'having a particular function'. But the only other examples of this past participial adj. are three from Florio, all applying to a church, and glossed by him as 'served with due office'—a sense which is clearly different from Shakespeare's use and is clearly one appropriate to the part participle of the verb. Shakespeare's use of the word in each passage, in fact, is best analyzed as a formation on the noun by means of the adjective-forming suffix *-ed*: the second would be adequately rendered as 'having a (serious) function to perform'. And Shakespeare's use was evidently an innovation.

The trend to a marginally new and different sense is also to be found in the following two examples, from *Othello*:

Yield up, O love, thy crown and *hearted* throne
To tyrannous hate! (III, iii, 452–3)

I hate the Moor. My cause is *hearted*: thine hath no less reason. (I, iii, 364–5)

The word is comparatively old, as a member of this class: it is first recorded soon after 1200, in the *Ancrene Riwle*. Three of the senses under which it is registered in the *O.E.D.* (s.v. 1, 2, and 3) are all examples of one or another aspect of the notion 'endowed with (heart, in one or another sense)'. The fourth is a nineteenth-century use—'having the shape of a heart'—and accordingly not of direct interest here. The only other sense is there defined 'fixed or established in the heart', and is illustrated by the first Shakespearian example quoted above and another text dated 1850. Where the second Shakespearian use is concerned, the full context, though not altogether decisive, is consistent with a gloss 'rooted in the heart' (and hence perhaps 'heart-felt') or 'passionately felt'. The *O.E.D.* has preferred to register this second use under the verb *heart* (i.e. as a past participle), in the sense 'to take to heart, fix or establish in the heart', on the strength of a clear example of this sense in an ordinary form of the verb, from a text of 1633. But the collocation with *is* in Shakespeare's use slightly favours the other analysis chosen above.

The third group of formations in *-ed* is, for the purposes of this study, the most important because the least well understood. The essential clue to an accurate understanding of the class and to the correct interpretation of individual members of it is available in the nature of words of Group II. The existence of adjectives formed on a word in very common use both as a noun and as a verb, such as *delight*, was evidently enough to provide a model for new formations on words which (because there was no noun of identical form) were unambiguously and exclusively verbs, such as *accept*. All that is involved is an analogical process of a familiar type: when a single linguistic form has two distinct grammatical functions, it may, when used in the one function, be interpreted by speakers of the language as being used in the other.

The example in *Troilus and Cressida*, III, iii, 30:

> and her presence
> Shall quite strike off all service I have done
> In most *accepted* pain

has not been registered by the *O.E.D.*, which does however recognize a '*ppl.a.*' of this form with a sense 2, glossed 'satisfactory, acceptable' and attested in three examples of 1500, 1611, and 1677. Moreover, *acceptedly* (which is likely to depend on and imply the existence of *accepted*) is recorded once in the corresponding sense 'acceptably' from Ben Jonson in 1599. The synonymous adj. *acceptable* is recorded from 1386, and was used once by Shakespeare; we must therefore, where Group III words are concerned, reckon with an equivalence of *-ed* and *-able*. To set up these 'equivalences' between one suffix and another implies merely that the second member of such a pair happens to be in English a means of expressing, *in the words concerned*, the main semantic implication contributed by the suffix to the formations in question. In words other than these much the same implication might be expressed by a different suffix, or by the use of the suffix with a synonymous base-word: there is no **bragful* alongside Shakespeare's *bragged* in *Coriolanus*, I, viii, 12 (though there might easily have been), but the synonymous *boastful* serves to show the force of the suffix.

It should be noted that, since a verb may be either transitive or intransitive (and very commonly both), a formation on a verb may have a passive or an active force respectively. Thus the two suffixes *-ed* and *-able* may be expected to mean either 'having the property of' (performing the action expressed in the verb) or 'having the property of being' (acted upon in the sense in question), 'such as to ...' or 'such as to be ...'. Everything that has been said here so far is of course meant to imply that in Group III formations *-ed* is necessarily by origin the adjectival suffix—not only because of the analogical process posited above, but because the meaning of such formations rules out the ending of the past participle. We may note in passing that the etymological statement in the *O.E.D.* under *accepted* merely names -ED, without specifying (and therefore perhaps without recognizing) that -ED[2] is what is in question.

When the base-word is a verb, and the context is not totally explicit, in the nature of things it is sometimes difficult or impossible to be sure that a formation in *-ed* contains the suffix and not the ending of the past participle. But in the following instance in *Romeo and Juliet*, III, ii, 77 one may perhaps have the temerity to dissent from the *O.E.D.*, which registers the Shakespearian word not only under a '*ppl.a.*' of the same form (as usual), but under a sense and a gloss which would classify it as a past participle ('looked down upon, contemned, scorned'):

Dove-feather'd raven! wolfish-ravening lamb!
Despised substance of divinest show!

This utterance of Juliet's is her reaction to the Nurse's information that Romeo has killed Tybalt; and it expresses an attitude to Romeo initiated in that moment, soon after the utterly different one of amorous ardour expressed in her words at the opening of the scene just before. Thus she cannot be thought to have previously despised Romeo; *despised* therefore cannot be the past participle, but must contain the suffix *-ed* and mean 'despicable'.

The excellent *Shakespeare–Lexicon* of Alexander Schmidt[1] lists seven or eight other examples of what he interprets as this same use; but most of them seem unsafe for contextual reasons. Matters are much the same for the use of *detested* in the sense that Schmidt glosses 'abominable', and for which he lists thirteen examples. Though several of these are contextually doubtful, the following seem reasonably secure examples of the suffix *-ed* and of the sense 'detestable, contemptible':

Abhorred villain! Unnatural, *detested*, brutish villain!
(*Lear*, I, ii, 74)

Persuade me rather to be slave and sumpter
To this *detested* groom. (*Lear*, II, iv, 216)

The *O.E.D.* however, does not recognize any such use. It registers the word, but as a '*ppl.a.*' in only one sense, which is without doubt meant to imply the interpretation of *-ed* here as the ending of the past participle: 'Intensely disliked ... etc.' And among the five examples given (from 1552 into the nineteenth century) is one from Shakespeare, which it would surely be wiser to treat as ambiguous:

Glory grows guilty of *detested* crimes.
(*L. L. Lost*, IV, i, 31)

Moreover, the *O.E.D.* registers the word *detestedly* (adv.) as the sole example (from a text dated 1836) in a sense glossed 'with detestation': this surely presupposes, if not the word *detested* itself, at least the pattern **detested* as an adj. in the corresponding sense 'feeling detestation'. That is to say, there is an implied knowledge of an equivalence of the suffix *-ed* with an adjectival use of the present participial *-ing* (an equivalence to be noticed below).[2]

The examples of Group III formations in which the suffix *-ed* can be equated with *-able* can of course be multiplied; but we need notice only one more, as a specially illuminating case, in *Measure for Measure*, III, ii, 55:

Ever your fresh whore and your powder'd bawd—an *unshunn'd* consequence; it must be so.

The *O.E.D.* registers this as usual as a '*ppl.a.*' and without a gloss; this is unfortunate, since the only other example, dated 1648, is from Hexham's *Dutch–English Dictionary* and is most likely to be a straightforward example of past participle. The context, however, makes it clear that Shakespeare's use is to be glossed 'unavoidable'.

Shakespeare also used the word *unshunnable*, once only, in *Othello*, III, iii, 279; and as the only other examples of this are two nineteenth-century ones, it is clear that both *unshunned* and *unshunnable* were coined by Shakespeare, and that the suffix *-ed* is here an equivalent of *-able*. An important and helpful further point is the existence of the word *unshunning*

[1] Fourth ed., revised G. Sarrazin (Berlin, 1923).
[2] P. 35.

(recorded once only, in 1593), which renders L. *inevitabili* and thus incontrovertibly means 'unavoidable', and which the *O.E.D.* classifies as a '*ppl.a.*'. That this abbreviation here (surprisingly) means '*present* participial adjective' appears from the accompanying reference to UN-[1] 10, an entry which is concerned with the use of *un-* in late nineteenth-century combinations with present participles. But this in turn is a mistaken or questionable analysis of *unshunning* by the *O.E.D.*: since the word means 'unavoidable', and *-ing* therefore in this instance contains the implication of a passive use of the verb used as base-word (which is not possible in the normal use of the present participle), it might well be the gerundial *-ing*. It is in fact matched in Shakespeare's usage by certain adjectival formations with gerundial *-ing*, such as *sweating* in *Antony and Cleopatra*, I, iii, 93; *feeling* in *King Lear*, IV, vi, 224, *Romeo and Juliet*, III, v, 74, and *The Winter's Tale*, IV, ii, 6; and probably *lamenting* in *Titus Andronicus*, III, ii, 62.

As it happens, there are formations of Group III that really do attest an equivalence of the adjectival *-ed* with the *-ing* of the present participle (used adjectivally). A simple instance occurs in *Coriolanus*, III, i, 292:

> Now the good gods forbid
> That our renowned Rome, whose gratitude
> Towards her *deserved* children is enroll'd
> In Jove's own book, like an unnatural dam
> Should now eat up her own!

This is the sole example in the *O.E.D.* of a use there glossed 'that has deserved; meritorious, worthy' and rightly equated with the present participial adj. *deserving*. Since the latter is recorded from 1576, and especially since Shakespeare used it himself (*Othello*, II, i, 143), *deserved* was probably struck out by him as an equivalent of *deserving*.

The one other reasonably assured example to be mentioned here of this equivalence of the suffix *-ed* in Group III formations with present participial *-ing* occurs in *The Comedy of Errors*, V, i, 298:

> And careful hours with time's *deformed* hand
> Have written strange defeatures in my face.

The contextually prescribed interpretation of *deformed* here is 'that deforms', i.e. 'deforming'. Neither this example nor any others of this use are registered in the *O.E.D.*; the word is thus evidently a Shakespearian innovation (in this sense), and a nonce-formation. The present participial adj. *deforming* is not recorded till 1870; but the pattern concerned in this use of *deformed* was of course available to Shakespeare.

The foregoing material for Group III, and especially the last two examples, suffice to show that Shakespeare's use of the form *becomed* (in the passage from *Romeo and Juliet* which was our starting-point) is in keeping with the mode of formation of at least some other Group III adjectives in *-ed*, and that it is entirely natural and intelligible. In fact, it is a third example of the equivalence of the suffix *-ed* with *-ing* (since the form *becomed* here means 'becoming'). It could not have been evolved by Shakespeare if there had been no such equivalence (at least as a relation latent in the implication contained in each—in *-ing*, of course, as the ending of the present participle).

These latter examples may just conceivably avail to provide an explanation of a word in *The Winter's Tale*, IV, iv, 524:

> And with my best endeavours in your absence
> Your *discontenting* father strive to qualify.

The *O.E.D.* records, in addition to this example, one slightly earlier and one slightly later (1605 and 1613 respectively), in this use, glossed 'feeling or showing discontent'. The verb *discontent*, however, is recorded only in two transitive senses, *viz.* 'to deprive of contentment, etc.' and 'to displease, vex'. These do not provide an orthodox basis for an adj. *discontenting* in the contextually required sense, as a formation on the verb. The word is therefore best explained as the inverse form of the equation of the suffix *-ed* (in Group III formations) with the present participial *-ing*. That is to say, the existence of the adj. *discontented* (which happens to belong to Group II) has led to the coinage of a word formed with the other member of the equation, as a legitimate synonymous equivalent of *discontented*. That this would be a typical practice in the late sixteenth and early seventeenth centuries is vouched for by the existence of *discontentful* (recorded 1615 to *c.* 1677, in three examples) and *discontentive* (recorded 1607–27, in three examples).

The methods applied above to the history and the uses of the suffix *-ed*, and the results worked out by means of them, can be used to bring certainty into the interpretation of a Shakespearian word which has been the subject of disagreement among authorities—indeed, between two who, as editors of the *O.E.D.*, might be regarded as maximally authoritative. The word in question occurs in *King Lear*, III, vii, 60:

> The sea, with such a storm as his bare head
> In hell-black night endur'd, would have buoy'd up
> And quenched the *stelled* fires.

Stelled is the first recorded example of this adjective, and is glossed in the *O.E.D.* '? Formed into stars; stellar'. The only others, dated 1628 and 1656, are evidently meant to be covered by the gloss *b.*: 'Studded with stars, starred'. The *O.E.D.* analyzes the formation as being on L. *stella* 'star', with the suffix -ED. This presumably expresses the view of Bradley, who edited the section of the *O.E.D.* dealing with words beginning in *st*. But Onions, in *A Shakespeare Glossary*, gives tentative priority to another view, while referring to the first: '*s. fires* (?) fixed stars (but often taken = stellate, starry)' It must be said that Onions' preferred view is mistaken, while Bradley was in error in invoking -ED[1] as the formant.

By a lucky chance, there is helpful evidence available within the vocabulary of English which points the way to a solution, at least if one has duly considered the uses of the suffix *-ed*. It may first be noted, as a piece of negative evidence, that the abundant examples of the verb *stell* in the sense 'to fix, post, place' (s.v. 2), in which it is recorded from *c.* 1470 into the twentieth century, all occur in works written in Scots or by Scotsmen or about Scottish life. This is a warning against any interpretation of *stelled* as a form of the verb *stell* and as meaning 'to fix in position'. But the clue that matters is the existence of the English adjective *stellate* and of the Latin adjective *stēllātus* (formed on *stella* 'star') that is given as its etymon in the *O.E.D.* The only pre-Shakespearian example of *stellate*, in which it bears the sense 'studded with stars' (applied to the sky), is recorded from a work in Scots (*c.* 1500). The next, dated 1661, is in the sense 'pertaining to or proceeding from the stars' (applied to 'influences'), and is the only example of this. The third sense, 'star-shaped', recorded abundantly from 1661 onwards, is in practice a technical term used in one or another of the sciences.

L. *stēllātus* (recorded since Caesar and Vergil) is a member of the class exemplified above by *caudātus* etc., with the difference that verb-forms were deduced from it: *stēllāns* (recorded since Cicero), *stēllō* and *stēllāre* (since Cicero and Lucretius). It thus illustrates the process by which such words were drawn into the system of verb-formation (though in this case the process stopped short of completeness), and themselves came to function as past participles. Since the pre-Shakespearian *stellate* is a unique example, and is known only from a work in Scots, Shakespeare's *stelled* is unlikely to have been suggested by it. On the other hand, it does seem very likely to have been struck out on the model of the L. adj. *stēllātus*, with replacement of the L. adjective-forming suffix by the native suffix *-ed* which was its equivalent. The native equivalent of Shakespeare's use is *-y* in *starry*, in the sense 'consisting of stars', 'of the stars'—with an implication that is recorded for the suffix *-y* in *furry* (s.v. 1). This is nearer the mark—in terms of the evidence given above and the conclusions drawn from it—than Bradley's gloss 'formed into stars; stellar'.

It follows, of course, from the foregoing analysis that *-ed* in *stelled* is the adjectival -ED², not the past participial ending; and that *stelled*, even though a calque on a Latin word, is an entirely orthodox member of our Group I formations. Though the two English words concerned (*stelled* and *stellate*) are so rare, one could hardly hope for a more felicitous example of the intimate connection between the English words of Group I and the corresponding type of Latin formation with which we began the attempt to elucidate them.

A word that involves an internal English equivalence (of a kind less open to certainty in interpretation) of the suffix *-ed* with *-ate* occurs in the Folio text of *King Lear*, IV, iv, 26:

> Therefore great France
> My mourning and *importun'd* tears hath pitied.

The surviving native equivalent, the adj. *importunate*, is recorded from 1477 in the required sense 'persistent (in soliciting), pressing'. This word is itself not altogether clear as a formation, since there is no L. adjective of corresponding form, but only *importun-us* (with the stem of which *-ate*, as a naturalized suffix, has been combined), and since the element *-ate* has a complex history. However, *importun'd* can be satisfactorily interpreted as a Group III formation, i.e. on the verb *importune* (which is recorded in the required sense from 1530, apart from the French verb of which it is an adoption). Accordingly, *importunate* (adj.) can be analyzed in the same terms, as a formation on the verb *importune*, with the suffix *-ate* used as its L. equivalent *-ātus* was originally used in the *caudātus* class to form adjectives from nouns.

SHAKESPEARE'S USE OF COLLOQUIAL LANGUAGE

KENNETH HUDSON

'Don't you think, deep down', wrote Paul Jennings, in a recent article about contemporary stage dialogue, 'reading almost any modern novel or looking at any modern play, "that's not the way people talk"? And don't you feel this especially when it's one of those realist plays?'[1] The short answer to Mr Jennings' question may well be 'Yes', but the short answer can be very misleading and largely beside the point. What we feel about a dramatist or a play depends to a great extent on what we want to feel. If, for social or cultural reasons, it is important for us to believe that Pinter or Charles Wood have an ear for conversation and an ability to write down what they hear that makes Shakespeare seem a blundering amateur, the dialogue of a Pinter or Wood play will no doubt appear highly convincing. If, on the other hand, we have no wish to accept what these playwrights are trying to tell us and if we find their attitude to life unappealing or repulsive, we are very likely to question their mental equipment and technical skill. The question is not merely, 'Is this dialogue convincing?' but 'convincing to what people, in what mood, under what circumstances?'

For half-a-century at least, the general opinion of Shakespearian critics has been that Shakespeare had an exceptionally good ear for the speech of his time and an exceptional ability to sift that speech and to absorb it into the language of his plays. Bernard Shaw believed that Shakespeare was a grossly over-worshipped national idol and declared that he himself had done all he could

> to open English eyes to the emptiness of Shakespeare's philosophy, to the superficiality and secondhandness of his morality, to his weakness and incoherence as a thinker, to his snobbery, his vulgar prejudices, his ignorance, his disqualification of all sorts for the philosophic eminence claimed for him.[2]

But Shaw understood perfectly well that, in England at least, Shakespeare's reputation did not rest on the quality or supposed quality of his philosophy. It was 'the mere word music which makes Shakespeare so irresistible in England', his 'prodigious literary power, his fun, his mimicry and the endearing qualities that earned him the title of "the gentle Shakespeare".'[3] This puts the emphasis where it properly belongs, on Shakespeare's power to entertain and impress an audience. A playwright with this power is, by definition, a successful playwright, whether his name is Shakespeare, Pinter or Shaw. It is not his raw materials that matter, but what he makes of them and what his audience thinks of the results. And the spoken language of his time is not the least of his raw materials.

Some remarkable claims have been made about Shakespeare's ability to mirror contemporary speech. Miss Muriel St Clair Byrne, for instance, has said that 'we know "by instinct"

[1] 'Actors' Eosh', *The Times*, 5 April 1969.

[2] Letters to V. Tchertkoff printed in *Tolstoy on Shakespeare*, ed. Tchertkoff (London, 1907), p. 114.

[3] *Ibid.*, p. 116.

that in Shakespeare we are listening to the real language of men'.[1] Professor F. P. Wilson is no less certain. He insists that Shakespeare's 'instinct for what was permanent in the colloquial language of his day is stronger than that of any contemporary dramatist'.[2] Statements of this kind are difficult to check or contradict, for the excellent reason that a time-machine has not yet been invented and that we have no recordings of Elizabethans talking. Miss Byrne and Professor Wilson may be absolutely right, but they are wholly dependent on written evidence and on this somewhat unreliable tool, 'instinct'. Shakespearian studies, like most others, have suffered a good deal from inbreeding and, although it is no disadvantage for a critic to like his subject and admire his author, extreme veneration is not always helpful. To a modern audience, Shakespeare can not infrequently appear dull, precious and long-winded, even when well-acted, and it is not impossible that his own contemporaries found his work patchy. There are times when he seems to have lost his grip on language and situation and others when he is marvellously effective. When Miss Byrne tells us that 'in Shakespeare we are listening to the real language of men', it is not unreasonable to ask, 'Always?'

Shakespeare is not, of course, the only great writer to have been distorted by his admirers. Adoration can produce curious forms of blindness. For many people today one of the great charms of Jane Austen is that her characters have the very non-twentieth-century habit of avoiding contractions and elisions in their speech. We say, 'I'm not', they say 'I am not'. But this is a pure convention, based on the way the novels were printed and on the willingness of radio and television to follow a convention, which helps to give a nice period flavour to the production. If we rewrite a piece of Jane Austen dialogue, replacing the full forms by contractions as we are fully entitled to do, we offend a very large number of people, for whom Jane Austen-as-printed represents a golden age of English speech, but we re-humanize and modernize the characters in the novel and do proper justice to the author's ear for conversation. A typical extract, modified only in this way, would be this, spoken by Mr Woodhouse in *Emma*:

> You'll make my excuses, my dear, as civilly as possible. You'll say that I'm quite an invalid, and go nowhere, and therefore must decline their obliging invitation—beginning with my *compliments*, of course. But you'll do everything right. I needn't tell you what's to be done. We must remember to let James know that the carriage'll be wanted on Tuesday. I shall have no fears for you with him. We've never been there above once since the new approach was made; but still I've no doubt that James will take you very safely. And when you get there you must tell him at what time you'd have him come for you again, and you'd better name an early hour. You'll not be staying late. You'll get very tired when tea's over.

Either with or without the contractions such a passage does not, of course, reproduce contemporary speech. The hesitations, the repetitions, the pauses, the little parentheses have been thrown away. What we are left with is shaped, cleaned-up speech, colloquial language after the artist has finished with it. But, by accepting and insisting on the 'we have never, you will get' forms, the twentieth century cleans up early nineteenth-century speech more than the original author did, and in this way helps to foster the myth that our well-bred ancestors spoke with immaculate precision and purist attention to detail, avoiding all concessions to the regrettable habits of the lower orders. A similar myth has been established in our own times with regard to the Royal family. During the 1950s, as Robert

[1] 'The Foundations of Elizabethan Language', *Shakespeare Survey 17* (Cambridge, 1964), p. 239.

[2] 'Shakespeare and the Diction of Common Life', *Proceedings of the British Academy*, XXVII (1941), 169.

Robinson has shrewdly pointed out, 'Royal asides at public functions were printed in newspapers with the verbal elisions carefully rubbed out. No Royal person was allowed to say "that's" or "it's". They were always heard to speak the words in full.'[1]

The tendency to interpret evidence in a way that meets a personal psychological need is widespread in all fields of scholarship and nowhere, perhaps, is it more marked than in work on the Elizabethan age. If the inclination is there, the modern researcher will find everything to satisfy him that the Elizabethans were supremely creative and skilled in everything they touched, literature, music, politics, exploration, commerce. Such an attitude can easily distort judgement, just as the conviction that Shakespeare was incomparably the greatest Elizabethan writer can lead to the belief that Shakespeare did everything incomparably well, which is not necessarily true.

If we are to examine Miss St Clair Byrne's proposition 'that in Shakespeare we are listening to the real language of men', we can reasonably begin by trying to assess the other evidence we have as to what this 'real language of men' may have been. This evidence is to be found mainly in letters, legal depositions and other court records, conversation manuals, and the works of other dramatists. The evidence we are looking for is of speech as it flowed from people's mouths, its rhythms, its shapes, its blending of the trite and the vivid, its circumlocutions, mistakes and fumblings, its communicability. Disconnected colloquialisms may be interesting in themselves, but they are not speech, in the sense in which we are using the term. As Miss Byrne has said, 'The touchstone for speech is speakability. Does the ear say Yes as we read?'[2]

The ear is more likely to say Yes if it discovers a number of examples, each closely echoing the other. This is often possible. In 1586, Lord Burghley wrote to Lord Walsingham, reporting the stupidity of the watchmen on the road to London who had been appointed to apprehend three young men concerned in Babington's plot. When the watchmen were asked how they proposed to identify the men, one of them answered, 'By intelligence of their favour', and, in order to explain what that meant, '"Marry," said they, "one hath a hooked nose".'[3] With this, we are immediately in the world of Dogberry, who had 'comprehended two aspicious persons', and whose misunderstanding of the word 'tedious' had ludicrous consequences.

The speech of the uneducated is a rich mine for the dramatist, with its fondness for high-sounding words, its frequently absurd repetitions and its comic lack of discipline. Shakespeare was well aware of the stage-possibilities of this kind of lovable, infuriating nonsense and used it to excellent effect. Juliet's Nurse, Mistress Quickly and Elbow and Pompey come particularly to mind. A comparison between Shakespeare's dialogue of this kind and with similar passages from other dramatists is interesting.

The author of the Parnassus Plays, performed 1598–1602, must have listened closely to the talk of humble people. It is skilfully reproduced in these plays. Two quotations will illustrate this. The first comes from Leonard, the carrier.

I thanke god Mr none of my kindred weere fooles, my father (god rest his soule) was wonte to tell me (god rest his soule, he was as honest a carier as ever whip horse) he tolde me, I saie (I rember at that time he sate upon a stoole by the fire warminge his bootes) that these yonge schollers woulde spend Gods Abbies, if they had them and then woulde sende there fathers home false notaires.[4]

[1] *The Listener*, 7 August 1969.

[2] 'Foundations of Elizabethan Language', p. 228.

[3] *Calendar of State Papers, Domestic Series, 1581–1590*, ed. R. Lemon (London, 1865), p. 344 (10 August 1586).

[4] *The Three Parnassus Plays*, ed. J. B. Leishman (London, 1949), pp. 137–8.

The second character of this type is Simson, the tapster.

O good morowe my good neighbours. By cocke the worlde squintes upon mee, it hath not lookt straight upon mee this good while, but nowe it hath giuen mee a bob will stick by mee. Wott yee what? Luxurio, as they say, a man of gods makinge, as they saye, came to my house, as they saye, & was trusted by my wife, a kinde woman, as they say, for a dozen of ale, as they saye; & he, a naughtie felow, as they saye, is run away, as they saye.[1]

The flavour of this talk is convincing, with the inability to keep to the point and the wearisome punctuation by such phrases as 'God rest his soul' and 'as they say'. It is amusing in small doses and no doubt the actors who presented it to the Inns of Court audience gave it full value. But it is not memorable, as the Elbow-Froth-Pompey exchanges in *Measure for Measure* are.

Elbow. Prove it before these varlets here, thou honourable man, prove it.
Escalus. (*to Angelo*) Do you hear how he misplaces?
Pompey. Sir, she came in great with child, and longing —saving your honour's reverence—for stewed prunes. Sir, we had but two in the house, which at that very distant time stood, as it were, in a fruit-dish, a dish of some threepence; your honours have seen such dishes; they are not China-dishes, but very good dishes.
Escalus. Go to, go to; no matter for the dish, sir.
Pompey. No indeed sir, not of a pin; you are therein in the right; but to the point. As I say, this Mistress Elbow, being, as I say, with child, and being great-bellied, and longing, as I said, for prunes: and having but two in the dish, as I said, Master Froth here, this very man having eaten the rest, as I said, and, as I say, paying for them very honestly —for as you know, Master Froth, I could not give you threepence again—
Froth. No indeed.
Pompey. Very well; you being then, if you be remembered, cracking the stones of the aforesaid prunes—
Froth. Ay, so I did indeed.

(II, i, 85–108)

Humble people are not, of course, always muddled, nor always comic to those whose minds have been disciplined by education. Their language can possess a great deal of directness, vigour and charm, qualities to which the Elizabethan dramatists were not indifferent. Most sixteenth-century prose, as L. C. Knights has pointed out, is based, in fact, on 'living idiomatic speech'. Compared with what came later, it is 'closer to folk speech, to the English of ploughing, carting, selling and small town gossip'.[2]

The legal records abound with examples of the forceful language of ordinary people. In the 1580s a Yorkshireman was trying to explain to an ecclesiastical court why he felt his parson was useless. 'The roaringe of an oxe in the toppe of an ashe tree is better', he said, 'than all the preachinge that he can preache'.[3] In 1607, one Wiltshireman complains of a neighbour 'that he hath neverthelesse of late threatened your suppliant to choppe a dagger into his side'.[4] Another is described by his neighbours, in a strange mixture of the grand and the colloquial, as 'an epicurious co'tempner of the service of God and would rather lye slugging in his bed on the lord's saboth than come to the church'. In 1596, Anna Belsye, wife of a small farmer, told the Canterbury Consistory Court:

ther came the arlat Hambrook from Canterbury and the arlat Hebbing met her in the street And there fell into veri whot and angry words and the said Hebbing his wife arlat began in the manner or the like effect viz speaking to the said Hambrook Art thou come thou arrant whore thou bloodsucking whore though

[1] *Ibid.*, p. 162.

[2] *Drama and Society in the Age of Jonson* (London, 1937), p. 303.

[3] *Tudor Parish Documents in the Diocese of York*, ed. J. S. Purvis (Cambridge, 1948), p. 140.

[4] *Extracts from the Records of Wiltshire Quarter Sessions*, communicated by R. W. Merriman, Clerk of the Peace, Publications of the Wiltshire Archaeological Society (Devizes, 1885), p. 19.

hedgehore then the said Hambrok asked the said Hebbing whose whore she was and she answered Thou art my husbands whore.[1]

In 1587, Anne Walton, a thirty-year-old spinster living at Warmouth, Co. Durham, gave her version of a disagreement between two of her neighbours. She said that

a little before Christenmas, comeing up the streat by George Smith his shopp, in the company of the said Isabell, Lawrence Thompson, 'will you presume to goe in a ladie's companie?' whereupon the said Isabell made aunswer, 'I may as tite be a ladye as thou a lord, as thou, pricklouse that thou arte.' Whereunto the said George made aunswere, 'Thou art a tantarband and a tantarbawde whore.'[2]

Simple people are often at their verbal best when they are angry, usually because of an insult or supposed insult, and the angry phrases they uttered usually found their way into the legal depositions verbatim, because the phrases were what the case was all about. Frequently, however, it is impossible to decide if we are reading the words of the witness or of the person taking down the deposition. The wife of the master of the Grammar School at Durham may have said 'I dwelt with him, but I did never know any dishonestie with him',[3] but this record of what was said may equally represent the clerk's version of some more homely phrase. On the other hand, no clerk would have tampered with the evidence of Peter Clifford, who charged Captain Parkinson with saying, 'that her Majesty was a very bitch and as bad as the old Queen of France'.[4]

Sometimes we are able to compare two or more versions of the same incident, as given by different deponents. These are likely to give the substance and flavour of the original speech, but probably few of the words that were actually spoken. This may also be true of the records of great trials, which may have been written from notes or from memory. They may not be verbatim, but probably give a reasonable impression of the style of speech used by the principal performers.

There is, for instance, a long account of the Essex and Southampton trial, which reads as if it had been written by an eye-witness. The prosecution was in the hands of the Attorney-General, Sir Edmund Coke.

Earl of Southampton. . . . ffor my p'te I knewe nothinge in the morninge when I came to Essex house of Or goinge into London. When I was in London I hard not the p'clamacon. I was not neare by the lengthe of the streete. Let my Lo. Burleigh speake (I knowe him honorable) whether he sawe me in London or not. I never drewe my sword all the daye. I am charged to carry a pistol: I had none when I went owte. When I came into London I sawe one havinge a pistoll. I desired it of him and had it. But it had never a stone nor cold it have hurte a flye.[5]

Mr. Attorney. Nay my Lo ... howsoever you goe aboute to cloake matters, and to make a p.tence of an innocente harte, these Deposicions of men of yor owne companye admytt noe contradiction; And I wonder not at yor denyall, for you will appeare to be of all religions, one while Papist, an other while a Puritaine, and that but to gayne unto yor selfe all sortes of people.[6]

At the trial of Sir Walter Raleigh the prosecuting counsel was once again Sir Edmund Coke. His bullying manner comes through here very much as in his attack on the Earl of Southampton, even though his words are transmitted to us by a different reporter.

[1] Canterbury Consistory Court Records, x/11/5, fol. 134ᵛ (1596).

[2] *Depositions and other Ecclesiastical Proceedings from the Courts of Durham*, Surtees Society Publications (London, 1845), p. 322.

[3] *Ibid.*, p. 316.

[4] *Manuscripts of the Marquis of Salisbury Preserved at Hatfield House, Part V*, Historical Manuscripts Commission (London, 1894), p. 51 (document dated December 1594).

[5] *The Dr. Farmer Chetham MS*, ed. A. B. Grosart, Chetham Society Publications, LXXXIX (Manchester, 1873), p. 11.

[6] *Ibid.*, p. 21.

Attorney. Nay I will prove all: thou art a monster: thou hast an English face but a Spanish heart ... Now then see the most horrible practices that ever came out the bottomless pit of the lowest hell ... All that he did was by thy instigation, thou Viper; for I thou thee, thou Traitor ...
Thou art the most vile and execrable Traitor that ever lived.

Raleigh. You speak indiscreetly, barbarously and uncivilly.

Attorney. I want words sufficient to express thy viperous Treason.

Raleigh. I think you want words indeed, for you have spoken one thing half a dozen times.

Attorney. Thou art an odious fellow, thy name is hateful to all the realm of England for thy pride.[1]

Occasionally the clerk who took down the deposition married quotation and paraphrase so skilfully that the whole passage runs pleasantly as a single unit. The Canterbury records contain a delightful example of this kind, which gives a convincing impression of the speech of the people concerned, Richard Bond and Prudence Bramelo, both servants in the household of William Tybbes, of Sturry. One day, Prudence said to Richard:

In fayth, Richard I would you coulde fynde in your hart to love me as well as I love you. Mary qd this rondent to hyr I love you exceedingly well. Mary Richard sayd she to this rondent you speake but in Jest and I speake yt to you ernestly Ernestly qd this rondent? Alas prudence I thinke yor freendes would be lothe to here you so ill bestowed upon so poore a fellowe as I am havinge nothinge but my poore occupacon. The sayd prudence Answered thys Richard sayinge As for yor estate Rychard That maketh no greate matter ffor my master will not stycke to gyve me XXti nobles to my maryage iff ye will have me. Thereupon this rondent sayd iff your mayster will be so well mynded and benefyciall to you I will tell you more here after and as this Rondent afterwards about III or IIII dayes happened to bee in hys masters stable dressinge of two geldings The sayd Tybbes her master being at the stable doore sayd to this rondent, I heer say Rychard ye shall have Prudence my mayde To whom this rondent answered Sr yt may pleese you to with, that shee hath layne at me a good while to have your good will in maryage wt her, well, sayd the sayd Tybbes to this rondent, as for my goodwill, ye shall have yt at all tymes, and the best I can doo for you, though you are but poore and have but lyttle substance. Neverthelesse yf ye be mynded to have hir, I will bee a friend unto you.[2]

Miss St Clair Byrne places great value on private correspondence as a reliable guide to the speech of the Elizabethan period. Many of the surviving letters certainly sound as if they could have been spoken without great changes needing to be made to them. One could instance John Chamberlain, who writes to Sir Dudley Carleton in 1598, 'I am growne so privat that I stirre not abrode, nor mean to do, but to live at home like a snaile in the shell',[3] or Mrs Montgomery, wife of the Bishop of Raffo, chatting about Ireland in a letter to John Willoughby.

We are setteled in the Derye, in a verye pretye litell house, byldyd after the Indglesh fashone, but somewhat whith the lest for our company; but we will make yt bigger if you and Piggie will promise to come and dwell with us ... The most that I do mislyke ys that the Iresh doth often troubell our house, and manye tymes they doth lend to us a louse, which makes me many tymes remember my daughter Jane, which tould me that yf I went into Irlande I should be full of lyse.[4]

There is plenty of evidence that the great used vivid language without any feeling of self-consciousness or of striving for effect. In 1596 Lord Admiral Howard wrote to Lord Burghley, describing a sea-action. At one stage, he recalled, 'All the gallies (were) still playinge on us but to their owne losse for they wer well peppered'. After this 'Their men leaped out like frogges (and) many of them

[1] *State Trials.*

[2] Canterbury Consistory Court Records, x/10/11, fol. 33 (1568).

[3] *Letters of John Chamberlain,* ed. Sarah Williams, Camden Society Publications (London, 1861), p. 36.

[4] *Trevelyan Papers, Part III,* ed. W. C. Trevelyan and C. E. Trevelyan, Camden Society Publications (London, 1872), p. 100.

were kylled'. 'All the rest of their shippes ... went upp to Port Royall where they were suer for us, as it were in a bagge.'[1]

Lord Admiral Howard wrote in a way that Montaigne would have approved:

It is a naturall, simple and unaffected speech that I love, so written as it is spoken, and such upon the paper as it is in the mouth, a pithie, sinnowie, full, strong, compendious and materiall speech, not so delicate and affected, as vehement and piercing ... Rather difficult than tedious, void of affectation, free, loose and bold, that every member it seeme to make a bodie; not Pedanticall, nor Frier-like, nor lawyer-like, but rather downe right, souldier-like.[2]

This 'naturall, simple and unaffected speech, so written as it is spoken' is frequently found among a wide range of writers. It is there, under perfect discipline and control, in William Turner's *Herbal* of 1551. Describing Epimedium Turner writes:

In the moneth of July I sawe thys herbe havyng IX or X leves comyng out of an roote ... and at that tyme I coulde fynde in it nother floure nor fruyte. The nexte yere folowyng in the myddes of Marche in the same place, I founde the same herbe, wyth leves, stalke and floure, lyke unto wylde valerian, and twoo handbredes from that place I found two or thre leves lyke unto violettes commyng out of the same roote, so that out of the one end of the roote came leves lyke violets, out of the other end leves, stalke, and floures lyke Valerian.[3]

It is there in parts of John Stow's autobiography. During the last days of his mother's life:

One tyme aftar I had longe tarryed thar, she cried out, as she dyd allwayes (when I was there) 'Ye lorde send me some drynke. O! that I had some kynd of drynke, what some evar it were.' And at ye last she sayd to Thomas his wyfe: 'Dowghter, for ye lordes sake gyve me some drynke.' Whereinto after many such allyngs she answeryd: 'I cannot tell what drynke I should gyve you, for yffe I seche eny of owre owne drynke ye wyll not lyke it.' 'Yes, dowghter, yes', quod she, 'ye lorde knows I would fayne have some drynke.' And then she fetchinge halfe a pynt of small drynke (beare as I supose) my mother sayd, 'good dowghter, for ye lordes sake loke in my cobard for a lytle gyngar, and put into it.'[4]

On the other hand, there was strong pressure on men with cultural and social pretensions to adopt an elaborately patterned, euphuistic style of speaking and writing, full of classical allusions as evidence that one was not a member of the herd. However extraordinary these flights of language may seem today, there is good reason to believe that, in court, legal and aristocratic circles, there were people who talked and wrote in this way. For the playwright, they were as much a stock-type, always at hand for satirical treatment, as the watchman, peasant, Irishman or Welshman.

If it is possible to catch the rhythms and phrases of Elizabethan speech by reading letters, manuals, legal records, and biographical material of various kinds, how does one assess the skill with which the dramatists made use of the colloquial raw material available? There is surely only one test—was the result dramatically and artistically effective? I have already suggested that Pompey and his friends are more satisfactory as stage characters than corresponding figures in the Parnassus Plays, and that this is due to Shakespeare's superior powers of selection and imagination. One remembers his characters as one does not remember the characters of other dramatists, and this is not only because, generation after generation, Shakespeare's plays have been more written about and more frequently performed than those of his contemporaries. It is not merely a matter of familiarity. The real reason is that Shakespeare has squeezed

1 *Manuscripts of the Marquis of Bath Preserved at Longleat, Vol. II,* Historical Manuscripts Commission (Dublin, 1907), pp. 45–9.

2 *Essayes,* translated by Florio, Book I, Chapter 25 (London, 1613), p. 83.

3 Quoted in C. E. Raven, *English Naturalists from Neckham to Ray* (Cambridge, 1947), p. 85.

4 *A Survey of London,* ed. C. L. Kingsford (Oxford, 1908), I, lvii.

colloquial speech harder, so that more of the tedious stuff has dropped out. He controls his characters' prattling and makes them bigger and brighter than they could ever have been in real life, rather as if one made a tape-recording of a man with a bad stammer and then painstakingly edited the stammers out of the tape.

One could make an anthology from Elizabethan plays of passages of dialogue which, with all the cautions mentioned above, sound like Elizabethans talking. Such an anthology might reasonably include extracts from Dekker, Beaumont and Fletcher, Middleton and Ben Jonson, all of whom appear to have had a good ear for the conversation around them. These extracts might be entitled to a place.

Middleton: *The Roaring Girl*

Gallipot. What, Pru! nay, sweet Prudence!

Mistress Gallipot. What a pruing keep you! I think the baby would have a teat, it kyes so. Pray, be not so fond of me, leave your city humours; I'm vexed at you, to see how like a calf you come bleating after me.

Gallipot. Nay, honey Pru, how does your rising up before all the table show, and flinging from my friends so uncivilly! fie, Pru, fie! come.

Mistress Gallipot. Then up and ride, i'faith!

Gallipot. Up and ride? nay, my pretty Pru, that's far from my thought, duck; why mouse, thy mind is nibbling at something, what is't? what lies upon thy stomach? (III, ii, 1–12)

Dekker: *The Shoemaker's Holiday*

Ralph. Who calls there? what want you, sir?

Serving-man. Marry, I would have a pair of shoes made for a gentlewoman against to-morrow morning. What, can you do them?

Ralph. Yes sir, you shall have them. But what length's her foot?

Serving-man. Why, you must make them in all parts like this shoe; but, at any hand, fail not to do them, for the gentlewoman is to be married very early in the morning.

Ralph. How? by this shoe must it be made? by this? Are you sure, sir, by this?

Serving-man. How, by this? Am I sure, by this? Art thou in thy wits? I tell thee, I must have a pair of shoes, dost thou mark me? A pair of shoes, two shoes, made by this very shoe, this same shoe, against to-morrow morning by four o'clock. Dost understand me? Canst thou do't? (IV, ii, 3–16)

Beaumont and Fletcher: *The Knight of the Burning Pestle*

Mistress Merrythought. Give thee my blessing! no, I'll ne'er give thee my blessing; I'll see thee hanging first; it shall ne'er be said I gave thee my blessing. Thou art thy father's own son, of the right blood of the Merrythoughts. I may curse the time that e'er I knew thy father; he hath spent all his own and mine too; and when I tell him of it, he laughs and dances, and sings, and cries, 'A merry heart lives long-a'. And thou art a waste-thrift, and art run away from thy master that loved thee well, and art come to me; and I have laid up a little for my younger son Michael and thou thinkest to bezzle that, but thou shalt never be able to do it—Come hither, Michael. (I, iv, 1–13)

Jonson, Chapman, and Marston: *Eastward Ho!*

Goulding. Why how now sir? doe yee know where you are?

Quicksilver. Where I am? why sblood you loulthead where I am.

Goulding. Go to, go to, for shame go to bed, and sleepe out this immodestie; thou sham'st both my maister and his house.

Quicksilver. Shame? What shame? I thought thou wouldst show thy bringing up: and thou wert a Gentleman as I am, thou wouldst think it no shame to be drunk. Lend me some money. (II, i, 95–104)

Why is it that these four dramatists, using and shaping Elizabethan colloquial speech in a highly professional way, produce results that are somehow flatter and less satisfying than those that Shakespeare obtained from the same material? There are, I believe, two reasons for the difference. One is that Shakespeare's instinct for imagery disciplined his writing to an extraordinary degree, and the other is that he had a more highly developed sense of satire. Like that great reproducer of ordinary people's speech in our own times, the broadcaster,

Mr Johnny Morris, Shakespeare always heard his contemporaries talking in inverted commas. He was never quite part of the world they inhabited, but kept himself sufficiently on the fringe of life to maintain everyone he saw and listened to in a slightly distorted shape, rather as if his favourite cinema seat had been at the end of the front row of the stalls. For most of the time the other Elizabethan dramatists were too much in the centre of the auditorium and well back, looking at the screen head-on.

One can put this another way by saying that Shakespeare's characters are rarely mere camera-pointing reproductions of people in real life, whereas those of his fellow-dramatists not infrequently are. The colloquial speech he gives his characters is speech that has been turned inside out, pared away and fortified. His effects, like those of any great artist, are obtained with a minimum of words. His characterization depends to a great extent on the proportion of paper he leaves white, a mark of genius that so many Shakespearian actors and producers do their best to ignore and conceal, by smudging the pattern and jumbling the words together so that they cram and flatten the picture.

Two examples of Shakespeare's economy of words in his colloquial passages are to be found in *Twelfth Night* and *Romeo and Juliet*.

Fabian. Here he is, here he is. How is't with you, sir?
Sir Toby. How is't with you, man?
Malvolio. Go off, I discard you. Let me enjoy my private. Go off.
Maria. Lo, how hollow the fiend speaks within him; did I not tell you? Sir Toby, my lady prays you to have a care of him.
Malvolio. Ah ha, does she so?
Sir Toby. Go to, go to. Peace, peace, we must deal gently with him. (*T.N.* III, iv, 82–90)

Nurse. I pray you sir, what saucy merchant was this that was so full of his ropery?
Romeo. A gentleman, nurse, that loves to hear himself talk, and will speak more in a minute than he will stand to in a month.
Nurse. An 'a speak any thing against me, I'll take him down, and 'a were lustier than he is, and twenty such Jacks; and if I cannot, I'll find those that shall. Scurvy knave, I am none of his flirt-gills, I am none of his skains-mates. (*To Peter*) And thou must stand by too and suffer every knave to use me at his pleasure?
Peter. I saw no man use you at his pleasure: if I had, my weapon should quickly have been out, I warrant you: I dare draw as soon as another man, if I see occasion in a good quarrel, and the law on my side. (*Rom. & Jul.*, II, iv, 141–55)

Perhaps Shakespeare's most impressive achievement in transforming colloquial language into something different and unforgettable is the play-upon-this-pipe passage in *Hamlet*. The words and the sentence structure are simple, but the image is skilfully and beautifully developed.

Hamlet. Will you play upon this pipe?
Guildenstern. My lord, I cannot.
Hamlet. I pray you.
Guildenstern. Believe me, I cannot.
Hamlet. I do beseech you.
Guildenstern. I know no touch of it my lord.
Hamlet. It is as easy as lying; govern these ventages with your fingers and thumb, give it breath with your mouth, and it will discourse most eloquent music. Look you, these are the stops.
Guildenstern. But these cannot I commend to any utterance of harmony; I have not the skill.
Hamlet. Why, look you now, how unworthy a thing you make of me. You would play upon me, you would seem to know my stops, you would pluck out the heart of my mystery, you would sound me from my lowest note to the top of my compass, and there is much music, excellent voice, in this little organ, yet cannot you make it speak. 'Sblood, do you think I am easier to be played on than a pipe? Call me what instrument you will, though you can fret me, you cannot play upon me. (III, ii, 341–62)

It is passages such as this which make one aware of the soundness of F. P. Wilson's judgement when he wrote that:

Shakespeare's drama is continually irrigated by the diction of common life. But it does not remain the diction of common life. It is transmuted ... It is no mannered simplicity such as we sometimes find in Webster when he is trying to write like Shakespeare; but it is as if the fire of genius had reduced language to its elements.[1]

And this power of using simple and direct language was, as Professor Ifor Evans has pointed out,[2] something that Shakespeare had to develop from his own resources:

In exploiting the resounding and elaborate elements in language he was answering the spirit of his age and the practice of his contemporaries, but the quiet language was a dramatic opportunity and necessity that he had to discover for himself, against the fashion of his time, and indeed in opposition to much that was dominant in his own temperament.

[1] 'Shakespeare and the Diction of Common Life', p. 191.

[2] *The Language of Shakespeare's Plays* (London, 1952), p. 48.

WORDS, ACTION, AND ARTISTIC ECONOMY

G. R. HIBBARD

'Here therefore is the first distemper of learning', wrote Bacon of the Renaissance Latinists, 'when men study words and not matter.'[1] Had he been interested in the drama of his own country, he might have said something similar about the best plays that were being written at the time when Shakespeare was composing his first extant works, somewhere around 1589. But, if he had been fair, he would have added that the copie which had such an appeal for Marlowe and Kyd was one of the things that helped to make their plays sing, where those of their predecessors had merely jingled. Still, the distemper was there; and, as many critics have noted, Shakespeare himself was not immune from it. There is something prodigal about his use of language in the early plays. Delighting in its Protean qualities, he often allows his fascination with a figure of speech to come into conflict with his dramatic purposes. Unlike his contemporaries, however, he also seems to have been aware of the danger from a very early stage, for there are times when he appears to be catching himself out, as it were. The opening of *3 Henry VI*, II, v, for example, presents the King soliloquizing while the battle of Towton goes on around him. He launches at once into an elaborate double simile, comparing the state of the battle first to the conflict of clouds with growing light at dawn, and then to that between the wind and the tide. The vivid sensuous picture that he paints extends over twelve lines; but, at the end of it, Shakespeare seems suddenly to have realized that his audience might well have forgotten what the point of the similes was, for, having begun with the line 'This battle fares like to the morning's war', he now has the King add 'So is the equal poise of this fell war'.[2]

Plainly, the capacity for self-criticism, so evident in the last line quoted, played a large part in the complex process that led from the early to the mature manner, but the process itself is singularly hard to chart or explain. In fact, M. C. Bradbrook has said of it that critics tend to evade the problem because 'It is too vast and intimidating'.[3] Nevertheless, it is possible to make a tentative beginning, provided that one can find some element running through much of Shakespeare's work that admits of valid comparisons being made between passages written at different times. One such common factor is, I think, his life-long interest in the great Renaissance commonplace of the opposition between light and darkness, day and night.[4] Its first impressive appearance is in *2 Henry VI*, IV, i, a scene that is generally accepted as Shakespeare's even by those who think that he is not the sole author

[1] *The Advancement of Learning*, Bk. I, IV, 3.

[2] All quotations from Shakespeare, unless otherwise stated, follow the text of Peter Alexander's edition of the *Complete Works* (1951).

[3] *Shakespeare Survey 7* (Cambridge, 1954), p. 1.

[4] For the significance of this opposition in Renaissance Art, see Erwin Panofsky, *Studies in Iconology* (Harper Torchbooks ed., New York, 1962), pp. 110–11.

of the play. It is the scene in which Suffolk, having been taken prisoner in a fight at sea, is murdered on the coast of Kent by Walter Whitmore, and it opens with the following words, spoken by the Lieutenant who commands Suffolk's captors:

The gaudy, blabbing, and remorseful day
Is crept into the bosom of the sea;
And now loud-howling wolves arouse the jades
That drag the tragic melancholy night;
Who with their drowsy, slow, and flagging wings
Clip dead men's graves, and from their misty jaws
Breathe foul contagious darkness in the air.
Therefore bring forth the soldiers of our prize;
For, whilst our pinnace anchors in the Downs,
Here shall they make their ransom on the sand,
Or with their blood stain this discoloured shore.
Master, this prisoner freely give I thee;
And thou that art his mate make boot of this;
The other, Walter Whitmore, is thy share.
(IV, i, 1–14)

Some sixteen or seventeen years later Shakespeare wrote *Macbeth*, where the hero tells his wife about the arrangements he has made for the murder of Banquo and Fleance in a dialogue that runs thus:

Macbeth. O, full of scorpions is my mind, dear wife!
Thou know'st that Banquo, and his Fleance, lives.
Lady Macbeth. But in them nature's copy's not eterne.
Macbeth. There's comfort yet; they are assailable.
Then be thou jocund. Ere the bat hath flown
His cloister'd flight; ere to black Hecate's summons
The shard-borne beetle with his drowsy hums
Hath rung night's yawning peal, there shall be done
A deed of dreadful note.
Lady Macbeth. What's to be done?
Macbeth. Be innocent of the knowledge, dearest chuck,
Till thou applaud the deed. Come, seeling night,
Scarf up the tender eye of pitiful day,
And with thy bloody and invisible hand
Cancel and tear to pieces that great bond
Which keeps me pale. Light thickens, and the crow
Makes wing to th' rooky wood;
Good things of day begin to droop and drowse,
Whiles night's black agents to their preys do rouse.
Thou marvell'st at my words; but hold thee still:
Things bad begun make strong themselves by ill.
So, prithee go with me. (III, ii, 36–56)

The first seven lines of the Lieutenant's speech in *2 Henry VI* and the speeches of Macbeth, especially the eight lines that begin with the words 'Come, seeling night', are obviously based on the same great commonplace and on the same association of ideas and images. As long ago as 1794, Walter Whiter pointed out the affinities between the Lieutenant's speech and other passages in *Macbeth*.[1] In each case the coming-on of night is equated with imminent crime, and more specifically with murder. The contrast between day and night is, in both passages, also a contrast between good and evil. Day is pitiful and kind; night is pitiless and cruel. Day reveals crime; night hides it. Even the figure of Hecate, queen of the night and goddess of witchcraft, is present in both passages, for though the Lieutenant does not mention her by name the 'jades' he refers to are clearly the dragons that drew her chariot. Moreover, in both cases day and night are endowed with human attributes. The characteristic Shakespearian economy is evident. The lines from *Macbeth* are a reworking, probably at an unconscious level, of the opening of the Lieutenant's speech. But they are anything but a repetition of it. Despite their marked similarities of idea and image, the two passages are as far apart in the dramatic impact that they make as are the scene in which York is first tormented and then killed by Queen Margaret and her supporters (*3 Henry VI*, I, iv) and that in which Gloucester's eyes are put out (*King Lear*, III, vii).

The seven lines with which the Lieutenant begins serve a double function. First, they indicate to the audience the time of day; it is late evening, and night is about to fall. But, secondly, they have a further and more important purpose: they are there to create

[1] Walter Whiter, *A Specimen of a Commentary on Shakespeare*, ed. Alan Over and Mary Bell (London, 1967), p. 137, n. 1 and p. 145.

atmosphere, to fill the spectators with a sense of gloom and foreboding, to raise their fears and expectations, and so to prepare them for the murder that is to follow. To achieve this effect, Shakespeare resorts to what were almost standard items of the tragic poet's stock-in-trade round about 1590. Hecate with her dragons would seem to come from Book VII of the *Metamorphoses*, where Medea cries at the end of her great invocation:

> Nec frustra volucrum tractus cervice draconum
> Currus adest. (lines 218–9)

There are also parallels with the work of Marlowe. A. S. Cairncross, in a note to his New Arden edition, cites Barabas' lines at the beginning of Act II of *The Jew of Malta*:

> Thus like the sad presaging Rauen that tolls
> The sicke mans passeport in her hollow beake,
> And in the shadow of the silent night,
> Doth shake contagion from her sable wings . . .
> (lines 640–3)

Even closer, I think, are these lines from the final speech of Bajazeth in *1 Tamburlaine*:

> O highest Lamp of euerliuing *Ioue*,
> Accursed day infected with my griefs,
> Hide now thy stained face in endles night,
> And shut the windowes of the lightsome heauens.
> Let vgly darknesse with her rusty coach,
> Engyrt with tempests wrapt in pitchy clouds,
> Smother the earth with neuer fading mistes:
> And let her horses from their nostrels breathe
> Rebellious winds and dreadfull thunderclaps . . .
> (lines 2071–9)[1]

The result is a piece of atmospheric writing which many critics have found impressive in a vague general sort of way, but not, I would suggest, a piece of true dramatic poetry. Ostensibly addressed to the men under his command, the Lieutenant's words are not really meant for them but for the audience. They are not part of the action. And, if one then goes on to ask how a brutal soldier comes to speak in these high-flown terms, no satisfactory answer can be given, because this is a matter, not of the Lieutenant talking to his men, but of the playwright speaking through him direct to the audience. When the Lieutenant ceases to be Shakespeare's mouthpiece and becomes a character in his own right, giving orders as to what is to be done, the tone of his speech changes radically. It becomes factual and practical, not atmospheric and 'poetical', apart from the one flourish provided by the proleptic use of 'discoloured'. There is, in fact, a marked discontinuity between the first seven lines and the rest of the speech—a discontinuity that is emphasized, not covered up, by Shakespeare's effort to paper over the crack with 'Therefore'. As a statement of logical consequence the word is painfully spurious, unless it can be taken as a kind of dramatic shorthand, standing for something like 'So, before it grows quite dark'.

In the seven lines that follow the Lieutenant comes to life. He is a man of action speaking to other men on the stage with him. His words now cover the ground quickly, especially in the last three lines, each of which contains a verb:

> Master, this prisoner freely give I thee;
> And thou that art his mate make boot of this;
> The other, Walter Whitmore, is thy share.

And, though the word order is not that of prose, the lines do have the prose virtues of lucidity and conciseness. The first seven lines, on the other hand, are consciously and deliberately 'poetical'. The most striking feature of them is their piling-up of adjectives in twos and even threes. The whole thing is static and pictorial; and the total impression it creates is of a striving for effect, rather than of an effect achieved. It is felt as something applied to the scene, not as something that leads into it and is part of it. Here Shakespeare's eye and his imagination are not fixed on the characters he has brought on to the stage and

1 References to Marlowe are to *The Works*, ed. C. F. Tucker-Brooke (Oxford, 1910).

the action they are involved in, but on the audience whose feelings he seeks to stimulate and manipulate.

This same sense of discontinuity and divided aims keeps on making itself felt throughout the rest of the scene. Whenever the Lieutenant gives orders or advice, he uses the direct utterance of the last seven lines of his first speech. This style is not only the dramatist's medium for keeping the action moving, but also a manner that fits the Lieutenant's nature. But Shakespeare also saddles him with the task of stating the moral significance of the scene, of putting into words the attitude to, and the judgement on, Suffolk and his actions that the play expresses, and of explaining why his death is fitting and deserved. When he has to fill this other role, the Lieutenant reverts to the manner of his opening lines. He quotes a Latin tag, refers to Sylla, and resorts to elaborate and carefully worked out figures, saying, for example, to Suffolk:

> And thou that smild'st at good Duke Humphrey's death
> Against the senseless winds shalt grin in vain,
> Who in contempt shall hiss at thee again;
> And wedded be thou to the hags of hell
> For daring to affy a mighty Lord
> Unto the daughter of a worthless king,
> Having neither subject, wealth, nor diadem.
> By devilish policy art thou grown great,
> And, like ambitious Sylla, overgorg'd
> With gobbets of thy mother's bleeding heart.
> (lines 76–85)

Considered as a piece of dramatic poetry, and judged against Shakespeare's later achievement, this scene is a jumble. The Lieutenant has three functions in it: to evoke atmosphere, to act in his own character, and to serve as the voice of history. But these three functions remain three disparate things that have not been fused into one thing. There is no economy here, no singleness of purpose or significant compression of experience. The dramatist rendering the action, the rhetorician moving his audience and guiding its responses, and the poet exercising his invention and ranging over his topics, are all present here. But they do not co-operate; they clash, because each goes his separate way.

In the dialogue between Macbeth and his wife there is no discontinuity, no confusion of dramatic purpose. The invocation to night, though obviously rhetorical in form, is not a set piece that can be detached from the rest of the scene as the Lieutenant's first seven lines can, but an integral part of it, arising naturally and unforcedly out of the action and leading back into it. Shakespeare's primary concern now is not, it seems to me, with his audience and with what he can do to them, but with the two figures on the stage, with the situation they are involved in, and with what happens between them. The information Macbeth gives to Lady Macbeth is not there to forward the plot. The audience knows already, having witnessed the interview between Macbeth and the Murderers in the previous scene, III, ii, that the murder is to be carried out 'to-night'. Much of the scene's significance lies in the fact that it is only now, when all the arrangements have been made, that Macbeth acquaints his wife with them. The relationship between them has undergone a radical change. It is now he who leads the way, while she follows with a weary acquiescence. Moreover, he is now at least as much interested in night and its attendant evils as he is in her. There is, surely, an element of sensual indulgence in the lines that begin 'Ere the bat hath flown her cloister'd flight', a deliberate embracing of evil that reaches its climax in the invocation itself, where Macbeth seems to forget the presence of his wife altogether in his contemplation of an action that absorbs his entire attention.

The invocation to night is far more precise, concrete, and terrifying than the Lieutenant's description of night's onset. It begins with an image that is implicit and active, not fully worked out and pictorial: that of night as a falconer and day as a falcon (no longer 'tow'ring in her pride of place'), which is contained in the technical word 'seeling'. The epithet produces an intense sense of pain and cruelty, which is heightened in the next line, 'Scarf up the tender eye of pitiful day'. The vividly evoked action from the daily life of Elizabethan England is much more shocking than the conventional paraphernalia of wolves and dead men's graves. Night as the falconer, and day as the suffering falcon, have taken on the attributes of living things through a kind of verbal shorthand that concentrates on action, as distinct from static description. The nouns 'falcon' and 'falconer' are not even used, but we see why night's hand is 'bloody and invisible'—'bloody' from its task and 'invisible' to the hawk—and we can then accept the sudden leap of the imagination from falconry to the law, perhaps suggested by the hinted pun on 'seeling' and 'sealing', that comes with the next lines:

> Cancel and tear to pieces that great bond
> Which keeps me pale.

And then, as though in answer to Macbeth's call, night does begin to fall, and the speech moves on to description, but a description that enacts what it describes. 'Light thickens'. How exact the word 'thickens' is to evoke a sense of the clear spaces of air filling with darkness! 'And the crow makes wing to th' rooky wood'. It is a familiar almost a homely image. We have all seen the crow doing it; it is a normal part of the evening scene. But here, as so often in *Macbeth*, the homely and the familiar carry sinister overtones. 'Thickens' takes the mind back to that earlier invocation of Act I, scene v, where Lady Macbeth called on 'thick night' to come down and hide the murder of Duncan, which she was planning, not only from the eye of the world but also from the very knife itself.

The contrast between day and night that has been so powerfully developed is finally summed up in the two lines:

> Good things of day begin to droop and drowse,
> Whiles night's black agents to their preys do rouse.

Here the contrasted rhythms reinforce the contrasted ideas. The first line is flagging and relaxed, with a heavy caesura after the word 'day'. The second is tense, keyed up, and mounts without a break. Goodness is ineffective; like the day, it is failing and in retreat. Evil is dynamic and on the attack. The antithesis between daylight, goodness and pity, on the one hand, and darkness, evil and ruthlessness, on the other, is now complete. To read these lines, or to hear them spoken, is to experience the contrast and the conflict as something real and tangible. They have this effect because Shakespeare is now working from within the consciousness of a particular man at a particular moment in time. The words could be spoken by no one but Macbeth. They are in his personal idiom, they are the product of his experience. The sense of horror in the face of cruelty, coupled with a fascinated attraction towards cruelty, and the hypnotized absorption in the effort to make the future present, all these are characteristic of Macbeth, evident in his speech and his actions from the moment that he meets the Witches. Equally characteristic is the way that he uses endearments and the familiar language of love to his wife when he reveals his sinister purpose to her, bidding her 'be jocund', calling her 'dear wife', and, most striking of all, making his plans a kind of love offering to her:

> Be innocent of the knowledge, dearest chuck,
> Till thou applaud the deed.

And, of course, the speech bears eloquent witness to the raw exposed nerves, so evident in everything Macbeth says and does at this stage in the action.

The lines can convey all this, because they

are deeply embedded in, and an indissoluble part of, that total experience which is the play. They stir echoes in the mind; they look back, and they look forward. The contrast they embody is not something laid on for the occasion, as it is in the Lieutenant's first seven lines, but something structural. As many critics have pointed out, the greater part of the action of *Macbeth*, up to the coming of Malcolm and the English forces, takes place in mist or darkness. Time after time, the hero and his wife call on the dark to hide what they are about to do, not merely from the eyes of others, but from their own eyes as well.

The Lieutenant's lines are not rooted in *2 Henry VI* as Macbeth's lines are in his play. The connecting links of image, association, and echo do not exist, because *2 Henry VI* as a whole, though its connections with *Macbeth* are many,[1] embodies no such precise yet complex experience as that which is to be found in the later play. Before Shakespeare wrote Macbeth's invocation to night even he, I venture to say, did not know how Macbeth would feel at this moment. In order to know, he had to find the words, to make his hero vocal. And these words are linked with all that has gone before, because what Shakespeare finds and reveals now grows out of what he has made of Macbeth and his situation earlier in the play. Macbeth speaks as he does here, because he is the man who has seen 'pity, like a naked new-born babe' (I, vii, 21), who has said 'Stars, hide your fires' (I, iv, 50) when contemplating the murder of Duncan, and who has voiced the moral confusion, raised in his mind by the Witches' prophecy, with the words:

> This supernatural soliciting
> Cannot be ill, cannot be good.
>
> (I, iii, 130–1)

The dialogue in *Macbeth* fulfills a whole series of closely inter-related functions. It sets the scene; it creates atmosphere; it prepares the way for the murder of Banquo; but simultaneously it dramatizes that isolation of husband and wife from each other, which is such an integral part of their tragedy; it expresses the state of mind of each of them; and, by implication, rather than explicit statement, it endorses those values of goodness and pity on which the play ultimately rests in the very process of realizing in concrete terms the menace of the forces opposed to those values. This, in fact, is supremely economical writing in which every word is doing a fantastic amount of work; and the difference in quality and in dramatic impact between it and the passage from *2 Henry VI* is an index of the extent to which Shakespeare's art had developed during the sixteen years or so that lie between the two plays.

How, then, did this growth in the capacity to knit words and action into a single indivisible entity take place? The best one can do in attempting an answer is to look at some of the sign-posts on the way. The same set of ideas and associations that appears in the first seven lines of the Lieutenant's speech is to be found again in *The Rape of Lucrece*, that 'graver labour' on which Shakespeare exercised such conscious art. There, after the rape has taken place and Tarquin has slunk away, Lucrece launches into a sustained tirade against Night, part of which runs thus:

> O comfort-killing Night, image of hell!
> Dim register and notary of shame!
> Black stage for tragedies and murders fell!
> Vast sin-concealing chaos! nurse of blame!
> Blind muffled bawd! dark harbour for defame!
> Grim cave of death! whisp'ring conspirator,
> With close-tongu'd treason and the ravisher! . . .
>
> O Night, thou furnace of foul reeking smoke,
> Let not the jealous Day behold that face
> Which underneath thy black all-hiding cloak
> Immodestly lies martyr'd with disgrace!
> Keep still possession of thy gloomy place,
> That all the faults which in thy reign are made
> May likewise be sepulcher'd in thy shade.

[1] See Kenneth Muir's edition of *Macbeth* (London, 1951), Appendix D.

Make me not object to the tell-tale Day.
The light will show, character'd in my brow,
The story of sweet chastity's decay,
The impious breach of holy wedlock vow;
Yea, the illiterate, that know not how
  To cipher what is writ in learned books,
  Will quote my loathsome trespass in my looks.

(lines 764–812)

The resemblance between this speech and the Lieutenant's opening lines are clear enough. Again night is associated with hell, murder, sin and concealment, while the day is described as 'tell-tale', the equivalent of 'blabbing' in the play. There are also marked similarities of manner. Shakespeare still relies heavily on adjectives, especially compound adjectives, and on a heaping-up of illustrative images. The mode is again highly rhetorical, particularly in the first stanza where there are nine exclamations. The total impression created is one of calculated study and artifice. Nevertheless, these lines are, I think, a great advance on those from *2 Henry VI*. In the first place, they occur, not in a dramatic context, but within the framework of an ornate Ovidian narrative poem, where the centre of interest does not lie in the story, but in the arguments, the laments, and the decoration for which the story provides the opportunity; and they do not slow up the movement of the narrative, because the whole thing is slow-moving by design. Secondly, the tirade against Night is firmly keyed to the structure of which it is part. It does not, like the Lieutenant's lines, erupt out of nowhere; it has been carefully prepared for, and it comes as the culmination of a sort of wave movement which has been gathering impetus for the previous seven hundred and fifty lines. In the first stanza Tarquin's lust is described as a 'lightless [hidden or smouldering] fire'. In the second Lucrece is equated with light when her face is referred to as

that sky of his [her husband's] delight,
Where mortal stars, as bright as heaven's beauties,
With pure aspects did him peculiar duties.

(lines 12–14)

Reaching Lucrece's house, Tarquin hides his purpose in coming there from her, praises her husband's exploits in the war, and appears as the perfect guest

Till sable Night, mother of Dread and Fear,
  Upon the world dim darkness doth display,
  And in her vaulty prison stows the Day.

(lines 117–19)

It is at this point that the main action of the poem begins; and from here onwards these initial references to dark and light are caught up and developed like a theme in a musical composition. Five lines later comes this:

Now leaden slumber with life's strength doth fight;
  And every one to rest themselves betake,
  Save thieves, and cares, and troubled minds that wake.

(lines 124–6)

And then, after forty lines of moral reflection, Tarquin's first move is heralded by the following stanza:

Now stole upon the time the dead of night,
When heavy sleep hath clos'd up mortal eyes;
No comfortable star did lend his light,
No noise but owls' and wolves' death-boding cries;
Now serves the season that they may surprise
  The silly lambs. Pure thoughts are dead and still,
  While lust and murder wake to stain and kill.

(lines 162–8)

The wolves have appeared already in *2 Henry VI*, but here they are something more than a conventional item of atmosphere, for soon Tarquin will be called a wolf and Lucrece a lamb. The images are being set to work; their connotations are being extended and interwoven with one another. Night has become the time for lust, theft, and pangs of conscience, as well as the time for murder. The wolf is on the way to becoming the 'universal wolf' of *Troilus and Cressida*. When Tarquin finally puts an end to Lucrece's pleas, Shakespeare writes:

This said, he sets his foot upon the light,
For light and lust are deadly enemies;
Shame folded up in blind concealing night,
When most unseen, then most doth tyrannize.
The wolf hath seiz'd his prey; the poor lamb cries . . .
(lines 673–7)

As a result of these recurrent waves of imagery, in which darkness and the crimes that accompany it are associated with Tarquin, while light and its suggestions of purity and innocence are attached to Lucrece, the tirade against Night comes as a fitting climax to what has gone before it. Working within a well-established narrative convention that demands studied artifice, Shakespeare finds it much easier to exploit the possibilities of the opposition between light and darkness than he does, at this stage in his career, within the more complicated framework of a play, where 'the two hours' traffic' of the stage allows little room for the elaboration of a figure, and where the poetry must be geared to the action in such a manner as to intensify it and to be intensified by it, instead of clogging and impeding it.

Perhaps the major artistic problem that confronted Shakespeare in the middle of the last decade of the sixteenth century was that of bringing his exuberant delight in words and figures of speech into harmony with the dependence of drama on action and character. In two plays, *Love's Labour's Lost* and *Richard II*, he even managed to make dramatic capital out of it, to have his cake as well as eat it. The first is a play about language, and the second places its central figure, from the time of his first appearance in Act III, in a position where the only freedom left him is that of uttering his thoughts and feelings. But these were necessarily temporary expedients. The lasting solution to the problem becomes evident in, among many other places, a passage from *King John* which takes up again the familiar opposition between day and night. In III, iii, John is at the height of his power. He has just defeated the French forces and taken his nephew Arthur prisoner. As the scene opens John hands Arthur over to the care of his grandmother, Queen Elinor, telling him:

Thy grandam loves thee, and thy uncle will
As dear be to thee as thy father was.

Then, after giving the Bastard orders to return to England, John turns to Hubert de Burgh, and, with Arthur present, though occupied, in the background, engages him in dialogue. Too long to be quoted in full, this dialogue begins with the King expressing his appreciation of Hubert's services to him in the most ingratiating terms, and drawing the admission from him: 'I am much bounden to your Majesty'. Taking full advantage of this response, John continues:

Good friend, thou hast no cause to say so yet,
But thou shalt have; and creep time ne'er so slow,
Yet it shall come for me to do thee good.
I had a thing to say—but let it go:
The sun is in the heaven, and the proud day,
Attended with the pleasures of the world,
Is all too wanton and too full of gawds
To give me audience. If the midnight bell
Did with his iron tongue and brazen mouth
Sound on into the drowsy ear of night;
If this same were a churchyard where we stand,
And thou possessed with a thousand wrongs;
Or if that surly spirit, melancholy,
Had bak'd thy blood and made it heavy-thick,
Which else runs tickling up and down the veins,
Making that idiot, laughter, keep men's eyes
And strain their cheeks to idle merriment,
A passion hateful to my purposes;
Or if that thou couldst see me without eyes,
Hear me without thine ears, and make reply
Without a tongue, using conceit alone,
Without eyes, ears, and harmful sound of words—
Then, in despite of broad-eyed watchful day,
I would into thy bosom pour my thoughts.
But, ah, I will not! Yet I love thee well;
And, by my troth, I think thou lov'st me well.[1]
(lines 30–55)

[1] I have, for obvious reasons, adopted Dover Wilson's readings of 'ear' for 'race' at line 39, and 'broad-eyed' for 'brooded' at line 52.

In this speech there are near-reminiscences of the Lieutenant's lines in *2 Henry VI*. Instead of being 'gaudy, blabbing, and remorseful', the day is 'all too wanton and too full of gawds'; later it is called 'broad-eyed' and 'watchful'. The 'dead men's graves' are replaced by 'a churchyard'. But, in spite of these resemblances, the total effect achieved is much closer to that of *Macbeth*. The whole dialogue is obviously dramatic in the sense that John is talking to Hubert, not to the audience. It is still more dramatic in the sense that John is thinking aloud, allowing a purpose to grow within his mind. And that purpose is one that he hardly dares to look at himself, much less reveal to Hubert who is to be the agent of it. John is testing and tempting himself, as well as the man he seeks to make his instrument. Night, the midnight bell, the churchyard, and the whole atmosphere of conspiratorial secrecy are evoked, not primarily to affect the feelings of the audience, though they do this as well, but as a kind of imaginative stimulus with which John attempts to encourage himself while working Hubert to his purpose. Compared with the detailed and carefully elaborated contrasts in *2 Henry VI* and *Lucrece*, the images here are barer and simpler. They derive much of their suggestiveness from their context, to which the presence of Arthur in the background contributes, from the ingratiating tone of John's address to Hubert, using his name time after time, and, above all, from the tentative probings of the speech, moving towards the decisive command, and then backing away from it before it is reached:

> I had a thing to say—but let it go.

The manner is altogether subtler and more flexible than that of *2 Henry VI*. The rhythm is varied by functional changes of pace that correspond to the to-and-fro movement of the mind. The speech will run rapidly ahead for a time, and then come to a sudden stop as John hesitates or changes direction. There is an interplay of the conversational and the formal, of the familiar and the 'poetical'. The contrast between day and night is not being developed for its own sake; it is being used and worked into the total situation. The sinister secrecy of the night, as it is conveyed through the verse, adds weight to, and is itself reinforced by, John's desire to communicate his purpose to Hubert without clothing it in words at all, or, indeed, without resorting to any of the senses for its transmission:

> Or if that thou couldst see me without eyes,
> Hear me without thine ears, and make reply
> Without a tongue, using conceit alone . . .

The sight of Arthur in his power plants the seeds of murder in John's mind; and we experience their growth as he experiences it. We are made aware both of his revulsion from it and of his attraction towards it, and we see the attraction gaining over the repulsion. Verse and action have fused together here and become one. The wealth of imagery is not a piece of self-indulgence on the part of Shakespeare the 'poet', it is a necessary part of the dramatic situation, establishing the atmosphere conducive to John's final order that Arthur be put to death, working on the emotions of Hubert in a manner that is designed to detach him from the daylight world of clear moral judgement and lead him into the dark world of John's imaginings, and, at the same time, revealing the devious nature of the King himself.

The Shakespeare who wrote *Macbeth* is already clearly recognizable in this passage, but a bridge leading from the one play to the other can be found in *Julius Caesar*. There, in II, i, the boy Lucius announces to Brutus that Cassius and several others are at the door. Brutus asks the boy whether he knows them, and is told that it is impossible to identify them, because their hats are pulled down to their ears and their cloaks cover the lower parts of their faces. While the boy is busy admitting them, Brutus soliloquizes:

> They are the faction. O conspiracy,
> Sham'st thou to show thy dang'rous brow by night.
> When evils are most free? O, then by day
> Where wilt thou find a cavern dark enough
> To mask thy monstrous visage? Seek none, conspiracy;
> Hide it in smiles and affability!
> For if thou path, thy native semblance on,
> Not Erebus itself were dim enough
> To hide thee from prevention. (II, i, 77–85)

The association of conspiracy with a cavern and with night seems to have been caught up from the corresponding passage in *The Rape of Lucrece*, where night is called

> Grim cave of death! whisp'ring conspirator,
> With close-tongu'd treason and the ravisher!
> (lines 769–70)

But the whole passage in its reliance on rhetorical questions is a forcible reminder that Shakespeare's mature manner was not achieved through an abandonment of such devices. What does seem to have happened is that the contrast between day and night is now handled in a more rapid and allusive fashion. It contributes to Brutus' realization of the true nature of the activities he is involved in, but it does not dominate the speech which is primarily about conspiracy. Moreover, heightened though the language is, it acquires a degree of naturalness and spontaneity from the informal structure and rhythm of the verse. The result is metaphorical writing—conspiracy is not compared to a monstrous criminal, but presented as a monstrous criminal—that is also flexible, and that can follow and render the curve of a passionate emotion or thought. The way lies open to the speech of a Lear or a Macbeth.

It is no accident that the signposts along the road that leads from *2 Henry VI* to *Macbeth* are to be found in *Lucrece*, *King John*, and *Julius Caesar*, for the poem and the two plays all contributed to the making of *Macbeth*. Tarquin is in many ways a first draft of Macbeth himself; John is the first of Shakespeare's tragic criminals, the man of power who gives way to temptation; and Brutus, though power is not his aim, is nonetheless another victim of temptation who, as Wilson Knight has shown,[1] has much in common with Macbeth. Consciously or unconsciously, Shakespeare was aware when he came to write *Macbeth* of what he had achieved in, and learnt from, his earlier works. Night, Hecate, murder, the wolf, Tarquin, John's self-stimulating thoughts, coupled with his desire for a secrecy beyond the reach of sense, are all fused together in one tremendous synthesis in the second half of the air-borne dagger speech (*Macbeth*, II, i, 49–60). These lines, like the play to which they belong, are both a distillation from much that he had written already and also something radically new, creating 'matter' of a very different kind from that which Bacon had in mind when he was writing *The Advancement of Learning*.

[1] *The Wheel of Fire* (London, 1930), pp. 132–53.

'ANTONY AND CLEOPATRA': THE LIMITS OF MYTHOLOGY

HAROLD FISCH

I

When critics speak of myth and ritual in Shakespeare they have in mind chiefly the symbolic structure of the plays. Thus *The Winter's Tale* which begins in winter ('a sad tale's best for winter', I, i, 25) and ends in high summer ('not yet on summer's death nor on the birth of trembling winter', IV, iv, 80) perfectly corresponds to the fertility rhythm. The accent on fertility in the sheep-shearing in Act IV gives to the structural form its emotional and spiritual content, whilst the symbolic revival of Hermione at the end rounds off the pattern of death and resurrection so basic to 'the myth of the eternal return'. Such an archetypal structure is older than Christianity (in spite of the Christian colouring) and perhaps older than the conscious memory of man.

In *King Lear* the symbolic structure of the play viewed as myth-ritual is defined by the image of the wheel. Lear speaks of himself as being bound on a wheel of fire (IV, vii, 47); Kent bids Fortune turn her wheel (II, ii, 173); the Fool speaking of the fate of his master bids himself 'let go thy hold when a great wheel runs down a hill' (II, iv, 71); whilst Edmund acknowledges at his death that 'the wheel is come full circle' (V, iii, 174). The circular movement thus intimated has behind it a sense of a cyclical order, the rise and fall of kings ordained as a means of guaranteeing the fertility of the land and the orderly sequence of the seasons. Such imagery, more than it is a statement about Lear as a Nature-god (though he is that too), is a statement about his predetermined fate, and about the structure of the play in which that fate is projected.

In *Antony and Cleopatra* the myth-ritual pattern is undoubtedly central. But one should add that it is not so much a structural principle (as in *King Lear*) as the actual subject of the play. Shakespeare is dealing *directly* in this play with a pair of characters who lay claim to mythological status and who at every turn adopt the posture of figures in a fertility ritual. The first such myth pattern is that connected with the names of Mars and Venus.[1] From the first scene the personalities of Antony and Cleopatra are mythologically inflated and presented in terms of the conjunction of the god of war and the goddess of love. Philo in the opening speech of the first scene declares that Antony's eyes 'have glow'd like plated Mars', and Antony's first speeches to Cleopatra introduce an allusion to the goddess Venus:

> Now for the love of Love, and her soft hours (I, i, 44)

—the reference being of course to the 'hours' and 'graces' which wait on the queen of love. It is because they are enacting the archetypal union of the god of war and the goddess of love that they may properly claim:

> Eternity was in our lips, and eyes,
> Bliss in our brows' bent; none our parts so poor,
> But was a race of heaven. (I, iii, 35–7)

[1] On this aspect, see Raymond B. Waddington, '*Antony and Cleopatra:* What Venus did with Mars', *Shakespeare Studies*, II (1966), 210–27, who also points out the link between Antony and his ancestor, Hercules (p. 216).

The full miming of this myth-pattern is achieved in Cleopatra's sailing on the Cydnus as described by Enobarbus: 'The barge she sat in, like a burnish'd throne, / Burn'd on the water' (II, ii, 199–200). The text continues with an explicit reference to Venus:

For her own person
It beggar'd all description: she did lie
In her pavilion—cloth of gold, of tissue—
O'er picturing that Venus where we see
The fancy outwork nature. (lines 205–9)

Plutarch, from whom this detail (like so much else in this speech) is derived, develops the link even further and remarks that Cleopatra's ladies were apparelled 'like the nymphes Nereides ... *and like the Graces*'; and he continues that on her arrival 'there went a rumor in the peoples mouthes, that the goddesse Venus was come to play with the god Bacchus, for the generall good of all Asia'.[1] Antony thus combines in himself aspects of both Mars and Bacchus, the god of war as well as the god of wine, Venus having been at various times the consort of both. The whole scene on the Cydnus naturally recalls the most famous scene associated in mythology with the goddess Venus, *viz.*, her riding on a sea-shell wafted by Zephyrs to the foot of mount Cythera. On that occasion she was accompanied by Nereids, Cupids, and Graces. Since she is traditionally produced by the foam of the sea, it is natural that she should thus first appear before Antony. Enobarbus' conclusion confirms once again the supernal, absolute character of her charms. She is not a lovely woman, simply, but the principle of love itself, love, so to speak, carried to the infinite degree. Hence in sober truth it may be stated that

Age cannot wither her, nor custome stale
Her infinite variety. (lines 243–4)

Her changeless, timeless character is also clearly marked in her own speech where she asserts her antiquity, her immortal, fixed and absolute quality:

Think on me,
That am with Phoebus' amorous pinches black,
And wrinkled deep in time. (I, v, 27–9)

Clearly she is not simply 'Miss Egypt', but the eternal feminine, Tiamat, Venus, Aphrodite. She is as old as the race of man, the source of passion, reproduction, and death.

Now whilst Shakespeare very clearly presents his two main characters in this inflated way, and has them claim all the divine honours, the transcendent status which belongs to them in their mythological capacities, he does so not without considerable irony. We may note here the same dialectical syntax as in Homer or as in *Troilus and Cressida* where the legendary theme of Helen and Paris becomes a subject for barrack-room jokes ('all the argument is a cuckold and a whore'). In the conversation of Agrippa and Enobarbus following the Cydnus passage we have the same deflating tendency. 'Royal wench' Agrippa calls her, whilst Enobarbus with as little sense of awe before the power of the queen of love describes how he once saw her 'hop forty paces through the public street'. Cleopatra's own servants also tend to burlesque the mythological theme:

Cleopatra. Hast thou affections?
Mardian. Yes, gracious madam.
Cleopatra. Indeed?
Mardian. Not in deed, madam, for I can do nothing
But what indeed is honest to be done:
Yet have I fierce affections, and think
What Venus did with Mars. (I, v, 12–18)

To think of the eunuch aping in his imagination the deeds of Mars and Venus produces the inevitable comic reaction at the expense of the whole mythological construction on which the personalities of the main characters are based.

The Mars–Venus theme is, however, not carried through to the end, and instead, the two

[1] G. Bullough (ed.), *Narrative and Dramatic Sources of Shakespeare*, v (London, 1964), p. 274.

main characters merge into another mythological grouping of much greater significance for Shakespeare's purpose, namely the Isis–Osiris–Set triangle with Cleopatra functioning as Isis, goddess of nature and fertility, and Antony as Osiris, the dying Sun-god who is resurrected in eternity.[1] Octavius Caesar seems in some sense to function as Set (or Typhon) the brother of Osiris who seeks to replace him with Isis, only to be thwarted by Isis who gathers the mangled remains of Osiris together and thus guarantees that he becomes immortal and reigns as king of the underworld. The blending of the two groups together—Venus–Mars–Bacchus and Isis–Osiris–Set is no accident, since Osiris has a close connection with Dionysus (Bacchus) being also the god of wine, and Isis is the ultimate goddess from whom all the lesser deities including Aphrodite (Venus) are derived. Typhon again is a war-god like Ares (Mars). Shakespeare could have gathered his knowledge of the myth from a number of sources. It seems natural to suppose that he drew on Plutarch's *Of Isis and Osiris* (still to this day the chief source of our information on the subject) since he had made use of Plutarch's *Lives* as the chief source for the play as a whole, and Philemon Holland had translated a version of this in 1603. He could also have read an account of the appearance of Isis and Osiris in Spenser. But a particularly tempting possibility is that he had read all about the goddess Isis in Apuleius' *The Golden Ass* which had reached four editions in the English translation of Adlington by the end of the sixteenth century. It is perhaps worth quoting the epiphany of the goddess as experienced by Lucius in his dream at the end of the book. Since Isis is the moon- and sea-goddess—just as Osiris is the Sun[2]—it is natural that she should reveal herself to Lucius as he lies on the beach in the light of the full moon, and that her garment should be stuck with fiery stars, with—in the middle—a full moon. It should also be noted that on the boat-like vessel which she holds in her hand 'an asp lifted up his head with a wide-swelling throat'. The association with Cleopatra is arresting. But the account of the goddess's claims are more to our present purpose:

> Behold, Lucius, I am come; thy weeping and prayer hath moved me to succour thee. I am she that is the natural mother of all things, mistress and governess of all the elements, the initial progeny of worlds, chief of the powers divine, queen of all that are in hell, the principal of them that dwell in heaven, manifested alone and under one form of all the gods and goddesses. At my will the planets of the sky, the wholesome winds of the seas, and the lamentable silences of hell be disposed... For the Phrygians that are the first of all men call me the Mother of the gods of Pessinus; the Athenians, which are sprung from their own soil, Cecropian Minerva; the Cyprians, which are girt about by the sea, Paphian Venus; the Cretans, which bear arrows, Dictynnian Diana; the Sicilians, which speak three tongues, infernal Proserpine... and the Egyptians... do call me by my true name, Queen Isis.[3]

Isis is no ordinary goddess. She is in fact the ultimate matrix of nature. She represents what

[1] The link with Isis as a more than casual feature of Cleopatra's personality was proposed by the eighteenth-century editors Capell and Warburton. (See M. R. Ridley (ed.), *Antony and Cleopatra* (London, 1954), notes to III, xiii, 153 and V, ii, 239.) It is surprising that present-day scholars have not shown more interest in this suggestion. But see M. Lloyd, 'Cleopatra as Isis', *Shakespeare Survey 12* (Cambridge, 1959), pp. 88–94.

[2] Cf. Spenser's description of the priests of Isis, *Faerie Queene*, V, vii:

> They wore rich Mitres shaped like the Moone,
> To shew that *Isis* doth the Moone portend;
> Like as *Osyris* signifies the Sunne.

Antony is also connected in the play with the sun-god Phoebus–Apollo. Cf. S. L. Bethell, *Shakespeare and the Popular Dramatic Tradition* (London, 1944), p. 127: '"Deep in time" gives her an infinite age: it does not suggest an old woman, but an immortal... she is an immortal lover of the sun-god, of Phoebus-Apollo'.

[3] *The Golden Ass*, trans. W. Adlington, with an essay by Charles Whibley (1927), p. 251.

Leslie Fiedler has called 'the huge, warm, enveloping darkness of unconscious life'.[1] But as well as her universal aspect she also has a distinct local connection with the Nile waters, the slimy, fertile ooze which through the annual rise and fall of the Nile guarantees life and sustenance to man and beast.

Shakespeare shows himself profoundly conscious of the full implications of the Isis–Osiris myth, and modern students of mythology could, if they were wise, learn of it in both depth and detail from this play. In Act III, scene vi, we are told that in the division of the middle east between their progeny, Cleopatra and Antony had been enthroned in chairs of gold, she enacting the part of the goddess Isis:

> she
> In the habiliments of the goddess Isis
> That day appeared. (lines 16–18)

Cleopatra's monument in which the latter part of the play takes place was (according to Plutarch) 'set up by the temple of Isis', and Shakespeare shows himself aware of the ritual framework. Antony's ritual death has all the slow elaborate ceremonial we would expect. His connection with the Sun is made clear. As he arrives in the monument, Cleopatra declares

> O sun,
> Burn the great sphere thou mov'st in, darkling stand
> The varying shore o' the world. (IV, xiii, 9–11)

And again:

> His face was as the heavens, and therein stuck
> A sun and moon, which kept their course, and lighted
> The little O, the earth. (V, ii, 79–81)

Mythological enlargement could not be more emphatic. She herself speaks of her own connection with the moon:

> Now the fleeting moon
> No planet is of mine. (V ii, 239–40)

And Antony had spoken earlier of her unflatteringly as 'our terrene moon' (III, xi, 153).

But all this is of minor interest compared with the vividness of Shakespeare's evocation of the principles of death and fertility as personified by Cleopatra, a conjunction closely tied in with the image of the Nile waters. She is the 'serpent of old Nile' (I, v, 25), and she swears by 'the fire/That quickens Nilus' slime' (I, iii, 68–9), the verb suggesting fertile life but also a swarming and insalubrious abundance, breeding produced by putrefaction. A later speech imaginatively stresses the link between death, putrefaction and fertility:

> Rather a ditch in Egypt
> Be gentle grave unto me, rather on Nilus' mud
> Lay me stark-nak'd, and let the water-flies
> Blow me into abhorring. (V, ii, 57–60)

The vivid sexuality of the image ('lay me stark nak'd') binds together its various components. Cleopatra joins in mythic union the principle of love and death: she represents the *Liebestod*, the downward drag of nature into unconsciousness and death. And this is entirely in keeping with her archetypal character: Enobarbus humorously remarks at the beginning of the play:

> I do think there is mettle in death, which commits some loving act upon her, she hath such a celerity in dying (I, ii, 152–4)

—whilst she herself testifies at the end to the same phenomenon:

> The stroke of death is as a lover's pinch,
> Which hurts and is desir'd. (V, ii, 297–8)

We recall that among the other *personae* of Isis (according to Apuleius) is the goddess Proserpine, and she is the bride of death ruling with him in the underworld. For Antony too death is 'a lover's bed' (IV, xii, 101). Modern psychologists would have no difficulty in identifying here the archetypal link between the *libido* and the death-wish which is so central for Shakespearian tragedy as a whole.

1 *Love and Death in the American Novel* (New York, 1960), p. 13.

But death is only one side of the coin: the other and sunnier side is immortality. For it is the peculiar achievement of the ancient Egyptians that they managed to swallow death in immortality. Osiris is a dying god who dies into eternity. And here at the climax of the play Shakespeare celebrates not so much the deaths of Antony and Cleopatra as their translation into immortal life. Antony himself declares:

> I come my queen . . . stay for me,
> Where souls do couch on flowers.
> (IV, xii, 50–1)

At the very heart of the Osiris legend is this notion of immortality, the mummified remains of the dead man living on eternally in 'the field of peace'. Shakespeare had somehow penetrated into this region of ancient belief; creating for us in the last act of the play a dramatic realization of the active attainment of immortality. It is achieved especially in the speeches of Cleopatra as she mourns over the mutilated Antony–Osiris, in this re-enacting perfectly the classic pose of Isis whose long lament over the dead Osiris is recorded by Plutarch. Behind all this we hear the echo of the lament for all the dead and rising gods, Adonis, Tammuz, and the rest. But here the accent is more especially on the revival of the dead hero. Shakespeare presents in the fifth act a ritual of apotheosis in which Antony and Cleopatra in the most ceremonial fashion put off mortality and announce their union as god and goddess eternally united in the field of peace. She performs a ritual marriage between herself and the dead Antony which is going to be consummated in the afterworld:

> Give me my robe, put on my crown, I have
> Immortal longings in me . . .
> Husband I come:
> Now to that name, my courage prove my title!
> I am fire, and air; my other elements
> I give to baser life. (V, ii, 281–3; 289–92)

It is an amazing piece of virtuosity, this latter-day dramatization of the most primitive and powerful of fertility myths; the one which holds within itself the key to the entire system of nature religion, linking the inner drives of flesh with the varying seasons of the world, and seeking by ritual and by magic ceremonies to overcome the most dreadful of all terrors—death itself, and convert it into love and sweetness, uniting the most disgusting of its aspects with the most alluring dream of which man is capable, *viz.*, the dream of eternal life.

But Shakespeare is no innocent and ingenuous worshipper of nature and fertility. He holds the entire archetypal pattern in his hand; he displays it to us; he penetrates to its inner heart, but there is no final identification either between us and the displayed forms, or between the author and his characters in their mythic personalities. There is a tonal distance. It is enough to quote Frazer's account of the manner in which the ancient Egyptians received the death of Osiris to realize how far away from such simple beliefs the play of Shakespeare takes us:

> In pity for her [Isis'] sorrow the sun-god Ra sent down from heaven the jackal-headed god Anubis, who, with the aid of Isis and Nephthys, of Thoth and Horus, pieced together the broken body of the murdered god, swathed it in linen bandages, and observed all the other rites which the Egyptians were wont to perform over the bodies of the departed. Then Isis fanned the cold clay with her wings: Osiris revived, and thenceforth reigned as king over the dead in the other world. There he bore the titles of Lord of the Underworld, Lord of Eternity, Ruler of the Dead.[1]

Shakespeare by contrast presents the whole apotheosis of Antony and Cleopatra within a framework of irony.

II

The entry of the Clown with his basket of figs in Act V, ii and the subsequent conversation in vulgar realistic prose between him and Cleopatra represents more than a comic defla-

[1] J. G. Frazer, *The Golden Bough* (London, ed. 1914), VI, 12–13.

tion of the whole mythic hyperbole on which much of the play is based: it brings a Biblical realism vigorously to bear on the dream-world of Paganism. The Clown functions like Edgar the bedlam-beggar in *King Lear*, or like the Porter in *Macbeth*, or like the Gravediggers in *Hamlet*. And like the Gravediggers he makes death real, showing it to us in a handful of dust. His opening words parody the Egyptian myth of immortality in the fields of peace—that Shangri-la escape from the absoluteness of human responsibility—which forms the very essence of the Isis–Osiris legend:

Cleopatra. Hast thou the pretty worm of Nilus there,
That kills and pains not?
Clown. Truly I have him: but I would not be the party that should desire you to touch him, for his biting is immortal: those that do die of it, do seldom or never recover.

The finality of death as in the Old Testament ('shall the dust praise thee?') is here given a comic form—'those that do die of it do seldom or never recover'; and in the phrase 'his biting is immortal' the whole notion of immortality is beheld in the perspective of irony. It is the death-bringing worm which becomes immortal. We are reminded of Isaiah 66:

And they shall go forth and look upon the carcases of the men that have transgressed against me: for their worm shall not die.[1]

But this is not the only Biblical *locus* which the Clown's immortal worm recalls to us. It is also the serpent of Eve in the garden of Eden: he tells us that he knew of an honest woman 'but something given to lie ... how she died of the biting of it, what pain she felt'. And he goes on—

truly she makes a very good report o' the worm: but he that will believe all that they say, shall never be saved by half that they do: but this is most falliable, the worm's an odd worm.

The man who believed what the woman said of the serpent (worm) but could not be saved by what she had done is of course Adam; just as Cleopatra is Eve, no longer the eternal feminine principle of fertility, goddess of love and nature, but the erring female who leads man into sin and consequently forfeits the gift of immortality. Even the fig-leaves fit into place in the new pattern. There is a reversal of values, a sudden refocusing of the whole dream within an archetypal frame entirely different from that which the Isis–Osiris–Set legend had provided. Here man is tested and found wanting within the limits of his brief span of three-score years and ten. Those who die of the worm—that is to say, the whole race of man—do seldom or never recover. A cold, sharp, but morally bracing wind of realism blows through this dialogue. At the end we have Cleopatra reduced to size; she is indeed 'no more but e'en a woman' (IV, xiii, 73)—a woman who might have been 'a dish for the gods' but who has been unfortunately marred by the devil. Here the worm (the serpent of Eve) has been—as in the standard Christian exegesis—enlarged into the devil. He has become the undying worm who preys on mortal man and woman. The whole ritual of apotheosis on which the latter part of the play is based is hereby exploded, and the hero and heroine become, for the moment, actors in the Judeo–Christian drama of salvation and damnation.

III

But the dialectical syntax is not provided just by this intrusion of Christian terminology in the speech of the Clown: it is there throughout in the juxtaposition of the Roman and Egyptian worlds. Both sides of the plot are Pagan: both the Egyptians and the Romans pursue a mythical grandeur, a cosmic delusion. In the one it is the delusion of an immortal feast of love, in the other, of an immortal feast of power. But there is a sharp distinction in ethical and dramatic content. The one world

[1] And see also Mark ix. 44 f.

is timeless, the other is governed by the inexorabilities of time—it is time-ridden. In Egypt, Antony's honour's 'prorogued ... Even till a Lethe'd dulness' (II, i, 26–7). Cleopatra seeks escape from time; she proposes to 'sleep out this great gap of time/My Antony is away' (I, v, 5–6). Her time is biological; it is the time of Nature; birth, copulation, and death. There is no advance. Lepidus, by contrast, expresses the urgency which characterizes the Roman sense of existence in his words on the forthcoming confrontation with Pompey:

> Time calls upon's.
> Of us must Pompey presently be sought,
> Or else he seeks out us. (II, ii, 164–6)

And in the race for Mount Misenum between Lepidus and Maecenas there is the careful synchronization of watches that we associate with Roman life. (We recall that Shakespeare's feeling for the Roman obsession with time had led him to his famous anachronism in *Julius Caesar* II, ii.) After peace is made between Pompey and the triumvirate, Menas makes his infamous proposition: he offers to kill Pompey's enemies now that they are in his power. Pompey's reply is that he is already too late:

> Ah this thou shouldst have done,
> And not have spoken on't. (II, vii, 80–1)

Caesar has the same sense of opportunity; he too like Pompey has his finger on the trigger. At Actium he declares that 'our fortune lies /Upon this jump' (III, viii, 5–6). Against the indolence, the drunkenness, and the sleepiness of the Egyptian world (shared paradoxically by the Romans in their Bacchanalian revels on Pompey's barge) there is the pressure set up by the need to act in the heat, the sense of a world in constant motion. It was a Roman poet who wrote 'Carpe diem', a love ditty composed by a man with one eye on the clock.

And behind this sense of the passage of time, its inexorability and quality of challenge, there is an awareness of the vaster historical process by which human life is governed. Caesar urging his active star at Misenum, at Actium, and in Egypt, is obeying a force mightier than himself: thus he knows no rest:

> Caesar through Syria
> Intends his journey, and within three days
> You with your children will he send before:
> Make your best use of this. (V, ii, 199–202)

Against this plan of world-conquest, the life and death of Cleopatra becomes almost an incident, sad, diverting, and remarkable, but hardly more than an incident. The world moves on, as it must, towards the 'time of universal peace' of which Octavius speaks in Act IV, vi, recalling to us Vergil's vision of the ages of the world in the fourth *Eclogue*. The drama of universal history sets up its rhythm in the play, and the ritual enactments of Isis and Osiris in their temporary incarnations as Cleopatra and Antony are accordingly diminished in size and significance. Their own tragedy observes the mythic unity of place; it is confined to one corner of Egypt: but the play as a whole, as is notorious, bursts the last fetters of classical restraint. The structure of the play does not mirror the 'myth of the eternal return'. In fact it is its opposite. The play lacks the rounded form, the satisfying, self-completed, cyclical rhythm of ancient tragedy which we still respond to in *King Lear* with its controlling image of the wheel of Fortune. Here in *Antony and Cleopatra* time and place extend so as to enclose the theme of universal history as it unfolds itself in power upon the vast amphitheatre of the world. The closed myth-world of tragedy is exploded, for the theme of world history has taken its place. And in this new epic context the mimic apotheosis of the two lovers shrinks to a little measure.

IV

This is the phenomenological paradox of the play, and on the whole Shakespeare is content to leave us (as he does in the other Roman plays) with the paradoxes unresolved, and with a sense of mutually contradictory value-systems.[1] And yet there is in the final act of *Antony and Cleopatra* a hint of resolution. As Cleopatra takes the centre of the stage for her final exit she is not only herself rehabilitated in a characteristically Shakespearian fashion, but the world of mythology is rehabilitated too. And this is achieved paradoxically through an injection of Roman 'virtue'. She chooses to die 'after the high Roman fashion'; and she chooses to conceive of her relationship to Antony under the Roman figure of marriage. The marriage between Antony and Octavia in Act II had been a marriage of convenience, another example of the Romans knowing how to seize opportunities and bend them to their will. Yet it had been weighted with moral responsibility, with a sense of the need to further the ends of an historical programme. This had charged it with an almost religious character: it had become an 'act of grace'.

Let me have thy hand.
Further this act of grace: and from this hour,
The heart of brothers govern in our loves,
And sway our great designs. (II, ii, 152–5)

But the words sound hollowly. The great designs are convincing, impressive, and real, but the brotherly love is not. The Romans lacked the affective content. They had discovered history, but they had failed to discover the individual spiritual force, the quality of human participation, which should give it meaning. They had no notion of dialogue. Cleopatra on the other hand knows what it is to love and be loved: in her relationship with Antony, and especially towards the close of the play, she glimpses a reality which raises man beyond the 'dull world':

Noblest of men, woo't die?
Hast thou no care of me, shall I abide
In this dull world, which in thy absence is
No better than a sty? (IV, xiii, 59–62)

These words would not have fallen from Roman lips, not even from Antony's. They point to love as a transcendent reality discovered within human relationships. Such love transcends the value-system of Romanism, but it equally transcends the Egyptian myth-world; for within the Isis–Osiris pattern proper there is no room for the marriage of true minds, but only for fertility and death. And yet it is in the notion of a marriage that this new-found transcendence finds its place in the last speech of Cleopatra:

Husband I come:
Now to that name, my courage prove my title.
(V, ii, 289–90)

Mr John Holloway points out that the two lovers in this play always seem to require an audience: when declaring their love to one another they desire to be the cynosure of all eyes.[2] This I would suggest is closely bound up with the ritual character of those appearances: they function in a fertility ceremony in which all are vitally concerned. But here at the end, it is surely the private character of the relationship which is uppermost. Cleopatra is withdrawing into that private mysterious world where only the still small voice of true love will be heard. She will deny Octavius his triumph: and she wishes for no more public appearances either of love or state in this 'vile world'.

Cleopatra's death is in one sense a ritual apotheosis: in another sense, it is a deserved punishment for a sinful life (this is the motif stressed in the conversation with the Clown): and in a third sense it is a marriage ceremony, in which Cleopatra rises above her conquerors showing them in the ceremony of love the true human dimension that they had missed. The

[1] Cf. J. F. Danby, 'The Shakespearean Dialectic: an Aspect of *Antony and Cleopatra*', *Scrutiny*, XVI (1949), 196–213, and comments thereon by L. C. Knights, *ibid.*, pp. 318–23.

[2] *The Story of the Night* (London, 1961), p. 102.

final words of Caesar underline the religious solemnity of Cleopatra's death:

> but she looks like sleep,
> As she would catch another Antony
> In her strong toil of grace. (v, ii, 347–9)

The word 'grace' has now a multiplicity of meaning: it suggests the irresistible beauty of Cleopatra, as goddess of love; but it also carries a suggestion of a heavenly and transcendent virtue.[1]

At this level we may look upon the deaths of the two chief characters not as an event which climaxes a fertility ritual, but as an event which brings the whole orgiastic world of Paganism to an end. It also brings to an end the sterile, world-conquering inhuman conception of time and history which the Romans had achieved, a history which had no room for salvation. If the Romans understood that history drives us on, if they felt its inexorable stress, its purposive direction, they had no means of discovering what that purpose was, to what end the labouring soul of man was striving. The final speeches of Cleopatra suggest not the meeting of Mars and Venus nor of Isis and Osiris, but rather of Cupid and Psyche—'latest born and loveliest vision far/Of all Olympus' faded hierarchy'. And at this point where the soul is born and its grace is discovered, Paganism transcends itself and glimpses those permanent and fundamental relations of love which give meaning not only to all human marriages but to the vast and seemingly impersonal march of history itself.

[1] Cf. Bethell, *Shakespeare and the Popular Dramatic Tradition*, p. 131. On the multiple meanings of *grace* (though without reference to this particular passage), see also M. M. Mahood, *Shakespeare's Wordplay* (London, 1965), pp. 150–3, 161.

SHAKESPEARE'S 'WAR WITH TIME': THE SONNETS AND 'RICHARD II'

MICHEL GRIVELET

The plausibility of a close connection between Shakespeare's Sonnets and his English history plays has long been recognized. *The Tragedy of King Richard II* in particular is one of the very first works to be noticed in several of the tables of parallels which, at various times, have been drawn up by students of the Sonnets for dating purposes.[1] It is the first and, in fact, the only one of the 'histories' to be mentioned—after six other Shakespearian plays or poems—in Tucker Brooke's edition of the Sonnets.[2] Yet, though—as Professor Mahood says—'the present trend of criticism is bringing Shakespeare's poems and his plays together',[3] *Richard II* has received little attention from critics concerned with this kind of approach. Miss Mahood herself, whose penetrating essay starts from a consideration of the 'sun/cloud' metaphor in Sonnet 33, soon dismisses as less significant the occurrence of the same metaphor in *Richard II*, III, iii, 62–8, to dwell upon that in *1 Henry IV*, I, ii, 220–6, and upon its context in both *Henry IV* plays. A similar emphasis is traceable in T. W. Baldwin's *The Literary Genetics of Shakespeare's Poems and Sonnets* and J. W. Lever's *The Elizabethan Love Sonnet.*

In 'Time's Subjects: The Sonnets and *King Henry IV, Part II*',[4] Professor L. C. Knights shows the same preference still more clearly. His point is that 'the sense of life's tragic issues' came to Shakespeare as 'a heightened awareness of what the mere passage of time does to man and all created things'. And just as

> there are many of the Sonnets that show the impact of time and mutability on a nature endowed with an uncommon capacity for delight ... it is surely no accident that one of the first plays in which we recognize the great Shakespeare—the second part of *King Henry IV*— is a play of which the controlling theme is time and change.

But the coupling together of the Sonnets with this play is not without effect upon the interpretation of the theme which both works have in common. Almost inevitably Professor Knights is led to stress the oppressive quality of the power of time and the subjection of man to its harsh necessity. He is further prompted to question the validity of whatever in the Sonnets conveys a sense of freedom from that oppression or claims that ultimately it is not to be feared. In his view, what Sonnet 116 maintains ('Love's not Time's fool ...'), is 'simply an assertion, rather than a final insight to which we are compelled by that honesty of imagination which takes everything into account'. In this, Professor Knights shares what would seem to be the common feeling about Shakespeare's Sonnets, a feeling so admirably expressed by J. B. Leishman when he writes that 'they are filled with a sadness different from Petrarch's and resembling that which

1 *The Sonnets*, ed. Hyder E. Rollins, New Variorum edition (Philadelphia, 1944), II, 63–9.

2 *Shakespeare's Sonnets* (London, 1936).

3 'Love's Confined Doom', *Shakespeare Survey 15* (Cambridge, 1962), p. 50.

4 *Some Shakespearean Themes* (London, 1959), pp. 45–64.

breathes from so much of the poetry of the ancient world: an almost overwhelming sadness at the fact of human transience'.[1] Though, of course, Leishman's position is perhaps slightly different, since he holds that 'Shakespeare always speaks of Time as an enemy to be defied, never as a power whose laws are to be accepted and submitted to'.[2] But whether there is submission or not, time in any case is felt to be essentially 'injurious'.

These pages are meant as an appendix rather than as a challenge to such authorized views; their purpose is to show that the study of the relationship between *Richard II* and the Sonnets is not irrelevant, and that perhaps it is indispensable, to a proper understanding of Shakespeare's attitude to time. Method itself requires it. There are good grounds for believing that the *Henry IV* plays, more than any other of the 'histories', belong to a dramatic conception which originates in *Richard II*. Therefore what the dramatic experience tells us about the 'fearfull meditation' pursued in the Sonnets can hardly be complete without reference to this origin. Textual evidence fully corroborates this theoretical requirement.

The following observations are not indebted to former tables of parallels nor can they claim to be due to any more modern technique than that of attentive reading. They point to a closeness with *Richard II* which appears particularly in the opening sequence of sonnets, the first seventeen, and even in some later sonnets. Similarities of metaphor and theme are found here and there, ranging from small, inconspicuous and hardly significant details to large and complex units of meaning.

It does not seem, for instance, that much importance should be attached to 'beauties *Rose*' (Sonnet 1, line 2) and 'My fair rose' (*Richard II*, v, i, 8). But in the same speech of Queen Isabel, 'thou most beauteous Inne' recalls the 'beautious roofe' of Sonnet 10, line 7, and line 10 of the same sonnet,

> Shall hate be fairer log'd then gentle love?

is very distinctly built on the same pattern as Isabel's

> Why should hard-favour'd grief be lodged in thee,
> When triumph is become an alehouse guest?
> (lines 14–15)

In Sonnet 2, line 4, 'totter'd weed', coming after the siege metaphor in line 1, has not a little in common with 'this castle's tottered battlements' (*Richard II*, III, iii, 52) from which Richard is expected to look at Bolingbroke's 'fair appointments'.

Sonnet 3, the first of the 'looking-glass' sonnets, concluding with '... thine Image dies with thee', can hardly fail to bring to mind the looking-glass episode in *Richard II*. But this is already one of the larger issues which will need more extensive treatment. However, before we come to the discussion of these main points, a few smaller echoes might as well be noted here.

There is, for instance, the use of 'vial' in Sonnet 6:

> Then let not winters wragged hand deface,
> In thee thy summer ere thou be distil'd:
> Make sweet some viall ... (lines 1–3)

and the more perfunctory, rather abrupt, comparison in *Richard II*, I, ii, 11–12:

> Edward's seven sons, whereof thyself art one,
> Were as seven vials of his sacred blood

These are, in fact, the only two occurrences in Shakespeare of 'vial' in this particular sense.

Sonnet 8 is, like *Richard II*, v, v, 41ff., on the theme of music, a theme frequent enough, one must admit, in Shakespeare. Yet there

[1] *Themes and Variations in Shakespeare's Sonnets* (London, 1961), p. 52.

[2] *Ibid.*, p. 100.

might be more than mere chance in the juxtaposition of 'truth' and 'concord' in the sonnet:

> If the true concord of well tuned sounds,
> By unions married do offend thine eare
>
> (lines 5–6)

and in the play:

> (I) ... for the concord of my state and time,
> Had not an ear to hear my true time broke.
>
> (v, v, 47–8)

Sonnet 14 ('Not from the stars do I my judgement plucke') deals with another commonplace of Elizabethan thought, and though the meaning of the sonnet is sharply antithetical to that of the relevant passage in *Richard II* (II, iv, 7–24), one can hardly fail to notice the echo 'fixed stars'/'constant stars' or the symmetry between:

> These signes forerunne the death or fall of Kings

and those lines of the sonnet in which the poet declares that he cannot

> say with Princes if it shal go wel
> By oft predict that I in heaven finde.
>
> (lines 7–8)

The link between Sonnet 22, line 3 ('But when in thee times forrwes I behould') and (*Richard II*, I, iii, 229) ('Thou canst help time to furrow me with age') has been noticed by T. W. Baldwin, who adds: 'The figure of Time plowing the furrow-wrinkles of age occurs, so far as I can find, in these two places only'.[1]

Sonnet 24, line 4, offers a very striking occurrence of 'perspective', the only one in the non-dramatic work of Shakespeare:

> And perspective it is best Painters art.

This is a difficult word of which there are only two instances in other plays (*All's Well*, v, iii, 48—*Twelfth Night*, v, i, 224) apart from the one in *Richard II*, by far the most explicit of all. What Bushy says to the weeping queen is indeed the best explanation of what the word means for Shakespeare, especially in the sonnet:

> ... Sorrow's eye, glazed with blinding tears,
> Divides one thing entire to many objects,
> Like perspectives, which, rightly gaz'd upon,
> Show nothing but confusion; ey'd awry,
> Distinguish form ...[2] (II, ii, 16–20)

None of the echoes which we have so far noticed is in itself conclusive, though as a whole perhaps they may be thought sufficient proof of a proximity of some kind between the early sonnets and *Richard II*. When, however, it comes to saying what kind of proximity, things grow more complex because other works, especially the two early narrative poems, must also be taken into consideration. There is, for example, an obvious connection between the theme of increase in the first sonnets and *Venus and Adonis*, lines 157–74. The image of the looking-glass or, more precisely, of the broken looking-glass is another notable instance. It is, as we have seen, faintly suggested in Sonnet 3. The proportions it takes in *Richard II* are those not of verbal only but of stage imagery also. What might seem to be an intermediate stage in the development of the figure occurs in *The Rape of Lucrece*, lines 1758–64, where old Lucretius addresses his dead daughter as follows:

> Poor broken glass, I often did behold
> In thy sweet semblance my old age new-born;
> But now that fair fresh mirror, dim and old,
> Shows me a bare-bon'd death by time outworn.
> O from thy cheeks my image thou hast torn,
> And shiver'd all the beauty of my glass,
> That I no more can see what once I was.

The conceit of the child as a mirror in which a parent sees himself is identical to that in Sonnet 3, or rather symmetrical with it, since in the sonnet it is a son who is his 'mother's glass'. At the same time, the stanza of *The Rape of Lucrece* is the nearest Shakespearian equivalent in words of the stage business in *Richard II*, IV, i.

[1] *On the Literary Genetics of Shakespeare's Poems and Sonnets* (Urbana, 1950), p. 224.

[2] See Peter Ure's notes on this passage in his edition of the play, the Arden Shakespeare (London, 1956).

Most important of all, however, and central to our purpose, is the evidence provided by the sun/cloud contrast and the more complex theme to which it is related. There is probably no play of Shakespeare which owes more to sun imagery than *Richard II*, where the fundamental opposition between light and dark, night and day, is not treated merely as a conflict of values but also as a rhythmic alternation, that of the diurnal course of the sun and of its nocturnal counterpart, by which we measure time. Throughout the play this complexity gives occasion for dramatic irony, for instance in the great speech in which an already-doomed sovereign boasts of the irresistible power of his kingship:

Discomfortable cousin! know'st thou not
That when the searching eye of heaven is hid
Behind the globe and lights the lower world,
Then thieves and robbers range abroad unseen
In murthers and in outrage boldly here;
But when from under this terrestrial ball
He fires the proud tops of the eastern pines,
And darts his light through every guilty hole,
Then murthers, treasons, and detested sins,
The cloak of night being pluck'd from off their backs,
Stand bare and naked, trembling at themselves?
So when this thief, this traitor, Bolingbroke,
Who all this while hath revell'd in the night,
Whilst we were wand'ring with the Antipodes,
Shall see us rising in our throne the east,
His treasons will sit blushing in his face,
Not able to endure the sight of day,
But self-affrighted tremble at his sin. (III, ii, 36–53)

While indeed Richard glories in the conceit of his royal splendour, the terms he uses inevitably involve the idea of the end of the day. They speak of his own downfall; they recall the vision which Salisbury had seen, not long before, 'with the eyes of heavy mind':

Ah Richard! ...
Thy sun sets weeping in the lowly west ...
(II, iv, 18–21)

Now there is a sonnet, Sonnet 7, which offers striking resemblances to this dramatic passage, dealing as it does both with the course of the sun and with its brightness:

Loe in the Orient when the gracious light,
Lifts up his burning head, each under eye
Doth homage to his new appearing sight,
Serving with lookes his sacred majesty ...

Of course, the sun-king analogy has behind it an immemorial tradition and, as a literary commonplace, it had become too frequent perhaps in Shakespeare's time to allow much originality or variety in the way a poet used it. So that often little room is left for evidence of a special likeness between two different occurrences of the commonplace. Here, however, the number of verbal echoes between the sonnet and the passage in the play is impressive. There is 'eastern pines' answering 'Orient', and, more remarkable in view of what we shall have to say of sources in a moment, the correspondence between 'He fires the proud tops' and 'Lifts up his burning head'. Noticeable also in both texts is the insistence on eyesight; in the sonnet: 'each under eye ... appearing sight ... Serving with lookes ... Yet mortall lookes ... The eyes ... looke another way'; in the play: 'searching eye of heaven ... Shall see us rising ... the sight of day'.

Additional proof of a link between these two texts is provided by parallel with yet another work. Claes Schaar, in *Elizabethan Sonnet Themes and the dating of Shakespeare Sonnets*,[1] has drawn attention to a resemblance between Sonnet 7 and a passage of the anonymous *Edward III*:

Comparest thou her to the pale queen of night?
Who being set in darke, seemes therefore light?
What is she when the sunne lifts up his head,
But like a fading taper, dym and dead?
My love shall brave the eye of heaven at noon,
And being unmaskt, outshine the golden sun.
(II, i, 143 ff.)[2]

[1] Lund, 1962.

[2] As printed in *The Shakespeare Apocrypha*, ed. C. F. Tucker Brooke (Oxford, 1908).

The parallel 'lifts up his burning head'/'lifts up his head' is certainly not negligible. But as far as the thought-pattern is concerned, the connection seems even closer with *Richard II*. And the more so as one reads further in *Edward III*:

> The king will in his glory hide thy shame;
> And those that gaze on him to finde out thee,
> Will loose their eie-sight, looking in the Sunne.
> What can one drop of poyson harme the Sea,
> Whose hugie vastures can digest the ill . . .
>
> (II, i, 398 ff.)

Not only does this recall the 'Not able to endure the sight of day' in Richard's speech but it also unquestionably echoes the lines in that speech which follow immediately upon those we have quoted:

> Not all the water in the rough rude sea,
> Can wash the balme off from an annointed King
>
> (lines 54–5)

It would seem to be an inescapable conclusion that whoever wrote the scenes in *Edward III*—and authoritative opinion is strongly in favour of Shakespeare himself[1]—he must have thought of the passage in *Richard II* and of Sonnet 7 as closely related. Besides, the story of Phaeton, as told by Ovid in book II of the *Metamorphoses*, is behind both texts, as Baldwin has shown for Sonnet 7[2] and as Shakespeare makes clear in the case of Richard.[3] This gives significance to the imagery of fire in sonnet and play where it implies the threat of a cosmic disaster like that which the world narrowly escaped when Apollo's sun-chariot was drawn too near it by Phaeton.

The idea of a disruption of universal order is also present and even more explicit in another instance of sun-imagery obviously related to those we have seen so far. It is a passage of *The Rape of Lucrece*, from the apostrophe of the distressed heroine to Night, Opportunity, and Time:

> O hateful, vaporous and foggy night,
> Since thou art guilty of my cureless crime,
> Muster thy mists to meet the eastern light,
> Make war against proportion'd course of time:
> Or if thou wilt permit the sun to climb
> His wonted height, yet ere he go to bed,
> Knit poisonous clouds about his golden head.
>
> With rotten damps ravish the morning air;
> Let their exhal'd unwholesome breaths make sick
> The life of purity, the supreme fair,
> Ere he arrive his weary noontide prick.
> And let thy musty vapours march so thick,
> That in their smoky ranks his smother'd light
> May set at noon and make perpetual night.
>
> (lines 771–84)

The cataclysm which Lucrece wishes for is no doubt very different from the conflagration of the Phaeton story. But in both cases there is the same notion of harm being done to the 'proportion'd course of time'. No passage moreover offers a better illustration than this of the imaginative link between the sun/cloud and the day/night themes. And, naturally enough, there are distinct verbal echoes with several of the sonnets as well as with *Richard II*.

With so many points of contact between these various texts, it is a tempting task to try and determine the chronological relationship in which they stand to one another. T. W. Baldwin has a general theory that an early group of twenty-six sonnets—the first of 'six approximately equal series' which make up the whole of the sequence—'appears certainly to date after *Venus and Adonis* (1593) but earlier than the completion of *Lucrece* at some time before May 9, 1594'[4] and that *Richard II* was written later than this early group of sonnets. But the basis of his argument is more often than not uncertain speculation. Concerning for instance the figure of 'Time's furrow' in

[1] Kenneth Muir, *Shakespeare as Collaborator* (London, 1960), pp. 31–55.

[2] Baldwin, *On the Literary Genetics*, p. 267.

[3] 'Down, down I come, like glist'ring Phaeton' (*Richard II*, III, iii, 178).

[4] Baldwin, *On the Literary Genetics*, p. 343.

Sonnet 22 and in *Richard II*—a figure derived from a passage in Ovid which is also used in Sonnet 12—he writes: 'Since the theme of Time belongs to the Sonnets, and Shakespeare used the original passage from Ovid in sonnet 12, the probability is that the figure was originated for sonnet 22 and later used in *Richard II*'.[1] Much of what this statement takes for granted cannot be really granted at all. It is, for one thing, as we shall presently show, an entirely unwarranted assumption that the theme of Time belongs to the Sonnets and not to *Richard II*. Baldwin's genetic demonstration appears in this and similar cases to be little more than an arrangement made to fit preconceived notions of Shakespearian chronology, a field in which few accepted beliefs can be received without a great deal of critical caution. The date 1595 for *Richard II*, here regarded as fact, rests on the conviction that the play is indebted to Daniel's *First Fowre Bookes of the civil warres*. However, though commonly held, this is not an unassailable doctrine. In a recent survey of the problem, Guy Lambrechts has made a strong case for the contrary view that Daniel is indebted to Shakespeare.[2] And if this is right, it may well be that 1593–4 rather than 1595 is the date of *Richard II*. The play would then be much closer to the two narrative poems and to the early sonnets. Can internal evidence lead us further? It does not seem so. As Claes Schaar writes: 'It is hardly possible, in the case of "myriad-minded" Shakespeare, to lay down rules as to how ideas or images develop, so that a study of such developments could help us towards a dating where other criteria are missing'.[3] But in the present case, this is really no loss if Schaar's suggestion that close resemblances should be treated as 'possible indications of a simultaneous date' can be retained. The dominant impression in the texts we have considered is indeed one of such intricacy—imaginative growth weaving several works together—that nothing seems more natural than to regard them as organically connected and to treat of *Richard II* as influencing, as well as influenced by, the early poems and sonnets.

Time is the stuff that drama is made on: the playwright's business is to give form and meaning to the 'two hours' during which the 'traffic of (his) stage' must hold our attention. Time—a certain period of the past—is also in a special way the stuff, or rather the subject, of a history play. It is not surprising therefore that time should be a major concern in *Richard II*. But in no other play of Shakespeare, in none of his 'histories', is the theme more explicit. From the first line to the last, from:

> Old John of Gaunt, *time*-honoured Lancaster,

to:

> In weeping after this *untimely* bier,

it is an ever recurring motive, a constant preoccupation. The first thing one notices about it, and it should be duly stressed, is that length of time is spoken of as a blessing. 'Many years of happy days' (I, i, 20) is what Bolingbroke first wishes his sovereign, and Mowbray clamorously concurs. The mark of royal happiness, length of time is also a token of royal power. A good deal of thought is given to this consideration after the banishment of the two nobles when Bolingbroke's sentence is reduced from ten to six years.

The irony of the drama lies in this that Richard will die young, that he who seemed to dispose so freely of time, his own and his subjects', will find himself short of it in his hour of need. 'Time will not permit' the duke of York to organize the defense of the realm against rebellion (II, ii, 119). When the king returns at last from Ireland, he is told that the Welsh have deserted his cause only the day

1 *Ibid.*, p. 224.

2 'Sur deux prétendues sources de *Richard II*', *Etudes Anglaises*, XX (1967), 118–39.

3 Schaar, *Elizabethan Sonnet Themes*, p. 174.

before, and this fatal blow prompts Salisbury to exclaim:

> One day too late, I fear me, noble lord,
> Hath clouded all thy happy days on earth
>
> (III, ii, 67–8)

his words offering a striking example of the connection between sun/cloud imagery and the idea of time. There is even greater irony in the fact that the blessing has become a curse. Once he is deposed and imprisoned, minutes, hours, and days are a torture to Richard. Though dying an untimely death, he has lived long enough to be made the plaything of time, a mere 'Jack of the clock' (v, v, 60).

But this irony is entirely in keeping with poetic justice, for Richard suffers wrongs that he himself had inflicted. As he must admit:

> I wasted time and now doth time waste me
>
> (v, v, 49)

And this is not just a superficial conceit, but the agonized recognition of a truth emerging from the hero's tragic experience. The injuriousness of time is a penalty which he has brought down upon himself. How deeply this truth has engaged the powers and conviction of the poet can be seen from the way in which it permeates the imaginative texture of the play. Time in this texture appears as belonging to the deeper harmonies of nature, as something which partakes of the essence of music. But emphasis is laid on the fact that it is a harmony specially perceived in the field of human relations. Time is also the times, that is to say the age with its characteristics of temper and spirit depending upon social life. It is this social sense of the word that Richard has in mind when he speaks of the 'concord of (his) state and time' and regrets that he 'had not an ear to hear (his) true time broke' (v, v, 47–8). The harmony is one not of sounds but of men. The same meaning is implied in the very first line of the play, in which 'time-honoured', far from being a mere amplification of 'old', indicates that Gaunt is what Richard is not, the life and soul of his age. Before long, indeed, Lancaster will speak for England as her 'prophet new inspired', having cherished the hope that his dying words would 'inforce' the young king's attention 'like deep harmony' (II, ii, 6). But all in vain, for the hearing of this harmony is what Richard has been most anxious to escape. 'Pray God we may make haste and come too late', are the words—so rich in dramatic ironies—with which he hurries to his uncle's death-bed (I, iv, 64).

In his wilful rejection of social harmony, Richard cannot but remind us of the fair youth of the Sonnets who, like him, is taught in vain a lesson in music:

> Music to hear, why hear'st thou music sadly?
> . . . Marke how one string, sweet husband to another,
> Strikes each by mutuall ordering;
> Resembling sire, and child, and happy mother . . .
>
> (Sonnet 8, lines 1, 9–11)

It is beyond doubt that the characterization of the King owes a great deal to the Friend. For Shakespeare, in the play, has gone out of his way in order to show Richard as a self-centred youth of whom it may also be said that he has 'unblesse(d) some mother' (Sonnet 3, line 4). Though without historical warrant, Bushy and Green are represented as having, in Bolingbroke's words:

> Made a divorce betwixt his queen and him,
> Broke the possession of a royal bed . . .
>
> (III, iii, 12–13)

And the suggestion is pathetically implied as early as Act II, scene ii, when Queen Isabel, all sadness and foreboding, sees her as yet 'unborn sorrow' as a grief begot without a father (II, ii, 34–6). Richard's fault is also indirectly but most severely denounced by Gaunt when he contrasts the degeneracy of the new reign with the legendary and quasi-paradisical perfection of the England of old, stressing the vitality of a 'happy breed of men', the fertility of the nation,

> This nurse, this teeming womb of royal kings,
> Fear'd by their breed, and famous by their birth
> (II, i, 51–2)

The fatal mistake which the king commits when, 'Tak(ing) Herford's rights away', he —as York points out—'take(s) from time/His charters and his customary rights ...' (II, i, 195–6), thus striking at the roots of his own legitimate power, is not just a political error, but an action entirely in character, flowing from Richard's absorption in the singleness of his kingly state.

On the other hand, it is the political tragedy which reveals the full implication, the grievous consequences of this self-regarding attitude. Devotion to the individual when it obscures the claims of society is ultimately an aggression upon time, an act of violence which causes further violence and disorder. It means war. Though Richard, when faced with defeat, first deceives himself with the illusion that he can easily give up his own brightness and order his followers to flee 'From Richard's night to Bolingbroke's fair day' (III, ii, 218), as if the course of time could go on as usual, his opponent has a more adequate view of their encounter:

> Methinks King Richard and myself should meet
> With no less terror than the elements
> Of fire and water, when their thund'ring shock
> At meeting tears the cloudy cheek of heaven.
> (III, iii, 54–7)

The imagery of light and dark ('fire' and 'cloud') is here charged with an additional sense of armed conflict obviously derived from the poet's meditation on Richard's disaster.

A comparable instance is that of Lucrece, preparing to do violence to herself in her desperate concern for her own integrity. She is, no doubt, above all a victim; but not entirely blameless. Though—unlike Heywood in his drama on the same subject—Shakespeare does not emphasize the heroine's proud chastity, her priggish regard for 'reputation', he does not either exculpate her from a share in what was, initially, her husband's error. The first stanzas of the poem make it clear that it was most unwise of Collatine to pride himself upon the beauty and virtue of his 'peerless dame' in the presence of Tarquin:

> Perchance his boast of Lucrece' sov'reignty
> Suggested this proud issue of a king.
> (lines 36–7)

But Lucrece shows little more wisdom in her decision to sacrifice everything to this high idea of herself:

> Let my good name, that senseless reputation,
> For Collatine's dear love be kept unspotted.
> (lines 820–1)

The resentment of moral uneasiness betrays itself in the curious phrase 'that senseless reputation', whatever the meaning one gives to it.[1] Throughout her long, tormented, expostulation with Night, Opportunity and Time, Lucrece does in fact accuse, as well as excuse, herself. It is as if, prompted by her husband, she was acting the part of a flatterer of her 'sov'reignty', thus lending a hand to the completion of its ruin. Tarquin, of course, is the main offender—all the more guilty as he destroys what he, as prince, ought to protect. And yet, by carrying her 'war with time' to the ultimate violence of death, she inflicts upon herself a far heavier penalty than the curse which she calls down upon him:

> And ever let his unrecalling crime
> Have time to wail th'abusing of his time.
> (lines 993–4)

[1] 'It is impossible', says F. T. Prince in a note to this passage (*The Poems,* the Arden Shakespeare (London, 1960), p. 105), 'to decide whether this means "that reputation which is based on hearsay, not knowledge"; or "that unfelt, impalpable reputation"; or "that reputation for being 'senseless', i.e. free from sensuality".' But it seems to me that in any case the note of disparagement cannot be missed.

This pattern of retribution is strikingly similar to that in *Richard II*. But the dramatic conception is less closely knit than in the history play. The role of Richard, both sovereign of beauty and tyrant, is here divided between Tarquin and Lucrece. She is not, as regards the paradox of time, in the central position which the king of England occupies. As a consequence the narrative poem offers no scope to the kind of moral recognition which one experiences, through Richard, at the end of the tragedy. In *The Rape of Lucrece*, Shakespeare's imagination seems to be moving towards—or still detained by—a dramatic truth more firmly grasped and adequately expressed in *Richard II*.

It remains to say, or at least to suggest, as a conclusion, how this may affect the interpretation of the theme in the sonnets. The notion of a 'war with time' is twice made explicit in the sequence (Sonnets 15 and 16) and the related figure of time the 'tyrant' appears also twice (Sonnets 8 and 115) in a manner which may seem reminiscent of, or at any rate illuminated by, Richard's drama. Shakespeare, of course, does not use the phrase later coined by historians who refer to the final crisis of the reign as the king's 'second tyranny'. The play nevertheless makes it clear that his conduct is tyrannical, so that the expression of his remorse at the end could be no less plausibly worded as: 'I played the tyrant to time and now doth time play the tyrant to me'. But this political and warlike phraseology seems on the whole rather sudden and unexpected in the early sonnets where its use is, in fact, remarkably oblique.

Consider, for instance, Sonnet 16:

> But wherefore do not you a mightier way
> Make war upon this bloody tyrant Time?

As the following lines explain, the 'mightier' war which is here advocated is no other than that which consists in marrying and begetting a son, the constant doctrine of the early sonnets. It is hardly necessary to point out how inadequate, how unconvincing a war this is. It might be argued perhaps that taking advantage of Time's power of 'increase' is a means of beating the enemy with his own weapon. But the evidence provided by the complex of imagery that we have explored shows that genuine hostility to time is something very different. It is not an attempt to outwit time but a determination to stop it. The real war is Richard's, who brings about his own undoing, or Lucrece's, who ceases to be in order to preserve at least the idea of her own unblemished self. Or, in the Sonnets, it is that of the Youth refusing to marry, since:

> If all were minded so, the times should cease
> (Sonnet 11, line 7)

The imagery of war used in Sonnet 16 betrays an ambiguity, not to say an equivocation, in the poet's attitude to time which is already perceptible in the preceding sonnet. The hostility here is genuine enough, though the way in which it is accounted for may be misleading. To a sober unimpassioned mind there is truly no tyranny, and therefore no sorrow, in the fact that 'swift-footed Time' is 'never-resting' and that neither 'brass, nor stone, nor earth, nor boundless sea' can resist his power. But a shadow is cast over the entire scope of nature because of 'one most heinous crime' which the poet would forbid time to commit, the crime against his 'love's fair brow' (Sonnet 19, lines 8–9). It is to the eyes and heart of a lover that the universal operation of time appears as fearful and iniquitous:

> When I consider every thing that growes
> Holds in perfection but a little moment
> ....
> Then the conceit of this inconstant stay,
> Sets you most rich in youth before my sight,
> Where wastfull time debateth with decay
> To change your day of youth to sullied night,
> And all in war with Time for love of you
> As he takes from you, I ingraft you new.
> (Sonnet 15, lines 1–2, 9–14)

Such is the passionate logic of love. The poet, however, is not ignorant of the retributive power that is here at work. Devoted as he is to the object of his love, he knows that such exclusive worship of an individual favours that individual's self-absorption. He knows that the proud cult of perfection in Lucrece has singled her out for the stroke of fate. And so, while the structure of the sonnet gives openly to understand that the poet's war is a decision taken at long last, after due consideration of the injuries received from 'wastfull time', the climactic phrase 'all in war with Time for love of you' concedes that love has a responsibility in the conflict, that it has in fact taken the initiative. Allowance is thus made, however furtive, for an outlook altogether different from that which the perspective of rhetorical progression defines.

A promise of relief is already alive in this incipient view. The poet's dawning awareness of what he does, in the urgency of his passion, to injure the harmony of time and provoke its invidiousness, makes the evil he has to suffer less unintelligible, if not less unavoidable. This is why the 'sadness at the fact of human transience' which pervades Shakespeare's Sonnets is not so 'overwhelming' as it is sometimes said. Nor is there sufficient reason to doubt the 'honesty of imagination' which, in later sonnets, denies the necessity of man's subjection to the oppressive power of time. The poet does not lack the power of selfless vision which belongs to the dramatist. If, as I have tried to show, the Sonnets are irradiated with an imaginative energy drawn from the drama of Richard, they can hardly be impervious to the spiritual awakening which he experiences when his soul opens at last to music. This music may be 'broke' but ''tis a sign of love'. A new moral poise emerges in a number of the later sonnets, a kind of visionary innocence, tinged with surprise and sorrow at having been kept in slavery so long. This is the sadness which prompts the poet to complain as he does in Sonnet 115:

Alas why fearing of times tiranie,
Might I not then say now I love you best,
When I was certaine ore in-certainty,
Crowning the present, doubting of the rest:
  Love is a Babe, then might I not say so
  To give full growth to that which still doth grow.
(lines 9–14)

The note is one of regret and even remorse because it is, more deeply, one of new-born freedom.

SHAKESPEARE AND CHRISTIAN DOCTRINE: SOME QUALIFICATIONS

EDWARD M. WILSON

Mr Roland Mushat Frye's brilliant and belligerent *Shakespeare and Christian Doctrine*[1] must be taken seriously; I have no wish to controvert much that he says. The passion for finding Christ-figures in Shakespeare is not one I share. The evidence he adduces is scrupulously presented, and I agree with many of his conclusions. At times, however, the evidence means something different to him from what it means to one who habitually reads other literatures than English.

I

I begin with his appendix on the Valladolid copy of the First Folio, castigated by Father William Sankey S.J. on behalf of the Spanish Inquisition.[2] Mr Frye regards these expurgations as evidence of how Shakespeare was officially regarded by the Roman church in the seventeenth century. If by that he meant how certain passages in Shakespeare were officially regarded by the Roman church I should endorse his opinion. Mr Frye takes Father Sankey's erasures, etc. in isolation; I want to try to compare them with the treatment of similar Spanish texts by Roman Catholic authors.

The censorship took place between the years 1641 and 1651. During this time the Spanish public theatre came under heavy ecclesiastical fire, and many of its most bitter opponents were Jesuits. Theatres in Spain were closed by law from 7 October 1644 until Midsummer 1645 and from 9 October 1646 until June 1649.[3] A censor from a different religious order and in another decade might conceivably have expurgated less. There was, of course, no ban on reading plays during this period, but the extreme anti-theatrical group would probably have tried to discourage it.

Mr Frye enables us to classify the main kinds of passages in Shakespeare to which Sankey took exception:

1. the use of oaths that involved Christian associations;
2. references to sexual intercourse;
3. expressions thought to be blasphemous;
4. reflections on ecclesiastical authority;
5. anti-papal arguments in *King John*;
6. praise of heretics (Cranmer and Queen Elizabeth) in *Henry VIII*;
7. the unexplained excision of *Measure for Measure*.

Perhaps the closest parallel in Spanish literature to the expurgation of Shakespeare was that of the works of the early dramatist Bartolomé de Torres Naharro. The inquisitorial Index of 1559 proscribed completely earlier plays by several authors, including his

[1] Princeton, New Jersey, 1963.

[2] 'Appendix: The Roman-Catholic Censorship of Shakespeare: 1641–51', pp. 275–93.

[3] For the controversies, see Emilio Cotarelo y Mori, *Bibliografía de las controversias sobre la licitud del teatro en España* ... (Madrid, 1904). For the closing of the theatres, J. E. Varey and N. D. Shergold, 'Datos históricos sobre los primeros teatros de Madrid: prohibiciones de autos y comedias y sus consecuencias (1647–51)', *Bulletin Hispanique*, lxii (1960), 286–325.

collected volume *Propalladia* (first edition, Naples, 1517, and six later editions) and the separate editions of his *Comedia Iacinta* and *Comedia Aquilana*. In 1573 a purged *Propalladia*, edited by Juan López de Velasco, was published in Madrid. By comparing this text with the earlier editions we can see what the inquisitors of 1559 had objected to. Joseph E. Gillet, the modern editor of Torres Naharro,[1] paid a good deal of attention to this matter in his bibliographical account of the 1573 edition in his first volume.

Torres Naharro wrote with considerable freedom, and his attacks on Rome, where some of his plays were originally performed, had all the old medieval violence. In 1557–8 a French sculptor named Esteban Jamete confessed under torture in an inquisitional prison that some of his heresies came from the *Propalladia*. Some of his quotations were inaccurate, and in others he obviously misunderstood the words he quoted. Naharro had attacked the vices of Rome and perhaps the private life of Alexander VI; but there is no reason to suppose that he was a crypto-Lutheran, an illuminist or a judaiser. His works were purged because what the papal ministers could tolerate during the first twenty years of the sixteenth century appeared intolerable to Spanish inquisitors who had seen—in the 1550s—the consequences of the writings of Erasmus, Luther and Calvin. The editor of the 1573 edition tells us that Torres Naharro was 'ageno de todo vicio, y muy dada a la virtud': that he was estranged from all vices and much given to virtue. He would not have used these words of a notorious heretic.[2]

1. If the Folio had appeared before the passing of the Blasphemy Act of 1605/6 Sankey would probably have had to expunge many more oaths from it. Mr Frye quotes only one: 'Falstaff's 'By the mass, lad'. The censor struck out the word 'mass'. Of the Spanish expurgations Gillet wrote: 'No oath is forgiven: every *Voto a Dios* is turned into *O gran Dios*, *si plaze a Dios*, *y sabe Dios*, *guarde os Dios*, *juriaños*, *voto a tal* or, at least into a dissimulated *pardiez*; references to ... the Mass ... are carefully sterilized'.

2. Neither censor was completely thorough in eradicating sexual allusions. A good deal of the coarseness of Naharro's countrymen survived; Sankey may never even have read *Romeo and Juliet*. Words like *cod-piece*, *maidenheads* and *prick* were removed from the Folio; López de Velasco suppressed several doubtful passages and changed all such words as *empreñar* (to inseminate), *desvirgar* (to deprive of virginity), *mear* (to piss), *regar* (lit. to water), *berraco* (boar) and *garañón* (a stone horse), to something less strong. Sometimes one suspects that he was moved also by a literary impulse—to remove from poetic compositions words he thought too plebeian for poetry.

3. Mr Frye notices Sankey's disapproval of phrases like 'Saint Cupid for Saint Dennis' (*Love's Labour's Lost*), 'his kissing is as full of sanctity as the touch of holy bread' (*As You Like It*), 'as the nun's lip to the friar's mouth' (*All's Well*) and even 'a holiday fool' (*The Tempest*). Gillet notes how in the *Propalladia* 'references to the Father, the Son or the Holy Ghost, to the Virgin, the Church, the saints and martyrs, the Pope, the Mass, the *frailes* [friars], even the *Cruzada* [lit. crusade; indulgences sold to support the crusades] are carefully sterilized'.

4. and 5. To parallel the cancellation by

[1] *Propalladia and other works of Bartolomé de Torres Naharro*, edited by Joseph E. Gillet (4 volumes, Bryn Mawr and Philadelphia, 1943–61). Unless otherwise stated my references are to the first volume.

[2] For the 1573 edition see Gillet, pp. 55–72; details about Jamete, pp. 66–7; Torres Naharro's virtue, p. 60. The details of textual changes by expurgation are summarized on pp. 69–71. I shall not give particular references to these as the different instances are easily found.

Sankey of words spoken to discredit the authority of Cardinal Beaufort in *1 Henry VI*, of the Pope in *King John* or the description of priests engaged in witchcraft in *2 Henry VI*, we may note the complete suppression of Torres Naharro's poem against Rome[1] and the scene in the *Comedia soldadesca* in which the Friar unfrocks himself to become a soldier. There was no protestantism here, but such passages could be considered a cause of scandal and used by heretics (as Esteban Jamete used the poem against Rome) to discredit the Papacy.

6. Favourable adjectives applied to Cranmer and to Queen Elizabeth were struck out of *Henry VIII* by Sankey. There is, I think, nowhere any praise of heretics in Torres Naharro. In another sixteenth-century work, however, we can find the removal of all mention of heretics in a book that otherwise circulated freely. In the Index of Madrid, 1677 (and presumably in earlier indexes), we find the following prohibition under the second class for the letter I:

Iuan Christoval Calvete de Estrella.
Su libro del *Viage del Principe*, se corrija.
Lib. 1, Tit. *Embarcacion*, fol. 5. pag. 2. y fol. 7 pag. 2. se quite todo lo que es en alabança de Constantino de la Fuente, Autor condenado. I en el lib. 4. fol. 325. se quite todo lo que tocare en alabança de Constantino, y de Augustin de Caçalla.[2]

The book was: *El felicissimo viaie d'el muy alto y muy Poderoso Principe Don Phelippe ... desde España à sus tierras dela baxa Alemaña* ... (Antwerp, 1552). Dr Constantino Ponce de la Fuente was imprisoned in 1558 and died in the inquisitorial prison in 1561; his works were condemned. Agustín de Cazalla was burned as a heretic at Valladolid in 1559. The three passages referred to run as follows:

I. 5v. El dotor Constantino muy gran Philosopho y profundo Theologo, y delos mas señalados hõbres enel pulpito y eloquẽcia que ha auido de grandes tiẽpos aca; como lo muestran bien claramẽte las obras que ha escrito dignas de su ingenio.[3]

I. 7v. Hizose el oficio diuino con gran solenidad, y predicò tan singularmẽte como lo suele hazer siempre el Dotor Constãtino.[4]

IV. 325v. Passose la Quaresma en oyr sermones delos grandes Predicadores, que en la Corte auia, en especial tres, los quales eran, el Doctor Constantino, el Comissario Fray Bernardo de Fresneda, el Doctor Augustin de Caçalla, Predicador d'el Emperador excelentissimo Theologo, y hombre de gran doctrina y eloquẽcia.[5]

Sankey's expurgations of *Henry VIII* are completely in line with the Inquisition's policy.

I return to the Torres Naharro edition of Madrid, 1573. I mentioned earlier that the 1559 Index banned the separate editions of the *Comedia Jacinta* and of the *Comedia Aquilana* along with the *Propalladia*.[6] The Biblioteca Nacional at Madrid has a copy of the 1573

[1] Its title is: *Capítulo III* and it begins 'Como quien no dize nada ...', I, 161–5.

[2] Juan Cristóbal Calvete de Estrella; his book *Viaje del Príncipe* should be corrected: Book 1, Heading: *Embarkation* fol. 5. second page and fol. 7. second page. Let all that is in praise of Constantino de la Fuente, a condemned author, be removed. And in book 4, fol. 325 remove everything to do with the praise of Constantino and of Agustín de Cazalla.

[3] Dr Constantino, a very great philosopher and profound theologian; for many years back he has been reckoned one of the men most distinguished for his eloquence in the pulpit, as his works, worthy of his genius, have clearly proved.

[4] The Divine Office was celebrated with great solemnity, and Dr Constantino preached with that singular eloquence he is always wont to employ.

[5] Lent was spent in hearing sermons from the great preachers who were at Court: especially three of them, who were: Dr Constantino, the commissary Fray Bernardo de Fresneda, Doctor Agustín de Cazalla, preacher to the Emperor, a most excellent theologian and a man filled with great doctrine and eloquence.

[6] I quote from the Spanish Academy's facsimile edition of *Tres índices expurgatorios de la Inquisición Española en el siglo XVI* (Madrid, 1952).

Comedia llamada Iacinta, compuesta & impressa con vna epistola familiar. fol. C4r.

Comedia llamada Aquilana, hecha por Bartholome de Torres Naharro. fol. C4r.

Propaladia, hecha por Bartholome de Torres Naharro. fol. C8r.

edition (R/4229) from which the *Comedia Jacinta* has been excised. The person responsible stated that he had corrected and emended the book, in accordance with the catalogue and index, according to the findings of the Inquisition, and that the comedy called *Jacinta* had been removed because it was thus decreed in the catalogue; dated 2 June 1585. His name was Fray Miguel de Sant Hierónimo, a professed friar in the monastery of St Jerome at Seville.[1] (The date is that of Fray Miguel's declaration, not that of the Index.) He added another note in which he stated: 'The comedy called *Jacinta* was taken out and torn up because it was prohibited in the catalogue printed in 1583'. The missing play, however, was later copied out by hand and bound up in the volume. Another man—almost certainly another agent of the Inquisition—wrote that the man who cut out the *Comedia Jacinta* from this copy and tore it up before showing the volume to the inquisitors (as he should have done in accordance with the catalogue's instructions) did so with hasty zeal and before the said catalogue came into his hands; in it he could have found out how to act in such circumstances. The play was wrongly excised; the censor took too literally a prohibition of a separate publication which clearly did not apply to the purged play in a collected volume. Another ecclesiastic mildly reproved him.

Here an indiscreet censor tore a whole play out of a volume published with full inquisitional sanction. It seems unwise, in view of this parallel, to dogmatize too much about the removal of *Measure for Measure* from the Valladolid Folio.

Further parallels can be found in other works listed in the various Spanish Indexes. There are some, for instance, very well documented, in the *princeps* of Góngora, printed in December 1627 and suppressed in June 1628.[2] But I doubt whether any example from that book makes any real addition to the others I have cited. There is more point in alluding to cases of theatrical censorship. Some light is thrown upon the consequences of inquisitorial interference in the case of Calderón's play about St Eugenia entitled *El José de las mujeres*. We do not know when this play was written, perhaps in the early 1640s. It was first printed in 1661. At the end of the first act the devil enters the dead body of Aurelio; he continues in this 'disguise' until the end of the play. There is a manuscript copy of this play dated 1669 in the Biblioteca Nacional at Madrid. At the end of the text there is a note by the Maestro Don Juan de Rueda y Cuebas, dated 18 November 1670. He here instructs the actors to observe his deletions and not to allow the devil to enter the corpse. This, he maintained, was heresy, a contravention of both the Old and New Testaments and the doctrine of the Fathers of the Church, as well as running counter to four General Councils. Doubtless the play was performed thus mangled.[3] But all the printed editions that I have seen continued to make the devil animate Aurelio's dead body. The same situation also occurs in a play named *El Fénix de España*, written to celebrate the canonization of St Francis Borja (or Borgia) in 1671; like its subject, its author was a Jesuit, Father Diego de Calleja.

Most of the examples of Sankey's cancellations, given, I am sure, accurately by Mr Frye, have parallels in works by orthodox Roman Catholics which underwent similar treatment. Let us not forget that the 1559 Index proscribed also the early works of Luis de Granada, of

[1] For the documents quoted in this paragraph see Gillet's edition, I, 62.

[2] See Luis de Góngora, *Obras en verso del Homero español*, Que recogió Juan López de Vicuña, Edición facsímil, prólogo e indices por Dámaso Alonso (Madrid, 1963). The *Prólogo* is very interesting.

[3] E. M. Wilson, 'Calderón and the Stage-Censor in the seventeenth century—A Provisional Study', *Symposium*, Fall 1961, pp. 165–84.

St Francis Borja and translations into any vernacular of Vida's *Christiados*. The purpose of the Index was to ban harmful books and to purge errors from books that were not harmful throughout. It had rules for so doing, and these rules were applied intelligently or stupidly according to the capacity of the particular censor. He was not asked to say what he thought of the uncensored parts of the books he dealt with. That was the business of ordinary civil or ecclesiastic persons appointed to read books before they were published or (in the seventeenth century) plays before they were acted. So the fact that a book was purged, or prohibited until it could be purged, did not necessarily mean that the rest of that book was unorthodox. The fact that Sankey purged Shakespeare, and the nature of his expurgations, cannot, in my opinion, be held to prove that Shakespeare was a thorough-going Protestant who had no sympathy whatever for the old religion.

The prohibitions of 1559 were obviously rigorously enforced. Books banned in that Index are usually very rare indeed and are to be found more often in foreign libraries than in Spain. But inquisitors were human and made mistakes. In my copy of Calvete de Estrella's *Viaje* the first passage quoted above is cancelled and can only be read with difficulty; against the second there is merely a + in the margin, and the third is not tampered with at all. The case of the *Comedia Jacinta* shows that mistakes were sometimes rectified as well as made; that of *El José de las mujeres* (and I can quote other cases here) that censorship could be purely local. The recommendations were not always acted on; single passages that appeared objectionable to a given officer none the less found their way into print or were reprinted. As long as certain general rules were observed (one could hardly expect Cervantes ro break into hymns of praise for Calvin) the Inquisition was less monolithic than is sometimes supposed. Another censor might have excised *Henry VIII* as well as (or instead of) *Measure for Measure*; or he might have left in more smut.

I doubt therefore whether I can accept Mr Frye's final words:

> What Sankey's expurgation may do is to put us on our guard, from yet another point of view, against the overly eager identification of Shakespeare's plays with Christian teaching in general and the Catholic tradition in particular.

II

Mr Frye, after summarizing Mr John Vyvyan's allegorical interpretations of *Romeo and Juliet* and *Hamlet*, says:

> So far as I know, there is no evidence from any source contemporary with Shakespeare to support the notion that Elizabethan audiences customarily allegorized the plays they saw or that Elizabethan dramatists (save, possibly in rare instances of clearly topical interest) allegorized the plays they wrote. Furthermore, anyone familiar with the public theater will doubt that *any* [my italics] audience, faced with a fast-moving stage play, could follow so elaborate and consistent a structure of double-entendres. To be understood, allegory (if it is at all characterized by subtlety) requires the study, or at least the parlor; popular drama, once it has moved beyond the charming simplicities of the medieval morality play, is too fast-paced a vehicle to convey it.[1]

I hold no brief for Mr Vyvyan, whose book I have not read. The passage quoted contains generalizations about allegorical drama which read very strangely to any one who has read a few Spanish *autos sacramentales*. I cannot help wondering also whether the 'charming simplicities of the medieval morality' were really so simple as Mr Frye says. In Spain, of course, the religious theatre was not suppressed in the sixteenth century, and the splendid spectacles of the Corpus Christi *autos*, performed in the open air with great lavishness of machines, scenery and music, were witnessed by far

[1] P. 33.

greater numbers of people than could be accommodated in any public theatre.

The splendour of the productions enabled the audience to see the relevance of the allegorical representation. Scenery and music, pleasurable in themselves, were subordinate to the action; all was carefully specified by the dramatist himself.[1] Short summaries cannot do justice to these complex and deeply moving plays, especially those written by their greatest master, Don Pedro Calderón de la Barca (1600–81). I mention only the titles of *La cena de Baltasar* (*Belshazzar's Supper*), in which the Biblical story is applied to any sinner who consistently smothers the voice of conscience, *A tu prójimo como a ti* (*Your Neighbour as yourself*), where the parable of the Good Samaritan is given its medieval interpretation, and *Los encantos de la Culpa* (*Guilt's Enchantments*), where the fable of Ulysses and Circe brilliantly shows the general nature of temptation and redemption.

Space does not allow me to bring out the many subtleties of allegory employed in these three plays (Calderón wrote about eighty altogether). The action at times is rapid enough. In seventeenth-century Spain, then, there was an allegorical theatre, which had no connections with study or parlour, but reached a wide audience: the king, the members of the royal councils, the ordinary inhabitants of many cities and towns. Calderón's success depended partly on his staging and his stagecraft, partly on the fact that he was dramatizing events or situations handed down by old traditions. The Elizabethans lacked the resources for such shows, it is true, but were all the old traditions killed outright by the energy and enthusiasm of three or four generations of reformers?

Some of these plays are based on an allegorical interpretation of Scripture. This was not entirely unfamiliar to Elizabethans and Jacobeans. Dr J. W. Blench, in his interesting book on fifteenth- and sixteenth-century sermons,[2] has dealt at length with the scriptural interpretations of Elizabethan preachers. He shows how these men subordinated the allegorical interpretation to the literal, but did not entirely reject it.[3] John Jewel interpreted the water from the rock as a figure of the blood of Christ, the manna of His body and the brazen serpent of the Crucifixion.[4] Something very like the medieval methods were used from time to time by Lancelot Andrewes, who, when preaching on Isaiah LXVI. I. exclaimed:

> Goe we then to the kernell, and let the huske lye: let goe the dead letter, and take we to us the spirituall meaning that hath some life in it. For what care we for the literall *Edom* or *Bozrah*, what became of them: what are they to us? Let us compare spirituall things with spirituall things; that is it must doe us good.
>
> I will give you a key to this, and such like scriptures. Familiar it is with the *Prophets* (Nothing more than) to speake to their People, in their owne language; than to expresse their ghostly enemies, the both mortall and immortall enemies of their soules, under the titles and termes of those Nations and Cities as were knowne sworne enemies of the Commonwealth of *Israel*.[5]

The Reformation in England, then, did not put an end to the allegorizing of Scripture.

Calderón's *Tu prójimo* is based on a traditional allegorization of the parable of the Good Samaritan; *Los encantos de la Culpa* on a moralization of a classical story. Juan Pérez de Moya, in a work first published in 1584, tells us that:

> Circe is the natural passion called unchaste love, which most often turns the wisest and most judicious men

[1] See A. A. Parker's *The Allegorical Theatre of Calderón* (Oxford, 1943), B. W. Wardropper's *Introducción al teatro religioso del siglo de oro* (*Evolución del Auto Sacramental: 1500–1648*) (Madrid, 1953), and N. D. Shergold and J. E. Varey, *Los autos sacramentales en Madrid en la época de Calderón, 1637–1681* (Madrid, 1961).

[2] *Preaching in England in the late Fifteenth and Sixteenth Centuries, A Study of English Sermons, 1450–c. 1600* (Oxford, 1964). See especially Chapter I.

[3] P. 57.

[4] P. 62.

[5] Quoted by Dr Blench, pp. 66–7.

into the wildest and most furious animals; sometimes she makes them more senseless than stones about the honour and reputation which they diligently preserved before they let themselves be blinded by this fiercest of passions. And as men who much delight in taking pleasure with common and filthy women are compared to swine; so the wise men feigned that Circe changed Ulisses's companions into these animals . . . By Ulisses is to be understood the part of our soul that shares in reason. Circe is Nature. The Companions are the powers of the soul who conspire with the affections of the body and disobey Reason. Nature, then, is the desire of unlawful things, and the good rule is the stay and bridle of the depraved mind. But Reason, typified by Ulysses, remains steadfast and unconquered against these seductions of appetite.[1]

Calderón has modified the details of Pérez de Moya's interpretation of the myth. But his treatment of it is similar. Mr Frye tells us that Golding saw in Ovid 'valuable and delightful instruction for the wise conduct of life';[2] so did Pérez de Moya. Calderón christianized Moya's moralisms but at the same time largely preserved them. I do not say that this happened also in Jacobean England. But to say that it could not have happened seems to me rash.

I think therefore that Mr Frye's general argument about allegory is refuted by the existence of Calderón's *autos sacramentales*. A better defence of his position would seem to lie in the fact that Shakespeare's 'fables are entirely secular and self-sufficient in their own plane'.[3] The same thing might be said of Calderón's purely secular plays (if we exclude not only the sacramental allegories but also all the *comedias* that deal with religious subjects), but if *Life's a Dream*, *Love the Greatest Enchantment* and even *The Painter of his Dishonour* could provide material for reworking into a sacramental allegory, the case for so considering them is considerably weakened. I am not entirely convinced that there is no possibility of any allegorical interpretation of any single play by Shakespeare.

[1] 'Circe es aquella passion natural que llaman amor deshonesto, que las mas vezes transforma a los mas sabios, y de mayor juyzio, en animales fierissimos, y llenos de furor, y algunas vezes los buelue mas insensibles que piedras, a cerca de la honra, y reputacion que conseruaban con tanta diligencia, antes que se dexassen cegar desta fierissima passion. Y porque el que mucho se deleyta de holgarse con las comunes, y suzias mugeres, es co[m]parado al puerco: por esto fingiero[n] los sabios, auer Circe conuertido los compañeros de Vlises en estos animales . . . Por Vlises se entiende la parte de nuestra anima que participa de la razon. Circe es la naturaleza. Los compañeros de Vlises, son las potencias del alma, que conspiran con los afectos del cuerpo, y no obedecen a la razon. La naturaleza pues es el apetecer las cosas no legitimas, y la buena ley es detenimiento, y freno del ingenio deprauado. Mas la razon entendida por Vlises, permanece firme sin ser vencida contra estos halagos del apetito.' Iuan Perez de Moya, *Filosofia secreta, donde debaxo de historias fabulosas, se contiene mucha doctrina prouechosa a todos estudios* . . . (Alcalá de Henares, 1611), pp. 449–50.

[2] P. 68.

[3] I owe this phrase to Dr Derek Brewer of Emmanuel College, Cambridge, who has been kind enough to criticize an early draft of this paper. But Mr Frye, who has also read the paper, comments that he would prefer to substitute 'essentially' for 'entirely' in Brewer's phrase. He also mentions that he has discussed Protestant allegorical interpretation of Scripture in the first chapter of his *Perspective on Man* and at many points throughout his book entitled *God, Man and Satan*. He adds: 'As for allegory, it can of course be assimilated on the stage *if* it is not so complicated by individualisation of the characters that it can no longer be followed on an allegorical plane. There is ample opportunity for following a simple (by which I do not mean simple-minded) allegory in *Everyman* and also in *A Game at Chess* (1624), but in both the religious and the political allegories the identifications of the characters are sufficiently clear and unambiguous to be followed in a fast-moving stage action. But even when ancient allegorical figures are referred to in connection with Shakespeare's characters as when Kent in *Lear* refers to Goneril as 'Vanity the puppet' and to her father as 'Royalty', or when Banquo plays a part comparable to that of 'Conscience' and Falstaff to that of 'Vice'—so much more is involved in the complexity of character and of situation that we in the audience are shut off from the effective possibility of a consistent allegorical interpretation.'

III

So far I have tried to show two things:

1. That Mr Frye's interpretation of Father Sankey's expurgation of the Valladolid Folio can be paralleled in the inquisitorial treatment of Spanish plays and other works by Roman Catholic writers.

2. That Mr Frye's generalizations about dramatic allegories are contradicted by the *autos sacramentales* of Calderón. I have also tried to show that some of the bases of their allegories were probably familiar to seventeenth-century Englishmen.

The impressively marshalled evidence of the central portion of Mr Frye's book does not admit contradiction, though it may perhaps require occasional qualification. Before I try to present my cavils I want to express my admiration for that part of his book. His account of the attitudes of Luther and Calvin towards classical literature and human ethics is extraordinarily revealing and shows the danger of identifying the attitudes of sixteenth-century Protestants with those of the more stupid nineteenth-century evangelicals and the wilder extremes of present-day nonconformity. I am most grateful for the third and fourth chapters of his Part Two and for the whole of his Part Three. These sections will save many of us from rash and uncharitable judgements on some sixteenth-century divines and sharpen our awareness of Shakespeare's debt to them.

Part of the difficulty I still find even in these chapters is due to the lack of a comparison with Roman Catholic thought on these topics. Parallels between Shakespeare on the one hand and the statements of Luther, Calvin and Hooker on the other, would have been even more revealing had he added in some representatives of sixteenth-century catholicism. Can we assume that the passages quoted from the three Protestants have no parallels in Catholic thought? Did the reformers jettison all the theological ideas that they had learned from earlier masters? Perhaps there was still a good deal of common ground between those who accepted, and those who rejected, transubstantiation, Purgatory, invocations of the saints, and justification by faith and works. We are not told which of the parallels adduced in Part Three could not be found in Aquinas or other Catholic authorities. His examples seem to me to prove that Shakespeare may have been an orthodox Protestant. They do not disprove that he could have had some sympathy for the religion of his ancestors. Hooker, after all, often quoted Aquinas with approval.

I also wonder whether Mr Frye has given due weight to some other considerations. It seems almost too obvious to say so, but not every Englishman was entirely convinced of the validity of reforming doctrine. On 9 May 1614 Gondomar reported to Philip III:

> In the kingdom of England, not counting Scotland and Ireland, according to the most reliable reports I have been able to obtain, there are three million five hundred thousand or six hundred thousand people... Of these it is understood that one in twelve are true catholics, who refuse the oath, refuse to go to church with heretics, but preserve themselves with caution (although they endure persecution) and by doing favours and giving money. According to my figures they will number about 300,000 catholics.
>
> Two twelfths are schismatics who know and believe the truth and at heart are catholics, but fear and false worldly prudence make them go to church and swear the oath. There are 600,000 of them. I am told that they most of all regret the persecution, for as they live with bad and unquiet consciences they are much hurt by not being able to abandon these cares.
>
> Another three twelfths are called 'well inclined' by the catholics, because they do not hate the catholic religion; but they do not believe in anything, nor do they want to talk or think about religious things. They try to live and to get by happily. They may be described as atheists. According to my reckoning they make up 900,000. So that these three groups come to form half the population of the kingdom.

The other six parts out of twelve are divided up into protestants [i.e. Lutherans] and puritans [i.e. Calvinists] . . .[1]

Gondomar probably exaggerated—his informers probably gave him the kind of figures he wanted to receive. He quotes too what he calls an English proverb: 'to live a protestant and die a catholic'.[2] But even if the numbers were halved or quartered there would still be a considerable group who, left to themselves, might have preferred the Roman allegiance. There must have been a good deal of crypto-catholicism in the early 1600s in England.

In so far as he neglects the hang-over of the old religion Mr Frye seems to me to cut Shakespeare off from his past. Were there no survivals of pre-Reformation spirituality in post-Reformation religion? Certain works by Mr Louis Martz, Miss Tuve and Dame Helen Gardner seem to point in another direction. Mr Frye's England seems too much an island. He does not consider continental influences at work in sixteenth-century England, except of course of the great reformers. But in the 1590s English Protestants could read Luis of Granada and Diego de Estella as well as Calvin's *Institutes*. According to Gondomar James used to talk of 'el reverendo Granada' and referred to him as 'an honoured divine'.[3] Those in England who were curious in such matters had some access to counter-Reformation writers. If we want to investigate Shakespeare's use of theological material, these matters are not entirely irrelevant.

Even if 'Elizabeth's proclamation of 1559 expressly forbade the stage to meddle' with religious changes,[4] religious subjects were chosen by a number of playwrights later in her reign. If Shakespeare carefully excluded religious messages from his plays, other writers hardly did so. *The Conflict of Conscience* seems to me essentially a theological play. *A looking-Glass for London and England* brings Hosea and Jonah on to the stage and makes them plead with London to imitate Niniveh:

O proud adulterous glorie of the West,
Thy neighbors burns, yet doest thou feare no fire.
Thy Preachers crie, yet doest thou stop thine eares.
Thy larum rings, yet sleepest thou secure.
London awake, for feare the Lord do frowne,
I set a looking Glasse before thine eyes.
O turne, O turne, with weeping to the Lord,
And thinke the praiers and vertues of thy Queene,
Defers the plague which otherwise would fall.

[1] En el reyno de Inglaterra, sin Escocia ni Irlanda, conforme a las relaciones más ciertas que he podido auer, ay tres millones y quinientas o seiscientas mil personas, que hazen treinta y seis veces cien mil; de éstas se entiende que una de doze partes son católicos uerdaderos, que no hazen el juramento ni concurren en las iglesias con los hereges, conseruándose con recato, y con tolerar las persecuciones y con fauores y dineros, y conforme a este presupuesto vendrán a ser trescientas mil personas los católicos.

Cismáticos ay dos partes de doze, que conocen y creen la uerdad y son católicos en su corazón, pero el temor y consideraciones de mala prudencia del mundo les haze ir a las iglesias y tomar el juramento, y éstos se entiende que son seiscientas mil personas, ye me dizen que son los que más sienten la persecución, porque como uiuen con mala y inquieta conciencia, dales gran pena no salir de este cuydado.

Ay otras tres partes de doze bien inclinados, que así los llaman los cattólicos, porque no aborrezen la religión católica, pero ni creen en nada ni quieren hablar ni pensar en cosa de religión, sólo procuran uiuir y pasar alegremente, y éstos se pueden llamar ateístas, y conforme al presupuesto que se lleua serán éstos nueuecientos mil, de manera que estas tres formas de gente vienen a ser la mitad del reyno.

Las otras seis partes de doze se diuiden entre protestantes y puritanos . . . *Correspondencia oficial de Don Diego Sarmiento de Acuña, Conde de Gondomar. Documentos inéditos para la historia de España*, publicados por los señores Duque de Alba . . . (four volumes, Madrid, 1945). My extract is from IV, 70–1.

[2] 'Es aquí refrán y dicho muy común, *uiuir protestante y morir católico*.' *Ibid.*, 71.

[3] 'De fray Luis de Granada me ha dicho el rey grandes uienes y que él lee, con gran gusto, sus obras; llámale el reberendo Granada, y hame dicho, muchas veces, que es muy honrado reberendo.' Gondomar to the Duke of Lerma, 28 July 1614. *Ibid.*, 226–7.

[4] George Sampson, *The Concise Cambridge History of English Literature* (second edition, Cambridge, 1961), p. 340.

Repent O London, least for thine offence,
Thy shepheard faile, whom mightie God preserue,
That she may hide the pillar of his Church,
Against the stormes of Romish Antichrist:
The hand of mercy ouershead her head,
And let all faithfull subiects say, *Amen.*[1]

The Blasphemy Act probably discouraged dramatists who had such tendencies. But I still find remarkable those two plays associated with Massinger: *The Renegado* and *The Virgin Martyr*. A good deal of other matter is contained in both; but they have religious intentions too. I doubt whether anyone could see in either play 'a universal rather than ... an exclusively Christian system of ethical values'.[2] Massinger and Dekker were lesser dramatists than Shakespeare; but if they could make effective religious appeals to their audiences, there seems no good historical reason why Shakespeare could not also have done so.

Mr Frye's central statement runs as follows:

> Shakespeare's standard of dramatic evaluation was the common ethical consensus of man, as that consensus was understood in his own time. Shakespeare did not any more appeal in his plays to an exclusively Christian ethic than he embodied in them an exclusively Christian theology. With the possible exception of *Measure for Measure* (and I am not convinced that an exception is to be admitted there as any more than a possibility), I find that an explicitly New Testament ethic is less relevant to Shakespeare's plays than an ethic of purely natural law, based equally in the Scriptures and the Greek and Latin classics. It is true that individual characters in the plays often rely upon or refer to elements of the Christian faith ... but the fact remains that Shakespeare's total dramatic structure could as well be supported by the ethics of the virtuous heathen as by those of the Christian church.[3]

The distinction exists clearly enough. It had been made by theologians long before the Reformation. But is it one of which the ordinary theatregoer or actor of the seventeenth century would have been aware? It might not always be very easy to keep the two apart or to avoid some intrusion of the exclusively Christian into the ethics of the virtuous heathen. In England no doubt legislation made dramatists careful; they could not write plays about the life of Christ or the actions of the apostles, nor could they show religious ceremonies on the stage. But Massinger was able to present a scene of confession and absolution in *The Renegado* and to portray martyrdom in *The Virgin Martyr*. In Spain no such prohibitions existed; there objections were raised against the profanity or lasciviousness of some of the scenes depicted, not to their religious associations. So Calderón was able to depict how, in *The Wonder-Working Magician*, the Grace of God converted Cipriano and how, in *The Devotion of the Cross*, repentance brought about the salvation of a reprobate. If we read *Life's a Dream* we can interpret it—as Mr Frye does *King Lear*—in terms of a purely human ethical system. But Calderón wrote years later an *auto sacramental* with the same title, based on the play. To read the *auto* back into the *comedia* is wrong, but the fact that the *comedia* could give rise to the *auto* hints at a possible interpretation of the *comedia* which might not exclude religious references. In Spanish plays the boundary between the ethic of natural law and that of Christianity was more often disregarded.[4]

Finally I should repeat that Mr Frye is probably right to warn critics to steer clear of introducing too many Christian suppositions into the interpretation of Shakespeare's plays. The fact remains that there existed at the same time a theatre that was sometimes explicitly

[1] Thomas Lodge and Robert Greene, *A looking-Glass for London and England* (1594), The Malone Society Reprints (Oxford, 1932), lines 2395–409.

[2] Frye, *Shakespeare and Christian Doctrine*, p. 108.

[3] P. 94–5.

[4] For the *auto* of *La vida es sueño*, see Professor A. A. Parker's excellent study in *The Allegorical Theatre of Calderón*, pp. 197–229. For the *comedia* see various studies in *Critical Essays on the Theatre of Calderón*, edited by Bruce W. Wardropper (New York, 1965), pp. 63–133.

Christian and that there still remained some common elements in the culture of England and Spain which might have enabled our greatest dramatist to use reflections of specifically Christian ideas had he wished to do so. I am not completely convinced that he never did.

SHAKESPEARE'S POETS

KENNETH MUIR

It has been observed by more than one critic that the poets depicted, and the references to poetry, in Shakespeare's plays seem to be by a man who regarded the art and its practitioners with irony, satire or contempt. But it is never safe to assume that Shakespeare shared the views of his characters, even of his virtuous characters; and the opinions expressed in his plays on the subject of poetry are all, in their various ways, suspect, because they are appropriate to the characters who speak them.

The earliest reference is in *The Two Gentlemen of Verona*, where Proteus instructs Thurio how to win Silvia. It must be remembered that Proteus is playing a double game since he wishes to win Silvia for himself. He is already false to Valentine and his advice to Thurio is insincere:

> But you, Sir Thurio, are not sharp enough;
> You must lay lime to tangle her desires
> By wailful sonnets, whose composed rhymes
> Should be full-fraught with serviceable vows.
>
> (III, ii, 67-70)

The Duke backs up Proteus' words with the remark:

> Much is the force of heaven-bred poesy.
>
> (III, ii, 72)

But the poetry advocated by Proteus is hardly heaven-bred: it is strictly utilitarian. Its object is the winning of Silvia, although Proteus does not wish it to succeed:

> Say that upon the altar of her beauty
> You sacrifice your tears, your sighs, your heart;
> Write till your ink be dry, and with your tears
> Moist it again, and frame some feeling line
> That may discover such integrity.
>
> (III, ii, 73-7)

Thurio, who is clearly incapable of genuine passion, is not really expected to weep, or even to be sincere in what he writes. He merely has to seem to be sincere, to give the illusion of 'such integrity'. Written at a time when scores of second-rate poets were turning out Petrarchan sonnets, the lines indirectly satirize the fashion. Yet Sir Sidney Lee, in one of his periodic attempts to show that Shakespeare did not express a genuine love or friendship for the recipient of the Sonnets, but was simply attempting to extort money by flattery, used Proteus' lines in support of his argument. Apparently Lee believed that time-serving insincerity would be less of a blot on Shakespeare's reputation than the faintest suspicion of homosexuality. He was writing after the trial of Oscar Wilde. But the sonnets Thurio is urged to write are the kind of poems that Shakespeare accused the Rival Poets of writing—the 'strained touches' of rhetoric and 'their gross painting'.

Proteus proceeds to advise Thurio to serenade Silvia

> With some sweet consort; to their instruments
> Tune a deploring dump. (III, ii, 84-5)

Thurio says he has 'a sonnet that will serve the turn'; but the song in praise of Silvia is hardly a 'deploring dump' and far too good to be supposed to come from Thurio's pen. Shakespeare, perhaps, could not resist the temptation of writing a good song. The same thing happens at the end of *Love's Labour's Lost*. The exquisite songs in praise of the owl and the cuckoo are supposed to be written by the two learned men, Holofernes and Nathaniel. But Holofernes' other poetic effusions are deliberately absurd and Nathaniel, though more modest, belongs to the same school of poetry. In one recent production of the play at Stratford-on-Avon, the director tried to conceal the beauty of the words by a deliberately feeble performance of a poor setting, thus effectively ruining one of Shakespeare's most exquisite endings.

In *Love's Labour's Lost*, which is, amongst other things, a play upon words, there are appropriately no less than eight amateur poets. Even Moth tries his hand at composition; and Armado, his master, who is drunk on figures of rhetoric, exclaims when he falls in love with Jaquenetta:

> Assist me, some extemporal god of rhyme, for I am sure I shall turn sonneter. Devise, wit; write, pen; for I am for whole volumes in folio. (I, ii, 177-81)

But we are given only six lines of Armado's composition, a postscript to his bombastic epistle.

The four poems by the King and his lords vary in quality. The King's own, being the weakest, was wisely omitted from *The Passionate Pilgrim*. Longaville's opens splendidly—

> Did not the heavenly rhetoric of thine eye—

but fails to live up to its promise. Berowne's, like the first sonnet in *Astrophel and Stella*, is in neatly turned alexandrines. But of the four poems Dumain's ode is the only one which is entirely charming and successful.

Berowne comments satirically on his fellow poets, but it is left to Holofernes to pronounce magisterially on Berowne's own poem: that it is not as good as Ovid's.

> Here are only numbers ratified; but, for the elegancy, facility, and golden cadence of poesy, *caret*. Ovidius Naso was the man. (IV, ii, 113-16)

Later in the scene he tells Nathaniel that he

> will prove those verses to be very unlearned, neither savouring of poetry, wit, nor invention. (lines 146-7)

What Holofernes understood by elegancy, facility and golden cadence, we can judge from his own extemporal verses on the death of the deer. Whereas the four lords are writing in the style of the nineties, Holofernes harks back to an earlier manner. He tells Nathaniel that he 'will something affect the letter, for it argues facility'.

> The preyful Princess pierc'd and prick'd a
> pretty pleasing pricket.
> (IV, ii, 54)

The poem depends, like a riddle, on an absurd conceit—adding L to sore to make sorel; but even more absurd than the poem is the author's complacent conviction, overlaid with mock modesty, that he is a genius:

> This is a gift that I have, simple, simple; a foolish extravagant spirit, full of forms, figures, shapes, objects, ideas, apprehensions, motions, revolutions. These are begot in the ventricle of memory, nourish'd in the womb of pia mater, and delivered upon the mellowing of occasion. But the gift is good in those in whom it is acute, and I am thankful for it. (IV, ii, 63-9)

Holofernes has one devoted admirer. The Curate speaks of his 'rare talent', declaring

> I praise the Lord for you, and so may my parishioners. (IV, ii, 70-1)

Shakespeare's best-known reference to the poet is in the speech of Theseus in the last act of *A Midsummer-Night's Dream*. Ever since Pollard pointed out the significance of the mislineation of these lines, it is generally accepted that they were a marginal insertion; but there is nothing to indicate whether they were written five minutes or five years after the rest of the speech:

The lunatic, the lover and the poet
Are of imagination all compact.
One sees more devils than vast hell can hold;
That is the madman. The lover, all as frantic,
Sees Helen's beauty in a brow of Egypt.
The poet's eye, in a fine frenzy rolling,
Doth glance from heaven to earth, from earth to heaven;
And as imagination bodies forth
The forms of things unknown, the poet's pen
Turns them to shapes and gives to airy nothing
A local habitation and a name. (v, i, 7-17)

Shakespeare's original intention was to make Theseus compare the lover and the lunatic. Then he inserted the lines about the poet, lines which are much more powerful than the surrounding ones.[1] At first sight, the association of poets with lunatics and equally frantic lovers seems to have a satirical purpose and this, doubtless, is Theseus' purpose. The 'fine frenzy' and the rolling eye recall the divine fury of which Plato, Sidney and others had spoken. The poet gives 'A local habitation and a name' to nothing. His creations, being the result of imagination, have no more connection with the real world than the delusions of the madman or the lover who cannot see his beloved as she really is. Theseus is ignoring Sidney's conjuration, at the end of his *Apology*, 'no more to scorn the sacred mysteries of poesy; no more to laugh at the name of poets, as though they were next inheritors to fools; no more to jest at the reverend title of a rhymer'. Theseus, in spite of his maturity compared with the young lovers in the play, should not be taken as Shakespeare's spokesman. He is, in fact, a bit of a Philistine. One has only to read the sonnets about the Dark Lady to realize that Shakespeare did not see Helen's beauty in a brow of Egypt.

Theseus is wrong, even about the lovers. He thinks their story is untrue; but as Hippolyta properly points out:

All the story of the night told over,
And all their minds transfigur'd so together,
More witnesseth than fancy's images,
And grows to something of great constancy;
But, howsoever, strange and admirable.
(v, i, 23-7)

The strange story of the lovers is, in the world of the play, true.

There is, I think, an additional irony. In his previous plays—historical, comical, tragical—Shakespeare had kept reasonably close to real life. The audience had to swallow plenty of improbable fictions—from the two pairs of identical twins severed by shipwreck to the methods used to tame the Shrew—but there had been no impossibilities. When Mercutio discourses on Queen Mab no one imagines that his account is meant to be taken seriously. But in *A Midsummer-Night's Dream* Shakespeare, as it were, took a leaf out of Mercutio's book and exhibited fairies on the stage; and even if many of his audience believed in fairies, *his* fairies were notoriously different. Not merely were they different from those of folk lore, but they varied in size from those able to wear bats' wings as coats or hide in acorn-cups to Titania herself who is large enough to embrace an ass. The audience, moreover, is asked to accept the magical effects of Oberon's juice and the transformation of Bottom; and, side by side with such things, there is placed the earthy absurdity of the amateur actors. Shakespeare had distanced *The Taming of the*

[1] Blake remarked that the lines are Theseus' opinion, not Shakespeare's, 'You might as well quote Satan's blasphemies from Milton & give them as Milton's opinions'. A. Thaler, *Shakespeare and Sir Philip Sidney* (1947), compares several passages from Sidney's *Defence*:

the poet . . . from Dante his heaven to his hell, under . . . his pen . . . the imagination and judging power . . . figured forth by the speaking picture of poesy . . .

forms such as never were in nature . . . The poets give names . . . to make their picture the more lively.

Shrew by presenting it before Christopher Sly, who imagines for a few hours that he is not a drunken tinker but a lord. In *A Midsummer-Night's Dream* Shakespeare relies only on his poetry to create the wood near Athens and what happens in it. He 'gives to airy nothing A local habitation and a name'. What Theseus intends as a gibe against poetry is a precise account of Shakespeare's method in this play. But what Theseus did not appreciate was that the poet who creates

> Forms more real than living man,
> Nurslings of immortality

may yet be making a valid comment on real life.

There is a poet called Lodowick in the anonymous *Edward III*. Many critics believe that the second act, in which he appears, was written by Shakespeare;[1] but Swinburne, who did not, referred to Lodowick as a pimp. He is employed by the King to write a poem to the Countess, as a means of seducing her; and he announces her arrival when she comes for her last interview with the King—in which virtue triumphs over adulterous passion. But there is nothing in Lodowick's part to suggest that he approves of the King's adulterous designs, nor even that he assists them. At the beginning of the act he describes how the King has fallen in love with the Countess. It is clear from the language he uses that he admires the Countess and deplores the King's adulterous love:

> If she did blush, 'twas tender modest shame,
> Being in the sacred presence of a King:
> If he did blush, 'twas red immodest shame,
> To vaile his eyes amisse, being a king:
> If she lookt pale, 'twas silly womans feare,
> To beare her selfe in presence of a king:
> If he lookt pale, it was with guiltie feare,
> To dote amisse, being a mighty king.

The King enters and orders Lodowick, who 'is well read in poetrie', to fetch ink and paper. He asks him to 'inuocate some golden Muse' and bring 'an enchanted pen'. Lodowick asks to whom he should write, though he presumably guesses that it is the Countess despite the fact that the King does not name her.

The technique of the scene is interesting. We hear only a line and a half of Lodowick's poem; but the King's instructions to him are like the rough draft of a poem, more poetical, indeed, than anything Lodowick writes. The King tells him:

> Better than bewtifull thou must begin,
> Devise for faire a fairer word than faire . . .
> For flattery feare thou not to be convicted;
> For, were thy admiration ten tymes more,
> Ten tymes ten thousand more the worth exceeds
> Of that thou art to praise, thy praises worth.

While Lodowick is composing his poem, the King peruses the Countess in his thoughts. He cannot compare her voice to music because

> To musicke every sommer leaping swaine
> Compares his sunburnt lover when she speakes.

Nor can he compare it to the nightingale, who sings of adulterate wrong,

> For sinne, though synne, would not be so esteemd,
> But rather, vertue sin, synne vertue deemd.

He then thinks of similes for her hair:

> far softer than the silke wormes twist,
> Like to a flattering glas, doth make more faire
> The yelow Amber.

He decides that the phrase *Like to a flattering glas* 'comes in too soon' because he wants to use it about her eyes. The King's speech gives a fair impression of a man composing a poem, accepting some similes and rejecting others, and thus suggests the silent process of Lodowick's composition.

Lodowick's first line—

> More faire and chast then is the Queen of Shades—

is criticized by the King on two grounds: that his love should not be compared to 'the

[1] See K. Muir, *Shakespeare as Collaborator* (London, 1960), pp. 10 ff.

pale Queene of night' and for the epithet *chaste*:

> I did not bid thee talke of chastitie,
> To ransack so the treasure of her minde, . . .
> Out with the moone line, I wil none of it;
> And let me have hir likened to the sun.

Lodowick continues:

> More bould in constancie . . . then Iudith was.

The King naturally objects to this line, as he remembers the fate of Holofernes.

It can hardly be doubted that Lodowick's lines were written deliberately to remind the King that he is proposing to commit a sin. Swinburne's word for Lodowick is quite undeserved. If Lodowick was Shakespeare's creation he is the only one of his poets who emerges with much credit.

Several characters in the plays written between 1595 and 1599 laugh at the fashionable absurdities of the sonneteers of the period. Mercutio, whose speech on Queen Mab shows that he has the instincts of a poet, quizzes Romeo about his conventional and sentimental love for Rosaline, though, unknown to him, Romeo is fully recovered:

> Now is he for the numbers that Petrarch flow'd in; Laura, to his lady, was a kitchen-wench—marry, she had a better love to berhyme her; Dido, a dowdy; Cleopatra, a gipsy; Helen and Hero, hildings and harlots; Thisbe, a gray eye or so, but not to the purpose. (*Rom. & Jul.*, II, iv, 38–42)

Benedick, before he acknowledges his love for Beatrice, scoffs similarly at Claudio, whose words are 'a very fantastical banquet, just so many strange dishes'; and, later in the play, he confesses that he cannot write verse to Beatrice:

> Marry, I cannot show it in rhyme; I have tried: I can find no rhyme to 'lady' but 'baby'—an innocent rhyme; for 'scorn', 'Horn'—a hard rhyme; for 'school', 'fool'—a babbling rhyme; very ominous endings. No, I was not born under a rhyming planet, nor I cannot woo in festival terms.
> (*Much Ado*, V, ii, 30-7)

Both Benedick and Beatrice are in reaction against the conventions of romantic love; and, in terms of the comedy, Benedick's inability to rhyme is a proof of his sincerity.

Hotspur, irritated by Glendower, expresses his dislike of ballad-mongers:

> I had rather hear a brazen canstick turn'd,
> Or a dry wheel grate on the axle-tree;
> And that would set my teeth nothing on edge,
> Nothing so much as mincing poetry:
> 'Tis like the forc'd gait of a shuffling nag.
> (*1 Hen. IV*, III, i, 131-5)

His similes prove Hotspur to be a poet in spite of himself; and though much of *1 Henry IV* is in prose, Hotspur speaks mainly in verse, appropriately enough for his 'huffing part'.

Yet Shakespeare seems to have become dissatisfied with verse in the last five years of the sixteenth century. He felt temporarily that it tended to blur the distinction between one character and another, and that it interfered with the greater realism he wished to introduce, both in the dialogue of his plays and in its delivery on the stage. So we have his major characters of this period—Shylock, Falstaff, Benedick, Beatrice and Rosalind speaking mainly in prose. When Orlando inadvertently speaks in verse—

> Good day, and happiness, dear Rosalind—
> (*A.Y.L.I.*, IV, i, 27)

Jaques immediately takes his leave with the words:

> Nay, then, God buy you, an you talk in blank verse.

Yet Jaques, the satirist, has spoken many lines of verse earlier in the play.

There are two poets in *Julius Caesar*, both of them mentioned by Plutarch. One of them, Cinna, appears in a short scene at the end of Act III. He is lynched by the mob because he shares his name with one of the conspirators. When he explains that he is not the conspirator, they decide to tear him for his bad verses. It is an effective little scene and it has an important dramatic function. In the previous scene Antony has whipped up the passions of the mob by appeals to pity and cupidity—by his increasingly sarcastic references to the honourable men, by his account of the assassination, by his reference to one of Caesar's victories, by the display of the blood-stained mantle and the mangled body, and, finally, by reading the will. The citizens rush off to burn the houses of the conspirators; Antony cries:

> Mischief, thou art afoot,
> Take thou what course thou wilt;
> (III, ii, 261–2)

and we hear that Brutus and Cassius have ridden 'like madmen through the gates of Rome'. What we need at this point is a scene to show the mob in action, in all its fury and irrationality: and the Cinna scene supplies this need to perfection.[1]

The second poet is introduced into Act IV, scene iii, for comic relief. The scene begins with a violent quarrel between Brutus and Cassius, a quarrel which ends with a reconciliation. After the scene with the Poet, Brutus reveals that Portia is dead. Although the intrusion of the poet is comic, his intentions are apparently serious and sensible. He has heard of the dispute between Brutus and Cassius and wishes to reconcile them. He is determined and he is brave. He tells Lucilius: 'Nothing but death shall stay me'. He addresses the generals as equals and annoys Brutus by his presumption. 'Saucy fellow, hence'. Cassius, on the other hand, is tolerantly amused by the Poet's—possibly unintentional—rhyming couplet:

> *Poet.* Love, and be friends, as two such men should be.
> For I have seen more years, I'm sure, than ye.
> *Cassius.* Ha, ha! How vilely doth this cynic rhyme! ...
> Bear with him, Brutus; 'tis his fashion.

To which Brutus replies:

> What should the wars do with these jigging fools?

Cassius is not sportive and never goes to a play, and Brutus is fond of music, so that the differing reactions of the two men are interesting. But Brutus, as we learn soon afterwards, has just heard of Portia's suicide.

The dialogue does not make clear, though it could be made clear in performance, that the Poet is a fool. Plutarch's account explains why Cassius calls him a cynic:

> Their friends, that were without the chamber, hearing them loud within and angry between themselves, they were both amazed and afraid also, lest it would grow to further matter: but yet they were commanded, that no man should come to them. Notwithstanding, one Marcus Phaonius, that had been a friend and follower of Cato while he lived, and took upon him to counterfeit a Philosopher not with wisdom and discretion, but with a certain bedlam and frantic motion: he would needs come into the chamber, though the men offered to keep him out. But it was no boot to let Phaonius, when a mad mood or toy took him in the head: for he was a hot hasty man, and sudden in all his doings, and cared for never a Senator of them all. Now, though he used this bold manner of speech after the profession of the Cynick Philosophers, (as who would say, Dogs,) yet his boldness did no hurt many times, because they did but laugh at him to see him so mad. This Phaonius at that time, in despite of the door-keepers, came into the chamber, and with a certain scoffing and mocking gesture, which he counterfeited of purpose, he rehearsed the verses which old Nestor said in Homer:
>
> My Lords, I pray you hearken both to me,
> For I have seen moe years than suchie three.
>
> Cassius fell a laughing at him: but Brutus thrust him out of the chamber, and called him Dog and counterfeit cynic. Howbeit his coming in brake their strife at that time.

It will be observed that Shakespeare ends the quarrel before the appearance of the Poet, and that he makes the intruder a poet rather

[1] In all the recent productions I have seen, Cinna has been lynched on the stage; and the horror is perhaps in this case legitimate and is not merely an attempt to show that Shakespeare was a forerunner of the Theatre of Cruelty. We need not suppose, as has been suggested, that the murder of a poet gives special satisfaction to an English audience, or even that the director is symbolically presenting his own butchery of the poet whose plays he 'adapts'.

than a philosopher, despite Cassius' term 'cynic'. His rhymed couplet is not of his own composition but a quotation from Homer, and ought, perhaps, to be put in inverted commas.[1]

Why Shakespeare turned the philosopher into a poet is impossible to determine with any certainty; but he may have wished to provide a scene to reinforce the one in which Cinna the poet appears and so comment ironically on the position of the poet in his own society. Shakespeare knew that art was made 'tongue-tied by authority'. He could not in his plays deal directly with great public issues. This was not due, as Orwell thought, to cowardice, making him express subversive views only through the mouths of fools and madmen, but to the conditions under which the dramatists wrote. Even the harmless and orthodox treatment of the anti-alien riots in *Sir Thomas More* prevented the play from being staged. If Shakespeare had presumed to advise Southampton or Essex he would have been treated as unceremoniously as the Poet is treated by Brutus. It is therefore difficult to accept the theory that the unflattering portrait of Achilles in *Troilus and Cressida* was intended as a warning to Essex before his rebellion—even though Chapman compared Essex to Achilles in his dedication of an instalment of his translation of the *Iliad*. Although Coleridge said that Members of Parliament in his day would do well to read Samuel Daniel for the lessons he gave on public affairs in his poems, there is no evidence that Daniel ever had any political influence in his own day; and *Philotas*, which was thought to refer to the Essex conspiracy, brought him into trouble.

Hamlet is an amateur poet who composed some lines to be inserted in *The Murder of Gonzago*. Which the lines were no one has settled beyond all controversy; and they may indeed belong to the part of the play we do not hear, where the murderer gets the love of the victim's wife. But we have a taste of Hamlet's quality as a poet in the verses he sends to Ophelia:

> Doubt that the stars are fire;
> Doubt that the sun doth move,
> Doubt truth to be a liar;
> But never doubt I love. (II, ii, 115–18)

We may deduce, perhaps, that Hamlet is not a Copernican; but we must agree with his own verdict that he is 'ill at these numbers'.

The letter containing these verses is something of a mystery. Was it written before Ophelia broke off their relations or afterwards? If it was written afterwards, was it designed to lend colour to Polonius' view that Hamlet had been driven mad by her rejection of him? If so, it is curious that there is no mention of this rejection. If it was written before, why is it written in such an affected style? We cannot assume that Hamlet was merely playing at love in view of his avowal at her grave. Perhaps the most probable explanation is this. Shakespeare had to write a letter which could be used by Polonius as a proof of madness; and he left the audience in doubt about the date of the letter. If they imagined it was written before Ophelia's rejection of him and before his visit to her closet, the letter could be taken as the effusion of a fashionable young man in love. One is tempted to say that the writer of the letter could scarcely afford to criticize Osric's style.

The next Shakespearian poet is the satirist, honest Iago. He is called on to show his skill in impromptu composition to entertain Desdemona while she is anxiously awaiting news of Othello. Iago professes to find the task difficult:

> my invention
> Comes from my pate as birdlime does from frieze—
> It plucks out brains and all. But my Muse labours
> And thus she is deliver'd. (*Oth.*, II, i, 125–8)

[1] No edition I have seen does this. Shakespeare alters the couplet but the general drift is the same; but it could be argued that he means it to be the bad poet's own rather than a quotation. This is supported by Brutus' 'jigging fools'. (Cf. Marlowe's 'jigging veins of rhyming mother wits'.)

The verses that follow consist of four epigrammatic couplets, each couplet devoted to a different character—the fair and wise, the black and witty, the fair and foolish, the foul and foolish—followed by a twelve-line epigram 'on a deserving woman indeed'. Compared with the couplets used by Elizabethan satirists—Lodge, Hall, Marston and Donne—Iago's are much smoother, much more polished, and much wittier. In some ways they are closer to those of the Augustan satirists, with the smart antitheses strengthened by alliteration. They reflect admirably the persona Iago wishes to impose on the world, the worldly wise debunker who is 'nothing if not critical', whose very cynicism is taken to be a proof of his honesty even though it is assumed to be something of a pose. He makes his acquaintances believe that he is pretending to be worse than he is in order to conceal the fact that he is worse than he pretends.

The fullest treatment of a poet is in *Timon of Athens*. He is given prominence in the first scene of the play as one of Timon's suitors; the poem he outlines to the Painter is clearly a mirror-image of the play; and he reappears in the last act because of the rumour that Timon has discovered gold. He and the Painter are both depicted as time-servers. The Poet's fourth speech is an aside, presumably part of a poem that has come into his head:[1]

> When we for recompense have praised the vile,
> It stains the glory in that happy verse
> Which aptly sings the good. (I, i, 16–18)

As Timon could not be regarded as vile, the lines may suggest that the Poet has in the past praised unworthy patrons in the hope of reward. In an age when poets depended largely on patronage it could hardly be expected that poets would dedicate their poems only to the virtuous. One wonders, for example, if all the people who received dedicatory sonnets to *The Faerie Queene* were worthy of Spenser's praises.[2]

The Painter asks the Poet if he is rapt 'in some dedication/To the great lord'. To which he replies:

> A thing slipp'd idly from me.
> Our poesy is as a gum, which oozes
> From whence 'tis nourish'd. The fire i' th' flint
> Shows not till it be struck; our gentle flame
> Provokes itself, and like the current flies
> Each bound it chafes. (I, i, 23–8)

This account of the creation of poetry as the spontaneous overflow of powerful feelings suggests that Shakespeare, for once, is speaking through his character. The oozing gum—which, however, depends on two emendations in the Folio text—looks forward to Keats' aphorism that 'if poetry come not as naturally as the leaves to a tree, it had better not come at all'.

The ensuing dialogue brings out the Poet's genuine interest in the Painter's work and the latter's oscillation between self-praise and mock-modesty, and, later on, his perfunctory interest in the Poet's allegory:

> *Painter.* 'Tis a good piece.
> *Poet.* So 'tis: this comes off well and excellent.
> *Painter.* Indifferent.
> *Poet.* Admirable. How this grace
> Speaks his own standing! What a mental power
> This eye shoots forth! How big imagination
> Moves in this lip! To th'dumbness of gesture
> One might interpret.
> *Painter.* It is a pretty mocking of the life.
> Here is a touch; is't good?
> *Poet.* I will say of it
> It tutors nature. Artificial strife
> Lives in these touches livelier than life.
> (I, i, 31–41)

The allegory of Fortune, the dramatic function of which is to prepare the audience for

[1] It can hardly refer to the remark of the Jeweller, as the Arden editor suggests, since the Poet tells the Painter that the 'thing' is poesy.

[2] J. Middleton Murry, *Countries of the Mind*, Second Series (London, 1931), p. 97, argued that Shakespeare was thinking of his own dedications to Southampton. The evidence, however, is slight.

Timon's fall, is introduced by an obscure passage in which the Poet disclaims malice or particular reference to Timon's case, although he admits that his subject was suggested by this:

> My free drift
> Halts not particularly, but moves itself
> In a wide sea of wax. No levell'd malice
> Infects one comma in the course I hold,
> But flies an eagle flight, bold and forth on,
> Leaving no tract behind. (I, i, 48–53)

It is not surprising that the Painter asks 'How shall I understand you?' The general drift of the speech, however, is plain enough. It is similar to Jaques' speech in *As You Like It* (II, vii, 70–8):

> Why, who cries out on pride,
> That can therein tax any private party?
> Doth it not flow as hugely as the sea,
> Till that the wearer's very means do ebb? . . .
> There then; how then? what then? Let me see wherein
> My tongue hath wrong'd him. If it do him right,
> Then he hath wrong'd himself. If he be free,
> Why then my taxing like a wild-goose flies,
> Unclaim'd of any man.[1]

Whatever we may think of the Poet's lack of integrity as revealed later in the play, his proposed poem is certainly neither venal nor flattering. It is a clear warning to Timon that when Fortune changes her mood he will be deserted by his friends. Later in the scene Apemantus tells the poet that he lies because he has feigned Timon to be a worthy fellow. The Poet retorts: 'That's not feign'd—he is so'; and there is no reason to doubt his sincerity. Apemantus may have been thinking of the common accusation, to which Sidney replied in his *Apology*, that poets were liars; and Apemantus receives the dubious support of Touchstone who contrasts 'poetical' with 'truthful', the truest poetry being the most feigning.[2]

The Poet and the Painter come to visit Timon when they hear that he is wealthy after all. The text of the play seems to be corrupt at this point, for Apemantus refers to the approach of the Poet and the Painter some 190 lines before they actually appear. In between there are scenes between Timon and the Banditti and between him and Flavius.[3] The Poet and the Painter in Act V, scene i, are seen through the eyes of Timon. They pretend that they are unaware of his discovery of gold; they are concerned not with the integrity of their respective arts, but only how they may be used for profit:

> Then do we sin against our own estate,
> When we may profit meet and come too late.
> (lines 39–40)

The Poet proposes to write 'a satire against the softness of prosperity, with a discovery of the infinite flatteries that follow youth and opulency'; and Timon, who overhears, asks: 'Wilt thou whip thine own faults in other men?' Once again we are reminded of Jaques, who is accused by the Duke:

> Most mischievous foul sin in chiding sin!
> For thou thyself hast been a libertine
> As sensual as the brutish sting itself
> And all th' embossed sores and headed evils
> That thou with licence of free foot hast caught
> Wouldst thou disgorge into the general world.
> (*A.Y.L.I.*, II, vii, 64–9)

[1] Alexander, on the strength of the penultimate line of this passage, emends *wax* to *tax* in the Poet's speech. But Shakespeare was presumably thinking of wax tablets and E. A. Armstrong associates it with two Icarus passages.

[2] Thaler, *Shakespeare and Sir Philip Sidney*, has shown that Shakespeare knew *The Defence of Poesy*, echoing Sidney's phrases in Menenius' fable, recalling perhaps his description of tragedy in the disease imagery of *Hamlet* and the effect of tragedy on tyrants in the prince's words on 'guilty creatures sitting at a play', and probably replying good-humouredly to Sidney's views on the unities through the mouth of Time in *The Winter's Tale*. It seems likely therefore, that the references to poetry as feigning or lying allude to Sidney's refutation of the view that all poets were liars.

[3] It would, perhaps, be possible for the Poet and Painter to be on the stage during these scenes, waiting for a suitable opportunity to approach.

Shakespeare appears to have been suspicious of the moral stance of such satirists as Marston.

Something may be said in extenuation of the Poet. From his own point of view, he can make a living only by patronage; a bankrupt patron is no use to him; and it was natural that he should unblushingly turn again to the generous Timon on hearing of the revival of his fortunes. He could at least say that he had warned Timon in the days of his prosperity that he would lose his friends if the wheel of Fortune were to turn. The point is, however, not that the Poet and Painter are exceptionally vile, but that in the Athenian society depicted by Shakespeare, poetry and art are mere commodities, just as the wares of the Jeweller and the Merchant in the opening scene of the play. This fact is brought out by the great speeches of Timon after his discovery of gold. Gold, he tells us, inverts the moral order of society, making

> black white, foul fair,
> Wrong right, base noble, old young, coward valiant.
> (*Timon*, IV, iii, 28–9)

It destroys religion, promotes thieves into senators, gives a second husband to the wappened widow, and thaws

> the consecrated snow
> That lies on Dian's lap!

It is the world of *Volpone* and *The Alchemist*, but painted in darker colours. Timon is brought to this understanding only after his downfall. In the days of his greatness he did not realize—perhaps he never realizes—that he himself was using his gold to buy love, and that he was therefore deeply involved in the perversion of values. The only characters in the play who emerge uncorrupted by the acquisitive society are Flavius and his fellow-servants.

Shakespeare's poets, whether amateur or professional, are never held up for our admiration; and his characters' remarks about poetry are uniformly disparaging. In his private sonnets he could proclaim that his powerful rhyme would outlast the monuments of princes, but he makes his characters speak each according to his kind, not according to the view of the author. In this, surely, he was wise. We are spared the embarrassment that Jonson sometimes gives us when he crowns his own head with laurel. Shakespeare's last word was to ask the indulgence of the audience to set him free.[1]

[1] Soon after I had completed this essay, I came across a chapter with the same title in *Shakespeare and Common Sense* by Edwin R. Hunter (Boston, 1954). Inevitably we cover much of the same ground, though with a very different emphasis. Mr Hunter's conclusion is that Shakespeare saw 'no reason for avoiding this comic and sceptical treatment of his own art ... Shakespeare thought too highly of poetry to have thought of its needing defenders, and he is just the sort of humorous man who does not mind having the jest come up occasionally against himself and his kind'.

THE TEXT OF COLERIDGE'S 1811–12 SHAKESPEARE LECTURES

R. A. FOAKES

When John Payne Collier moved house in Maidenhead in 1854, he discovered a set of shorthand notes he had taken more than forty years earlier at the lectures on Shakespeare and other poets given by S. T. Coleridge in 1811–12. He also, as he testified in the preface to *Seven Lectures on Shakespeare and Milton by the late S. T. Coleridge* (1856), found 'transcripts in long-hand of some of the said notes', on turning out a 'double chest of drawers', although diligent search on a number of previous occasions had failed to locate them.[1] Collier announced his discovery in a series of four short contributions to *Notes and Queries* in July and August 1854.[2] In the first two he printed excerpts from a diary he had kept at the time he attended the lectures, asserting that 'only fragments remain' of it,[3] and he also reprinted the prospectuses of both the 1811–12 and the 1818 lectures given by Coleridge. In the last two he included some passages from his notes of the lectures. Of his 'memoranda' of seven lectures (numbers 1, 2, 6, 7, 8, 9 and 12 of the seventeen Coleridge gave in the series), he claimed that they were 'generally very full, and in the *ipsissima verba* of the author'.[4]

The publication of these extracts received favourable notice in *The Athenaeum*, which in turn provoked the retort of 'A Detective' in a pamphlet called *Literary Cookery with Reference to Matter attributed to Coleridge and Shakespeare* published in 1855. The editor of *The Athenaeum*, W. H. Dixon, like Collier himself a lawyer and antiquary, remained his loyal supporter, and had refused to print the contents of this pamphlet when the author submitted it as a letter to his periodical. It is mainly devoted to an attack on Collier's dating in 1812 of the prospectus for Coleridge's lectures of 1811–12, and proves, citing James Gillman's *Life of Coleridge*, that the prospectus was issued in 1811. In fact this was an oversight on Collier's part, for the prospectus is not dated, and he had not troubled to check the year of its issue; nevertheless, the insinuations of *Literary Cookery* were enough to persuade him to attempt proceedings for libel, and in January 1856 he moved for a criminal information against the publisher of the pamphlet. This led to nothing, except that on 8 January 1856 Collier filed an affidavit in the Court of Queen's Bench recounting the history of his attendance at Coleridge's lectures, and of how he took notes, mislaid them for forty years, and recovered them in 1854.

Later in the same year (the dedication is dated 10 July 1856), Collier published *Seven Lectures on Shakespeare and Milton*. The full text of the lectures from which excerpts had been printed in *Notes and Queries* occupies about half of the volume, which includes a substantial preface, and is padded out with a

[1] *Seven Lectures*, pp. iii, xi.

[2] *Notes and Queries*, x (July–August, 1854), 1–2, 21–3, 57–8, and 117–19.

[3] *Ibid.*, p. 2.

[4] *Ibid.*, p. 1.

reprint of the manuscript notes and emendations Collier claimed to have found in a copy of the Second Folio of Shakespeare's plays. These *Notes and Emendations* had been printed under this title for the Shakespeare Society in 1852, had already been the subject of much commentary, and had been attacked as spurious by a number of scholars, including J. O. Halliwell and S. W. Singer.[1] Collier could rely on the support of *The Athenaeum*, but the weight of scholarship and of evidence was against him. After a further sharp attack on him by Alexander Dyce in 1859, C. M. Ingleby published in 1861 *A Complete View of the Shakspere Controversy*, showing, in a recapitulation of the whole affair, that the emendations in the Folio had been fabricated, and were written in Collier's own hand. Dr Ingleby provided a substantial bibliography, listing twenty-two books and pamphlets published on this matter between 1852 and 1860, besides a number of essays in periodicals.[2]

In relation to this, the matter of the Coleridge lectures was a minor one, and Dr Ingleby supposed that 'the finishing stroke in the demolition of the genuineness of the "Seven Lectures", which Mr Collier in 1856 published as Coleridge's, had already been delivered'.[3] The final blow, he thought, had been given in *Collier, Coleridge and Shakespeare. A Review*, published as by the author of *Literary Cookery* in 1860. In the event, he was quite mistaken. When Thomas Ashe gathered Coleridge's notes and lectures on Shakespeare and other poets for Bohn's Library in 1883, he was pleased to be able to reprint much of Collier's 1856 preface, and all of the lectures from his text. In the meantime, extracts from the diary of Henry Crabb Robinson had been published, confirming that Collier had indeed attended Coleridge's 1811–12 lectures, and helping to corroborate his notes.[4] Furthermore, the notices of the lectures which had been printed in the *Morning Chronicle* were discovered, and some of them were included by Ashe in his edition; these too tended to validate Collier's *Seven Lectures*. These notices we now know had been written either by J. P. Collier himself, or by his father, John Dyer Collier, who was a journalist, or by Henry Crabb Robinson, as the last-named states in a letter to Thomas Robinson of 16 December 1811.[5] By the time T. M. Raysor came to present his definitive edition of Coleridge's *Shakespearean Criticism* in 1930, he could see no reason for troubling to defend the authenticity of Collier's reports, and he was able to point to a number of further links and overlaps between Collier's text and fragments of authentic Coleridge manuscripts now published for the first time.[6]

In other words, Collier's text has been accepted into the canon of Coleridge's works, and provides the only substantial record we possess of the lectures he gave on Shakespeare. Raysor argued, reasonably enough, that to suppose Collier invented lectures so 'characteristic of Coleridge in his greatest excellences as well as his faults is to attribute to the great literary forger genius rather than dishonesty'.[7] However, a study of *Collier, Coleridge and Shakespeare* shows that the matter is not quite so straightforward. Although the author

[1] J. O. Halliwell, *Curiosities of Modern Shaksperian Criticism* (1853), and S. W. Singer, *The Text of Shakespeare Vindicated* (1853). Singer later changed his views and accepted some of Collier's emendations.

[2] *Complete View of the Shakspere Controversy*, pp. 339–48.

[3] *Ibid.*, p. 343.

[4] Ashe included extracts from Crabb Robinson's diary in his *Lectures and Notes on Shakspere and other English Poets*. By Samuel Taylor Coleridge. Now first collected by T. Ashe' (1883), pp. 20–9.

[5] *Lectures and Notes*, pp. 55–9, 118–19. Ashe did not know that Collier had himself had a hand in reporting lectures for the press; for the evidence regarding this, see T. M. Raysor, *Coleridge's Shakespearean Criticism* (second edition, Everyman Series, 1960), II, 160 n., 166, and 180.

[6] Raysor, II, 22.

[7] *Ibid.*

of this, Andrew Brae,[1] was not able to substantiate his charges of 'literary fraud' and 'fabrication'[2] against Collier, he succeeded in exposing some absurdities and disturbing features in Collier's text, often by comparing passages in *Seven Lectures* with similar passages in Coleridge's *Literary Remains* (1836). Coleridge sometimes used the same material in a variety of contexts, but with differences of wording, and variations in the formulation of ideas, so that similarities may provide inconclusive textual evidence, and Brae presses some trivial points too hard. At the same time, he had a sharp eye, as one example of his method may indicate. He noticed that in Lecture 6 Coleridge said, according to Collier,[3]

> Not long since, when I lectured at the Royal Institution, I had the honour of sitting at the desk so ably occupied by Sir Humphry Davy, who may be said to have elevated the art of chemistry to the dignity of a science.

Now Brae could show that Humphry Davy had not been knighted when the lecture was delivered on 5 December 1811, so that Coleridge would certainly not have referred to '*Sir* Humphry Davy'.[4] In addition, he pointed to the absurdity of the words attributed here to Coleridge, asking 'who, that knows anything of the history of chemistry could believe that Coleridge ever said anything so silly as that *the art* of chemistry might be said to have been elevated in the nineteenth century to the dignity of *a science*?'[5] The question is a good one, and, together with other criticisms made by Brae, might lead us to question Collier's claim to be presenting the '*ipsissima verba*' of Coleridge.

In point of fact, Collier's statements about what he was doing with the text of the lectures are confusing and somewhat contradictory. In the preface to *Seven Lectures*, he modified his earlier claim to be offering Coleridge's '*ipsissima verba*'. At one point he asserts,[6]

> I am certain, even at this distance of time, that I did not knowingly register a sentence, that did not come from Coleridge's lips, although doubtless I missed, omitted, and mistook points and passages, which now I should have been most rejoiced to have preserved. In completing my transcripts, however, I have added no word or syllable of my own.

A little later, however, he confesses that 'in some cases I relied upon my recollection to fill up chasms in my memoranda'.[7] Then, too, he acknowledges that while he took down his notes in the third person, he has put them all into the first person to make them 'consistent with each other'.[8] At another point he claims, 'I present my notes merely as they are'.[9] Collier does not seem to have been clear in his own mind as to what he was about, and Brae's demonstration that the 'Sir' given to Humphry Davy must be a later addition demolishes Collier's claim to have added 'no word or syllable of my own'. The question raised by all this is not whether Collier fabricated the lectures, as Brae and Ingleby thought, for so much in them is characteristic of Coleridge that Raysor's argument stands: if Collier invented them he must have been a genius. The question is rather, just how much did Collier alter, re-write, or add to his original notes? Continuing from this, one might also ask whether Brae was justified in asserting that the reader of Collier's versions would 'seek in vain for that vivid and peculiar phraseology he has been accustomed to associate with' Coleridge.[10]

It so happens that Collier's long-hand transcriptions of his notes have survived, and

[1] The book was published anonymously, but the identity of the author was known to Dr Ingleby by the time he published *A Complete View of the Shakspere Controversy* in 1861.

[2] *Collier, Coleridge and Shakespeare*, p. 43.

[3] *Seven Lectures*, p. 31; Raysor, II, 82.

[4] *Collier, Coleridge and Shakespeare*, p. 41. Davy was knighted in April 1812.

[5] *Ibid.*, p. 42. [6] *Seven Lectures*, pp. vi–vii.

[7] *Ibid.*, p. xiii. [8] *Ibid.*, p. xiii. [9] *Ibid.*, p. xiii.

[10] *Collier, Coleridge and Shakespeare*, p. 19.

are now listed as MSS. M.a. 219–28 in the Folger Shakespeare Library.[1] These 'brochures', as Collier called them,[2] consist of ten sewn gatherings, each containing between 22 and 30 leaves, measuring approximately $7\frac{1}{4}$ by 4 inches. All have one gilt edge, but it seems that they were never bound together as a book; indeed, they are not made up from one stock of paper, for Brochures 9 and 10, which are slightly taller than the others, have leaves watermarked with the date 1806, while Brochure 1 is watermarked 1811, and Brochures 5 to 8 are watermarked 1807. Perhaps not surprisingly, they do not conform to Collier's particular description of them in his preface to *Seven Lectures*. There he spoke of 'fragments' of a diary, and other brochures containing 'partial transcripts'[3] of Lectures 1, 2, 6 and 8; in fact, the brochures appear to contain the complete diary he kept between 10 October and 27 November 1811, and full transcripts of the lectures. The first two lectures, delivered on 18 and 21 November, are written out as part of the diary, which occupies four brochures. Collier also said that Lectures 9 and 12 were found 'entirely untranscribed',[4] and had to be written out, when in fact the transcriptions continue in the same way, and in the same hand to a point late in Lecture 12.[5] Here a different ink, a more rapid and slanting hand, a flurry of deletions and corrections, the turning round of the brochure to write across, not down the page, and a pencilled entry referring to a shorthand notebook, all seem to indicate the place where the original transcript broke off, and Collier had to complete it later. If this is so, then all the shorthand notes, except perhaps for a few pages of Lecture 12, had been transcribed into long-hand by Collier in 1811 or 1812.

In any case, Collier's accounts of the 'brochures', like his account of what he printed in *Seven Lectures*, is plainly inaccurate. Perhaps he did not intend to mislead, and really did not realize that what he was claiming to do bore little relation to what he was actually doing. The same habit of mind is reflected in the transcripts themselves. In his preface, Collier cited long extracts from his diary, where he records various meetings with Coleridge, and said of them, 'That these were Coleridge's *ipsissima verba* I cannot, at this distance of time, state; but they are the *ipsissima verba* in my Diary'.[6] Even this is false, for he revised and elaborated almost every sentence. One example may suffice to illustrate his method; Coleridge was commenting, on 17 October 1811, on Southey's *The Curse of Kehama*:

Brochure 1, p. 53

He thought it a work of great talent but not so much genius & he drew the distinction between talent & genius that there is between a Watch and an Eye: each were beautiful in their way but the one was made the other grew.—Talent was a manufactured thing: genius was born.

Preface to 'Seven Lectures', p. xxv

He looked upon 'The Curse of Kehama' as a work of great talent, but not of much genius; and he drew the distinction between talent and genius by comparing the first to a watch and the last to an eye: both were beautiful, but one was only a piece of ingenious mechanism, while the other was a production above all art. Talent was a manufacture; genius a gift, that no labour nor study could supply: nobody could make an eye, but anybody, duly instructed, could make a watch.

Here Collier justifies the complaint of Andrew Brae; what in the manuscript seems close to

[1] T. M. Raysor could not have had access to them when he prepared the first edition of his *Coleridge's Shakespearean Criticism* (1930); the Folger Shakespeare Library was opened to the public in 1933.

[2] *Seven Lectures*, p. xii.

[3] *Ibid.*, p. xii.

[4] *Ibid.*, p. xii.

[5] This point occurs in Brochure 10, p. 21, after the quotation ending 'My stooping duty tenderly shall show' (Raysor, II, 149).

[6] *Seven Lectures*, p. xxv.

Coleridge's 'vivid and peculiar phraseology' is expanded in the preface, where the characteristic opposition of the mechanical and organic is sadly weakened. If Collier could so meddle with the wording of his diary, it is hardly surprising to find him taking even greater liberties with the text of Coleridge's lectures. So, for example, the absurdity Brae noted in the passage cited above[1] concerning Humphry Davy turns out to be Collier's reworking of what Coleridge said; the text in the manuscript runs as follows:

Brochure 5, p. 5

Coleridge then paid a high compliment to Davy (at whose desk he had had the honour of lecturing—at the Royal Institution) who had reduced the art of Chemistry to a science.

This makes clear Coleridge's meaning, namely, that Davy had given method and discipline to chemistry, and in rewriting it, Collier seems quite to have missed the point of his early note.

Before going on to cite some of the more notable alterations relating to Shakespeare, it is worth observing that in 1811–12 when Collier attended the lectures and met Coleridge in his father's home and as a guest of Charles Lamb, he was a very young man, aged twenty-two, rather uncertain of himself, to judge by various entries in the diary, and much overawed by the brilliance of the poet. Two unpublished excerpts from the diary may illustrate this. The first immediately precedes the conversation of 17 October 1811 Collier printed in his preface to *Seven Lectures*:

Brochure 1, pp. 47–8

Yesterday Evening at C. Lambs I met S. T. Coleridge of whom I have made previous mention. I had previously made up my mind that if I saw him I would set down everything that he said worthy of recollection. I went into the room where he & many more were at ½ past 8 & before a quarter past 9 my mind was so burdened with the things worthy of recollection that he said that I was obliged to relieve myself by quitting his company and not attending to him for the remainder of the night. When I returned however do all I could I found it impossible to keep my attention off him: it is as impossible for a man that can see to avoid being sensible that the sun shines on a clear midsummer day as it is to be in company with Coleridge and not to attend to him.—The following, as well as memory serves me, is the substance of what he said tho' I fear that I shall fall short of giving even the substance of what he expressed with a *before unknown felicity of language.*

The second passage precedes the report in the manuscript of Lecture 2, delivered on 21 November 1811:

Brochure 4, p. 7

This Evening Coleridge delivered his second Lecture which is not only beyond my praise but beyond the praise of any man, but himself. He only is capable of speaking of himself. All others seem so contemptible in comparison. I felt myself more humble if possible than the meanest worm before the Almighty, and blessed my stars that I could comprehend what he had the power to invent.

By the time he came to print his notes in *Seven Lectures*, Collier was a mature scholar in his sixties, who could more easily take liberties with a poet who had been dead now for more than twenty years. This may partly explain, though it does not excuse, Collier's cavalier treatment of the notes which, as a young man, he had hurried to set down in order to preserve as accurately as possible the very words of one he called 'the greatest man of the present day & in some respects unrivalled in any former age'.[2]

A comparison of the manuscript brochures with Collier's printed text shows that he made continual small changes, frequently adding adverbs, adjectives, and qualifying phrases, in such a way as to weaken or distort the sharper and more sinewy statements recorded in the notes. He is fond of inserting 'as it were', 'generally', 'some of', 'may be said to', and suchlike phrases, where the notes speak boldly

[1] See above, p. 103. [2] Brochure 2, p. 15.

and without qualification. He duplicates words, so that 'attribute' (MS.) becomes 'trace and attribute'; 'with especial pleasure' is altered to 'with peculiar pleasure and satisfaction'; 'an age of high moral feeling' becomes 'an age of high moral feeling and lofty principle'; and 'England overflowed' is changed to 'England may be said to have then overflowed'.[1] These examples illustrate Collier's constant expansion of the notes. His object may have been to make them sound more mellifluous and smooth, or to soften what appeared dogmatic to the mature scholar, and certainly at times he sought to clarify and elaborate what remained obscure or fragmentary. At one or two points he introduces complete new paragraphs, and adds allusions not in the manuscript; an instance is the reference to Richard Hooker's *Laws of Ecclesiastical Polity* in Lecture 1.[2] This may be an example of Collier relying upon 'recollection to fill up chasms in my memoranda', or possibly he included where appropriate some of the 'scattered and unconnected memoranda' he made of Coleridge's 1818 lectures, which he also attended.[3] At other places Collier omits or drastically changes what is in the manuscript; sometimes there seems to be no reason for the changes, but at some points he appears to have forgotten the significance of an allusion, or simply not to understand the meaning of his notes.

The selection of passages I now present from Coleridge's remarks in his lectures of 1811–12 all relate to Shakespeare, and show some of the more significant changes made by Collier when he revised his notes. In each case the text of the manuscript notes is printed first, with the number and page of the relevant brochure, and the text of *Seven Lectures* follows, with page references both to this volume, and to Raysor's revised Everyman edition of *Coleridge's Shakespearean Criticism* (1960). Each selection is accompanied by an explanatory note in the form of an afterword.

1. *Lecture 6; Brochure 5, pp. 13–14: on Shakespeare's art*

This was the great art by which Shakespeare combined the Poet & the gentleman, throughout borrowing from his own most amiable character that which only could combine them, a perfect simplicity of mind a delight in what was excellent for its own sake without reference to himself as causing it & by that which distinguished Shakespeare from all others which is alluded to by Drummond in a short poem in wch he tells us that while he had the powers of a man, & more than man yet he had all the feelings & manners which he painted in an affectionate young woman of 18.

Collier, Seven Lectures, *p. 38; Raysor*, II, *86*

This is the great art by which Shakespeare combines the poet and the gentleman throughout, borrowing from his most amiable nature that which alone could combine them, a perfect simplicity of mind, a delight in all that is excellent for its own sake, without reference to himself as causing it, and by that which distinguishes him from all other poets, alluded to by one of his admirers in a short poem, where he tells us that while Shakespeare possessed all the powers of a man, and more than a man, yet he had all the feelings, the sensibility, the purity, innocence, and delicacy of an affectionate girl of eighteen.

No poem by Drummond alludes to Shakespeare in this way, and Collier, puzzled no doubt by what seems an error in his original notes, dropped the name, and substituted 'one of his admirers'. The last sentence of the passage is

[1] These examples are taken from Lecture 6 in Brochure 5, pp. 8–11 (*Seven Lectures*, pp. 33–5; Raysor, II, 83–4).

[2] Raysor, II, 34. Collier here quotes a passage from Hooker, an author Coleridge read carefully and cited elsewhere, and he may well be filling out the rather thin notes of the first lecture with genuinely Coleridgean material. It is curious that Collier omitted from the printed text of Lecture 8 two substantial quotations from Hooker which are written out in the manuscript (Brochure 6, pp. 45–6 and Brochure 7, p. 3), substituting a footnote in which he says the manuscript 'contains only a hint' of the passage he remembers Coleridge citing (*Seven Lectures*, p. 82n.; Raysor, II, 113n.).

[3] *Seven Lectures*, p. lv.

noteworthy for the expansion, which alters the sense, and also reduces to sentimentality a fine comment by Coleridge.

2. *Lecture 6; Brochure 5, pp. 26–7: on Shakespeare's wit*

The wit of Shakespeare was like the flourishing of a mans stick when he is walking along in the full flow of animal spirits. It was a sort of overflow of hilarity which disburdened us & seemed like a conductor to distribute a portion of our joy to the surrounding air by carrying it away from us. While too it disburdened us it enabled us to appropriate what remained to what was most important and most within our direct aim.

Collier, p. 46; Raysor, II, *91*

The wit of Shakespeare is, as it were, like the flourishing of a man's stick, when he is walking, in the full flow of animal spirits: it is a sort of exuberance of hilarity which disburdens, and it resembles a conductor, to distribute a portion of our gladness to the surrounding air. While, however, it disburdens, it leaves behind what is weightiest and most important, and what most contributes to some direct aim and purpose.

The minor alterations Collier made in this passage are characteristic. He adds 'as it were' to qualify the boldness of a simile; he substitutes 'exuberance' for 'overflow', and 'resembles' for 'seems like'; he omits altogether the phrase 'by carrying it away from us', perhaps thinking it redundant; and he alters the last sentence, possibly in an effort to clarify, and only succeeds in changing the sense.

3. *Lecture 8; Brochure 7, pp. 20–4: on Romeo as a lover*

Surely Shakespeare the philosopher, the grand Poet who combined truth with beauty and beauty with truth, never could have dreamed that it was a mode of interesting the affections of his audience by making his Romeo a mere weathercock, who having seen one woman, became the victim of melancholy, eating away his own heart, concentring all his hopes & fears in this form, in an instant changes and falls as madly in love with another being: Shakespeare surely must have meant something more than this & Romeo tells us what it was. He says that he had a different feeling towards Juliet from that he had towards Rosaline—He adds that Rosaline was the object to wch his overbuilt heart attached itself; that our imperfect nature in proportion as our ideas are vivid they seek after something in which they may appear realized—As men of genius conscious of their own weakness are ready to believe persons whom they meet the modes of perfection when in truth they are worse than themselves: they have formed an ideal in their minds & they want to see it realized; they want it something more than shadowy thought: their own consciousness of imperfection makes it impossible for them to attach it to themselves but the first man they meet they only see what is good & thus have no conjecture of his imperfections & they fall down and adore almost one greatly inferior to themselves.

Such is frequently the case in the friendships of men of genius and still more frequently in the first loves of ardent feelings and strong imaginations; but still for a man, having had the experience, without any inward feeling demonstrating the difference to change one object for another seems without example. But it is perfectly accordant with life: in a life of such various events, such a shifting of scenes and such a change of personages we may have mistaken in thinking, that he or she was what in truth he or she was not: we may have suffered unnecessary pangs and have felt idley directed hopes and then a being may arise who has more resemblance to our ideal: we know that we loved the former with purity and yet it was not what we now feel: our own mind tells us that the former was but the yearning after the object in the latter we have found the object correspondent to the idea we had formed.

The same thing arises in every circumstance of taste. What is meant by taste? The inward faculties make a demand. There is a feeling in every man: there is a deviation, & he knows it, between that which is common to all mankind and that which individualizes him.

Collier, pp. 91–3; Raysor, II, *119–20*

Surely Shakespeare, the poet, the philosopher, who combined truth with beauty and beauty with truth, never dreamed that he could interest his auditory in favour of Romeo, by representing him as a mere weathercock, blown round by every woman's breath; who, having seen one, became the victim of melancholy, eating his own heart, concentrating all his hopes and fears in her, and yet, in an instant, changing, and falling madly in love with another. Shakespeare must have meant something more than this, for this was the way to make people despise, instead of admiring his hero. Romeo tells us what was Shakespeare's purpose: he shows us that he had looked at Rosaline with a different feeling from that with which he had looked at Juliet. Rosaline was the object to which his over-full heart had attached itself in the first instance: our imperfect nature, in proportion as our ideas are vivid, seeks after something in which those ideas may be realised.

So with the indiscreet friendships sometimes formed by men of genius: they are conscious of their own weakness, and are ready to believe others stronger than themselves, when, in truth, they are weaker: they have formed an ideal in their own minds, and they want to see it realised; they require more than shadowy thought. Their own sense of imperfection makes it impossible for them to fasten their attachment upon themselves, and hence the humility of men of true genius: in, perhaps, the first man they meet, they only see what is good; they have no sense of his deficiencies, and their friendship becomes so strong, that they almost fall down and worship one in every respect greatly their inferior.

What is true of friendship is true of love, with a person of ardent feelings and warm imagination. What took place in the mind of Romeo was merely natural; it is accordant with every day's experience. Amid such various events, such shifting scenes, such changing personages, we are often mistaken, and discover that he or she was not what we hoped and expected; we find that the individual first chosen will not complete our imperfection; we may have suffered unnecessary pangs, and have indulged idly-directed hopes, and then a being may arise before us, who has more resemblance to the ideal we have formed. We know that we loved the earlier object with ardour and purity, but it was not what we feel for the later object. Our own mind tells us, that in the first instance we merely yearned after an object, but in the last instance we know that we have found that object, and that it corresponds with the idea we had previously formed.

In this famous passage about Romeo, the numerous minor changes perhaps speak for themselves. Especially notable are the phrases Collier has added to his original note, such as 'blown round by every woman's breath', and 'for this was the way to make people despise, instead of admiring his hero', both unnecessary expansions, and no doubt further instances of Collier relying upon his recollection.[1] More significant are changes such as the weakening of 'concentring' to 'concentrating', and the softening of Coleridge's no doubt very personal remarks on men of genius. However, there seems to be no reason for Collier's omission of 'but still for a man, having had the experience, without any inward feeling demonstrating the difference, to change one object for another seems without example', for this passage helps to make clear the drift of Coleridge's argument. Collier also omitted altogether the last brief paragraph on taste. The notes of this lecture are incomplete, and break off at this point, leaving almost half of Brochure 7 blank. It seems that Coleridge turned his attention away from *Romeo and Juliet* at this point, and Collier silently omitted the last paragraph simply, it may be, for the sake of tidiness.

4. *Lecture 9; Brochure 8, pp. 16–17: on Shakespeare's genius*

Some of his contemporaries appear to have understood him and in a way that does him no small honour: the moderns in their prefaces praise him as a great genius but when they come to their notes on his plays they treat him like a Schoolboy—Coleridge went on to ridicule the modern commentators still further asserting that they only exercised the most vulgar of all feelings—that of wonderment—They had maintained that Shakespeare was an irregular poet that he was now above all praise and now if possible below contempt & they reconciled it by saying that he wrote for the mob.—No man of genius ever wrote for the mob; he never wd consciously write that which was below himself. Careless he might be or he might write at a time when his better genius did not attend him but he never wrote anything that he knew would degrade himself. Were it so, as well might a man pride himself on acting the beast or a Catalani, because she did not feel in a mood to sing, begin to bray.—

[1] As he says he did at times in the preface to *Seven Lectures*, p. xiii.

Collier, pp. 102–3; Raysor, II, *126*

Some of Shakespeare's contemporaries appear to have understood him, and imitated him in a way that does the original no small honour; but modern preface-writers and commentators, while they praise him as a great genius, when they come to publish notes upon his plays, treat him like a schoolboy; as if this great genius did not understand himself, was not aware of his own powers, and wrote without design or purpose. Nearly all they can do is to express the most vulgar of all feelings, wonderment—wondering at what they term the irregularity of his genius, sometimes above all praise, and at other times, if they are to be trusted, below all contempt. They endeavour to reconcile the two opinions by asserting that he wrote for the mob; as if a man of real genius ever wrote for the mob. Shakespeare never consciously wrote what was below himself: careless he might be, and his better genius may not always have attended him; but I fearlessly say, that he never penned a line that he knew would degrade him. No man does anything equally well at all times; but because Shakespeare could not always be the greatest of poets, was he therefore to condescend to make himself the least?

It seems that by 1856 Collier thought the reference to Catalani would seem pointless, or had himself forgotten who she was. Angelica Catalani, an Italian soprano, had a great vogue in London for some years after her debut there in 1806. Possibly Collier was troubled by the radical change made in this passage, or possibly he thought a comment here might add a touch of authenticity to his text; at any rate, he appended the following footnote to the end of the passage in 1856:[1]

It is certain that my short-hand note in this place affords another instance of mishearing: it runs literally thus—'but because Shakespeare could not always be the greatest of poets, was he therefore to condescend to make himself a beast?' For 'a beast' we must read *the least,* the antithesis being between 'greatest' and 'least', and not between 'poet' and 'beast'.

This rather meaningless note at least verifies that the word 'beast' was in the original.

Lecture 9; Brochure 8, pp. 42–3: on Ariel in 'The Tempest'

Coleridge now returned to the introduction of Ariel prepared as he had explained—If ever there could be a doubt that Shakespeare was a great Poet acting by laws arising out of his own nature and not acting without law as had been asserted it would be removed by the character of Ariel. The very first words spoken by Ariel introduced him not as an Angel above men, not as a Gnome or a Fiend but while the Poet gives him all the advantages all the faculties of reason he divests him of all moral character not positively but negatively. In air he lives, from air he derives his being. In air he acts and all his colours & properties seem to be derived from the clouds.—There is nothing in Ariel that cannot be conceived to exist in the atmosphere at sunrise or sunset: hence all that belongs to Ariel is all that belongs to the delight the mind can receive from external appearances abstracted from any inborn or purpose. His answers to Prospero are either directly to the question and nothing beyond, or if he expatiates which he does frequently it is upon his own delights, & the unnatural situation in which he is placed tho' under a good power and employed to good ends.

Collier, pp. 118–19; Raysor, II, *136*

But to return to 'The Tempest', and to the wondrous creation of Ariel. If a doubt could ever be entertained whether Shakespeare was a great poet, acting upon laws arising out of his own nature, and not without law, as has sometimes been idly asserted, that doubt must be removed by the character of Ariel. The very first words uttered by this being introduce the spirit, not as an angel, above man; not a gnome, or a fiend, below man; but while the poet gives him the faculties and the advantages of reason, he divests him of all mortal character, not positively, it is true, but negatively. In air he lives, from air he derives his being, in air he acts; and all his colours and properties seem to have been obtained from the rainbow and the skies. There is nothing about Ariel that cannot be conceived to exist either at sun-rise or at sun-set: hence all that belongs to Ariel belongs to the delight the mind is capable of receiving from the most lovely external appearances. His answers to Prospero are directly to the question, and nothing beyond; or

[1] *Seven Lectures,* p. 103; Raysor, II, 126.

where he expatiates, which is not unfrequently, it is to himself and upon his own delights, or upon the unnatural situation in which he is placed, though under a kindly power and to good ends.

Here, apart from the usual minor alterations and elaborations, Collier alters the sense of the passage radically by changing 'moral' to 'mortal', and omitting the phrase 'abstracted from any inborn or purpose'. There is a space in the notes here, where a word Collier presumably could not reconstruct from his shorthand is left out, as if to be added later; the sense, however, is clear, and in 1856 he seems wilfully to have corrupted the text at this point.

6. *Lecture 9; Brochure 9, pp. 8–10: on Miranda's first view of Ferdinand*

But Coleridge was content to try this passage by its introduction: How does Prospero introduce it? He has just told Miranda a story which deeply affects her and afterwards for his own purposes lulled her to sleep, & Shakespeare wholly inattentive to the present when she awakes & dwelling only on the past. The Actress who truly understands the character should have her eyelids sunk down & living as it were in her dreams.—Prospero then sees Ferdinand and wishes to point him out to his daughter not only with great but almost scenic solemnity himself always present to her and to the spectators as a magician.—Something was to appear on a sudden which was no more expected than we should look for the hero of a Play to be on the stage when the Curtain is drawn up: it is under such circumstances that Prospero says

> 'The fringed curtains of thine eye advance
> And say what thou seest yond.'—

This solemnity of phrazeology was in Coleridge's opinion completely in character with Prospero who was assuming the Magician whose very art seems to consider all the objects of nature in a mysterious point of view and who wishes to produce a strong impression on Miranda at the first view of Ferdinand—

It is much easier to find fault with a writer merely by reference to former notions & experience than to sit down and read him & to connect the one feeling with the other & to judge of words & phrazes in proportion as they convey those feelings together.

Miranda possessed in herself all the ideal beauties that could be conceived by the greatest Poet altho' it was not Coleridge's object so much to point out the high Poetic powers of Shakespeare as his exquisite judgment. But to describe one of the female characters of Shakespeare was almost to describe the whole for each possessed all the excellencies with which they could be invested.—

Collier, pp. 124–5; Raysor, II, *139–40*

But I am content to try the lines I have just quoted by the introduction to them; and then, I think, you will admit, that nothing could be more fit and appropriate than such language. How does Prospero introduce them? He has just told Miranda a wonderful story, which deeply affected her, and filled her with surprise and astonishment, and for his own purposes he afterwards lulls her to sleep. When she awakes, Shakespeare has made her wholly inattentive to the present, but wrapped up in the past. An actress, who understands the character of Miranda, would have her eyes cast down, and her eyelids almost covering them, while she was, as it were, living in her dream. At this moment Prospero sees Ferdinand, and wishes to point him out to his daughter, not only with great, but with scenic solemnity, he standing before her, and before the spectator, in the dignified character of a great magician. Something was to appear to Miranda on the sudden, and as unexpectedly as if the hero of a drama were to be on the stage at the instant when the curtain is elevated. It is under such circumstances that Prospero says, in a tone calculated at once to arouse his daughter's attention,

> 'The fringed curtains of thine eye advance,
> And say what thou seest yond.'

Turning from the sight of Ferdinand to his thoughtful daughter, his attention was first struck by the downcast appearance of her eyes and eyelids; and, in my humble opinion, the solemnity of the phraseology assigned to Prospero is completely in character, recollecting his preternatural capacity, in which the most familiar objects in nature present themselves in a mysterious point of view. It is much easier to find fault with a writer by reference to former notions and experience, than to sit down and read him, recollecting his purpose, connecting one feeling with another, and judging of his words and phrases, in proportion as they convey the sentiments of the persons represented.

Of Miranda we may say, that she possesses in herself

all the ideal beauties that could be imagined by the greatest poet of any age or country; but it is not my purpose now, so much to point out the high poetic powers of Shakespeare, as to illustrate his exquisite judgment, and it is solely with this design that I have noticed a passage with which, it seems to me, some critics, and those among the best, have been unreasonably dissatisfied.

Andrew Brae cited the 1856 version of this passage in his attack on Collier, remarking, 'It is difficult to imagine that Coleridge ever could have uttered such fustian as this'.[1] He clearly disagreed with Coleridge over the interpretation of the scene from *The Tempest* but a comparison of the two versions does show Collier, in his elaboration of the last paragraphs, at least verging on 'fustian', as, for example, in changing 'whose very art' to 'recollecting his preternatural capacity'. In elaborating Coleridge's advice to the actress playing Miranda, and altering 'eyelids sunk down' to 'eyes cast down, and her eyelids almost covering them', Collier again subtly changes the sense, especially as he adds a phrase about her 'downcast appearance'.

These sample passages may be enough to show that the brochures containing Collier's longhand transcripts of his shorthand notes taken at Coleridge's lectures provide a much better guide than the text of *Seven Lectures* to what Coleridge actually said. The full text will be printed in an edition of the transcripts now in preparation, but even that will have to be treated with some caution. A study of the preface and notes of *Seven Lectures*, and a comparison of the two texts of the lectures, confirms G. F. Warner's conclusion in his judicious account of Collier in the *Dictionary of National Biography*: 'None of his statements or quotations can be trusted without verifying, and no volume or document that passed through his hands can be too carefully scrutinised'.[2] As a young man eagerly striving to record what Coleridge said, he clearly sought to be as accurate as possible, and had not yet become the literary forger of later years; but in view of the claims he makes for his memory or recollection in supplying material 'to fill up chasms in my memoranda' in *Seven Lectures*,[3] and the fact that all of the conversations of Coleridge reported in his diary, and possibly some part of the notes of the lectures, were set down from memory, it is worth remarking the comment he made about himself in a confessional moment on 1 November 1811: 'I have been greatly disheartened in all my studies by many things, but principally by two—1 That my memory is so bad and 2 that my ability is so small'.[4] If he exaggerates in self-criticism here, he was certainly attempting in this comment to be quite honest.

1 *Collier, Coleridge and Shakespeare*, p. 20.
2 *Dictionary of National Biography*, XI (1887), 351.
3 *Seven Lectures*, p. xiii.
4 Brochure 3, p. 13.

SHAKESPEARE STUDIES IN GERMAN: 1959–68

WERNER HABICHT AND HANS WALTER GABLER

For practical rather than for nationalistic reasons most German and many Swiss publications on Shakespeare continue to be in German. Writings on the most popular dramatist on the German stage may legitimately hope for a response by German readers; and the more their authors adopt critical methods, the more they tend to rely on their command of the nuances of their native language. On the other hand an increasing unawareness of these studies in the English-speaking world has become evident, and German Shakespearians are sometimes overcome by a feeling of isolation, or, at best, of the onesidedness of their contribution to the critical dialogue. Naturally enough, they take due account of what has been done in English and are at times confident—rightly or wrongly—that they have hit upon a new answer to a problem, or a modification to an opinion current in Shakespeare criticism generally. But if they remain unheeded on the other side of the Channel (or the Atlantic), much independent grappling with parallel problems is, as the following pages may well suggest, the inevitable result. The present survey of German Shakespeare studies published roughly between 1959 and 1968 can hardly expect to remedy this state of affairs. It merely hopes to draw attention to some general trends and to some individual achievements and is therefore intended to be informative rather than critical. In order to avoid an accumulation of titles it covers independent publications only and excludes articles. Doctoral dissertations, however, are included; for as a rule these either appear as regular books or else get privately printed; and even though some of them may prove to be more original than others, the theses taken as a body and in conjunction with the work of those who inspired them may be said to be fairly representative of the variety of German endeavours.

General Studies

Nothing really comparable to the rivalry between scholarly and critical approaches that prevailed on the British scene has taken place. Still, the German tradition of philological scholarship has undergone its reorientations; a readiness to turn to the close reading of individual plays and to the microscopic study of specific aspects of Shakespeare's art has developed. The key word, ever since the 'fifties, has been 'interpretation'; and interpretation is felt to be a matter of both imaginative criticism and historical scholarship. More recently, however, a reaction against the interpretative preoccupation with detail seems to have set in—in Germany no less than elsewhere—and has generated a desire for a synthesis of the results which the age of interpretation has yielded.

Two major contributions, coming from quite different quarters and in themselves too weighty to be done justice to in a rapid survey, may illustrate these tendencies and at the same time mark the limits of our period. Wolfgang

Clemen's commentary on *Richard III*, which was first published in 1957 and had to wait for more than ten years before it became available in a drastically shortened English version,[1] is clearly more than just another study of a single play. This comprehensive scene-by-scene analysis not only provides a lucid account of the texture and artistry of a history play of the formative period, but by placing all its facets into the context of pre-Shakespearian and Shakespearian development, permits acute insights into the genetics of Shakespeare's dramatic form and thus raises many points of specific and general interest, many of which have since been further developed. Towards the other end of our period came Robert Weimann's book,[2] which, though primarily concerned with the popular elements in the plays and their medieval background, is in fact a well-balanced summing-up of much that has been discovered and pondered over in the past ten years. Commanding a vast knowledge in social history and folk lore as well as in theatrical history, Professor Weimann re-assesses the popular drama from the Mime down to Tarlton, sets into focus its salient features such as parody, satire, realism, word-play, anachronism, audience response, etc., and spots traces of these within the context of even the maturest plays of Shakespeare, always stressing the integration of popular dramaturgy and literary ambition. That Shakespeare here continues a historical development becomes evident from Weimann's chapters on medieval and early Tudor drama, which throw light on the interrelation between social climate and stage practice.

Close interpretations of the texts or of specific aspects of the texts on the one hand, and repeated attempts at synthesizing such observations on the other: these are the polarities between which recent Shakespeare studies have oscillated. To realize this one only has to look into the various collections of essays by some leading scholars, however divergent their individual lines of approach may be. Horst Oppel's volume,[3] for example, contains articles on single scenes and passages, such as the banquet scene in *Macbeth*, or Gonzalo's Utopian vision—and to these may be added the same author's more recent separate study of the mad trial scene in *King Lear* (III, vi).[4] In each of these a significant detail is illuminated from the structural and thematic context of the entire play and held against the Elizabethan background. And there are surveys of basic features such as will-struggle, or contrast and counterpoint. But Professor Oppel also draws a picture of Shakespeare's position in Elizabethan literature—how far can he be said to be the mouthpiece of his epoch?—and discusses the currents of critical opinion on these matters. Professor Clemen, too, in a recent volume of miscellanea[5] on the one hand takes up topics like appearance and reality, or music, in Shakespeare, and on the other attempts comprehensive views of the nature of Shakespearian drama. Rudolf Stamm in two different volumes of essays[6] has a number of studies, both general and specific, which assess the theatrical qualities of Shakespeare's texts (word scenery, gesture, etc.) or deal with problems of modern production, adaptation and translation. Max Lüthi[7] offers a series of observations on various aspects of the general theme of reality and illusion, including an

[1] *Kommentar zu Shakespeares Richard III* (Göttingen, 1957); English edn, London, 1968.

[2] *Shakespeare und die Tradition des Volkstheaters* (Berlin, 1967).

[3] *Shakespeare: Studien zum Werk und zur Welt des Dichters* (Heidelberg, 1963).

[4] *Die Gerichtsszene in 'King Lear'*, Akademie der Wissenschaften und der Literatur in Mainz, Abhandlungen der geistes- und sozial-wissenschaftlichen Klasse, Jg. 1968, No. 8 (Wiesbaden, 1968).

[5] *Das Drama Shakespeares* (Göttingen, 1969).

[6] *Zwischen Vision und Wirklichkeit* (Bern, 1964); *The Shaping Powers at Work* (Heidelberg, 1967).

[7] *Shakespeare: Dichter des Wirklichen und des Nichtwirklichen* (Bern, 1964).

essay on the play within the play and a discussion of the fairy-tale qualities of the plays. To these collections one may add a printed series of lectures (delivered at Tübingen University in honour of the quater-centenary)[1] whose contributors are specialists in various fields and have therefore outlined a panorama of Shakespearian influence.

Dramatic Art

Many a single aspect or device of Shakespeare's dramatic art, dealt with at book length, has been used as a clue to insights into the fabric of the plays and to observations on Shakespeare's development as a dramatist. E.Th. Sehrt[2] (another author who has had influence in Germany) draws attention to the beginnings of Elizabethan tragedies and breaks away from their traditional consideration as mere expositions of the plot. Tracing the devices for opening a play from the prologues, dumb shows and inductions of pre-Shakespearian drama down to initial *coups de théâtre* to be found in later Jacobean plays, Professor Sehrt unfolds the range of possibilities at the dramatists' disposal in order to show, in his thorough interpretations of the first passages in all of Shakespeare's tragedies and of their relation to the entire plays, at how many levels the audience is introduced into the total effect. At the same time Shakespeare's virtuosity in these matters becomes evident; the individuality of each play is matched by so many different methods of employing and intensifying traditional opening techniques.

Few of the studies undertaken on similar methodical lines share Sehrt's combination of wide scope and detailed observation. Many, however, are useful for the material they contribute to an assessment of Shakespeare's dramatic form. Brigitte Thaler,[3] for example, raises problems of scene division and scenic structure. Though 'scene' is defined as a section of action between two clear-stage moments (not necessarily identical with the scenes marked in modern editions), the author feels that this purely mechanical criterion is in itself insufficient for recognizing scenes as structural units. Her main concern is with the opening and closing passages of several types of scenes, with the methods of linking scenes together, of effectively filling and clearing the stage, of motivating entrances and exits. As Shakespeare's art develops, these methods gain importance in supplying the overall texture of the plays. Recurring scene-types and their variations have had a particular attraction for authors of theses and articles alike. The 1966 volume of the *Shakespeare Jahrbuch* (*West*) is devoted to essays of this kind—on scenes of persuasion (E. Th. Sehrt), ghost scenes (S. Korninger), scenes of temptation (D. Mehl), etc. On the scale of a thesis, Anne-Marie Tauber[4] investigates dying scenes, describes the various ways in which the stage death of a character can be placed into the scenic framework, considers the distribution of death scenes in each play and of the gamut of effects aroused by them, and adds an inventory of causes of death and motives for murder. The author diagnoses a decrease in the numbers of deaths in Shakespeare's dramatic development, which is matched by an intensified artistry of presentation. Surveying the same kind of material, but extending his study to include pre-Shakespearian drama, Rudolf Böhm[5]

[1] *Shakespeare: Seine Welt—Unsere Welt*, ed. Gerhard Müller-Schwefe (Tübingen, 1964).

[2] *Der dramatische Auftakt in der Elisabethanischen Tragödie*, Abhandlungen der Akademie der Wissenschaften in Göttingen, phil.-hist. Klasse, 3. Folge, No. 46 (Göttingen, 1960).

[3] *Szenenschluß, Szenenanfang und Szenennaht in Shakespeares Historien und Tragödien*. Diss. (München, 1965).

[4] *Die Sterbeszenen in Shakespeares Dramen*, Diss. (Bern, 1964).

[5] *Wesen und Funktion der Sterberede im elisabethanischen Drama*, Britannica et Americana, 13 (Hamburg, 1964).

concentrates on dramatic speeches uttered by characters immediately before dying. He reminds us of the historical background of public executions and then proceeds to a detailed analysis of such speeches gathered from twenty-two representative plays, including all of Shakespeare's histories. A systematic classification of his findings encourages the author to declare that the dying speech is a set convention in Elizabethan drama, which, however, admits of many variants and elaborations, and which in Shakespeare is intricately woven into the total meaning of a play. A fresh account of Shakespeare's art of the soliloquy is offered by Wolfgang Clemen in an expanded German version of his presidential address to the Modern Humanities Research Association.[1] There are sensitive readings of representative monologues, ranging from the opening speech of Richard III to Lear's mad manifesto ('every inch a king'); they serve to demonstrate the experimental character of Shakespeare's art and the effect of extensiveness increasingly achieved by the soliloquy. The interplay of convention and experiment, and in particular of realistic and symbolical presentation, is the subject of Margareta Braun,[2] who considers mainly Elizabethan and Jacobean history plays (including *Henry VI* and *Henry VIII*), as these on the one hand pursue didactic ends and thus call for symbolical presentation, but on the other hand deal with historical subject matter that requires realistic portraiture. Paying attention to soliloquies, asides and audience-address, this thesis traces the changing attitudes of authors and audiences to dramatic illusion by which the evolution from medieval to Elizabethan and Jacobean drama is marked. Shakespeare's asides in particular are studied by Wolfgang Riehle.[3] He starts by considering conventional uses of the device, but soon becomes aware that in Shakespeare the aside serves other ends besides providing a link between actor and audience: it may point to a discrepancy in awarenesses, or it may stress the divergence of appearance and reality. The most fascinating type is the emotionally charged aside, where a character is made to express his secret thoughts and feelings; this comes close to the soliloquy, except that the speaker is not alone on the stage and knows he must conceal his utterance from others present. The temptation scene in *Macbeth* (I, iii) is a case in point; there the asides suggest the hero's progressive isolation. Methods of creating and maintaining suspense in single scenes and entire plays are analyzed by Friedrich Ungerer.[4] In the early tragedies suspense is seen to be bound up with the plot; in plays like *Hamlet* or *Othello* the thrill of events is superseded by an interest in the characters and their motives. Suspense is eventually replaced by different ways of arousing the audience's sympathies, antipathies or moral responses.

The significance of the visual element in drama is emphasized by Dieter Mehl,[5] who with admirable completeness surveys dumb shows in the Elizabethan and Jacobean period. The Shakespearian sections contain a discussion of the dumb show of the mousetrap scene in *Hamlet*, which stresses the fact that, for all its exaggerated style, it alone presents the entire action of Claudius' murder and its consequences. Günter Reichert's study of the sub-plot[6] has mainly the pre-Shakespearian

[1] *Shakespeares Monologe* (Göttingen, 1964).

[2] *Symbolismus und Illusionismus im englischen Drama vor 1620*, Diss. (München, 1962).

[3] *Das Beiseitesprechen bei Shakespeare*, Diss. (München, 1964).

[4] *Dramatische Spannung in Shakespeares Tragödien*, Diss. (München, 1964).

[5] *Die Pantomime im Drama der Shakespearezeit*, Schriftenreihe der Deutschen Shakespeare-Gesellschaft West, N.F., 10, (Heidelberg, 1964), translated as *The Elizabethan Dumb Show* (London, 1965).

[6] *Die Entwicklung und die Funktion der Nebenhandlung in der Tragödie vor Shakespeare*, Studien zur englischen Philologie, N.F., 11 (Tübingen, 1966).

development in view (Kyd, Peele and Marlowe are fully discussed), but adds a chapter on *King Lear*, hoping to relate the double plot and its range of effects to various stages of earlier experimentation. As comedy is excluded, Reichert's treatise is necessarily incomplete. There are two works, published almost simultaneously, which consider, from rather different angles, the sonnet element within the plays. Karl-Heinz Wendel[1] shows that such familiar examples as the meeting sonnet in *Romeo and Juliet* (I, v) are in fact representative of an ubiquitous phenomenon. He detects some 500 passages in the canon which appear to be sonnets or variations of the sonnet form. That *Romeo and Juliet* in particular is deeply indebted to the sonnet tradition is suggested by Inge Leimberg.[2] Whereas a comparison of *Romeo and Juliet* with earlier English love tragedies (*Gismond of Salerne*, *Soliman and Perseda*) yields only few points of contact, it is the influence of Elizabethan sonneteering which, according to Professor Leimberg, accounts both for the particular nature of tragedy in *Romeo and Juliet* and for many of its characteristic forms of expression. This is maintained on the basis of, for example, the play metaphors and the tragic potentialities contained in contemporary sonnets, and also on the strength of typical motives (Icarus, Acteon), reminiscences of which can be spotted in Shakespeare's play.

Shakespeare's language and style, too, have been studied as part of his dramatic technique. Karen Schmidt di Simoni's monograph on *Troilus and Cressida*[3] describes the uses of vocabulary, verse, imagery, irony, allusion, word-play, etc. in each important scene and thus unravels the kaleidoscopic mixture of styles, the stylistic clashes and the transitions from cynicism to lyricism, which create the play's ambivalent intellectual atmosphere, besides serving to delineate characters and to emphasize central themes. Others have traced the dramatic effects of one or several stylistic features through all, or part of, the canon. Norbert Kohl[4] writes on word-play in the early comedies and in the last plays and maintains that contemporary jest books and courtesy books are one of the sources of Shakespeare's low comedy. On the basis of a theory of the word-play, which takes into consideration literary traditions as well as semantic and rhetorical aspects, he analyzes the functions of the pun and concludes that the self-sufficient uses of word-play in the artificially organized punning combats of the early comedies gave way, in the later comedies, to an art of the word-play more closely linked to its dramatic context and to the plays' thematic patterns. Elisabeth Weber[5] pays exclusive attention to the oxymoron, lists some 200 Shakespearian examples of this figure, comments on its traditional or original employment and looks out for links with characters, subjects, and the genres of the plays. Horst Weinstock[6] investigates Shakespeare's use of proverbs, proverbial sayings and sententiæ. A background discussion of Renaissance attitudes to the proverb is the foil against which the dramatic qualities of the phenomenon are evaluated. Shakespeare's early plays in putting proverbs and sententiæ mainly to ornamental uses follow a tradition established ever since the moralities. But even there new

[1] *Sonettstrukturen in Shakespeares Dramen*, Linguistica et Litteraria, 1 (Bad Homburg, 1968).

[2] *Shakespeares 'Romeo und Julia'*, Beihefte zu Poetica, 4 (München, 1968).

[3] *Shakespeares 'Troilus and Cressida'*, Schriftenreihe der Deutschen Shakespeare-Gesellschaft, N.F., 8 (Heidelberg, 1960).

[4] *Das Wortspiel in der Shakespeareschen Komödie*, Diss. (Frankfurt, 1966).

[5] *Das Oxymoron bei Shakespeare*, Diss. (Hamburg, 1963).

[6] *Die Funktion elisabethanischer Sprichwörter und Pseudosprichwörter bei Shakespeare*, Annales Universitatis Saraviensis: Reihe Phil. Fak., 6 (Heidelberg, 1966).

coinages, and re-fashionings of traditional proverbs, are discernible, and the proverb increasingly serves to motivate the action, to stress dramatic situations, to foreshadow future events and to establish contact with the audience. Shakespeare often evokes traditional proverbs by mere hints and allusions, and on the other hand knows how to furnish his own coinages with a typically proverbial flavour. There are useful observations on Hamlet's prognostic, and Iago's suggestive, use of proverbs, and on proverbial leitmotifs in *King Lear*. Maria-Beate von Loeben[1] selects out of the forms of irony in drama what has been described as 'Sophoclean verbal irony', whose counterpart consists in 'moralizing of two meanings in one word', in order to determine the extent to which such basically verbal patterns strengthen the dramatic structure of the serious plays from *Romeo and Juliet* to *Antony and Cleopatra*. Hans Walter Gabler[2] in his thesis on parody in Elizabethan drama has a chapter on *Love's Labour's Lost* which shows that Shakespeare's art of stylistic differentiation has one of its roots in parodistic adoptions of earlier literary styles. Gabler also adduces instances of dramatized parody; thus, Pistol is described as a dramatic embodiment of pre-Shakespearian tragic style. Dietrich Buntrock[3] studies the style of prose dialogue from linguistic angles and emphasizes Shakespeare's originality in vocabulary, sentence structure and imagery. A specific contribution to the study of imagery comes from Alexander Augustin,[4] who, by relating a considerable number of recurring images and motifs mainly from the tragedies to Shakespeare's sources, corrects and complements those views that attribute Shakespeare's imagery to the poet's subconscious creative energy.

Themes and Ideas

That the meanings of Shakespeare's words are in need of detailed study has been stressed by Ernst Leisi, who in his Old-Spelling Edition of *Measure for Measure*[5] renders a linguist's service to Shakespeare's text. He equips the play with a running commentary on the vocabulary, which on the strength of the *OED*, parallel passages and grammatical and stylistic contexts aims at establishing the specifically Shakespearian meanings and associations of the words, as distinguished from both current and period meanings. Leisi's methods have been brought to bear on studies of certain Shakespearian key words and ideas. Kurt Jetter[6] bases his exploration of 'wrath' on both semantic analyses and observations on rhetoric, verse, gesture, and dialogue, and also considers the psychological background of the term 'wrath' and related concepts (anger, rage, fury, madness), in order to elucidate the importance these phenomena have for plot, characters and themes of *King Lear*. Lear's wrath, the author concludes, is the germinal point from which his tragic destiny develops. 'Madness', on the other hand, has received Petra Böse's attention,[7] who studies some fourteen terms denoting insanity, again supplementing contextual and historical study of meaning by sidelights on religious, philosophical and psychological ideas of the period, and in each case adds statistics of word frequencies as well as some remarks on Shakespeare's literary

1 *Shakespeares sprachliche Ironie und die Entwicklung seiner Dramatik*, Diss. (München, 1966).

2 *Zur Funktion dramatischer und literarischer Parodie im elisabethanischen Drama*, Diss. (München, 1966).

3 *Die Entwicklung des englischen Lustspieldialogs vor 1640*, Diss. (Hamburg, 1962).

4 *Der Einfluß der Quellen auf Shakespeares Bilder und Motive*, Diss. (Hamburg, 1966).

5 Heidelberg, 1964. Cf. Leisi's article, 'Zur Bestimmung Shakespearescher Wortbedeutungen', *Shakespeare-Jahrbuch*, 100 (1964), 209–26.

6 *Der Zorn in der Shakespeareschen Tragödie*, Diss. (Frankfurt, 1959).

7 *'Wahnsinn' in Shakespeares Dramen: Eine Untersuchung zu Bedeutungsgeschichte und Wortgebrauch*, Studien zur englischen Philologie, N.F., 10 (Tübingen, 1966).

achievement, for instance on the uses of these words as leitmotifs, or on the choice of synonyms. Rainer Lengeler,[1] whose book on the grotesque in the great tragedies is, as it were, a historically conceived counterpart of Jan Kott's modernistic approach, has a preliminary lexicological study of the word 'antic'. But his more significant point of departure is the Neoplatonic vision of the conflict between cosmos and chaos, which implies that but for the action of divine providence the ordered world would fall back into chaotic unreality. Behind this unreality there are demonic forces, and these manifest themselves dramatically in grotesque, fantastic, unnatural, monstrous and ludicrous elements, in transformations of human life into an evil dream, into madness, into a stage play; in short, they create an 'alienated world', which in the great tragedies is haunted by the ludicrous terrors of chance, of the occult, etc., while on the level of the dramatic action the hero is estranged from his ideal nature—whence his insanity, his antic disposition, his possession by vices and passions.

There are two treatises on the concept of humour; the more recent one by Jürgen Schäfer[2] traces the popularization of the physiology of humours and observes that around 1600 the protean scope of the use of the word 'humour' was more considerable than at any other time. Though not specifically devoted to them, this study throws incidental light on Shakespeare's comedies, which are seen as a link in the development of the dramatic exploitation of the humour concept and its imaginative associations, a development that culminates in, but certainly does not begin with, Ben Jonson. Two earlier theses, on the ideas of space and time respectively, also establish a relationship between concept and dramatic technique. Karl Emunds[3] explores the implications of 'space'. The function of locality, distance and travel in the plots, images of the sea or of unlimited space, and the illusion of a wide world as created on the stage, come within the range of this study, which also refers to Elizabethan literature of travel. Inge Leimberg[4] collects allusions to time and uses them to explain 'dark metaphors' in the tragedies. For example, Lear's attitude to time involved in his resignation and suffering is compared to the experiences of Henry VI, Richard II and Achilles, all of which teach the audience explicitly that resignation implies a revolt against, and a punishment by, time; Lear's 'monster ingratitude' is thrown into relief by Ulysses' warning: 'time has, my Lord, a wallet at his back ... a great-sized monster of ingratitudes'. From examples of this kind—Hamlet's procrastination, prophecy in *Macbeth* and occasion and mutability in *Timon of Athens* are considered on similar lines—the author works her way towards an appraisal of Shakespearian tragedy.

This kind of work comes within the range of topos studies, to which Claus Uhlig's learned book[5] is a more explicit contribution. Its author extracts from Renaissance writings an enormous quantity of evidence illustrating the background of stereotyped patterns of moral thought which underlie Shakespeare's tragic art, in particular the ideas of 'conscience', 'time' and 'suffering', or the antinomy of 'love' and 'lust'. Shakespeare's creative process is seen as an actualization in dramatic

[1] *Tragische Wirklichkeit als groteske Verfremdung bei Shakespeare*, Anglistische Studien, 2 (Köln, 1964).

[2] *Wort und Begriff 'Humour' in der elisabethanischen Komödie*. Neue Beiträge zur englischen Philologie, 6 (Münster, 1966). Cf. Anneliese Huber, *Die Bedeutungsgeschichte von englisch 'humour' in der Zeit der Wende vom 16. zum 17. Jahrhundert*, Diss. (Erlangen–Nürnberg, 1961).

[3] *Der Raum bei Shakespeare*, Diss. (Köln, 1959).

[4] *Untersuchungen zu Shakespeares Zeitvorstellung als ein Beitrag zur Interpretation der Tragödien*, Diss. (Köln, 1961).

[5] *Traditionelle Denkformen in Shakespeares tragischer Kunst*, Britannica et Americana, 15 (Hamburg, 1967).

terms of these traditional ideas and commonplaces, which give moral significance to the action on the stage. Attempts towards a definition of Shakespearian tragedy include Gerhard W. Kaiser's dissertation,[1] which evokes classical Greek drama as a foil for a discussion of *Romeo and Juliet*, *King Lear*, *Macbeth* and *Othello*, whereas Klaus Gruhn[2] in what he calls a theological study in literature offers a contribution to the controversy on the Christian element in Shakespeare. Analyzing Shakespeare's religious terminology and phraseology, Gruhn recognizes the avoidance of contemporary theological controversy and the absence of specified dogmatic positions, and stresses the poet's 'anthropological' concern. *Hamlet* serves as a paradigm, a mirror-like demonstration, in which the theme of conscience and the vision of order are seen as aspects of the religious character of Shakespeare's tragic intention.

Shakespeare's political ideas are explored in two books, one on the histories, the other on *Measure for Measure*. The former, by Erich Braun,[3] deals with Shakespeare's attitude towards kingship and the right of opposition. An examination of Shakespeare's deviations from his historical sources, and from Elizabethan historiography in general, leads the author to the assumption that the dramatist's tenets must have changed in the course of his work: the York-tetralogy and *Richard II* are firmly based on a principle that allows the legitimate pretender to the throne the right to oppose the usurping king, whereas later on, especially in *Henry V*, personal qualification is a valid criterion of kingship. Manfred Gross[4] maintains that *Measure for Measure* can be better understood if seen as a reflection of King James' political theory and practice (and the dichotomy of the two). On the strength of the parallels with the *Basilikon Doron* the author thinks that the opposition of Duke Vincentio and Angelo exemplifies James' juxtaposition of the good ruler and the tyrant, and that *Measure for Measure* is an exploration of the political situation after Elizabeth's death, characterized by rigorous theory and political instability. More daringly, he accounts for the break in Act III, scene i by interpreting the two halves of the play as an allegory of the Elizabethan and the Jacobean age.

In a small but comprehensive book on the comedies, E. Th. Sehrt[5] focuses on the element of play and game and, discussing the comedies in their chronological order, traces the changes of comic mood it reveals. In the very early comedies the characters rarely play games; they are rather played with by Fortune. But gradually the element of play and game becomes central, it becomes humanized, and in the 'romantic' comedies there are tissues of sportive constellations; man through playing a part may discover his true being or make manifest his delusion. The great tragedies, where the hero's fate is indissolubly bound up with the game of the world, account for the more sombre mood of the 'dark' comedies. Explorations of specific ideas in the comedies include Hans Rudolf Matthäi's thesis[6] on the love theme and its structural relevance. The early comedies exemplify traditional concepts of love; in *A Midsummer Night's Dream* and *The Merchant of Venice* techniques of introducing the natural element are developed, and the 'romantic' comedies are enriched by a

[1] *The Substance of Greek and Shakespearean Tragedy*, Diss. (Freiburg, 1963).

[2] *Der religiöse Gehalt in der Deutung des Tragischen bei Shakespeare*, Diss. (Kiel, 1963).

[3] *Widerstandsrecht: Das Legitimitätsprinzip in Shakespeares Königsdramen*. Schriften zur Rechtslehre und Politik, 26 (Bonn, 1960).

[4] *Shakespeares 'Measure for Measure' und die Politik Jakobs I.*, Kieler Beiträge zur Anglistik und Amerikanistik, 2 (Neumünster, 1965).

[5] *Wandlungen der Shakespeareschen Komödie* (Göttingen, 1961).

[6] *Das Liebesmotiv in den Komödien Shakespeares*, Diss. (Frankfurt, 1965).

criticism of pastoral clichés, an individualization of the heroines, by extended sub-plots and contrasts of court and country, and a concern with 'fancy' tends to supersede the traditional love themes. The 'dark' quality of the comedies after 1600 is attributable to the preponderance of the antagonist and to a strain of scepticism. Eckhard Auberlen[1] devotes himself to the supernatural and the 'unbelievable' in the last plays and tries to show that Shakespeare surpasses romance conventions by involving his audience in the revelation of a symbolic significance of wonderful events and by thus driving home the truth of improbabilities which before had been accepted only by temporary suspension of disbelief.

The narrative poems, together with contemporary short epics, have received attention by Helmut Castrop,[2] who discerns in these works the programmatic expression of differing views of the nature of love. Shakespeare and Marlowe are singled out as the main contestants; against Marlowe's Ovidian theme in *Hero and Leander* Shakespeare retaliates by exploring, in *Venus and Adonis*, the same material in a somewhat grim and gloomy manner, and at the same time criticizes the erotic language of the day; in *Lucrece* he subjects the genre of the complaint to a similar castigation.

Authorship, Text, Translation, Illustration

That detailed analysis of Shakespeare's dramatic art, its developments and its conceptual background may fruitfully be brought to bear on problems of authorship has been demonstrated in two monographs of Horst Oppel. In his book on *Titus Andronicus*[3] this indefatigable author produces fresh arguments for Shakespeare's sole authorship by reading the play against the traditional tragedies of blood on the one hand and in the light of the later development of Shakespearian tragedy on the other. On his way he settles many a point of interpretation; he claims Marlowe's influence (more so than Seneca's) for the banquet scene in Act v, scene iii, points out the emblematic quality of the imagery and the skilful handling of the initial contrast, and describes Titus' renouncing the crown (I, i, 189) and the fly-scene (III, ii, 80) as poetic centres. The play, in short, emerges as a product of the change of dramatic style which occurred around 1590. A similar study of the banquet scene in *Henry VIII*[4] leads the same author to assume a share from John Fletcher's hand.

It is perhaps due to the perennial pre-occupation with problems of translation that there have been next to no recent contributions to the rigid discipline of textual criticism. Some curious signs of sympathy with the Quarto texts might, however, be noted. Paul Gerhard Buchloh (in a controversy with G. I. Duthie)[5] tries to account for the differences between the Quarto and Folio versions of *King Lear* by adducing political reasons: if the Quarto version (designated as 'history') was intended as a tribute to James I, this intention in 1623 would have lost its topical pregnancy and hence became obliterated in the Folio. More provokingly, Hans Rothe[6]

[1] *Das Unglaubliche in Shakespeares späten Stücken*, Diss. (Frankfurt, 1967).

[2] *Shakespeares Verserzählungen: Eine Untersuchung der ovidischen Epik im elisabethanischen England*, Diss. (München, 1964).

[3] *'Titus Andronicus': Studien zur dramengeschichtlichen Stellung von Shakespeares früher Tragödie.* Schriftenreihe der Deutschen Shakespeare Gesellschaft, N.F., 9 (Heidelberg, 1961).

[4] *Shakespeare oder Fletcher?: Die Bankett-Szene in 'Henry VIII' als Kriterium der Verfasserschaft.* Akademie der Wissenschaften und der Literatur in Mainz, Abhandlungen der geistes- und sozialwissenschaftlichen Klasse, Jg. 1965, No. 7 (Wiesbaden, 1965).

[5] George Ian Duthie und Paul Gerhard Buchloh, *Shakespeares 'King Lear': Historie oder Tragödie? Untersuchungen zur Textkritik.* Veröffentlichungen der Schleswig-Holsteinischen Universitätsgesellschaft, N.F., 35 (Kiel, 1965).

[6] *Shakespeare als Provokation* (München, 1961).

gathers arguments old and new to denigrate the Folio editors' competence and thus justifies his own rather free translations, which he calls 'The Elizabethan Shakespeare'[1] and to which many German producers are still addicted. With more display of learning (the relevance of which is not always easy to see) Ludwig Berger[2] attempts to restore the 'bad' quarto of *Hamlet* to dignity and advances the theory that it represents Shakespeare's early and vigorous version.

The period under review has seen some twenty new editions of the plays in German translation, including four paperback series with one or several plays per volume (some of them equipped with appreciative essays), not to mention numerous school editions of single plays. In most cases the classical Schlegel–Tieck translation is used, sometimes with slight revisions. Of the modern translators, Rudolf Alexander Schröder added some more plays to his earlier efforts,[3] and at least two new names have firmly established themselves, both in print and on the stage: Rudolf Schaller[4] and Erich Fried.[5] While the necessity of providing a German Shakespeare is accompanied by a continuous flood of occasional comment and controversy,[6] a comprehensive and up-to-date study of the history of translation and adaptation in Germany is still unwritten. New material has, however, been made accessible. Heinrich Huesmann[7] bases his exhaustive treatment of Goethe's involvement in Shakespearian production at Weimar—which he considers seminal—on promptbooks, playbills and other original material, some of it re-discovered. Hans Georg Heun[8] takes a specific look at Goethe's adaptation of *Romeo and Juliet*, attributing the changes—among them severe cuts in the comic passages—to a classically inspired desire for concentration and pathetic heightening. A. W. Schlegel's methods of translation are studied by Hans Georg Koyro,[9] who analyzes with especial thoroughness the language and style of this translator's *Julius Caesar*. Frank Jolles has edited the early version of Schlegel's *A Midsummer Night's Dream*,[10] which, as is explained in the introduction, was inspired by the young author's contact with G. A. Bürger, though it is Schlegel's re-translation of 1797 that eventually became standard. Another remarkable translation that has been unearthed is Theodor Fontane's *Hamlet*,[11] apparently an early effort (never before published) of this author to whom we owe vivid descriptions of Kean's productions. From the point of view of stage-history, Heide Nüssel[12] surveys the conscious attempts by the German theatre of the nineteenth and early twentieth centuries to present Shakespeare on 'reconstructed' Elizabethan stages; these began with Ludwig Tieck's memorable production of *A Midsummer Night's Dream* (1843) and led to the perhaps

1 *Der elisabethanische Shakespeare* (1955; revised edn, 4 volumes, München, 1963–4).

2 *William Shakespeare: 'Hamlet' 1603* (Frankfurt, 1967).

3 Rudolf Alexander Schröder, *Gesammelte Werke*, vol. 7 (Frankfurt, 1963).

4 Shakespeare, *Werke*, übersetzt und erläutet von Rudolf Schaller (third edn, 3 vols., Berlin, 1964).

5 *Shakespeare-Übersetzungen: 'Romeo und Julia', 'Julius Caesar', 'Hamlet'* (München, 1968).

6 See the bibliographies by Hans Georg Heun, *Shakespeare-Jahrbuch*, 92 (1956), 450–63; 95 (1959), 403–10; 102 (1966), 273–87.

7 *Shakespeare-Inszenierungen unter Goethe in Weimar*, Österreichische Akademie der Wissenschaften, philosophisch-historische Klasse, Sitzungsberichte, 258 (Graz, 1968).

8 *Shakespeares 'Romeo und Julia' in Goethes Bearbeitung*, Philologische Studien und Quellen, 24 (Berlin, 1965).

9 *August Wilhelm Schlegel als Shakespeare-Übersetzer*, Diss. (Marburg, 1966).

10 *A. W. Schlegels 'Sommernachtstraum' in der ersten Fassung vom Jahre 1789*, Palaestra, 244 (Göttingen, 1967).

11 *Shakespeares Hamlet*, übersetzt von Theodor Fontane (Berlin, 1966).

12 *Rekonstruktionen der Shakespeare-Bühne auf dem deutschen Theater*, Diss. (Köln, 1967).

best-known example—the Munich Shakespeare Stage, which significantly coincided with Poel's activities in London.

Last but not least, mention should be made of the contributions by Horst Oppel to the history of Shakespearian illustration. They are based on a collection of reproductions assembled for the Shakespeare-Bildarchiv of the Akademie der Wissenschaften und Literatur in Mainz. In a preliminary treatise Oppel sets down the guiding principles of his approach.[1] His aim is an analysis of the artists' contribution to the interpretation of the plays. Oppel distinguishes various types of relationship between Shakespeare's text and pictorial comment—the illustrator may level or compress the action; he may visualize offstage events, lyrical passages or imagery; he may idealize, stylize, etc.; and there are interesting points of contact with the history of stage design and costume. While Professor Oppel has applied his method in the context of his studies of *Titus Andronicus* and *King Lear* mentioned above, Heidemarie Spangenberg, in a thesis on *Macbeth*,[2] gives a systematic account of nineteenth-century illustrations relating to each scene and evaluates her findings with a view to establishing links between pictorial and verbal criticism.

[1] *Die Shakespeare-Illustration als Interpretation der Dichtung*, Akademie der Wissenschaften und der Literatur in Mainz, Abhandlungen der geistes- und sozial-wissenschaftlichen Klasse, Jg. 1965, No. 2 (Wiesbaden, 1965).

[2] *Illustrationen zu Shakespeares 'Macbeth'*, Diss. (Marburg, 1967).

A NEGLECTED JONES/WEBB THEATRE PROJECT: 'BARBER–SURGEONS' HALL WRIT LARGE'*

D. F. ROWAN

The drawings, which are reproduced in Plates I and II, form part of the 'Jones/Webb Collection' in the Library of Worcester College, Oxford, and must be of paramount interest to theatrical scholars. Part of a series numbered 7, 7A, 7B, and 7C, their neglect is particularly surprising as they are now found in the same large scrapbook volume, *Drawings by Inigo Jones and John Webb, Nos. 1–61*, as number 27, the important Jones/Webb drawing of 'The Cockpit-in-Court'. Drawings 7 and 7A are plans and elevations of Jones' famous oval 'Theater of Anatomie' completed for the Company of Barber–Surgeons in 1638. Drawing 7B (Plate I) is an exterior elevation of a building which may, with an explicit caveat, be tentatively and temporarily called 'Barber–Surgeons' Hall', and a plan view of the same building. Drawing 7C (Plate II) offers two interior elevations of the opposite ends of the same 'Hall'. Both 7B and 7C are carefully finished ink drawings, 'show drawings' in fact, on sheets of fine quality paper which measure approximately 12½ by 16½ inches. (Number 27, the 'Cockpit' drawing, is only slightly larger, measuring 13½ by 17 inches.) The unknown compiler of this volume—perhaps C. H. Wilkinson—has associated, through his numbering, the four sets of drawings with 'The Mystery and Commonality of Barbers and Surgeons of London'.

The location of the first Barber–Surgeons' Hall, destroyed in the Great Fire, can be fixed with precision, for its western end rested on the foundations of a tower of Old London Wall, between Aldersgate and Cripplegate, and it is this use of the old tower foundation which gave to both the first and the second halls their distinctive shape—a shape which was perhaps the dubious ground for the association of drawings 7B and 7C with the Company. The evidence for 7 and 7A is indisputable, but the association of 7B and 7C with the Company and the Livery Hall is tenuous indeed. If one takes the scale beneath the plan on drawing 7B as representing yards (an unusual scale in the seventeenth century) the diameter of the semi-circular termination, and thus the width of the playhouse, is almost exactly 23 feet, the figure arrived at by actual measurement of the existing tower foundation. However, this can be nothing more than a curious coincidence. Even bearing in mind the tiny measurements of the Rutland House stage, such a scale renders other dimensions of the drawing impossible. It is much more likely that the large divisions on the scales of both drawings indicate five feet, and that the small divisions which are still clear on 7C are foot marks. There is a very slight discrepancy between the scales on the two drawings but this is unintended, as actual measurements on the two sets of drawings are identical. Can one

* This synopsis is abstracted from the original article which appeared in *New Theatre Magazine*, IX (1969), 6–15, and is Part I of a two-part study of the drawings. Part II will appear in *The Elizabethan Theatre*, II, ed. David Galloway (Toronto, 1970).

conjecture on the facts to hand: Inigo Jones designed the Theatre and the Great Parlour of the Barber-Surgeons in 1635 and 1636; there are striking similarities between the playhouse of these drawings and the 'Cockpit-in-Court'; the shape and proportions, but not the dimensions, of this unknown building accord almost perfectly with the foundations now remaining behind the present Hall. I can only suggest that the drawings represent an imaginative theatre project from the teeming mind of Inigo Jones, perhaps suggested to him by the unique proportions of the first Barber–Surgeons' Hall. It is, however, certain that the designs were never executed by the Company. The records, so full of items pertaining to the Theatre and the Great Parlour, make scant mention of the Hall, and the commentators who praised the Theatre and the Great Parlour could not have passed with complete silence over another work of the incomparable Jones.

Occurring as they do in the 'Jones/Webb Collection' the authenticity of the drawings seems beyond dispute. Webb bequeathed his entire library along with all his 'prints and cutts and drawings of Architecture' to his son William with strict injunctions that they should be kept together. The descent of a large portion of the drawings to Dr George Clarke of All Souls College is well documented and Clarke, on his death in 1736, left them to Worcester College with the proviso that they 'may be preserv'd with care in their Library, as the Books and Prints are to be'. There can be little doubt that drawings 7B and 7C were part of Webb's original collection.

I have attempted to avoid the more difficult question of the hand which actually held the pen by referring to them as Jones/Webb drawings. Although recent work has proved that the Cockpit design is primarily the work of Jones, the actual drawing has not been attributed with certainty to either of the two architects. Despite the obvious similarities of the design of the two stages, the manner and execution of the drawings is different. The clearest distinction is in the shading; drawings 7B and 7C use an ink-wash and their overall tone is lighter and more delicate than that of the Cockpit drawings where lines and cross-hatchings are used. These drawings have, as well, a finished quality which is lacking in the Cockpit drawings where erasures and pencilled additions are visible in the original. Reluctantly I must abandon this question to those more expert than myself in the history of architectural drawing, but I cannot resist the hazardous negative suggestion that drawings 7B and 7C are *not* in the hand of Webb.

I have been unable to find any records of another building with this unusual shape, although such negative evidence is not proof that such a playhouse was not built. The meticulous and detailed execution of the drawings suggests that they were intended as something more than a toy; yet certain structural discrepancies suggest that they could not have been based on fully developed working drawings. Were they perhaps part of a 'show collection' presented as credentials by an aspiring architect? A careful examination of the evidence in such works as Adams' *Shakespearean Playhouses* and volume six of Bentley's *Jacobean and Caroline Stage* has yielded no clues toward the certain or even tentative identity of this playhouse. I cannot believe that a stage of such 'conventional' design would have been considered by any of the post-Restoration theatrical entrepreneurs, and for this reason I dismiss the converted tennis courts, and the 'new' theatres of Davenant and Killigrew. I cannot be so certain about the repairs and reconstructions carried out at the Phoenix and Salisbury Court in the years immediately before 1660, but the existing evidence is far too slight to support more than a bare possibility. Davenant's projected theatre of 1639 is more attractive; Jones and Davenant were closely associated and the date is appropriate but, in Bentley's words, 'such evidence as the license presents implies a large house, not a small private theatre like Blackfriars or the Salisbury Court'.[1]

I have suggested that Jones was intrigued by the unusual shape of the first Barber–Surgeons' Hall, which he certainly viewed no later than early 1636, and that in response to the stimulus to his imagination he designed this playhouse. The year 1636 indicates a development out of and after the 'Cockpit', but Jones may have known the first Barber–Surgeons' Hall long before he built the Company's Anatomical Theatre, and the plans may well antedate those of the 'Cockpit'. In fact, the evidence of watermarks points to an earlier date. Drawings 7B and 7C carry a watermark of a family illustrated by Edward Heawood.[2] The mark is a crowned fleur-de-lis with a pendant monogram, 'WR', clearly in the series listed by Heawood as figures 1761, 1762, 1768 and 1769. This series has a chronological range from 1592 to 1616. If this evidence be accepted, then one cannot dismiss out of hand the early seventeenth-century triumvirate of the Blackfriars, the Phoenix and the Salisbury Court which, according to Wright in his *Historia Histrionica*, 'were all three built almost exactly alike, for Form and Bigness'. It is, however, difficult to believe that if one of these theatres had had such an unusual shape it would not have been noted.

On the basis of the evidence at my disposal I must regard the case for any of these theatres as not proved and I have chosen to reserve further discussions of provenance, date and identity for the second part of my study, turning now to an examination of the drawings themselves. If we accept the scales as representing 5 feet and 1 foot we have a small, unusually shaped 'private' playhouse with a maximum interior width of 37 feet and a length of 53 feet. A fine sense of proportion places the front edge of the 4-foot-high stage precisely at the midpoint: 26 feet and 6 inches from the back wall of a tiring-house just slightly over 10 feet in depth and stretching the width of the theatre. Galleries on each side of the stage, measuring 6 feet and 9 inches, leave a stage 23 feet and 6 inches wide, and 15 feet deep. The front wall of the tiring-house is broken by an arched central door 8 feet high and 4 feet wide, flanked on either side by rectangular doors 6 feet high, and 2 feet and 6 inches wide. From the floor of the pit to the curved ceiling is a distance of 26 feet and 9 inches. In this height the architect has placed two galleries, the first of which rises 11 feet above the level of the stage, and the second, an additional 7 feet.

These galleries are broken at the midpoint of the playhouse: both the upper and lower galleries of the 'house end' of the building have four degrees and space for a walkway behind the last row. The lower galleries of the 'stage end' appear to terminate against the tiring-house wall, and also have four degrees but no walkway behind. The upper galleries at this end have, as well, four degrees and no walkway, and may (the drawing is not clear on this point) continue unbroken around the upper stage corner. There are, however, only three degrees of seats above the stage and they are interrupted by a classically ornamented 'window' 4 feet wide. In the pit are oval degrees gracefully reflecting the curve of the playhouse wall. Divided by a central gangway, they probably rise to the 4-foot level of both the stage and the floor of the first gallery.

I must at this point direct attention to Richard Hosley's recent remarkably perceptive paper, 'A Reconstruction of the Second

[1] G. E. Bentley, *The Jacobean and Caroline Stage* (Oxford, 1942–68), VI, 306.

[2] E. Heawood, *Watermarks* (Hilversum, 1950), Plate 238.

Blackfriars'.[1] It is hardly an exaggeration to say that drawing 7C could serve as an illustration for this excellent study. A detailed comparison may best be left to the reader but there is an exciting agreement on several important points: a gallery over the stage for both actors and spectators; a stage running the narrow dimension of the playhouse; seats for spectators along the side of a stage with almost precisely an eight to five ratio; a tiring-house façade with three doors. There are some minor points of difference: Hosley's stage is some six inches higher, and our drawing does not suggest side stage-seats converted into a number of boxes. One major difference is the number of galleries and their vertical arrangement. The solution proposed in these drawings is architecturally sounder than that suggested in the reconstruction of the Blackfriars, and my own feeling is that the builder of that theatre might well have chosen to place the floor of the first gallery at stage level and to reduce the height of his galleries in order to achieve simplicity of construction. However, as the architect of our playhouse was content with two galleries within an overall height of slightly over 26 feet, his problems were not as severe as those of an architect who attempted three galleries within 32 feet. Nevertheless, one may question the existence of stepped galleries in the Second Blackfriars.

I have noted above that the drawings, although elegantly finished, present a number of unresolved problems—problems which presumably would have had to be resolved before actual construction began. The most serious is perhaps, the absence of any indication of entrances to the lower galleries. The oval seating in the pit, which appears on 7B, does not appear on 7C, and there is a seemingly insoluble confusion of levels in the plan view on 7B. A tentative explanation for these inconsistencies is that the drawings are not fully worked out; further evidence, perhaps, that the playhouse was never built. Be that as it may, the very fact that such plans could be mooted vests them with significance for the study of the Elizabethan stage, and one may perhaps proceed to a more general discussion of the drawings.

Since the publication of the Swan drawing in 1888, a vexing question concerning the use of the 'upper area' over or above the stage has exercised scholars. Most recently Herbert Berry in his carefully documented paper, 'The Playhouse in the Boar's Head Inn, Whitechapel',[2] has offered much interesting evidence about the use of the area in that theatre. At the centre of a long and involved lawsuit rests the question of who should have the profits from the 'galleries over the stage'. One document uses the phrase six times and there can be no doubt that the area was highly prized by spectators at the Boar's Head. Mistakenly, to my mind, Professor Berry goes on to suggest in passing, on the basis of this evidence, that the case for an upper acting area is not much stronger than that for the 'inner stage'. I cannot agree. Evidence for the 'inner stage' is so slight and uncertain that it is virtually negligible; evidence for the use of an upper acting area fills the plays of every professional company, of every theatre, both public and private, for over half a hundred years. Because of the special nature of the Cockpit-in-Court there was no provision for spectators over the stage, but an upper acting area was provided. I have recently completed a detailed study of over twenty plays produced at the 'Cockpit' between 1630 and 1638, and of these plays at least eight demand the use of the upper area. Surely the answer to this question is found in a multi-purpose upper area used by spectators, actors or musicians as circumstance permitted or occasion demanded. Such an 'upper area' is

[1] In *The Elizabethan Theatre*, ed. David Galloway (Toronto, 1969), pp. 74–88.

[2] *Ibid.*, pp. 45–73.

PLATES

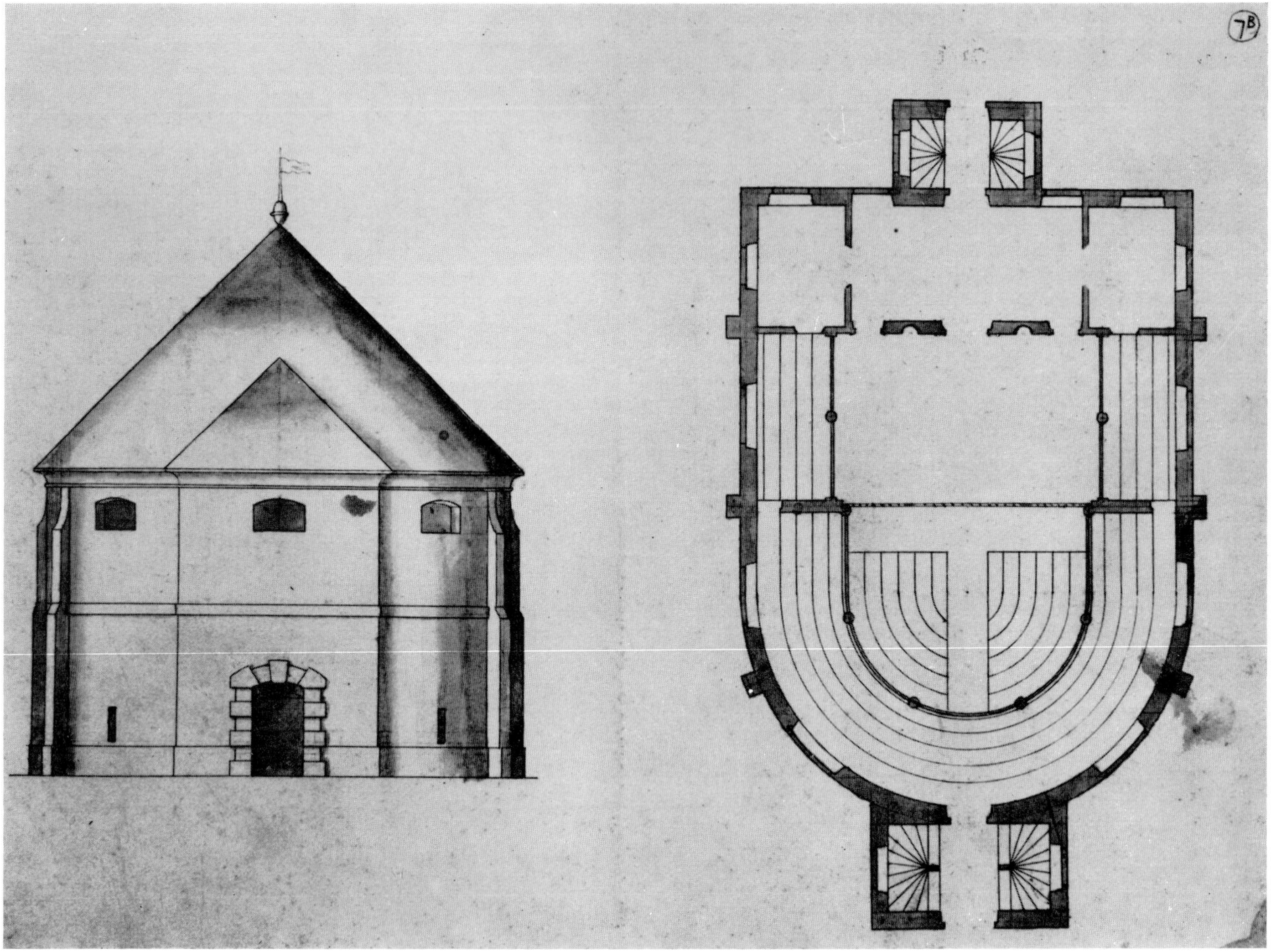

I & II Jones/Webb designs for a theatre project

I exterior elevation and a plan view of 'Barber-Surgeons' Hall'

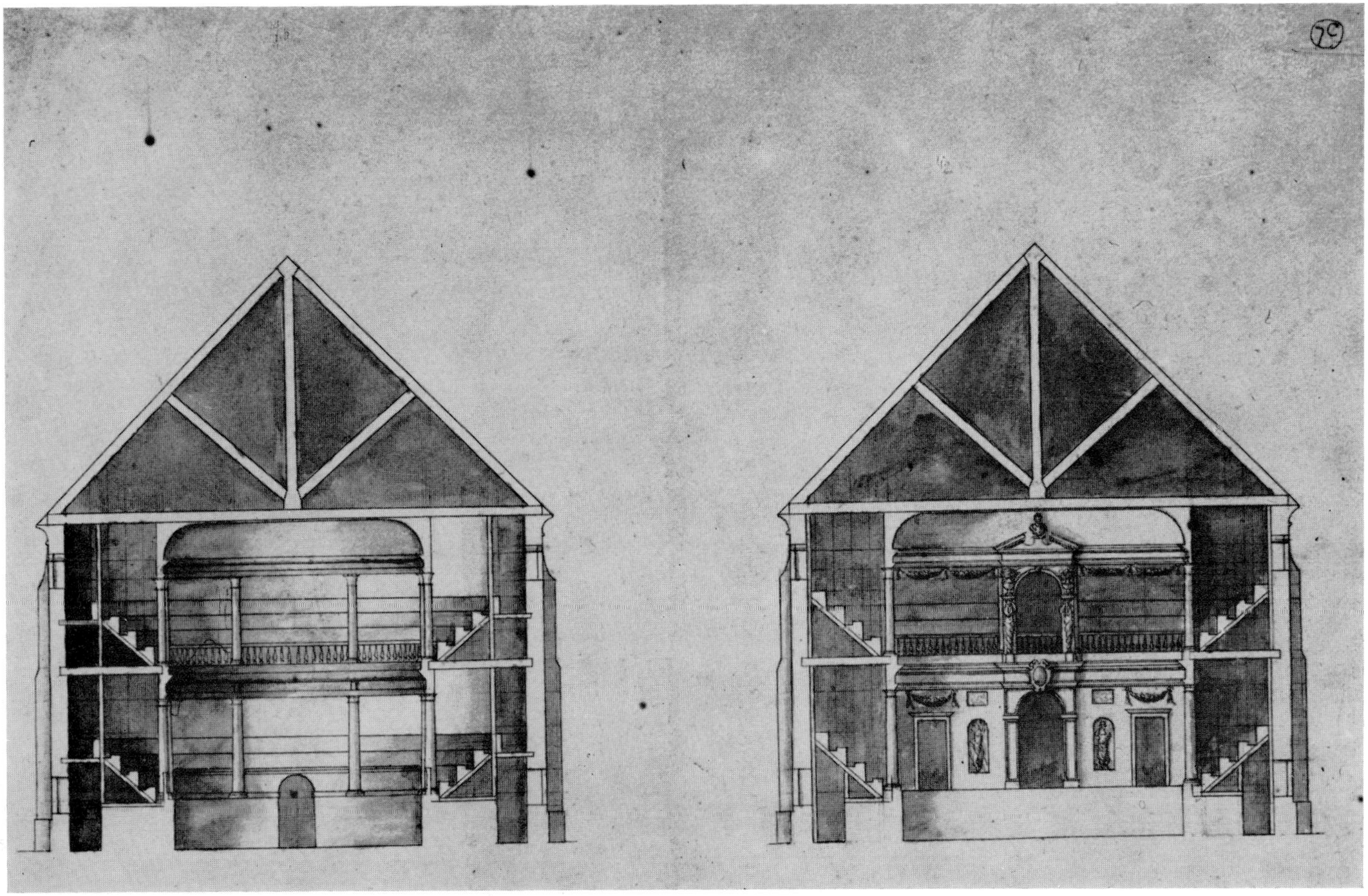

11 Two interior elevations of the opposite ends of the same 'Hall'

III *Pericles*, Royal Shakespeare Theatre, 1969. Directed by Terry Hands, designs by Timothy O'Brien.
Ian Richardson as Pericles and Susan Fleetwood as Thaisa

IV *Women Beware Women* (Thomas Middleton), Royal Shakespeare Theatre, 1969. Directed by Terry Hands, designs by Timothy O'Brien. Judi Dench as Bianca and Brewster Mason as the Duke of Florence

v *Twelfth Night*, Royal Shakespeare Theatre, 1969. Directed by John Barton, designs by Christopher Morley. Left to right: Brenda Bruce as Maria, Emrys James as Feste, Barrie Ingham as Sir Andrew Aguecheek, and Donald Sinden as Malvolio

VI *Women Beware Women.* Left to right: Derek Smith as Guardiano, Anne Dyson as the Widow, Judi Dench (Bianca) and Elizabeth Spriggs as Livia

VII *The Winter's Tale*, Royal Shakespeare Theatre, 1969. Directed by Trevor Nunn, designs by Christopher Morley. Judi Dench as Hermione, Jeremy Richardson as Mamillius and Barrie Ingham as Leontes found in 7C where there is clearly a small ornamented 'window' or upper stage and, just as clearly, degrees for spectators. That the horizontal lines along the back of the upper area over the stage are not mere remnants of the draughtsman's guide lines is proved by the concession to the area's difficult sight lines; there are only three tiers of seats. One must note as well the care with which the drawing shows that the seats do not carry through behind the 'window'.

Neither this drawing (7B) nor the Cockpit drawing shows a trapdoor, but there can be no doubt concerning the actual use of a trap. Plays such as *Bussy D'Ambois* and *Aglaura*, both produced at the 'Cockpit', have as a central element in their plot the use of a special exit to and entrance from below which is specially noted in the stage directions. None of the views of the Elizabethan stage (with the probable exception of the 'Messalina' drawing) shows a trap but the evidence of the plays is incontrovertible. There is similar evidence for the use of flying-machinery in both the public and private theatres, although there is no visual evidence in any of the drawings. Certainly the sturdy rafters shown in 7C could have supported the necessary gear.

Finally I must note the general resemblances between this theatre and the 'Cockpit'. Most striking of all is the remarkable similarity of the two tiring-house façades. The fine proportions of all features, the rounded central doors with square flanking doors, the decorative medallions and statuary, the classical pediments above the oval upper windows combine to produce the irresistible impression that both stages are the work of a single architect, Inigo Jones. As in the 'Cockpit' there can be no question of the use of the central door as anything more than a 'discovery space'. Apart from the differences in the shapes of the stages (the unusual shape of the Cockpit stage was forced on Jones by the existing structure) and the number of doors, the single feature lacking in this unknown theatre is the stage railing. The seating in the pit of both theatres is also similar, but in the 'Cockpit' Jones has solved the problem of the central corner seats by simply doing away with them. Is this a later solution to an earlier problem; does this theatre antedate the 'Cockpit'? Although the suggested association with Barber–Surgeons' Hall may, as noted above, point to a date after 1636, Jones might well have seen the Company's Hall at a much earlier date. On balance, the evidence of the early watermarks on the drawings and the more elaborately developed classical façade of the 'Cockpit' suggest that it is the later design, but of this I cannot be certain.

Having reserved for a later study the vital and crucial questions of provenance, date and identity, I must indicate my intense awareness of the dangers of arguing *in vacuo*. The greatest caution must be exercised in moving backwards, forwards or even sideways from an unknown point. Nevertheless, I suggest that the visual evidence of these previously unpublished drawings must be taken into account in any future reconstructions or discussions of the Elizabethan theatre.

INTERPRETATION OR EXPERIENCE? SHAKESPEARE AT STRATFORD

GARETH LLOYD EVANS

In a recent review of the interpretations of Edward II and Richard II by the exciting young actor, Ian McKellen, Ronald Bryden quoted Richard Mansfield. The capacity required for the great Shakespearian roles is described thus:

> When the fire-bell rings, the horses have got to come out and rattle and race down the street, and rouse the town.[1]

It is heartening to note such words being used to indicate a young actor's quality yet, with a start, we realize how rarely they can be applied now. On the other hand, it is not long ago that we found them echoing in our minds when we experienced the best of Wolfit, Gielgud and Olivier.

In the summer number of *Flourish*[2] J. C. Trewin amplifies the evidence of past glory. He recalls Ernest Milton's 'orchestration of the "Rogue and Peasant slave" soliloquy', and Maurice Evans' 'sweeping gesture at "Northumberland thou ladder"'. Richard Mansfield's strident image is matched by Trewin's recalling of 'Edith Evans' Millamant voice—fan spread and streamers out'.

Trewin is not indulging in romantic nostalgia. His point is firmly made.

> Today, in Shakespeare particularly, there is a curious reluctance to 'give'. It is as if an actor or actress were in the ante-room, refusing to go further, refusing to fling the door wide... It is curious, for there are many current actors of high spirit and intelligence. Can it be that they and their directors—who so often have the final word—are intent on interpreting a play to us rather than letting us experience it.

This is an important statement and its validity is worth examining in the context of the R.S.C.'s way with Shakespeare. Probably very definite reasons could be given as to why, since the advent of the younger directorial generation at Stratford, those actors and actresses who 'make the fire-bells ring', have been conspicuous by their absence. Olivier's and Edith Evans' last appearances at Stratford were years ago. Wolfit never passionately darkened the place in the last decade. Gielgud's last appearance (as Othello) was unhappy—a displaced Saturn. Alone, of an older generation, Peggy Ashcroft has held her own with the young Hyperions. Whatever the reasons (good or expedient) the simple fact is that Trewin's 'givers' have been absent. A young theatregoing generation is growing up, exposed to the world's most influential Shakespearian theatre, without experiencing such players. They have, of course, perhaps unconsciously, heard echoes of music and passion, and seen images of thrustful dramatic energy in the work of players like Ian Richardson, Elizabeth Spriggs, Donald Sinden and Charles Thomas; but when it comes to counting, the hands still have fingers left.

The replacement for 'giving' actors has been, to use Trewin's words, 'interpretation' for 'experience'. It is well to be clear, however, whose interpretation we are considering.

It is with a shock that we realize, when we

[1] *The Observer*, 28 September 1969.

[2] Published by the R.S.C. (Summer 1969).

consider the Hyperion era at Stratford, that it is much easier to recall directors than actors. Hall, Williams, Barton, Nunn, Brook and *their* histories, comedies, tragedies and what-have-you are remembered more clearly than individual acting interpretations. Who played Katharine in the Hall/Barton *Henry V*, and who the King of France (it wasn't Harcourt Williams was it? certainly not, but who?). Suddenly we recall with joy Vanessa Redgrave's Rosalind, but who was her Celia and Orlando? Again, we recall, not without pleasure (but perhaps for reasons unconnected with Shakespeare), that Diana Rigg played one of the lovers in Hall's *Dream*. Yet, which lover did she play, and who were the other three—was one of them David Warner?

Trevor Nunn's first full season as artistic director nears its close and already such shades of forgetfulness begin to incline. Judi Dench we will remember for her urgent, husky lyricism, Ian Richardson for the piercing agony in his voice in part two of *Pericles*, Brewster Mason's unguent Duke in *Women Beware Women*, Donald Sinden's liver-faced, thick-tongued anguished Malvolio; other moments of consequence may linger—Charles Thomas' first speech as Orsino, Emrys James' bringing of the play to an end as Feste, but 'experience' is already being overmounted by 'interpretation'.

It has three aspects: one, academic, two, visual, three, 'contemporary'. They all grow from the athletic imaginativeness, energetic cleverness and competent skill of the young group around Mr Nunn—John Barton, successfully making good with the new dispensation, Terry Hands, swept quickly into directorial stardom by his peripatetic intelligence, David Jones, a more cautious but still adventurous man. In the background, part *éminence grise*, part *enfant terrible*, lurks Peter Brook—but then, he has always seemed young and could never be accused of courting a traditionalism he had not himself invented, or eschewing perilous exploration.

They are representative of the 'academic' spirit which, both for much good and some ill, has penetrated Shakespearian production. They will turn the bazaars and museums of scholarly exegesis upside down to find a good bargain (the R.S.C. programmes are stuffed with their better buys—Traversi, Wain, Mahood, Salingar, Leech—and with some of their worst). They 'know' their texts, even if they do not always use all of them. They are meticulous in historical detail—when they decide to be. You can now say, as you could not, only a few years ago, that Shakespearian production is in the hands of the most knowledgeable directors of all time.

The extent of directorial committal to the 'academic' is indicated by Ann Barton's programme note to her husband's production of *Twelfth Night*:

> This comedy prefigures the final romances. Like Marina in *Pericles* or Perdita in *The Winter's Tale*, Viola simply accepts her strange situation. She does not transform it as Rosalind and Julia did.

This season is, in its major productions, an attempt to link the 'romantic' comedies with the last plays. Indeed, it might be said that the 'gravity' of Barton's *Twelfth Night* tacitly redefines the chronological boundaries of what we used to call the 'last' plays—they start earlier, so to say. The effect of the attempted link is to give an overall emphasis to the symbolic and allegorical in the earlier play as well as in the two later ones. A small but trenchant example is the doubling of Marina and Thaisa and of Hermione and Perdita. The justification for the former is supported in the programme notes—by Traversi:

> Through her [i.e. Marina] past and present, death and life, temporal servitude and spiritual freedom are fused in a single organic process tending to the affirmation of a new state of being.

The 'new state of being' is Marina/Thaisa/Susan Fleetwood. The theatregoer, however, may be excused for not remembering Traversi or directorial academicism when, in the last scene, another actress has to help such high concepts along by aiding the exquisite Miss Fleetwood in her dichotomy. 'Willing suspension' is a difficult thing to achieve in an audience and the R.S.C. have a long way to go before they do so. In this context they are done a disservice by their highly efficient pre-production advertising, and by assiduous journalists hot for a scoop. The 'doubling' this year was announced at an early stage—the effect was to incite the curious to look for it, and to note its process.

The spirit of 'academicism' is seen too, in Terry Hands' *Pericles*. There is nothing outrageously dashing about his programme notes which fairly and succinctly present reasonable possibilities about dating and authorship. He is frank about the ultimate source of his text—the First Quarto—and about the inclusion of blank verse passages from Wilkins' *The Painfull Adventures of Pericles Prince of Tyre*. It is ironic that his attempt to realize the play dramatically is less impressive than the obvious academic speculation that accompanied its preparation.

There is hardly need to record that John Barton's *Twelfth Night* is based upon the most assiduous and, in this theatre, undoubtedly the deepest academic preparation. This shows most obviously in the text. Not only is there an avoidance of this theatre's most persistently annoying foible—the glossing of words and phrases with modern emphasis and innuendo—but there is a triumphantly successful revelation of the rich seams of meaning, music and rhythm of the original. Mr Barton, in this production, has read his Folio without arrogance and with much wisdom.

So far as the second (the visual) aspects of the season are concerned, there has been an attempt to unify the visual style by the use (in *The Winter's Tale*, *Pericles* and *Women Beware Women*—a *very* late play?) of a large-seeming space bounded on sides and back by fly-aspiring walls. The effect is of vast emptiness and a de-localization of action and hence a de-naturalizing of the picture. Inside this space movement aspires to ritual. Terry Hands is specific about this:

> I think Shakespeare may have written *Pericles* as a fresh attempt to rebalance words and spectacle. If so he would need to abandon naturalism, use simple verse, formula phrasing and dumb-shows. Why else choose Gower with his terse metre and medieval wisdom? Why else combine allegorical masque, with archetypal fairy-tale?

Amidst the plethora of question-begging it is clear that Mr Hands is more interested in movement than words.

The R.S.C., since the early Hall days, has never, with certain exceptions, been notable for giving its audiences round and singing verse-speaking (an aural 'experience') which older theatregoers remember but younger ones have never heard. Can it be that the mark of the Nunn era will be a further diminution of the aural by policy where, in the Hall era, it seemed often meagre by default?

The third (contemporary) aspect of the season is best illustrated by Trevor Nunn's *The Winter's Tale*.

Jung and Freud seem to have been his bedside reading. In order to embrace Mr Nunn's interpretation one has to forget about kings and princes and about melody and rhythm. It is incumbent to think, rather, of psychology, psychiatry and 'pop'. It is a brilliantly realized study of a mind suddenly fractured by reasonless jealousy and slowly healed by love, time and the ministrations of a priestess/female analyst (Paulina). The best achievement of the interpretation is to give theatrical cogency to Leontes' jealousy. The first scene is like a white-hued visual aid to the Freudian notion that in childhood lies the source of adult complex. Leontes and his world are seen in a nursery whose equipment is either a slightly larger or slightly warped version of the real. In this Leontes' jealousy becomes psychologically justified. His relationship to Polixenes is based on a pathetically immature failure to realize that growing up destroys both images and innocence. He lives a Peter Pan inner life; his wife, friend and child are almost part of the nursery furniture of which nothing more is expected than that it should continue to perform an unchanging function. Leontes' sudden jealousy is a terrible realization that relationship is a subtle thing—he cannot face it. His descent (superbly counterpointed by the lighting) into the twilight world of mental illness is noted and watched by Paulina. She becomes the main agent in the healing process, standing at his side, prompting him, so to say, to 'talk out' his illness. This relationship is most poignantly maintained by Brenda Bruce.

The more brazen contemporary elements of the production are in the pastoral scenes. Shocked academics have been heard to cry 'out, harrow' at an Autolycus who sings apparent 'pop', at dancers who 'twist' their way through a sheep-shearing ceremony. In fact, it is not simply 'pop'—within the brash sounds there are subtle dying falls; neither is the dancing entirely 'twist'—it has some movement-phrases of great grace, in one of which Perdita looks exquisitely Botticelli-like.

The production is lively, superbly-paced; it intermittently lights up areas of the text with astonishing clarity; yet, one comes away dazzled with interpretation and musing upon what happened to experience. Barrie Ingham, battening his mind upon psychiatry, gives us meaning without melody, exposition without characterization; Judi Dench, with her mind intent upon both Hermione and Perdita, gives us a moving display of her characteristically vulnerable style of movement and facial expression, but falters at the details of character, the nuances of meaning. They both seem engulfed by interpretation.

The penultimate production of the season—*Twelfth Night*—was awaited with interest and perhaps some trepidation, in view of the published announcements that it was to be linked with the last plays. Expectation was utterly confounded. John Barton has created the most visually graceful, most intelligently ordered production of this season. The vast stage area is gone, replaced by an elegant set, resembling an angular tunnel in perspective, but, with its candelabra and suggestion of wattle, redolent of an Elizabethan Hall. Illyria, unlike Bohemia, *is* somewhere. No *musique concrète* or 'pop' astound the air; the aural background to Orsino's part of Illyria is the dim sound of the sea and curlews crying.

Mr Barton has taken his interpretation from the text and not dressed it in contemporary reach-me-up-or-downs. It seems a simple thing to declare that when Shakespeare is allowed to speak to the director, the actors themselves seem to find it easier to 'give' without worrying about how much of Shakespeare they are expected to withhold; yet, on the evidence of *Twelfth Night* this would seem to be almost a law of nature. There is indeed a distinct contrast between the general acting standard of this production and the others of the season—much to the detriment of the latter.

The tone of the interpretation is gravely lyrical. The comedy is an *obbligato* and not a *raison d'être*. Andrew Aguecheek's zaniness is here encased in a Scots accent—a procedure which itself gives a quality of lurking melancholy to the character. His by-play with the bagpipes is stridently funny, but always controlled. This Aguecheek (Barrie Ingham's finest performance at this theatre) is no mere daft gull. His hopeless affection for Olivia is emphasized by pathetic gifts of flowers; his need for friendship, devoid of Toby's commodity, is suggested by his pathetic but curiously dignified appeals in the eyes and his occasional snatching up of the nearest female hand to kiss. Toby Belch is very much the black sheep of a noble family, aware of his precarious station and, indeed, of his alcoholic fecklessness. He spends his time in Illyria on a slippery slope and has much of self-reproach in him. Maria stands, either actually or in spirit, at his side, throughout. She herself, is ageing, left on the shelf; she waits desperately for the word from him, and what she often gets is a dusty answer. The words 'Tis too late to go to bed, now' are spoken to her. Olivia is bewildered and very young, giving the sense that unexpected family responsibility has sapped her youth of the opportunity to learn judgement and, indeed, real love. Orsino broods upon his love with dark melancholic brows. In the end he seizes his chance, not like a covetous and peremptory prince, but like a youngster (a Romeo) who has mewled about ideal love and compromises with a sweet actuality which, unknown to him, is as near to the ideal as he will ever achieve.

Love, of all kinds, gravely finds its own places in Barton's Illyria. Even Viola seems to be part of an inevitability rather than, as is customary, a prime agent in the ordering of Illyria's heart.

Time and time again the production illuminates the text, not only by the intelligent and lyrical speaking and the sharpness with which the wit is observed, but in by-play and the intelligent placing of lines. Malvolio (who, alone, is unsought by the spirit of love and therefore Illyria can have none of him) cannot remove the ring from his finger to give to Viola; 'We three' are hear, speak and see no evil; Viola's hand intermittently pulls her doublet down over her pubic areas with shy fright.

This production is a superb demonstration of the difference between imposed and acquired interpretation. The truth is that, in this case, because the director himself has 'experienced' the text rather than forced it to experience him, we in the audience 'share' the production. This 'sharing' is an important matter. One of the weaknesses of the kind of directorial interpretation which is more imposed upon, than acquired from, the text, is that it often places a gap between audience and realized performance. On a simple level this can be described as a process in which the audience is forced to come to conclusions on matters which do not grow from the text—hence they are sometimes left darkling. On another level, an audience sometimes feels that, after leaving the theatre, something has been 'taken away' rather than 'added to' them. Imposed interpretation almost always diminishes not only the quality of audience experience but also the potency of the play.

Twelfth Night is not the sort of play which induces actors to make the fire bells ring and the horses run. Yet, in Barton's production, because the play is respected, the actors find faith in themselves, and we hear, from them, the sounds of lutes and viols—this is as it should be.

THE YEAR'S CONTRIBUTIONS TO SHAKESPEARIAN STUDY

1. CRITICAL STUDIES

reviewed by G. R. HIBBARD

Good reference books are invaluable. Stanley Wells' *Shakespeare: A Reading Guide*[1] is a model of its kind. Designed to replace the English Association's Pamphlet 61, *A Shakespeare Reference Library*, it contrives, while being of necessity highly selective, to cover an enormous amount of ground in a brief space, listing significant critical writings from the time of Doctor Johnson right down to the year of its appearance. Patrick Murray's *The Shakespearian Scene*[2] is both more restricted and more discursive than Wells' pamphlet. Its avowed purpose is to offer some guidance to the general reader and the student by examining some of the major trends in Shakespearian criticism over the past forty years. Divided into four sections, it comments in a sensible and fair-minded manner on the controversy over character, the interest in imagery, the religious aspect of the plays, and the historical approach to Shakespeare's work. Almost inevitably there is some overlapping, and the dangers of repetition are not avoided. A more serious shortcoming is that the centre of discussion is largely confined to the great tragedies and the problem plays. It is arguable that over the last fifteen years or so it is the emergence of new interpretations of Shakespearian comedy that has proved the most valuable addition to Shakespeare studies, yet the reader will look in vain for the names of Northrop Frye and C. L. Barber, while those of J. R. Brown and Bertrand Evans appear only in the Bibliography.

Like the good reference book, the good general survey is no easy thing to write. *Shakespearian and Other Studies*, by the late F. P. Wilson,[3] will be treasured for two admirable pieces of this sort. Edited by Helen Gardner, it is made up of some previously published essays—notably 'Shakespeare and the Diction of Common Life', 'Shakespeare's Reading', 'The Proverbial Wisdom of Shakespeare' and 'The Elizabethan Theatre'—and two chapters from the volume in the *Oxford History of English Literature* that he did not live to complete. These chapters, on the 'English History Play' and 'Shakespeare's Comedies', are distinguished for their unfailing grasp of essential matters, their wisdom, and the authority that comes from a profound and intimate knowledge of the subject. Never obtrusive yet always present, this knowledge enables Wilson to place Shakespeare's histories within the context not only of the history plays written by other dramatists but also of the writings of the chroniclers, the historiographers, and the pamphleteers of the time. Without tilting at the theories of other critics, he can say with confidence that what Shakespeare does is to present history 'not in terms of political doctrines but of human agents', and assert that 'the dignity and seriousness of purpose apparent in Shakespeare's history plays are in sharp contrast to many of the productions

[1] The English Association, 1969.

[2] Longmans, 1969.

[3] Oxford University Press, 1969.

by other hands'. His treatment of the comedies is equally thorough and illuminating. He sees *Love's Labour's Lost* as marking the point at which Shakespeare begins to find his own unique comic vision, praising it for its 'assured strength of diction and musical phrasing'. Not afraid to say what happens in a particular play or what it is about, he can throw a sudden shaft of new light on it by a shrewd and telling reference to the text. Thus he defines the comparative failure of *The Two Gentlemen of Verona* in a couple of sentences. He writes: 'Never again did [Shakespeare] create a "hero" like Proteus. Launce sums him up in a word: "my master is a kind of knave".'

Another book offering a broad general view is *The World and Art of Shakespeare*, by A. A. Mendilow and Alice Shalvi,[1] both teachers at the Hebrew University of Jerusalem. The first section, by Mendilow, deals with such topics as Shakespeare's life, the theatre that he wrote for, the intellectual climate of the time, and so forth. Much of this is, of course, familiar ground, but it is handled competently and succinctly, though the author seems to think that Shakespeare learnt how to write history plays from Marlowe, ignoring the strong case, so well put by F. P. Wilson, for regarding this as the reverse of what actually happened. The main body of the work is a survey, by Shalvi, of the plays. Here the emphasis falls on the mature comedies, the problem plays, and the great tragedies, with *Timon of Athens* relegated to a mere note. The histories receive much briefer treatment, being shuffled together in one rather conventional chapter; and the same thing happens to the romances. The Sonnets and the Poems are left out of account. The implicit judgement as to what matters most is interesting, but it is hard not to feel that less than justice is done to the achievement of *Henry IV*. The nature of the book leaves little room for originality, but it has the great virtue of being eminently fair. Where there is a wide divergence of critical opinion, both sides of the argument are properly represented. The chapters on *The Merchant of Venice* and on *Hamlet*, which is ingeniously paired with *Titus Andronicus*, are particularly good in this respect. The third and final part, by Mendilow, is devoted to the significance of music both in the plays and in Shakespeare's thinking, leading on to a useful discussion of his use of forms and patterns. *Aspects of Shakespeare*, by Erik Frykman and Göran Kjellmer,[2] is similar in purpose but more limited in scope. Intended primarily for Swedish university students of English, it excludes literary analysis. Frykman provides a section on background matters, including the history of the Tudor period, while Kjellmer deals with the vocabulary, the grammar, and so on.

The range of Glynne Wickham's *Shakespeare's Dramatic Heritage*[3] is well indicated by its sub-title, 'Collected Studies in Mediaeval, Tudor and Shakespearean Drama'. Of the four sections into which it falls, the last will be of most immediate interest to the Shakespearian scholar, since it contains detailed studies of *Richard II*, *A Midsummer Night's Dream*, *Hamlet*, *Macbeth*, *Coriolanus* and *The Winter's Tale*, but it would be a mistake to ignore the earlier part of the book which makes out a strong case for continuity and puts forward some challenging ideas about the origins of secular drama in the Middle Ages. It is, in fact, this preoccupation with the dramatic heritage, together with the author's constant concern for problems of production, that gives a certain unity to what would appear at first sight as a rather miscellaneous collection of essays, several of which have already been published separately. The most impressive of the Shakespearian pieces is that on *Hamlet*, where

[1] Israel Universities Press, Jerusalem, 1967 (distributed by H. A. Humphrey, Ltd).

[2] Almqvist and Wiksell, Stockholm, 1969.

[3] Routledge and Kegan Paul, 1969.

Wickham finds his way into the play by considering the character of the Prince as it presents itself, not to the critic at his desk, but to the actor who has to play the part. He is also pleasingly emphatic about the achievement of *Coriolanus*, and puts forward the exciting suggestion that this play, because of the exacting demands it puts on the acting company, was probably written for some occasion when both halves of the King's Men, the London ensemble and the provincial touring company, were in the City at the same time. In the essays on *The Winter's Tale* and on *Macbeth* it seems to this reviewer that the theory of the medieval heritage is being driven rather hard; but this may well be the reaction that Wickham was looking for, since the work is clearly meant to be provocative in the best kind of way.

Paul N. Siegel goes to work after another fashion; his aim is not to provoke reasoned opposition but to steam-roller it. The assumption on which his collection of essays, *Shakespeare in His Time and Ours*,[1] rests is that informed critics today are cognizant of 'the ideas and expectations of the Elizabethan audience'. It is a large assumption to make at a time when many not altogether uninformed critics are as doubtful of the reality of 'the Elizabethan audience' as they are about the existence of 'the Elizabethan theatre', but it serves to provide some under-pinning for the main argument which is that Shakespeare in his writing was intent on expressing a Christian outlook on life. The chief evidence adduced for this view is that the great tragic figures do not simply die. They are either rewarded in heaven (which is what Siegel maintains happens to Lear) or they are doomed to everlasting damnation (the ultimate fate, in his opinion, of Othello). The 'proof' offered involves some violence to the text, not to mention a dismissal of opposing views that can hardly be said to breathe the spirit of Christian charity. We are told that Lear, at the end of his play, is 'reconciled to the order of things', as though the anguish of the last speech did not exist. We are also informed that the 'picture of himself eternally and agonizedly separated from Desdemona and subject to the tortures of hell which Othello paints in his final speech' is the culmination to the dramatic pattern of the play. In fact, however, the speech in question comes more than fifty lines before the final speech, which is very different in tone. Indeed, Othello's last words and actions are very similar to those of Romeo and Juliet, who also 'die upon a kiss'; but Siegel exempts the two young lovers from the damnation to which he consigns Othello because they are devotees of the Religion of Love. It all seems illogical as well as distinctly repellent.

It is a relief to turn from this kind of dogmatism to the more tentative and sensitive probings of Philip Edwards in his *Shakespeare and the Confines of Art*.[2] Beginning with the sonnets addressed to the Dark Lady and ending with a discussion of *The Two Noble Kinsmen*, this book is an attempt to establish the relationship of the work of art to the material of raw experience, and, in the process, to explore the creative dynamism that led to a continuous series of dramatic experiments extending over a quarter of a century. Edwards' starting point is the observation that men in general have a double attitude both to life and art; one aspect of it is the faith that leads to the heroic view of life, the other the doubt that finds its characteristic expression in burlesque. Shakespeare, he goes on to suggest, had this double vision to an unusual degree; so that the writing of the first sequence of the Sonnets, with their celebration of 'the marriage of true minds', called into being the second sequence, analyzing the moods generated by sheer physical desire. Similarly, when he looks at the comedies, it is what Edwards calls 'the

[1] University of Notre Dame Press, Notre Dame, Indiana, 1968. [2] Methuen, 1968.

minority voice' that catches his interest—the 'unfair' intrusion of the fact of death into the comic world of *Love's Labour's Lost*, the figure of Jaques who rejects the festive ending of *As You Like It*, and the uncomfortable element in *Twelfth Night*. *Hamlet* is presented, in an essay that is all the more effective for its brevity, as a play about action, dramatizing the conflict between the notion that the impulse to act should be obeyed and the contrasting idea that no action should be undertaken before the reasons for it become clear. Dissatisfied with *All's Well That Ends Well* and with *Measure for Measure*, both of which he concludes to be failures, Edwards sees *Troilus and Cressida* as the play in which Shakespeare yielded entirely to the sceptical voice within him, and produced a 'work of art designed to show life before the poetic imagination moulds it into a meaningful shape'. The epic answer to this drama he finds in *Othello* and, above all, in the figure of Desdemona, about whom he writes particularly well. In *Timon of Athens* it is the Poet that he concentrates on, wondering whether he may not reflect certain feelings of Shakespeare's own about the problems that the exercise of his art may have led him into. This, indeed, is one of the most attractive features of the book. Unlike those who rest content with the idea of 'negative capability', Edwards is ready to speculate about Shakespeare the artist, and to relate the plays to what he sees as a developing vision of human life, attained through a continuous process of trial and error.

There is something in common between Edwards' picture of Shakespeare and that which emerges from *Shakespearean Meanings*,[1] by the late Sigurd Burckhardt. Behind this collection of essays, most of which have been published before, there is a consistent attitude and method. Burckhardt's case is that Shakespeare's plays have messages; that these messages are precise; and that the clue to them is close detailed reading, especially of anything that seems at first sight to be odd, unnecessary, or out of place. Starting from an unusual phrase, or an anachronism—the striking clock in *Julius Caesar*, for example—he finds his way to the heart of the play he is dealing with. The Shakespeare he presents is one who was ready at all times to expose himself to the disorder of reality, of the raw material of experience, but who was equally prepared to fight his way, as it were, through this disorder to the apprehension of some new kind of order created by the poet out of the flux. At times the intense concentration on the word and its ambiguities can lead to some eccentricity, as when the 'wand'ring bark' in Sonnet 116 is taken to refer, among other things, to the barking of a dog, but more often it results in new insights, particularly where the political plays are concerned. For Burckhardt, *King John* and the plays of the second tetralogy ask the questions that Tudor political theory failed to ask, and, in so far as they offer any answers, these answers are pragmatic not orthodox. Nor is it only the political plays that yield to the method; perhaps the finest of these subtle and discriminating essays is '*King Lear*: The Quality of Nothing', where the differing reactions of Lear and Gloucester to the word 'nothing' are made the basis for a careful distinction between the two characters and their roles.

As long ago as 1938 Derek Traversi published his *Approach to Shakespeare*. It was a short stimulating book, concerning itself almost entirely with the plays written after 1600, to which the earlier work was regarded as preparatory, and it worked from a careful consideration of the verbal texture. Since then he has written a study of the romances, another dealing with the second tetralogy of the histories, and a third on the Roman plays. Now comes *An Approach to Shakespeare*,[2] surveying

[1] Princeton University Press, Princeton, New Jersey, 1968.

[2] Hollis and Carter, 1968.

the entire *oeuvre*, apart from the narrative poems and *Henry VIII*. This reproduces the body of the original book substantially as it stood, conflates the findings of the other two works, and adds new material on the earlier plays, *All's Well That Ends Well*, and *Timon of Athens*. The author states in his Introduction that he has sought to take advantage of new kinds of thinking that have grown up since 1938, and in particular that he has worked with the requirements of Shakespeare's theatre very much in mind. In fact, however, there are few marks of this re-orientation in the book itself. It is still the verbal texture that is at the centre of Traversi's thinking, and the attitude taken towards the early work has not changed in any radical way. There are obvious gains in having his criticism brought together, but it seems a pity that he has not made more use of the best work that has been done since 1938 and that the old error about the date of Montemayor's *Diana* (Vol. I, p. 90) has not been put right.

Wolfgang Clemen has brought together five of his lectures and essays in a volume entitled *Das Drama Shakespeares*,[1] including 'Schein und Sein bei Shakespeare' (1957), an essay that makes the useful distinction between the comedies, where the difference between seeming and being is usually obvious, and the tragedies, where it is by no means so easy to see and has disastrous consequences. Seeking to account for the fact that Shakespeare is, above all others, the international author, T. J. B. Spencer[2] attributes his capacity to please men everywhere to his intellectual agility, his concern with basic human experience, his verbal skill, and his sense of theatre. Moreover, there is, Spencer thinks, the attraction that he is not our contemporary. Harold Fisch comes to a not dissimilar conclusion in his article 'Shakespeare and "The Theatre of the World"',[3] where he advances the thesis that the stage metaphors in the plays, which have aroused so much attention in recent years, suggest 'the infinite meaningfulness and reality of life', as well as something of its illusory nature. Hardin Craig, too, emphasizes Shakespeare's closeness to life in 'Shakespeare and the All-inclusive Law of Nature',[4] arguing that he and Marlowe thought of drama as a natural thing concerned with the telling of the truth, whereas for Ben Jonson it was an artifact. In an address given to the Deutsche Shakespeare-Gesellschaft Josef Frings[5] looks at Shakespeare's work in relation to the Platonic triad of the True, the Good, and the Beautiful, concluding that the dramatist's main concern was with the truth about man; that his general outlook was moral rather than religious; and that his mastery of language endows all that he touches with grace. In a more technical article[6] Rolf Soellner relates Shakespeare's use of the word 'soul' to the complex notions about the relation between body and soul at the time when he was writing, and then applies his findings to an analysis of what happens in *King Lear*. The gist of Donald Neil Friesner's article about Shakespeare's politics is adequately represented by its title, 'William Shakespeare, Conservative'.[7] Taking up the question of Shakespeare's anachronisms, Anselm Schlösser[8] decides that they are, in the main, functional devices, serving to connect

1 Vandenhoeck und Ruprecht, Göttingen, 1969.

2 'Shakespeare the International Author', *The Future of the Modern Humanities*, ed. J. C. Laidlaw (The Modern Humanities Research Association, Cambridge, 1969), pp. 31–50.

3 *The Morality of Art*, ed. D. W. Jefferson (Routledge and Kegan Paul, 1969), pp. 76–86.

4 *Studies in Honor of DeWitt T. Starnes*, ed. Thomas P. Harrison, James Sledd, *et al.* (The University of Texas Press, Austin, 1967), pp. 77–87.

5 'Ansprache zur Jahrestagung der Gesellschaft', *Deutsche Shakespeare-Gesellschaft West Jahrbuch* (1968), pp. 9–12.

6 'Shakespeare, Aristotle, Plato, and the Soul', *ibid.*, pp. 56–71.

7 *Shakespeare Quarterly*, XX (1969), 165–78.

8 'Zur Bedeutung der Anachronismen bei Shakespeare', *Shakespeare Jahrbuch*, CV (1969), 7–24.

events in the past with the living present; and Armin-Gerd Kuckhoff[1] holds that the tension in the plays between accident—which is never pure accident—and necessity is an essential part of their meaning. Another antithesis which Shakespeare explores and exploits, that between tears and laughter, has caught the eye of Werner Habicht who works out some of its implications in his 'With an Auspicious and a Dropping Eye. Antithetische Mimik in Shakespeares Dramen.'[2]

Shakespeare's Early Tragedies, by Nicholas Brooke,[3] is a consistently fresh and lively piece of thinking. It springs from the conviction that many critics are far too prone to pontificate about 'pure' tragedy, basing their conception of it on the work of Shakespeare's maturity, and then to complete the circular process of argument by dismissing the early tragedies that he wrote as prentice-work. Brooke prefers to look at each play for what it is in itself, with the result that for him the variety of Shakespeare's achievement in the tragic mode is more impressive than the development of the tragic sense about which so much has been written already. The plays he deals with are *Titus Andronicus*, *Richard III*, *Romeo and Juliet*, *Richard II*, *Julius Caesar* and *Hamlet*. In the light of what he makes of them it seems a pity that he did not choose to bring in *3 Henry VI* as well. Opposed though he is to theorizing and generalization, Brooke nevertheless has a method of going to work. At the back of what he says lies the conviction that Shakespeare's tragedies are essentially poetic dramas, and that an excessive preoccupation with 'character' on the part of the critic can be very misleading. This does not mean, however, that his central interest is in imagery. What he concentrates on far more is the style, or rather the varieties of style, that Shakespeare employs in a particular play. It is through the contrasts of style which he perceives that he reaches his critical conclusions. Setting the formal rhetoric of the rest of *Richard III* against the lively individualized speech of Richard himself, he is led to the view that the drama is paradoxical in that Richard the villain emerges as something like the tragic hero, because he is the one character who fights against the divinely sanctioned yet nevertheless mechanical movement of history. Similarly, the rhetorical strength of Richard II's utterance in the early scenes is used as an effective counter to the notion of the King as a kind of ineffectual poet. In fact, the general conclusion Brooke seems to be moving towards is that all the plays he treats of are deeply ambiguous. He goes so far as to criticize the endings of *Julius Caesar* and *Hamlet*, because they emphasize the more positive side of the vision the plays themselves present—especially the idea of nobility—at the expense of that more sceptical view of the events portrayed in them which is so evident in both tragedies. In so far as any generalization can be drawn from a book that sedulously avoids it, it would seem to be that these plays portray a conflict between a divine order on the one hand and man's imperfections, which make that order unobtainable on earth, on the other.

In 'The First Step of a Giant'[4] Todor T. Kirov examines the imagery of the four earliest comedies, *Henry VI*, *Titus Andronicus*, and the Sonnets. His finding is that in general the images in these works lie on the euphuistic plane of thought and lack human substance, but that in *Henry VI* Shakespeare's response to the situations created and to the characters of York and Richard endows them with more depth and vigour. Taking *Titus Andronicus* as wholly Shakespeare's and dating it about 1589, Anselm Schlösser[5] sees Aaron as an adumbra-

[1] 'Zufall und Notwendigkeit in Drama William Shakespeares', *ibid.*, 121–39.

[2] *Anglia*, LXXXVII (1969), 147–66.

[3] Methuen, 1968.

[4] *Shakespeare Jahrbuch*, CIV (1968), 109–40.

[5] '*Titus Andronicus*', *ibid.* 75–84.

tion of Richard III and points to elements in it that will recur, in various forms, in some of the subsequent works. Ruth Nevo's 'Tragic Form in *Romeo and Juliet*'[1] is a good essay putting forward the idea that the play embodies two traditional views of tragedy, the providential and the fatal, yet avoids falling into either category, because of its central concern with the concrete fact of the love relationship. The fencing match in the play is the subject of a technical article by Adolph L. Soens[2] who thinks that Tybalt fights in the Spanish style and Mercutio in the Italian.

Apart from the splendid essay by F. P. Wilson that has already been mentioned, the main work on the comedies has taken the form of articles on specific points and issues. T. W. Baldwin[3] draws attention to two jests in *The Comedy of Errors* which were also used in the Marprelate Controversy; and Anne C. Lancashire[4] adds to his comments on 'Respice Finem: Respice Funem' by offering evidence that 'rope' could mean 'penis'. Writing on 'The Structural Unity of *Two Gentlemen of Verona*'[5] William Leigh Godshalk suggests that the use of classical myth, of love letters, and of journeys in the play serves to give it artistic cohesion.

Peter Alexander's 'The Original Ending of *The Taming of the Shrew*'[6] is a fascinating mixture of literary and textual criticism, arguing in a most persuasive manner that the final scene in the pirated *A Shrew*, where Sly wakes and goes off to tame his wife, preserves an essential part of Shakespeare's original design that has disappeared from the text of *The Shrew*, though the exchanges between Sly and the 'Lady' at the end of Act I, scene i, which were part of the same design, were accidentally allowed to stand in the manuscript handed to Jaggard for the printing of the Folio.

'Pattern in *Love's Labour's Lost*',[7] by William Leigh Godshalk, dwells mainly on those elements in the play that serve to break up its ordered symmetry; while J. Hasler points to the use of repetition and enumeration in it.[8] In his 'Berowne and the Progress of *Love's Labour's Lost*'[9] Gates K. Agnew sets out to show how this comedy achieves its peculiar effect by constantly flouting expectation, but the demonstration becomes so lengthy and involved that nothing clear-cut emerges from it.

Taking up the question of how 'the sweet witty soul of Ovid lives in mellifluous and honey-tongued Shakespeare', Dietrich Klose, in his 'Shakespeare und Ovid',[10] picks out Holofernes' words about 'the golden cadence of poetry' as the key to Ovid's appeal for Shakespeare, and then moves on to a valuable discussion of the close relationship between *A Midsummer Night's Dream* and the *Metamorphoses*. Robert Weimann's lecture, 'Puck und Ariel: Mythos und Poetische Fantasie'[11] ranges widely but comes back to the same starting point. As he sees it, the two figures have their origins in a union of popular belief and classical myth, especially as transmitted by Ovid. The element of terror and nightmare in the comedy is studied in Michael Taylor's 'The Darker Purpose of *A Midsummer Night's Dream*';[12] and Roger Warren's 'Three

1 *Studies in English Literature*, IX (1969), 241–58.

2 'Tybalt's Spanish Fencing in *Romeo and Juliet*', *Shakespeare Quarterly*, XX (1969), 121–7.

3 '*Errors* and Marprelate', *Studies in Honor of DeWitt T. Starnes*, pp. 9–23.

4 'Lyly and Shakespeare on the Ropes', *JEGP*, LXVIII (1969), 237–44.

5 *Studies in Philology*, LXVI (1969), 168–81.

6 *Shakespeare Quarterly*, XX (1969), 111–16.

7 *Renaissance Papers 1968*, pp. 41–8.

8 'Enumeration in *Love's Labour's Lost*', *English Studies*, L (1969), 176–85.

9 *Shakespeare Studies*, IV (1968), 40–72.

10 *Deutsche Shakespeare-Gesellschaft West Jahrbuch* (1968), pp. 72–93.

11 *Shakespeare Jahrbuch*, CIV (1968), 17–33.

12 *Studies in English Literature*, IX (1969), 259–73.

Notes on *A Midsummer Night's Dream*'[1] are helpful and very much to the point.

The Merchant of Venice continues to be something of a critical battleground. Marvin Felheim[2] notes that the melancholy of the play does not touch Bassanio, proceeds to develop the familiar notion of contrast as the basis of the action, and concludes that the unifying element is Shakespeare's realism. Alan Holaday, on the other hand, regards it as an allegory based on the metaphor of the Parliament in Heaven, and entitles his essay on it 'Antonio and the Allegory of Salvation'.[3] 'Shakespeare's Caskets: Unity in *The Merchant of Venice*',[4] by Herbert S. Donow, takes the line that the love of Portia, not the bond, is the central issue; but John P. Sisk, writing on 'Bondage and Release in *The Merchant of Venice*',[5] interprets the drama as a conflict between bonds that are good (that which binds Antonio to Bassanio, for instance) and bonds that are bad (that with which Shylock binds Antonio). Finally, Herbert Bronstein observes that Shakespeare's Jew is literary and traditional, not the product of first-hand knowledge, but he then goes on to argue, in 'Shakespeare, the Jews, and *The Merchant of Venice*',[6] that the playwright found it impossible to rest content with the literary stereotype.

In an essay entitled 'Love, Appearance and Reality: Much Ado about Something'[7] B. K. Lewalski advances the theory that *Much Ado*, underneath its surface gaiety, is essentially Neoplatonic in that it deals with different levels of love in the terms made familiar by Bembo's discourse in the fourth book of *The Courtier*. Discussing the significance of the wounded stag in *As You Like It*, Claus Uhlig contends, in 'Der weinende Hirsch: *As You Like It*, II, i, 21–66, und der historische Kontext',[8] that critics have been on the wrong track in looking for a pictorial emblem as the source of the scene, and that they are equally mistaken in relating it to emblems dealing with unrequited love. The theme is the cruel inhumanity of the chase, as described by humanists such as More and Erasmus. Not satisfied with the notion that love at first sight and sudden conversion are merely theatrical conventions, Sylvan Barnet sets out to demonstrate that the improbabilities of *As You Like It* are an important part of its meaning. His article, '"Strange Events": Improbability in *As You Like It*',[9] draws attention to the fact that Shakespeare makes Lodge's tale even more unlikely than it was, and deduces that in this comedy Shakespeare is much concerned with conversion and with things absurd to reason. The ambiguities inherent in 'what is' and 'what is not', so well exploited by Feste, provide the basis for Walter N. King's 'Shakespeare and Parmenides: The Metaphysics of *Twelfth Night*',[10] a piece that would, no doubt, have given much pleasure to the old hermit of Prague.

There have been two general books about the histories. H. M. Richmond's *Shakespeare's Political Plays*[11] deals with all of them, except for *Henry VIII*, and with *Julius Caesar* and *Coriolanus* as well. Unfortunately, the justification for the book is not evident. No attempt is made, despite the affirmation in the Preface that commentators have paid too little attention to Shakespeare's political intelligence and have failed to see that he was a 'subtle political philosopher' (there is significantly no mention of the writings of L. C. Knights in the list of books for Further Reading), to relate his

[1] *Notes and Queries*, N.S., XVI (1969), 130–4.

[2] '*The Merchant of Venice*', *Shakespeare Studies*, IV (1968), 94–108.

[3] *Ibid.*, 109–18. [4] *Ibid.*, 86–93.

[5] *Shakespeare Quarterly*, XX (1969), 217–23.

[6] *Ibid.*, 3–10.

[7] *Studies in English Literature*, VIII (1968), 235–51.

[8] *Deutsche Shakespeare-Gesellschaft West Jahrbuch* (1968), pp. 141–68.

[9] *Shakespeare Studies*, IV (1968), 119–31.

[10] *Studies in English Literature*, VIII (1968), 283–306.

[11] Random House, New York, 1967.

political ideas to those of his contemporaries. In so far as the book has a thesis, it amounts to no more than the comfortable assumption that Shakespeare had an instinctive sense that English society has always tended to be evolutionary rather than revolutionary, and that he was therefore something of a pragmatist, sharing many of the ideas of Machiavelli and Hobbes. In fact, the author does not appear to have much interest in political ideas as such, and nowhere does he seek to define what Shakespeare's conception of the state and its function was. Instead, he gives some rather impressionistic views about what each play is doing, committing himself in the process to such curious *apercus* as that *Henry IV* is in many ways 'a return to the symbolic methods of *Richard III* after the comparative realism of *Richard II*'. The possibility that *Henry IV*, in its depiction of the life of the people, may be a radically new kind of history does not seem to occur to him, because he concentrates on the relationships between the big figures, following in the footsteps of Dover Wilson. In the process he writes well about Hotspur, but sadly reduces the stature of Falstaff who appears at one point (p. 149), in what looks very like a Freudian slip, as Flagstaff.

Both the title of James Winny's *The Player King*[1] and the dust-jacket give the impression that Richard III is to figure largely in it. In fact he does not. The main subject of this book is the second tetralogy, not the first, though Winny himself would probably object to the use of the word 'tetralogy', since part of his thesis is that the plays are not linked with each other in the manner suggested by Tillyard and others. Insisting that they are 'essentially imaginative in character', he prefers to see them as so many disparate dramatic essays, bound together by a common interest in the image of the King as an actor called on to fulfil a role on the stage of life. Richard II is the legitimate King who has not the personal qualities that his part demands of him. Henry IV is better equipped in this respect, but he has no right to the throne, with the result that his reign becomes a hollow performance. Henry V has both the right and the personal qualities, but, intermittently, the play begins to question the value and even the validity of the act that he carries through with such an appearance of panache. That this is indeed part of what these plays are about few would deny. Una Ellis-Fermor said it all in a much more succinct fashion some twenty-five years ago in Chapter III of her *The Frontiers of Drama* (1945). But the plays are also concerned with the state of England and with the need for good government. To deny that they have any political content of the kind that Tillyard finds in them is to reduce their richness. Similarly, by hammering away too insistently at the ironies of *Henry IV* Winny misses the spontaneous delight in the variety of human beings and of human behaviour which is one of its most compelling characteristics. He is right to stress the imaginative nature of the histories, but here, as in his book on the Sonnets to be noticed later, he seems to be in danger of under-rating the extent to which the imagination is dependent on, and can be stimulated by, the raw material of experience.

'The World of *Richard III*',[2] by A. L. French, argues that the play is not a straightforward moral history and seeks to demonstrate some of its ambiguities by concentrating on the character and the role of Stanley. In 'The Troublesome Ending of *King John*'[3] Gunnar Boklund suggests that while the play is dominated by the idea of commodity, the young people in it offer some kind of alternative to self-interest. Nevertheless, the partial solution is the result of Pandulph's activities, not of divine intervention, and, in these

[1] Chatto and Windus, 1968.
[2] *Shakespeare Studies*, IV (1968), 25–39.
[3] *Studia Neophilologica*, XL (1968), 175–84.

circumstances, the final speech is somewhat questionable, since commodity remains the guiding principle of political action.

Robert Rentoul Reed, Jr has written an admirable monograph, *Richard II: From Mask to Prophet*,[1] that restricts itself to Shakespeare's portrayal of the King, who is, Reed holds, the first of the tragic heroes to look forward to Hamlet and Lear. The work falls into four parts. In the first it is suggested that because Shakespeare relied primarily on Holinshed he had to make the reason for Richard's failure to meet the challenge of Bolingbroke psychological. The second and most interesting chapter deals with the problem of divine right which, it is argued, Richard has to begin with but then forfeits by his failure to act justly. Turning to the psychology of the King, Reed puts a good case for his suffering from a form of psychosis that leads him to indulge in self-pity when he discovers that he has lost the love of his subjects by which he set such store. But this is not the end of the story. Behind the arrogant public figure there is a kindly loving private man who comes into his own when the public persona is destroyed. Richard the man arrives at a genuine knowledge of himself and of his position, so that at the end he is capable of winning a spiritual victory over his materially successful but morally bankrupt rival. In marked contrast to the careful thinking that informs Reed's study, A. Norman Jeffares[2] states magisterially that 'the play is essentially a study of Richard's character', but offers no proof beyond a singularly tedious and pedestrian recapitulation of the action, scene by scene. 'History and Tragedy in *Richard II*', by John R. Elliott, Jr,[3] examines the play with a view to discovering whether it has a political or historical purpose, and, if it has, whether this purpose affects the dramatic structure. He decides that the play is political, because its end is not concerned solely with Richard, as it would be, he says, conveniently ignoring the endings of the major tragedies, if the play were a tragedy. 'The Dimension of Time in *Richard II*', by Robert L. Montgomery, Jr,[4] leads to the conclusion that the references to time in the play serve to illuminate the situations of the characters, and especially of the King who comes to see himself clearly by thinking of himself in relation to time.

'Wingless Victory: Michelangelo, Shakespeare, and the "Old Man"'[5] is a fascinating work that opens up fresh areas of thinking. The thesis advanced by Lawrence J. Ross is that Michelangelo's statue and Shakespeare's *Henry IV* both illustrate, in their different ways, 'the collision of medieval Christianity with the Renaissance'. For Saint Paul 'the old man' is an image of unregenerate human nature; therefore Michelangelo's 'Victory' offers a unified image of the soul's terrestrial state as the Neoplatonists thought of it, striving upwards yet still attached to the material world. Similarly, the author finds elements of 'the old man', probably derived from the morality tradition, in Falstaff. But in *Henry IV*, as in the sculpture, there is nothing simple and clear-cut about the relationship between the Young Man and the Old Man. Working at a less exalted level, Alan Gerald Gross[6] argues that through both parts of *Henry IV* Hal shows a moral stability which fits him for the task of government, and George Walton Williams writes 'Some Notes on

1 Pennsylvania State University, University Park, Pennsylvania, 1968.

2 'In One Person Many People: *King Richard the Second*', *The Morality of Art*, pp. 50–66.

3 *Studies in English Literature*, VIII (1968), 253–71.

4 *Shakespeare Studies*, IV (1968), 73–85.

5 *Literary Monographs*, Vol. 2, ed. Eric Rothstein and Richard N. Ringler (University of Wisconsin Press, Madison, Milwaukee, and London, 1969), pp. 3–56.

6 'The Justification of Prince Hal', *Texas Studies in Literature and Language*, X (1968), 27–35.

Shakespeare's *Henry IV*',[1] demonstrating the artistic economy of Part I.

Charles Barber's 'Prince Hal, Henry V, and the Tudor Monarchy'[2] relates the plays dealing with the Prince to the conflict of medieval and capitalist values that was emerging during Queen Elizabeth's later years. He holds that Hal, like Elizabeth, tries to strike a balance between old-fashioned chivalry (Hotspur) and new cynicism (Falstaff). *Henry V* he takes to be an uncritical glorification of the Tudor monarchy. Elsa Sjoberg is also interested in the continuity of these plays. Her essay, 'From Madcap Prince to King: The Evolution of Prince Hal',[3] is designed to demonstrate that any change in the Prince is merely outward. His inner purpose remains constant, and he always knows how to act when the time for action comes. It is precisely this idea that Thomas H. Jameson cannot tolerate. Vigorously rebutting all suggestions that the Prince of *Henry IV* shows any proclivities for Machiavellianism, he finds it impossible to reconcile this figure with the bellicose patriotic king of *Henry V*. The solution for this dilemma which he proposes in *The Hidden Shakespeare*[4] is that *Henry V* is not the play that Shakespeare would have written had he been left to his own devices. It is, instead, his response to the censorship that was being exercised around 1599. He writes a 'safe' play, at least on the surface, but his treatment of his subject, making it a travesty of what it should have been, expresses his contempt for the received ideas of the time. The Shakespeare presented in this lively, though somewhat erratic book, is a subversive artist engaged, to quote part of the sub-title, in 'Undercover Activity in the Theatre'. Marilyn L. Williamson, on the other hand, thinks that 'The Episode with Williams in *Henry V*'[5] serves as a reminder, particularly in the way that it ends, that something of the wild prince of Eastcheap still survives in the King at Agincourt; and Robert L. Kelly[6] asserts that the King's condemnation of his 'bedfellow' shows his political insight and maturity, since the record of the entire Scroop family, as depicted in *Richard II* and *Henry IV*, is a treacherous one. The dispute about the play and about the character of the King is, of course, an old one. Taking note of this fact, C. H. Hobday, in his 'Imagery and Irony in *Henry V*',[7] comes to the reasonable conclusion that the division among critics corresponds to a division in Shakespeare's own mind. Called on to present Henry as a hero, he took refuge, Hobday thinks, in irony, juxtaposing honour and religion with greed and cruelty.

Geoffrey Brereton's *Principles of Tragedy*[8] is a wide-ranging, clear, yet undogmatic attempt to make, in the words of its sub-title, 'A Rational Examination of the Tragic Concept in Life and Literature'. Starting from an analysis of the manner in which the word 'tragic' is employed in daily use, the author moves on, by way of Aristotle, to a consideration of *Oedipus*, *Hamlet*, *Macbeth*, and *Phèdre*. The negative conclusions this leads to are: that there is no fixed pattern of interaction between the hero and the community he belongs to; that none of the actions can be reduced to the simple idea of retribution; and that the tragic situation need not necessarily include any problem of choice. What the four plays do have in common is an individual hero and a deep concern with power, whether external in the shape of the gods or Fate, or internal in the form of innate drives and passions, as it exerts its effect on the hero. Above all, this

1 *Renaissance Papers 1969*, pp. 49–53.
2 *The Morality of Art*, pp. 67–75.
3 *Shakespeare Quarterly*, XX (1969), 11–16.
4 Funk and Wagnalls, New York, 1969.
5 *Studies in English Literature*, IX (1969), 275–82.
6 'Shakespeare's Scroops and the "Spirit of Cain"', *Shakespeare Quarterly*, XX (1969), 71–80.
7 *Shakespeare Survey 21* (1968), 107–14.
8 Routledge and Kegan Paul, 1968.

concern always takes the form of a moral exploration, not a moral demonstration. Brereton does not stop at the seventeenth century; he carries his analysis through, by way of selected examples, to the present day. Refreshingly sceptical about the large abstractions, such as 'the tragic view of life' and the sacrificial theory, he is, nonetheless, ready to risk generalizations of his own. As befits 'A Rational Examination', the whole book is characterized by good sense, but the method followed leaves no scope for any consideration of the language of tragedy, which seems a pity. The relevance of Aristotle is also emphasized by Matthew W. Black in his 'Aristotle's Mythos and the Tragedies of Shakespeare'.[1] He bases his interpretation of *The Poetics* on Gerald F. Else's *Aristotle's Poetics: The Argument* (1957), where *hamartia* is taken to be 'an ignorance or mistake as to certain details... pregnant with disaster for the hero' and *catharsis* is defined as 'the purification of the hero from his guilt, not the purification of the audience'. With the key terms given these meanings, the convergence between Greek theory and Shakespearian practice becomes much closer than it has been hitherto. Fredson Bowers, however, taking *hamartia* to be a critical error of judgement, differentiates, in his 'Death in Victory: Shakespeare's Tragic Reconciliations',[2] between Greek tragedy, where the hero repeats his initial mistake, and Shakespearian tragedy, where he comes to see its true nature, either before or at the moment of catastrophe, and thus succeeds in reconciling his will to God's purpose. Resting his case largely on a reading of *Hamlet*, Bowers affirms that the killing of Polonius is the turning point in the play, and states, with a confidence that not all would wish to imitate: 'Without question this error is Hamlet's alienation from Heaven by his inability to wait upon a non-criminal revenge that God would in due course have arranged for His minister.' It is exactly this kind of dogmatism that Roland Mushat Frye attacks in 'Theological and Non-theological Structures in Tragedy',[3] where he compares *Doctor Faustus* with *Macbeth* to make the point that Marlowe's play is explicitly theological both in its terms of reference and in its structure, whereas Shakespeare's play is not. The line of thought opened up by D. J. Gordon with his 'Name and Fame: Shakespeare's Coriolanus' (1964) is pursued further by Manfred Weidhorn in 'The Relation of Title and Name to Identity in Shakespearean Tragedy';[4] and Matthew N. Proser's *The Heroic Image in Five Shakespearean Tragedies* (1965), which was reviewed in *Shakespeare Survey 20*, is now available in paperback form.[5]

Leonard F. Dean has brought together a useful, if somewhat bitty, anthology of modern criticism in his *Twentieth Century Interpretations of 'Julius Caesar'*.[6] The editorial Introduction strikes a rather jarring note in its jaunty effort to be up-to-date, but the selection of essays and parts of essays is sensible, representative, and, on occasions, entertaining, as when Leo Kirschbaum clashes head-on with Mark Van Doren. In '*Julius Caesar*: An Experiment in Point of View'[7] Rene E. Fortin, developing an idea put forward by Ernest Schanzer, argues that the play is a dramatization of the notion that truth cannot be objective. Two critics consider the part that the assumption of roles plays in this tragedy. J. L. Simmons[8] thinks that the use of

1 *Deutsche Shakespeare-Gesellschaft West Jahrbuch* (1968), pp. 43–55.

2 *Studies in Honor of DeWitt T. Starnes*, pp. 53–75.

3 *Shakespeare Studies*, IV, (1968), 132–48.

4 *Studies in English Literature*, IX (1969), 303–19.

5 Princeton University Press, Princeton, New Jersey, 1965.

6 Prentice-Hall, Englewood Cliffs, N.J., 1968.

7 *Shakespeare Quarterly*, XIX (1968), 341–7.

8 'Shakespeare's *Julius Caesar*: The Roman Actor and the Man', *Tulane Studies in English*, XVI (1968), 1–28.

theatre imagery is a means of conveying Shakespeare's sense that the actor on the stage of the world is another being from the same man in private life; and John W. Velz, in his '"If I Were Brutus Now...": Role-playing in *Julius Caesar*',[1] regards the characters' adoption of roles as a structural element that helps to give unity to the whole. Antony's speech in the Forum scene is analyzed by Eduard Kurke, who sees it as a turning point in the development of Shakespeare's dramatic art, because, as he puts it in 'Zur Darstellung von Redner und Rede in Shakespeares Dramen',[2] it is here that the playwright, like his Antony, abandons cultivated artifice for rhetoric that is truly part of the play's action.

Fully aware of the differences between a tragedy and a poetical discourse on ethical and philosophical problems, Alur Janaki Ram points, with proper precautions, to some striking parallels between the situation of Hamlet, called on to avenge his father, and that of Arjuna, faced with the demands of an exacting warrior code which entail the shedding of his kinsmen's blood. The idea he arrives at in 'Arjuna and Hamlet: The Moral Dilemmas'[3] is that in the end both heroes come to submit themselves to the cosmic will in a sober acceptance of the human condition, where any action to secure justice brings with it involvement in guilt. Keith Brown, writing about 'Moral Quality and Moral Content',[4] uses *Hamlet* as the test case for his theory, mainly derived from Bradley, that the moral quality of tragedy comes to us through the patterning, and is exploratory rather than explicit, thus agreeing, without knowing it, with Geoffrey Brereton. This position does not, however, satisfy Herbert Randolph Coursen, Jr, whose monograph, 'The Rarer Action: Hamlet's Mousetrap',[5] comes very close to expressing the wish that Shakespeare had made a different play of *Hamlet*. Taking *The Tempest* as Shakespeare's last word on revenge, he tries to look at *Hamlet* in the light of it. Essentially the argument amounts to the assertion that the Prince by stopping the play-within-the-play—does he stop it or merely interrupt it?—prevents it from having its full effect on the conscience of the King and causing him to reveal his guilt in public. Quite apart from the fact that no theatre audience, surely, has ever envisaged this possibility, because it is not what Hamlet has asked them to look for, the Prayer scene which, according to Coursen, shows that Claudius' character is susceptible to open confession, has precisely the opposite effect, since it reveals unequivocally that repentance and the giving-up of the crown are actions of which the King is incapable. Difficulties of this kind are, however, ignored or glossed over, because Coursen wants the tragedy to be more explicitly Christian than it is, and to demonstrate 'what can happen to a supremely gifted man who ignores the way offered by "our Saviour"'. Myron Taylor's 'Tragic Justice and the House of Polonius'[6] maintains that the hand of Providence is clearly visible in the fate of Polonius and his family, all of whom thoroughly deserve the retribution that comes to them, including poor Ophelia who is guilty of living in a 'moral vacuum'; critics can be harsh. For a long time Clifford Leech has been interested in the influence of Marlowe on Shakespeare. Now, in 'The Hesitation of Pyrrhus',[7] he argues that the Pyrrhus speech is a piece of pastiche, recalling an earlier manner without showing contempt for it, whereas the mode adopted in 'The Murder of Gonzago' is deliberate burlesque. He then proceeds to

1 *Shakespeare Studies*, IV (1968), 149–59.

2 *Shakespeare Jahrbuch*, CIV (1968), 175–91.

3 *Philosophy East and West (Hawaii)*, XVIII (1968), 11–28.

4 *English Studies*, L (1969), 248–54.

5 *Literary Monographs*, Vol. 2, pp. 59–97.

6 *Studies in English Literature*, VIII (1968), 273–81.

7 *The Morality of Art*, pp. 41–9.

relate the situation of Pyrrhus, who has a father to avenge, with that of the Prince. 'Hamlet's Place on the Map',[1] by Keith Brown, is an unusual and interesting piece of work. It seeks to demonstrate that Shakespeare, when he wrote his tragedy, was familiar with maps which made Denmark the centre of Northern Europe. This central position may well have contributed, it is claimed, both to the play's claustrophobic atmosphere and to the awareness shown in it of places outside Denmark. 'Der französische *Hamlet* des Marquis d'Argens (1744)'[2] is praised by Hans Mattauch for coming nearer to the sense and feel of the passages it translates than any other French version of the eighteenth or early nineteenth century.

Critics of *Troilus and Cressida* have been much occupied with its stylistic peculiarities. Patricia Thomson's 'Rant and Cant in *Troilus and Cressida*'[3] rests on the premise that the Elizabethans, less sceptical about rhetoric than we are, were very much aware of its tendency to run to the excessive on the one hand and the trite on the other. Her case is that much that is said in the play, especially by and about the lovers, is either excessive or platitudinous, and would have been recognized as such. Working along a parallel line in 'Language, Style, and Meaning in *Troilus and Cressida*',[4] T. McAlindon thinks that the characters offend against decorum by losing the style appropriate to their traditional reputations, and that these stylistic dissonances are meant to endorse the play's preoccupation with chaos, inadequacy, and disorder. As Katherine Stockholder views it, in her 'Power and Pleasure in *Troilus and Cressida*, Rhetoric and Structure of the Anti-Tragic',[5] the characters employ rhetoric only for their self-glorification, not for the common cause. She argues further that Shakespeare raises expectations by means of an action that suggests irrevocable consequences, but then negates them by depicting figures whose sole concern is with the immediate present. Her verdict that there is a deep cleavage between thought and action is fully endorsed by Arnold Stein, whose '*Troilus and Cressida*: The Disjunctive Imagination'[6] concentrates on the gross discrepancy in the play between what is said and planned and what is actually done. Stein finds that the play engages the mind but not the feelings. It comes nearer to tragedy than to anything else, but it is not tragic, since it ensures that we remain detached from it. August Rüegg, however, after trying to determine what had happened to the spirit of Homer's epic by the time that Shakespeare wrote his play, comes to the conclusion of his 'Homerisches und Unhomerisches in Shakespeare's *Troilus und Cressida*'[7] with the firm conviction that the drama can only be explained as an outright parody of Homer's epic, of the chivalric poems of the Middle Ages, and of war and war poetry in general. Looking at it from another angle in her 'Bemerkungen zu Shakespeares *Troilus and Cressida*',[8] Dorothea Siegmund-Schultze sees it as a manifestation of the spiritual and intellectual crisis of the early seventeenth century; and W. W. Bernhardt, after discussing what Dryden did to Shakespeare's play, ends his 'Shakespeare's *Troilus and Cressida* and Dryden's *Truth Found Too Late*'[9] by presenting his own view of Shakespeare's Troilus as an 'adolescent hero', whose language expresses his confused state of mind and his capacity for deluding himself.

[1] *Shakespeare Studies*, IV (1968), 160–82.

[2] *Deutsche Shakespeare-Gesellschaft West Jahrbuch* (1968), pp. 179–92.

[3] *Essays and Studies*, XXII (1969), 33–56.

[4] *PMLA*, LXXXIV (1969), 29–43.

[5] *College English*, XXX (1968–9), 539–54.

[6] *ELH*, XXXVI (1969), 145–67.

[7] *Deutsche Shakespeare-Gesellschaft West Jahrbuch* (1968), pp. 28–42.

[8] *Zeitschrift für Anglistik und Amerikanistik*, XVI (1968), 352–61.

[9] *Shakespeare Quarterly*, XX (1969), 129–41.

The Unfortunate Comedy,[1] by Joseph G. Price, is the first full-length study of *All's Well That Ends Well*, and it has the virtue of being thorough. The first section of it reviews the unhappy stage history of the play, and the second brings together and comments on the views expressed by critics from the middle of the seventeenth century down to 1964. Enthusiastic approval is hard to find. Finally, in the last section, Price gives his own reading of the work. And he sees it, *All's Well*, unlike *Twelfth Night* or *As You Like It*, lacks a distinctive mood or atmosphere. This deficiency he attributes to the fact that it contains elements of farce, fable, melodrama, realism, satire and symbolism, none of which is sustained throughout. Nevertheless, it is, he decides, a comedy that can work in its own terms of human interest, provided that none of the elements that have gone into its making is elevated to the central place in it at the expense of the rest. It is a charitable conclusion, for it involves a certain glossing over of some of Price's own misigivings, not to mention the disturbing impact of such lines as Bertram's bitter comment on his marriage 'War is no strife/To the dark house and the detested wife'. The puzzling matter of 'Helena's Pilgrimage' is the subject of a useful note by J. C. Maxwell[2] who thinks that Shakespeare meant us to have a suspicion that Helena did not arrive in Florence by chance, and that she was in some way responsible for the story of her own death.

Wilson Knight's interpretation of *Measure for Measure* is challenged by A. D. Nuttall in '*Measure for Measure*: Quid Pro Quo?'.[3] Nuttall sees the play as a dialectical drama in which there is a substructure providing the counterpoint to the superstructure that Knight is interested in. The Duke is a Machiavel as well as being the presiding genius, and Angelo, though he becomes a devil, is also a character of real moral stature. Michael P. Hamburger,[4] on the other hand, looks for a historical explanation of the Duke's oddities, and finds it in the now fashionable tendency to connect the Duke with James I. Jonathan R. Price concludes his '*Measure for Measure* and the Critics: Towards a New Approach'[5] by asking the question: how has Shakespeare 'made us care so passionately about the drama of *Measure for Measure*?'. The only possible response, in the light of what he has to say about it, is 'How, indeed?'.

Othello is the main theme of *Shakespeare Survey 21*, to which Helen Gardner contributes a survey of twentieth-century criticism of the play, entitled '*Othello*: A Retrospect, 1900–67'.[6] Making Bradley's uneasiness about this tragedy her starting point, she goes on to show that even those who thought of themselves as opposing him nonetheless felt with him that the play lacks universal significance, shrewdly adding the suggestion that the First World War created a climate of opinion in which the Othello type came to be deeply distrusted. But while she understands the reasons that have made critics suspicious of Othello, she never disguises her own admiration for the play and is in no doubt about the nature of the much disputed ending. Ned B. Allen breaks some new ground with his 'The Two Parts of *Othello*'.[7] Examining Shakespeare's debt to Cinthio, he observes that it is far greater in Acts III–V than it is in I–II. Moreover, the 'short time' in the play is confined to the first two acts, while 'long time' is found in the rest of it. From this he deduces that the two parts of the play were written at

[1] Liverpool University Press; University of Toronto Press, 1968.

[2] *RES*, XX (1969), 189–92.

[3] *Shakespeare Studies*, IV (1968), 231–51.

[4] 'Besonderheiten der Herzogsfigur in *Measure for Measure*', *Shakespeare Jahrbuch*, CV (1969), 158–67.

[5] *Shakespeare Quarterly*, XX (1969), 179–204.

[6] *Shakespeare Survey 21* (1968), 1–11.

[7] *Ibid.*, 13–29.

different times and in different frames of mind, and he further finds reasons for deciding that III–V was written before I–II. In '*Othello*: A Tragedy Built on a Comic Structure'[1] Barbara Heliodora C. de Mendonça relates the play to the *commedia dell'arte*, seeing a close connection between Iago and the inventive Harlequin and between Brabantio and the Pantalone. But, she adds, Othello himself does not, and is not meant to, belong to this scheme of things. G. R. Hibbard writes on '*Othello* and the Pattern of Shakespearian Tragedy';[2] and Leah Scragg finds herself disagreeing to some extent with Bernard Spivack's view that Iago is a descendant of the Vice, and argues in 'Iago—Vice or Devil'[3] that he has more in common with the Devil of the Morality plays. 'Thomas Rymer and *Othello*',[4] is a splendid piece of disposal work that is a joy to read. Taking up T. S. Eliot's statement about his never having seen 'a cogent refutation' of Rymer's attack on the play, Nigel Alexander deals with each of Rymer's objections to the play in turn, and then comes back to Eliot's remark with the unanswerable retort: 'He had most certainly read at least one, for it was written by William Shakespeare and it is called *Othello, the Moor of Venice*'. G. K. Hunter's British Academy Lecture, 'Othello and Colour Prejudice,'[5] sets out to determine Shakespeare's theatrical purpose in making his hero a black man. After pointing out the ill-omened and evil associations which the colour had for the ancients, the early Christians, and the Middle Ages, Hunter observes that the essence of Iago's technique is to play on these prejudices and, ultimately, to make Othello himself conform for a time to this stereotype, though the hero does recover his true whiteness of character at the end. In conclusion, he suggests that critics are wrong to see the play solely in terms of personal encounters. Othello represents, he argues, the outgoing aspect of the Renaissance, while Iago embodies its more cynical and empirical side. This idea receives some independent support from Georg Meri who sees the play, in his '*Othello*',[6] as a dramatization of the tragedy of humanism. Othello is the Renaissance individualist, looking for the self-development that Venetian society denies him but which he gains from Desdemona. Iago, on the other hand, represents the acquisitive and destructive form of individualism. Y. Shvedov takes issue with Bradley's judgement that *Othello* is the darkest of the tragedies. The main contention of his *Shakespeare's Tragedy 'Othello'*,[7] which is in Russian, is that the ultimate victor in the struggle is Desdemona. Othello himself is seen as a 'noble savage' who comes into conflict with a society, represented by Iago, that is inimical to the ideals of truth and honesty which he and Desdemona cherish. Seeing a connection between Iago and the Jesuitical Machiavel notorious in England at the time when *Othello* was written, Daniel Stempel explains 'The Silence of Iago'[8] by arguing that although he thinks he is exercising his own will, Iago has, in fact, been mastered by a radically evil will that he cannot understand. Peter Mercer's '*Othello* and the form of heroic tragedy'[9] criticizes the response to tragedy made by T. S. Eliot, F. R. Leavis, and L. C. Knights, and finds heroic reassertion in Othello's final speech. Noting that there is no 'middle voice' in Othello's speeches which are either lofty or vulgar in tone, Peter Cronin, in his 'Language and Character in *Othello*—Part One',[10] takes the two modes of utterance as an index of the division in Othello

[1] *Ibid.*, 31–8. [2] *Ibid.*, 39–46.
[3] *Ibid.*, 53–65. [4] *Ibid.*, 67–77.
[5] *Proceedings of the British Academy*, LIII (1967), 139–70.
[6] *Shakespeare Jahrbuch*, CIV (1968), 85–108.
[7] Moscow, 1969.
[8] *PMLA*, LXXXIV (1969), 252–63.
[9] *Critical Quarterly*, XI (1969), 45–61.
[10] *The London Review*, V (1969), 3–19.

between the noble but primitive essence of the man and the 'civilized' Venetian superstructure he has incompletely acquired. Robert A. Watts argues that 'The Comic Scenes in *Othello*',[1] i.e. the Drinking scene and the two Clown scenes, are thematically connected with the rest of the play; and Robert Rogers[2] offers a psychological reading of the drama, with Othello and Iago as the two parts of a composite character.

Nahum Tate's *The History of King Lear* can claim to be the most radical, and certainly the most influential, indirect criticism of Shakespeare's tragedy that has ever been made. Moreover, the Dedication carries some of the earliest significant critical comment. It is good therefore to be able to report that the original text of 1681 is now available in a handsomely produced facsimile,[3] being one of an 86-volume facsimile series of Restoration and eighteenth-century acting versions of Shakespeare's plays. The opening scene of *King Lear*, which Tate regarded as improbable, is studied by John Roland Dove and Peter Gamble in '"Our Darker Purpose": The Division Scene in *Lear*',[4] where they argue that until Lear announces his 'darker purpose' it is taken for granted that Britain will be divided between the two elder daughters. The point of Lear's scheme is, they think, to offer Cordelia a bait, in the form of a coronet and the dukedom that goes with it, to stay in Britain and look after him. Sandra Hole considers that the tragedy is religious rather than secular, because, as she puts it in 'The Background of Divine Action in *King Lear*',[5] there is a 'continuous suggestion that the actions of all the characters stem from the influence of, or are to be judged in relation to, a background of supernatural, or divine, activity'. Linking Gloucester's use of the word 'sport', in Act IV, scene i, with his use of it in I, i, Lawrence Rosinger's 'Gloucester and Lear: Men Who Act Like Gods'[6] suggests that Gloucester's outburst against the gods, in IV, i, marks a significant point in the process by which he ceases to think of himself as godlike and comes to realise his humanity. 'The Role of Edmund in *King Lear*', by Waldo F. McNeir,[7] is concerned primarily with Edmund's actions in the final scene, where, it is argued, he tries to repent but fails. Robert J. Bauer, on the other hand, in 'Despite of Mine Own Nature: Edmund and the Orders, Cosmic and Moral',[8] maintains that Edmund does ultimately come to recognize some kind of moral order. 'Edmund's Conception and Nativity in *King Lear*',[9] by Harry Rusche, resorts to Ptolemy's *Tetrabiblos* in an attempt to demonstrate that, since Edmund was begotten 'under the dragon's tail', he was bound to be 'rough and lecherous'. The references to Cordelia's return that occur in Acts II and III have the effect, Waldo F. McNeir thinks,[10] of adding to the ironic pattern by raising expectations of a happy outcome. Finally, A. L. Soens, in a note entitled '*King Lear* III, iv, 62–65: A Fencing Pun and Staging',[11] considers that the word 'pass' in Lear's question 'What, have his daughters brought him to this pass?' is probably a fencing term, meaning 'trick', as well as carrying its normal sense of 'dilemma'.

Agostino Lombardo's *Lettura del Macbeth*[12] is precisely what its title implies: a close, well-informed, and sensitive reading of the play,

[1] *Shakespeare Quarterly*, XIX (1968), 349–54.

[2] 'Endopsychic Drama in *Othello*', *Shakespeare Quarterly*, XX (1969), 205–15.

[3] The Cornmarket Press, 1969.

[4] *Neuphilologische Mitteilungen*, LXX (1969), 306–18.

[5] *Studies in English Literature*, VIII (1968), 217–33.

[6] *ELH*, XXXV (1968), 491–504.

[7] *Studies in English Literature*, VIII (1968), 187–216.

[8] *Texas Studies in Literature and Language*, X (1968), 359–66.

[9] *Shakespeare Quarterly*, XX (1969), 161–4.

[10] 'Cordelia's Return in *King Lear*', *English Language Notes*, VI (1968–9), 172–6.

[11] *Ibid.*, 19–24.

[12] Neri Pozza, Vicenza, 1969.

moving forward scene by scene, and, for much of the time, line by line. It is essentially a product of the study, because Lombardo is reading the play backwards, with an ear for repetitions of phrase and an eye for ironic anticipation that no theatre audience could bring to bear on it. He is at his best, perhaps, in the section he devotes to Act IV, where he has some excellent things to say about the scene in which Lady Macduff's son is murdered and about the scene in England, allowing his commentary to expand into a consideration of general ideas of a kind that he normally excludes. This part of the book leaves one regretting that he has not said more about the play's place among the tragedies. Writing on 'Two Aspects of Ambition in Elizabethan Tragedy: *Doctor Faustus* and *Macbeth*',[1] Kristian Smidt emphasizes the narrowness of the boundary that separated plain ambition (bad) from virtuous ambition (good). In *Doctor Faustus* Marlowe avoids the word 'ambition' while portraying the drive sympathetically. Shakespeare does not avoid the word in *Macbeth*, but, even so, he hesitates about making Macbeth an out-and-out villain. *The Tragic Cycle in Shakespeare's 'Macbeth'*,[2] by Toshikazu Oyama, is a free-wheeling piece of exegesis, based on the notion that the play dramatizes the mental state in which 'to be' is 'not to be'. The function of the witches is examined by Ian Robinson in 'The Witches and Macbeth'.[3]

The way in which Shakespeare, when writing *Antony and Cleopatra*, bestows life and movement on what is comparatively static and pictorial in North is studied by Peter Günther in 'Shakespeares *Antony and Cleopatra*: Wandel und Gestaltung eines Stoffes'.[4] Observing that two scenes in the play are concerned with fortune-telling and that the word 'fortune' frequently occurs, Marilyn L. Williamson looks at the imagery of fortune and its place in the total design.[5] An interesting contemporary reference to *Antony and Cleopatra* has been picked up by Reginald Saner from an anonymous black-letter pamphlet of 1614. He describes it in '*Antony and Cleopatra*: How Pompey's Honor Struck a Contemporary'.[6] Some evidence to show that Shakespeare may have had Elizabeth in mind when creating his Egyptian queen is offered by Helen Morris in her 'Queen Elizabeth I "Shadowed" in Cleopatra'.[7]

The primary concern of H. D. F. Kitto's 'The Classical Heritage of the Modern Humanities'[8] is with the Greeks, not Shakespeare, but he concludes his discourse with some penetrating words on *Coriolanus*. His view is that in Act V, scene iii, both the hero and Volumnia yield, not to each other, but to Nature. Committing himself to the assertion that Shakespeare was 'interested in history mainly for its practical application', Clifford Davidson argues, in his '*Coriolanus*: A Study in Political Dislocation',[9] that the tragedy is about the proper relationship between the individual and the state, and that it depicts a national rather than a personal disaster. A fragment of an eighteenth-century translation of *Coriolanus* into German is printed by Martin Bircher, along with some biographical information about the translator, in 'Die früheste deutsche *Coriolan*-Übersetzung. Ein Fragment des Zürchers Johann Jakob Kitt (1747–96)'.[10]

Describing *Timon of Athens* as the 'most

1 *English Studies*, L (1969), 235–48.

2 Seijo University, Tokyo, 1968.

3 *The Critical Review*, XI (1968), 101–5.

4 *Deutsche Shakespeare-Gesellschaft West Jahrbuch* (1968), pp. 94–108.

5 'Fortune in *Antony and Cleopatra*', *JEGP*, LXVII (1968), 423–9.

6 *Shakespeare Quarterly*, XX (1969), 117–20.

7 *Huntington Library Quarterly*, XXXII (1968–9), 271–8.

8 *The Future of the Modern Humanities*, pp. 31–72.

9 *Shakespeare Studies*, IV (1968), 263–74.

10 *Deutsche Shakespeare-Gesellschaft West Jahrbuch* (1968), pp. 121–40.

puzzling of Shakespeare's plays' and taking into account the incompatible readings of it that critics have produced, L. C. Knights[1] adopts what is, by and large, the attitude of Apemantus towards the protagonist. Admitting the force and power of the invective that Timon utters in the woods, he stresses the fact that in these speeches there is far more about sex than about money. He deduces from this that in the early scenes Timon is really using his wealth to feed his self-esteem, with the result that when his money has gone and he is thrown back on himself, he discovers that there is nothing there, except a self-contempt which he then projects on to the world about him. It is a challenging interpretation of the play, but it does leave one wondering what is the point, if Knights is right, of the scene with the three Strangers (III, ii) which would seem to owe its existence to Shakespeare's desire to make it clear that there is something positive and valuable about Timon's behaviour before disaster overtakes him.

The romances continue to attract critical attention. John P. Cutts regards it as a long-standing error to use the word 'romances' about them. His *Rich and Strange: A Study of Shakespeare's Last Plays*[2] sets out to correct this aberration by offering four essays, one on each play, designed to show that they are, in fact, psychological dramas of a hitherto unrealized complexity. His main thesis is that critics have been taken in by the benevolence of Prospero, the chastity of Imogen, the purity of Perdita, and so forth, because these qualities, so evident to the uninitiated eye, are merely so many masks behind which the characters concerned hide their true motives from themselves as well as others. The essays supporting this thesis are—at least to this reviewer—entirely unconvincing, and have the effect of turning the plays into curious hybrids, sired by the detective story on the psychological novel. The general air of zaniness is endorsed by the patent inaccuracy of many of the statements that are made—for example, Cutts places the *O lente, lente currite noctis equi* passage of *Doctor Faustus* in the Helen scene, not the final scene—and by the ineptitudes of a prose that is as fecund in unrelated clauses as the general thesis is in unsubstantiated judgements.

Cymbeline continues to be intractable. Geoffrey Hill's essay '"The True Conduct of Human Judgment": Some Observations on *Cymbeline*'[3] is intended to demonstrate that Shakespeare's main interest is 'in certain kinds of immaturity, and in the inaccuracy and imbalance affecting relationships'. But nothing very clear or tangible emerges from it. Nor does '*Cymbeline*: "Lopp'd Branches" and the Concept of Regeneration'[4] help very much, for the conclusion that William Barry Thorne reaches in this consideration of the play is that it is 'a national play, presenting in artistic and sophisticated terms the theme of regeneration which can be seen in the prototypal mummers' play'. Naseeb Shaheen, writing on 'The Use of Scripture in *Cymbeline*',[5] presents a more definite finding. Asserting that scriptural references are used more freely in *Cymbeline* than in any other play, he goes on to show that they do not support any allegorical reading of the drama but are employed, as Shakespeare employs classical references, for purely dramatic ends.

Fitzroy Pyle's '*The Winter's Tale*': *A Commentary on the Structure*[6] is a welcome change from much that has been written on this play recently. Not unsympathetic to those who see it as the dramatization of an allegory or the exploration of a myth, he prefers to take it as a play about human beings immersed in the

1 '*Timon of Athens*', *The Morality of Art*, pp. 1–17.
2 Washington State University Press, 1968.
3 *The Morality of Art*, pp. 18–32.
4 *Shakespeare Quarterly*, XX (1969), 143–59.
5 *Shakespeare Studies*, IV (1968), 294–315.
6 Routledge and Kegan Paul, 1969.

ordinary business of life. His main concern is with 'the beauty of its plotting', which he approaches through a consideration of the way in which it transforms its primary source, *Pandosto*. The patient, thorough, and detailed commentary that the method leads to yields most valuable results. Pyle is not convinced that the initial jealousy of Leontes is already present when the play begins, or that it arises without motivation. His view is that while Hermione is talking to Polixenes Leontes is playing with Mamillius, but that he overhears the last part of her speech to the King of Bohemia which, to one who has not heard the rest of it, readily lends itself to distortion and rapidly leads to the creation of that fantasy world in which Leontes lives up to the death of Mamillius. Similarly, Pyle takes up and deals with the two other major critical problems that the play poses: the use of Time as the Chorus, and the transformation of the statue into a living woman. His main interest is in the coherence of the plotting and in the events as a convincing rendering of human experience. The results are impressive. Kenneth Muir,[1] too, defends the last scene against the attacks of those who think it 'unrealistic', acutely pointing out that such critics tend to be readers, rather than spectators, and that stage history finds the scene an unqualified success. He also provides an answer to the question of why Shakespeare deceives his audience into thinking that Hermione is dead. Barbara Adams Mowat's 'A Tale of Sprights and Goblins'[2] advances the theory that the first three acts are not meant to be tragic but grotesque, and that their 'warped comedy' becomes pure comedy in the second half of the play. Charles Lloyd Holt[3] deals with the movement of time in the play, as it is to be found in the imagery; and Lee Sheridan Cox, considering 'The Role of Autolycus in *The Winter's Tale*',[4] thinks that the rogue's activities are 'a springlike variation of the winter story of Leontes'. Writing on 'Polixenes and the Winter of his Discontent',[5] A. Bonjour makes the useful point that while there is a parallel between Leontes' outburst of jealousy in Act I and the anger of Polixenes in IV, iv, there is also the basic difference, that we know the threats of Polixenes will not be carried out. 'The Language of Leontes',[6] by Jonathan Smith, is a sensitive examination of Shakespeare's use of diction to express Leontes' varying states of mind. It also makes the interesting observation that a number of the rare words Leontes employs also appear in Henry Cockeram's *The English dictionary* (1623), which was published just before the First Folio.

'Prospero and the Drama of the Soul',[7] by Herbert R. Coursen, Jr, is in effect a continuation of his monograph on *Hamlet*, arguing that *The Tempest* is about Prospero's abandonment of revenge, and his manipulation of the other characters into a state of grace, causing them to realize that freedom without responsibility is a form of bondage. The potentially disturbing qualities of the play are emphasized by John Fraser in '*The Tempest* Revisited';[8] and John Tyree Fain writes 'Some Notes on Ariel's Song',[9] the song in question being 'Full fathom five'. The structural relationship of Gonzalo's picture of the ideal commonwealth to the rest of the play is explored by Verena Stalder in 'Zur Utopie des Gonzalo in Shakespeares *Tempest*, II, i, 139–64'.[10] The suggestion that *The Seven*

[1] 'The Conclusion of *The Winter's Tale*', *The Morality of Art*, pp. 87–101.

[2] *Shakespeare Quarterly*, XX (1969), 37–46.

[3] 'Notes on the Dramaturgy of *The Winter's Tale*', *ibid.*, 47–51.

[4] *Studies in English Literature*, IX (1969), 283–301.

[5] *English Studies*, L (1969), 206–12.

[6] *Shakespeare Quarterly*, XIX (1968), 317–27.

[7] *Shakespeare Studies*, IV (1968), 316–33.

[8] *The Critical Review*, XI (1968), 60–78.

[9] *Shakespeare Quarterly*, XIX (1968), 329–32.

[10] *Deutsche Shakespeare-Gesellschaft West Jahrbuch* (1968), pp. 169–78.

Champions of Christendom (published in 1638, but written and acted in 1613–14) is a contemporary burlesque of *The Tempest* is made in 'Shakespeare's *Tempest* and *The Seven Champions*',[1] by John Freehafer.

'Shakespeare's *Henry VIII*: Romance Redeemed by History',[2] by H. M. Richmond, argues that the trial scenes in the play show the King becoming progressively more aware of himself, more understanding of others, and more alive to his responsibilities as chief magistrate. Like the romances, the play sets a high value on mercifulness, but in an overtly political context.

Don Cameron Allen's valuable essays on *Venus and Adonis* and *The Rape of Lucrece* are included in the second and enlarged edition of his *Image and Meaning*,[3] along with the essay on *The Tempest* that appeared in the first edition of 1960. The main argument of 'Shakespeare's Gaudy: The Method of *The Rape of Lucrece*',[4] by Robert L. Montgomery, Jr, is that the rhetoric of the poem is designed to convey what Lucrece and Tarquin feel.

Three books on the Sonnets have come out during the period under review, and not one of them, happily, is about Mr W. H. Brents Stirling's *The Shakespeare Sonnet Order: Poems and Groups*[5] is a work of fundamental importance which will, if its conclusions receive anything like general assent, have a profound effect on the future evaluation and understanding of the Sonnets. The idea on which it rests is that the Sonnets ought, like the rest of the poet's works, to be models of organization. Signs that such organization once existed are not lacking. They are to be found, not in any hints of a continuous story, but in the fact, long recognized, that about three quarters of the sonnets, as they stand in the 1609 Quarto, fall into groups of two or more linked to each other by the carry-over of a phrase, an image, or an idea. A number of sonnets fitting together to form a coherent whole Stirling calls a poem, and when two or more such poems can be linked they become a group. Thus, the familar group 1–17 is made up of two poems: 1–14 and 15–17. The criteria used to establish the other poems and groups are linkage by multiple interconnections of theme, recurring metaphor or phrase, and logical dependence. The book falls into three parts. First comes the outline of the method, complete with a series of test cases. Then come the Sonnets themselves, rearranged as poems, and, where the justification for it exists, with these poems brought together in groups. Finally, there is the verification, where the evidence is gone over once more and buttressed by bibliographical hypotheses. The entire argument hangs together remarkably well; and the kind of reward that the book offers is the superb poem that emerges when 91, 92, 93, 69, 70, 95, 96 and 94 are brought together in that order. The eight sonnets do make an independent and coherent unit, to which 94 comes as a devastating climax. Not the least of Stirling's virtues is that he does not try to push things too far. Confronted by 20, for example, which does not hook on to anything else by the criteria he is employing, he is content to leave it as an independent poem. At the end of his labours the Sonnets are still a miscellany, but it is a miscellany made up of five groups and six poems.

Stephen Booth, in his *An Essay on Shakespeare's Sonnets*,[6] takes the opposite view to Stirling, stating flatly that the Sonnets cannot be re-ordered and holding that the 1609 edition 'seems to need interpretation or reorganization not because it is disordered but

[1] *Studies in Philology*, LXVI (1969), 87–103.

[2] *Shakespeare Studies*, IV (1968), 334–49.

[3] The Johns Hopkins Press, Baltimore, 1968.

[4] *Studies in Honor of DeWitt T. Starnes*, pp. 25–36.

[5] University of California Press, Berkeley and Los Angeles, 1968.

[6] Yale University Press, New Haven and London, 1969.

because it is so obviously ordered'. However, there is no indication that Booth has Stirling's work in mind when he makes these pronouncements and, in any case, it does not matter because his concern is with the experience of the careful analytical reader seeking to come to terms with the sonnet form as Shakespeare develops it. Sticking close to the text, he examines the various interlocking structural patterns—rhyme, rhetoric, sound, diction, paradox—and demonstrates how these multiple patterns overlap in an unobtrusive yet highly complex fashion. The result of this art is not confusion but a continuous forward drive that attains its goal—and its clarification—in the final couplet, producing both an awareness of the manifold nature of experience and a sense of unity and coherence. The book is, perhaps, the most illuminating analysis yet made of the principles on which the Sonnets are constructed, and it goes far towards explaining, and reconciling, the apparently contradictory views of John Benson, who thought the Sonnets 'Seren, cleere and eligantly plaine', and of the many modern critics who have found them difficult and ambiguous.

Compared with these two books, each of which has a clear-cut thesis and a definite method, James Winny's *The Master-Mistress*[1] seems diffuse, though it contains some good things. It really divides into two parts. The first is an attack on those who see the Sonnets as the account of something that actually happened. Winny says acutely that 'If there is a story, it develops irregularly', he gives some good reasons for doubting whether Shakespeare and the poet of the sequence are the same person, and he points to inconsistencies in the character of the friend. The conclusion to which these observations lead is that the central concern of the Sonnets is with Shakespeare's own interior life, of which they are a kind of projection. Seeing them in this way, he proceeds in the second part of his book to make some connections between them and the narrative poems, together with some of the plays. It is here that one becomes aware of a certain fuzziness. There is too much play with the big abstractions—'Truth and Falsehood', 'Increase and Creation'—and the attention is centred almost exclusively on the sonnets that lend themselves to explication in terms of irony and ambiguity. Those which make strong positive statements are largely ignored; there is nothing at all about 146, and 116 is merely mentioned in passing. What seems to be missing here is any feeling for that quality in the Sonnets that C. S. Lewis defines so well when he writes that in them Shakespeare 'sings (always sings, never talks)'. Sonnet 146 is the subject of a rather lengthy article by Charles A. Huttar, the content of which is adequately defined by its title, 'The Christian Basis of Shakespeare's Sonnet 146'.[2]

'Dramatic Time versus Clock Time in Shakespeare'[3] is studied by Irwin Smith, who comes to the conclusion that theatre conventions prevent any real clash between the two forms of measurement. Peter Bilton, writing on 'Shakespeare Criticism and the "Choric Character"',[4] decides that the choric character, in the true sense of the word, is a very rare figure in the plays. 'The Operatic Character of Background Music in Film Adaptations of Shakespeare',[5] by Charles Hurtgen, reviews the use of music in film adaptations, ranging from *As You Like It* (1935) to *Richard III* (1956), and finds that the general tendency of such music is to turn speech into *recitative*.

The connections between Shakespeare and other writers are the subject of two articles. Michail Pawlowitsch Alexejew[6] shows the effect

[1] Chatto and Windus, 1968.

[2] *Shakespeare Quarterly*, XIX (1968), 355–65.

[3] *Ibid.*, XX (1969), 65–9.

[4] *English Studies*, L (1969), 254–60.

[5] *Shakespeare Quarterly*, XX (1969), 53–64.

[6] 'Shakespeare und Puschkin', *Shakespeare Jahrbuch*, CIV (1968), 141–74.

that the histories had on *Boris Godunov*, and Yu D. Levin's 'Tolstoy, Shakespeare, and Russian Writers of the 1860s'[1] goes far towards explaining Tolstoy's notorious essay 'On Shakespeare and the Drama' by pointing out that Tolstoy's attitude was already established in the 1850s when he was moving in a literary circle, including Chernyshevsky, that found Shakespeare's work lacking in psychological realism.

'Shakespeare in Litauen',[2] by Alfonsas Šešplaukis, is a historical study, packed with information, that connects the translations into Lithuanian with the movement for self-determination. Volume VI of the translation of Shakespeare into Estonian[3] contains versions of the five later tragedies. Georg Meri is responsible for *King Lear*, *Antony and Cleopatra*, *Coriolanus*, and *Timon*, while *Macbeth* is the work of Jaan Kross. The volume includes a critical essay on each play and also explanatory notes.

Elmer Edgar Stoll's *Poets and Playwrights*,[4] originally published in 1930, is now available in paperback form.

1 *Oxford Slavonic Papers*, n. s., I (1968), 85–104.

2 *Deutsche Shakespeare-Gesellschaft West Jahrbuch* (1968), pp. 193–206.

3 *William Shakespeare, Kogutud Teosed*, VI, 'Eesti Raamat' (Tallin, 1968).

4 University of Minnesota Press, Minneapolis, 1967.

© G. R. HIBBARD 1970

2. SHAKESPEARE'S LIFE, TIMES, AND STAGE

reviewed by LEAH SCRAGG

The question of Shakespeare's identity, always so rewarding for the imaginative writer, has provided the year's most entertaining item among many delightful contributions to the study of the dramatist's life—William Honey's *The Shakespeare Epitaph Deciphered.*[1] Mr Honey's beginning was, he tells us, with Shakespeare's end, more precisely, with the bard's doggerel epitaph which, he discovered, was capable of being deciphered as follows (spelling has been modernized):

> Good friend who wishes for Shakespeare
> To dig the dust: entombed here:
> Plays by the man, verses his sonnets
> And Christopher Marlowe's bones.

From this starting point, we are told, the author proceeded to 'bolster up' his discovery with historical facts. These include the murder of the actor William Shakespeare, Marlowe's impersonation of him, and his subsequent acceptance by Shakespeare's degenerate family (including Anne Hathaway) and (more puzzlingly) his associates. The reviewer was charmed but unconvinced. Delight has also been afforded by another imaginative work of a very different kind, Ivor Brown's *The Women in Shakespeare's Life.*[2] Taking the scraps of information available to us about Shakespeare's mother, wife and daughters as his point of departure, the author has woven round them his considerable knowledge of the period with characteristic charm, creating a graceful 'family portrait' which cannot fail to enchant its anticipated audience of 'Avonside tourists ... under the influence'. A rather more ambitious effort at reconstruction is made in G. P. V. Akrigg's *Shakespeare and the Earl of Southampton*,[3] which attempts to trace the growth

1 The Mitre Press, 1969.

2 The Bodley Head, 1968. Perhaps one should note here that the same author has produced an elementary illustrated life of the dramatist (*William Shakespeare*, International Profiles, 1968).

3 Hamish Hamilton, 1968.

and decline of Shakespeare's relationship with his patron. Of prime importance in the history of this relationship of course are the Sonnets, which, Akrigg suggests, were published by Shakespeare himself when considering retirement, were dedicated by him to Southampton, and were the cause of Southampton's decision to terminate the friendship. Akrigg's identification of Mr W. H. as Wriothesley, Henry, runs counter to the views of Messrs I. R. W. Cook[1] and Robert F. Fleissner,[2] both of whom have advanced their own candidates for the role. Cook has identified William Hervey, the third husband of the Countess of Southampton, with Hervey of Chessington, and thus, as both Shakespeare's contemporary and a member of the Southampton circle, with Mr W. H., supporting his argument with evidence based on the original, unpunctuated version of the dedication. Fleissner, on the other hand, while also content to leave the text of the dedication intact, questions the force of the word 'begetter', arguing for the sense 'bringer forth', and advancing William Houghton as the 'bringer forth' of the Sonnets for Thorpe. All three suggestions are as convincingly unconvincing as the results of W. H. investigations are wont to be. The spirit of detection has also infused itself into Peter Milward[3] who suggests that documents relating to Shakespeare, including letters by the dramatist, may be in existence today, and into Franklin B. Williams, Jr,[4] who speculates that Shakespeare and Zachary Jones may have known each other. Guy Lambrechts[5] (providing a useful link between biographical and canonical studies) has heaped hypothesis on hypothesis in an attempt to aportion sections of *1 Henry VI* to Nashe, Greene and Shakespeare (without reference to Kirschbaum's work in this field), and hence to throw light on the dramatist's relationship with one of his less admiring contemporaries. Of those concerned to augment the canon rather than disintegrate it, John P. Cutts[6] has joined the ranks of the many distinguished scholars who have detected Shakespeare's hand in *The Two Noble Kinsmen*, while on less firm ground, Warren Stevenson[7] has discussed the authorship of the additions to *The Spanish Tragedy*, dismissed the claims of Jonson and Webster, and argued that on both internal and external evidence Shakespeare is the likeliest candidate.

Speculation gives place to scholarship in the less heady atmosphere of source studies. Undoubtedly the year's most important contribution to the field is Richard Hosley's selective, modern spelling edition of Holinshed's *Chronicles*.[8] Hosley has departed from the practice of earlier editors (cf. the newly republished edition of Boswell-Stone) by preserving the chronology of the original rather than rearranging the material to provide comparison with the relevant Shakespearian play. Consequently the reader comes much closer to seeing Shakespeare at work than has previously been possible, while enjoying Holinshed's narrative for its own sake (though it must be noted that the presentation of the material is marred by a distinctly unattractive type face and unnecessarily obtrusive reference numbers). The edition is equipped with maps

1 'William Hervey and Shakespeare's Sonnets', *Shakespeare Survey 21* (1968), 97–106.

2 'A Plausible Mr. W. H.', *Notes and Queries*, CCXIV (1969), 129.

3 'Some Missing Shakespeare Letters', *Shakespeare Quarterly*, XX (1969), 84–7.

4 'Spenser, Shakespeare, and Zachary Jones', *ibid.*, XIX (1968), 205–12.

5 'La Composition De La Première Partie De *Henri VI*', *Bulletin de la Faculté des Lettres de Strasbourg*, XLVI (December 1967), 325–54.

6 'Shakespeare's Song and Masque Hand in *The Two Noble Kinsmen*', *English Miscellany*, XVIII (1967), 55–85.

7 'Shakespeare's Hand in *The Spanish Tragedy* 1602', *Studies in English Literature 1500–1900*, VIII (1968), 307–21.

8 *Shakespeare's Holinshed* (G. P. Putnam's Sons, New York, 1968).

and genealogical tables for the general reader, and a full bibliography for scholars. Also worthy of note is *Shakespeare Studies*' selective reproduction of Sandys' Commentary on Books I–IV of the *Metamorphoses*,[1] a commentary which, it is suggested, contributes to our understanding of Shakespeare's attitude to Golding since it 'preserves for us some traditional ways of understanding what it was that Golding translated'.

Numerous minor points relating works to source material have been made during the year. J.C. Maxwell[2] has contributed another item to T. W. Baldwin's analysis of Shakespeare's debt to Plautus in *The Comedy of Errors*; W. Schrickx[3] has considered the implications of Shakespeare's use of *The Unfortunate Traveller* for details of the rape of Lavinia; T. W. Baldwin,[4] in an elegantly turned essay, has demonstrated the characteristically Shakespearian fusion of classical learning and first hand experience in the pedigree and description of the royal hounds in *A Midsummer Night's Dream*; Jürgen Schäfer[5] has suggested that Falstaff's jocular claim to have cracked his voice singing anthems derives from Erasmus' *Moriae Encomium*; Geoffrey Creigh[6] has examined Munday's *Zelauto*, one of the sources of the pound of flesh plot, refuted the suggestion that the third part is based on a lost English Jew play, and postulated an Italian dramatic original; Claus Uhlig[7] has compared *As You Like It* II, i, 21–66 with emblem material, relating the play to contemporary and post-Renaissance attitudes to hunting; D. M. Gaunt[8] has advanced Plutarch's *Moralia* in place of the *Life of Pelopidas* as the source of the anecdote Shakespeare had in mind during Hamlet's reflections on the Players in Act II, scene ii; August Rüegg[9] has discussed the Homeric element in *Troilus and Cressida*; and P. Michel-Michot[10] has found Iago's original in the person of Sir Walter Raleigh. (However, though she demonstrates successfully that in many respects Iago and Raleigh are the same *kind* of man, she fails to produce convincing evidence that one is based upon the other, rather than upon the Jacobean 'new man' in general.) Finally, Plutarch's *Morals* (essay on 'Isis and Osiris'),[11] Ovid's *Metamorphoses* (Book 14),[12] and *Fedele and Fortunio* 293–9[13] have been advanced as the sources of the phrase 'infinite variety', Caliban's fear of being turned into an ape, and the chaser-chased image of Sonnet 143 respectively; parallels have been cited between a Chapman letter and Hamlet's 'pipe' speech to Guildenstern,[14] and also between Montaigne's essay 'Of the Inconsistencie of Our Actions' and Sonnet 124;[15] and the choice of historical

[1] 'Shakespeare's Other Ovid: A Reproduction of Commentary on Metamorphoses I–IV', *Shakespeare Studies*, III (1967), 173–256.

[2] '*The Comedy of Errors* and *Menaechmi*', *Notes and Queries*, CCXIV (1969), 128–9.

[3] '*Titus Andronicus* and Thomas Nashe', *English Studies*, L (1969), 82–4.

[4] 'The Pedigree of Theseus' Pups. *Midsummer-Night's Dream*, IV, i, 123–130', *Deutsche Shakespeare-Gesellschaft West Jahrbuch* (1968), 109–20.

[5] 'Falstaff's Voice', *Notes and Queries*, CCXIV (1969), 135–6.

[6] '*Zelauto* and Italian Comedy: A Study in Sources', *Modern Language Quarterly*, XXIX (1968), 161–7.

[7] 'Der weinende Hirsch: *As You Like It*, II, i, 21–66, und der historische Kontext', *Deutsche Shakespeare-Gesellschaft West Jahrbuch* (1968), 141–68.

[8] 'Hamlet and Hecuba', *Notes and Queries*, CCXIV (1969), 136–7.

[9] 'Homerisches und Unhomerisches in Shakespeares *Troilus and Cressida*', *Deutsche Shakespeare-Gesellschaft West Jahrbuch* (1968), 28–42.

[10] 'Sir Walter Raleigh as a Source for the Character of Iago', *English Studies*, L (1969), 85–9.

[11] J. H. Walter, 'Four Notes on *Antony and Cleopatra*', Note I, II. ii. 236, '*Her infinite variety*', *Notes and Queries*, CCXIV (1969), 137.

[12] A. B. Taylor, 'Shakespeare and the Apes', *ibid.*, 144–5.

[13] Douglas Hamer, 'Shakespeare: Sonnet 143', *ibid.*, 129–30.

[14] Robert D. Parsons, 'Chapman's letter to Mr. Sares: A *Hamlet* Parallel', *ibid.*, 137.

[15] Sacvan Bercovitch, 'Shakespeare's Sonnet CXXIV', *The Explicator*, XXVII (1968–9), item 22.

setting for *Othello* has been ascribed[1] to a desire to please James I who had written a poem on the Turkish wars.

Bridging the gap between Shakespeare's life and his times come two lavishly illustrated books from Paul Hamlyn[2] and Faber and Faber.[3] The former is a glossy publication presenting a brief life of Shakespeare, the time-worn pictures of Stratford, and the familiar faces of the dramatist's more obvious contemporaries. Faber's *Shakespeare's Life and Times*, however, is in an entirely different class. Beautifully produced and intelligently organized, it presents a wealth of factual information in a highly attractive form.[4] The Da Capo Press[5] have also been concerned with 'The English Experience', in this case in the form of photographic reproductions of Renaissance books. Da Capo and, to an even greater extent, the Scolar Press[6] have effected an over-night revolution in the lives of Renaissance students of all ages by placing within their reach a mass of well-produced, moderately priced primary material.[7]

Our understanding of Renaissance thought has been increased by a wide variety of studies. In the political sphere, Francis Oakley[8] has distinguished between the 'ordinary' and 'absolute' powers of the king; J. A. W. Gunn[9] has analyzed the implications behind changing attitudes to the word 'interest'; Robert Hale Ltd have published a translation of *Machiavelli anticristo* (Rome, 1954), Guiseppe Prezzolini's profoundly pessimistic work on the thought of Machiavelli, his 'adversaries, followers, interpreters and appropriators';[10] and Katherine S. Van Eerde[11] has discussed the fluctuating attitudes of a representative Englishman to the projected Spanish marriage.[12] In the ecclesiastical sphere, two articles have been of particular interest—James A. Devereux's 'The Primers and the Prayer Book Collects'[13] and E. J. Devereux's 'The Publication of the English *Paraphrases* of Erasmus'.[14] The former traces the history of English collects prior to 1549, concluding that Cranmer made little discernible use of any existing collect-translating tradition, while the latter considers the history of the attempt to found an Erasmian Church in England on the basis of the *Paraphrases*, *Homilies* and *Prayer Book*. Also worthy of note

[1] Emrys Jones, '*Othello*, *Lepanto* and the Cyprus Wars', *Shakespeare Survey 21* (1968), 47–52.

[2] Maria Pia Rosignoli, *The Life and Times of Shakespeare*, translated by Mary Kanini (1968).

[3] Roland Mushat Frye, *Shakespeare's Life and Times* (1968).

[4] Another illustrated book attempting to convey a sense of Elizabethan England to the general reader is Martin Holmes, *Elizabethan London* (Cassell, 1969). This starts with the city as a whole, gradually moving closer to view the lives of its inhabitants. This is a book which might well be of interest to schools.

[5] *The English Experience. Its Record In Early English Books*. Published in Facsimile, Da Capo Press, New York, and Theatrum Orbis Terrarvm Ltd (Amsterdam, 1969).

[6] Menston, England.

[7] Two articles concerned indirectly with primary material should probably be noted at this point. Katharine F. Pantzer ('The Serpentine Progress of the STC Revision', *The Papers of the Bibliographical Society of America*, LXII (1968), 297–311) has informed us that 91% of the entries in the STC have now been revised, and that the new edition will give further information on format, variations between copies, etc., and J. A. Lavin ('Additions to McKerrow's *Devices*', *The Library*, XXIII (1968), 191–205) has produced a long list of additions to McKerrow's *Printers' and publishers' devices 1485–1640*, with illustrations of previously unrecorded examples.

[8] 'Jacobean Political Theology: The Absolute And Ordinary Powers Of The King', *Journal of the History of Ideas*, XXIX (1968), 323–46.

[9] '"Interest Will Not Lie": A Seventeenth-Century Political Maxim', *ibid.*, 551–64.

[10] *Machiavelli* (1968).

[11] 'The Spanish Match through an English Protestant's Eyes', *The Huntington Library Quarterly*, XXXII (1968–9), 59–75.

[12] Scholars may also find interesting R. B. Outhwaite's *Inflation in Tudor and Early Stuart England* (Macmillan, 1969).

[13] *The Huntington Library Quarterly*, XXXII (1968–9), 29–44.

[14] *Bulletin of the John Rylands Library Manchester*, LI (1968–9), 348–67.

is an article by Joseph E. Duncan[1] exploring the growth of the concept that Paradise was not to be found in any specific location but embraced the whole earth[2] (i.e. that the expulsion was to be seen not as a change of place but as a change of state).[3] Philosophy, the physical sciences, and the philosophy of medicine have all been the subject of extremely valuable studies this year.[4] Sister Patricia Reif[5] has made an extensive examination of European textbooks of natural philosophy, established precisely what was taught, and determined to what extent the contemporary charge that the subject consisted of 'poring continually upon a few paper Idols' was justified; S. K. Heninger, Jr,[6] has produced the first part of an extensive survey of Tudor publications on the physical sciences; C. D. O'Malley[7] has published a full account of English medicine during the Tudor period, covering all aspects of the subject from surgery to medical botany, discussing individual works and accounting for the type of books produced; and Massachusetts Institute of Technology Press[8] have republished William Barclay Parsons' fascinating (and, we are informed, still reliable) book on Renaissance engineers and engineering.

Moving from scientific works, through a book on engineering which devotes considerable space to Leonardo, we arrive at the arts. On the literary front, two scholars have been concerned with the boundary between truth and fiction, one[9] describing the Renaissance attempt to distinguish fiction from history and to define an area in which 'falsehood' was legitimate, the other[10] attempting to reach an understanding of what 'the imitation of history and its accompanying rhetorical performance meant to the Renaissance poet'. A third writer on Renaissance literary thought[11] has examined the failure of humanist scholarship whereby satire was regarded as an off-shoot of the Greek satyr-play. Two studies have been devoted to the changing emphasis given to popular fables. David G. Hale's 'Intestine Sedition: The Fable of the Belly'[12] surveys traditional interpretations of the tale, distinguishes two main lines of approach to it, and discusses its use in *Coriolanus*, while Kenneth R. R. Gros Louis' 'The Triumph and Death of Orpheus in the English Renaissance'[13] compares allusions to Orpheus in the sixteenth and seventeenth centuries to show 'the decline

1 'Paradise as the Whole Earth', *Journal of the History of Ideas*, XXX (1969), 171–86.

2 The growth of this concept is ascribed by the writer to the Renaissance desire to reconcile the findings of reason with scriptural revelation. Similarly Michael Hattaway ('Paradoxes of Solomon: Learning in the English Renaissance', *Journal of the History of Ideas*, XXIX (1968), 499–530) has seen the 'impulse towards enquiry' and the confines of 'theological sanctions' as productive of ambivalent attitudes to learning in the Renaissance, reflected in the treatment of the figure of Solomon.

3 Church music too has received a share of scholarly attention, cf. Alan Smith's assessment of the large and important body of material relating to musical practice in Ludlow from the Reformation to the Restoration ('Elizabethan Church Music at Ludlow', *Music and Letters*, XLIX (1968), 108–21).

4 Also a useful first introduction to the work of some humanist philosophers has been published (S. Dresden, *Humanism in the Renaissance*, World University Library (Weidenfeld and Nicolson, 1968)).

5 'The Textbook Tradition in Natural Philosophy, 1600–1650', *Journal of the History of Ideas*, XXX (1969), 17–32.

6 'Tudor Literature of the Physical Sciences', *The Huntington Library Quarterly*, XXXII (1968–9), 101–33.

7 'Tudor Medicine and Biology', *ibid.*, 1–27.

8 *Engineers and Engineering in the Renaissance* (1968).

9 William Nelson, 'The Boundaries of Fiction in the Renaissance: A Treaty Between Truth and Falsehood', *ELH*, XXXVI (1969), 30–58.

10 Anthony LaBranche, 'Poetry, History, and Oratory: The Renaissance Historical Poem', *Studies in English Literature 1500–1900*, IX (1969), 1–19.

11 D. J. Shaw, 'More about the "Dramatic Satyre"', *Bibliothèque D'Humanisme et Renaissance*, XXX (1968), 301–25.

12 *Comparative Literature Studies*, V (1968), 377–88.

13 *Studies in English Literature 1500–1900*, IX (1969), 63–80.

of the humanists' vision of a new golden age led by poet-philosophers'. One of the year's most potentially useful books for the student of Shakespeare's times is Lee A. Sonnino's *A Handbook to Sixteenth-Century Rhetoric.*[1] The bulk of the work consists of an alphabetical list of rhetorical figures, each entry comprising the name of the figure, some Renaissance definitions of it and examples of its use. This procedure is then reversed in a descriptive index of tropes and schemes so that, ideally, the reader, however ignorant of rhetorical theory, should be able to identify any figure of speech with which he is presented. Unfortunately the approach fails to take into account the various guises in which Renaissance rhetorical figures are apt to appear. For example, would the average reader have enough knowledge to identify *anacoenosis*, if he encountered it, with Sonnino's *anachinosis?* (Or, more pertinently perhaps, would he think of looking for *homoioteleuton* under *omoeoteleuton?*) At the same time the usefulness of the book is diminished by indexing errors. *Antenagoge*, for example, appears in the text (p. 46) but not in the index, while *antisagoge* appears in the index but is not mentioned by name in the text. Nevertheless, this is a helpful handbook to a complex field.[2] Finally, analysis of a different kind is the subject of an article by R. M. Cummings,[3] who supports Fowler's argument that 'Renaissance poets were more familiar than had been commonly supposed with the principles of numerical composition' by citing two Renaissance critics who saw a numerological structure in the *Aeneid.*

Aspects of Renaissance musical theory and practice have concerned a number of writers. Howard B. Barnett[4] has discussed the life and work of John Case, the author of one of the two major sources of our knowledge of Renaissance attitudes to music, and argued that he was also the author of the other; Putnam Aldrich[5] has summarized the principles according to which Renaissance musicians analyzed their music and suggested that these principles can be used to direct our attention to once important and now neglected features; and Gwilym Beechey[6] has described a seventeenth-century manuscript in the National Library of Scotland containing a number of pieces of keyboard music unique to this source, several of which have been ascribed to John Blow. For the general reader, Friedrich Blume's survey of Renaissance and baroque music[7] (which covers such topics as the characteristics of the Renaissance as a period of musical history, the achievement of the period, etc.) has been translated into English.

Miscellaneous information on Shakespeare's times has been afforded by a host of scholars in an assortment of journals. The activities of a notable plagiarist,[8] the origin of the Pegasus emblem of the Inner Temple,[9] the possible influence of Near Eastern cosmogonies on Elizabethan thought,[10] changing attitudes to Italy,[11] the justice of describing Stanyhurst's

1 Routledge and Kegan Paul, 1968.

2 Perhaps one should note here a modern analysis of one aspect of written Renaissance English, Frederick Bowers' 'A Transformational Description of the Elizabethan *be*+V-*ing*', *Orbis*, XVII (1968), 23–33.

3 'Two Sixteenth-Century Notices of Numerical Composition in Virgil's *Aeneid*', *Notes and Queries*, CCXIV (1969), 26–7.

4 'John Case—An Elizabethan Music Scholar', *Music and Letters*, L (1969), 252–66.

5 'An Approach to the Analysis of Renaissance Music', *The Music Review*, XXX (1969), 1–21.

6 'A New Source of Seventeenth-Century Keyboard Music', *Music and Letters*, L (1969), 278–89.

7 *Renaissance and Baroque Music*, translated by M. D. Herter Norton (Faber and Faber, 1968).

8 Walter R. Davis, 'The Plagiarisms of John Hynd', *Notes and Queries*, CCXIV (1969), 90–2.

9 D. S. Bland, 'Pegasus at the Inner Temple', *ibid.*, 16–18.

10 Blossom Feinstein, '*The Faerie Queene* and Cosmogonies of the Near East', *Journal of the History of Ideas*, XXIX (1968), 531–50.

11 George B. Parks, 'The Decline and Fall of the English Renaissance Admiration of Italy', *The Huntington Library Quarterly*, XXXI (1967–8), 341–57.

translation of the *Aeneid* (1582) as 'the common sewer of the language',[1] the costumes of thirty-six seventeenth-century trades and professions,[2] Renaissance fashions,[3] and the jocular 'safe conduct' given by the Mermaid Club to one of its members in 1612[4] have all been discussed, described or illustrated. Four of these miscellaneous studies have particular relevance to Shakespeare. Cynthia Griffin Wolff's 'Literary Reflections of the Puritan Character'[5] shows why the 'Puritan' character-type is capable of a variety of interpretations; T. M. Gang's 'The Quarrel Between Edward Fairfax and his Brother'[6] provides us with an exact analogy to the Edmund/Edgar situation in 1599–1600; B. Kniazevsky's 'Russia in Shakespeare's Plays'[7] examines Shakespeare's references to Russia and discusses Elizabethan awareness of things Russian; and Creighton Gilbert's thought-provoking essay 'When Did a Man in the Renaissance Grow Old?'[8] brings to light information suggesting that Shakespeare may well have been regarded as a very old man when he retired.

Conveniently spanning those studies concerned with the thought of the time and those more directly related to Shakespeare's non-dramatic contemporaries is John Wardroper's *Love and Drollery*,[9] a collection of some 400 items of witty and amatory verse (appropriately clad in purple covers) allowing us, as the editor suggests, to hear the voice of an age 'rude, phantastical, absurd, insolent, indiscreet'. Mr Wardroper has avoided the obvious material, canvassed manuscript collections, song books, verse miscellanies, etc., and brought to light numerous entertaining items which haven't seen the light of day since the seventeenth century. Altogether a delightful anthology which one suspects will rapidly be seen in provocative paper-back form! A full account of the year's work on Shakespeare's non-dramatic contemporaries would be out of place in this context, but a number of studies have thrown light on the thought, politics, or literary history of the period and are thus worthy of mention. Ambivalent attitudes to the word 'fancy' in the Renaissance, its association with perturbation and chaos but also with the imaginative powers of the mind are discussed by Donald M. Friedman in an interesting article on Wyatt,[10] in which analogies are suggested between Wyatt's thought and Shakespeare's. F. W. Brownlow[11] has attempted to make more perspicuous the nature of Skelton's satire on English politics around 1521 in *Speke, Parrot*; a new date (c. 1580) has been suggested for Breton's *Mavillia*;[12] and the pronunciation of Dowland's name has been reconsidered[13] (though it must be admitted that little reliance can be placed on the linguistic scholarship here—cf. the assumption that modern English 'doe' contains phonetic [o:]).

A spate of articles have appeared on Sidney. Four writers have discussed aspects of the

1 'Ruffe Raffe Roaring: A Sixteenth-Century Virgil' (Editorial article), *Arion*, VII (1968), 296–7.

2 Nicolas de L'Armessin and Gerard Valck, *Fantastic Costumes Of Trades and Professions* (Holland Press, 1969).

3 R. Broby-Johansen, *Body And Clothes* (Faber and Faber, 1968). Also, a sidelight is thrown on the costumes of the Caroline period by Gail S. Weinberg in 'Herrick's *Upon Julia's Clothes*', *The Explicator*, XXVII (1968–9), item 12.

4 Edgar Hinchcliffe, 'Thomae Coriati Testimonium', *Notes and Queries*, CCXIII (1968), 370–5.

5 *Journal of the History of Ideas*, XXIX (1968), 13–32.

6 *Notes and Queries*, CCXIV (1969), 28–33.

7 *Shekspirovski Cbornik*, ed. A. A. Anikst (Moscow, 1967).

8 *Studies in the Renaissance*, XIV (1967), 7–32.

9 Routledge and Kegan Paul, 1969.

10 'Wyatt and the Ambiguities of Fancy', *Journal of English and Germanic Philology*, LXVII (1968), 32–48.

11 '*Speke, Parrot*: Skelton's Allegorical Denunciation of Cardinal Wolsey', *Studies in Philology*, LXV (1968), 124–39.

12 Charles Crupi, 'The Date of Breton's *Mavillia*', *Notes and Queries*, CCXIV (1969), 27–8.

13 Victor Reed, 'Doleful Dowland', *English Language Notes*, VI (1968–9), 17–19.

Arcadia in relation to existing literary traditions, and hence have seen the work as in some way illuminating traditional ways of thought. Thus we have Elizabeth Dipple[1] suggesting that the *Old Arcadia*, while seeming to operate within the pastoral convention, is concerned with the destruction of 'the false delicacy of literary modes' and the substitution of 'the kind of viability real action calls for in the time ordered world of external responsibility'; Franco Marenco,[2] also concerned with the *Old Arcadia*, has seen the work in terms of the 'soul's pilgrimage' tradition and hence as analogous with *The Faerie Queene*; Alan D. Isler[3] has emphasized Sidney's concern with degree, with order within the family and state, thus stressing his affinities with numerous other Renaissance writers including Shakespeare; and the same writer has urged that the heroes of the *Arcadia* embody the two aspects of the Renaissance ideal man, courage and wisdom.[4] Various facts have come to light with regard to Sidney's life. It has been suggested that he (and his family) were hostile to Irish poets;[5] Fulke Greville's intentions with regard to his tomb and epitaph have been illuminated;[6] and an author has been suggested for the pseudonymous life prefixed to the 1655 edition of the *Arcadia*.[7] Of the usual plethora of Spenserian studies, one has been of particular interest to the student of Shakespeare's times, Douglas A. Northrop's 'Spenser's Defence of Elizabeth'.[8] Northrop argues that in *The Faerie Queene* Spenser justifies Elizabeth's internal and external policy in terms of Renaissance political theory. He distinguishes between various kinds of kingship recognized during the period, discusses the obligations incumbent upon each, and shows the way in which Elizabeth's practice conforms to the theory of her time. On the fringes of Spenserian scholarship, E.K., that dim figure who exists only in relation to the author of the *Shepherd's Calendar*, has been tentatively linked[9] with an E.K. who contributed Latin congratulatory verses to a book on the art of learning to swim! Another dim figure, Thomas Peend, has been brought out of the shadows to some extent by two articles by A. B. Taylor. Taylor suggests[10] that Peend's *The Pleasant Fable of Hermaphroditus and Salmacis*, far from being a sample of the translation of Ovid he claimed to have abandoned on hearing of Golding's work, in fact shows the influence of Golding's translation. Whether Peend had translated Ovid or not, his *Pleasant Fable*, Taylor claims, was not without influence. In his second article,[11] he attempts to demonstrate that Marlowe's *Hero and Leander* is indebted to Peend's work, but the 'parallels' drawn are too slight and too few to be convincing. The works of Samuel Daniel have inspired a massive critical study by Pierre

1 'Harmony and Pastoral in the *Old Arcadia*', *ELH*, XXXV (1968), 309–28.

2 'Double Plot in Sidney's *Old Arcadia*', *The Modern Language Review*, LXIV (1969), 248–63.

3 'Moral Philosophy and the Family in Sidney's *Arcadia*', *The Huntington Library Quarterly*, XXXI (1967–8), 359–71.

4 'The Allegory of the Hero and Sidney's Two *Arcadias*', *Studies in Philology*, LXV (1968), 171–91.

5 Katherine Duncan-Jones, 'A Note on Irish Poets and the Sidneys', *English Studies*, XLIX (1968), 424–5.

6 Joan Rees, 'Fulke Greville's Epitaph on Sidney', *The Review of English Studies*, XIX (1968), 47–51.

7 Daniel H. Woodward, 'Thomas Fuller, William Dugard, and the Pseudonymous Life of Sidney (1655)', *The Papers of the Bibliographical Society of America*, LXII (1968), 501–10.

8 *University of Toronto Quarterly*, XXXVIII (1968–9), 277–94. Also concerned with Spenser and Elizabeth is Lawrence Rosinger ('Spenser's Una and Queen Elizabeth', *English Language Notes*, VI (1968–9), 12–17) who argues that the name 'Una' refers explicitly to Elizabeth, being derived from her motto 'semper eadem' (apparently interchangeable with 'semper una').

9 René Graziani, 'Verses by E. K.', *Notes and Queries*, CCXIV (1969), 21.

10 'Thomas Peend and Arthur Golding', *ibid.*, 19–20.

11 'A Note on Christopher Marlowe's *Hero and Leander*', *ibid.*, 20–1.

Spriet,[1] *Delia* has been related to the emblem tradition,[2] and the same poem has been advanced as 'the high-water mark of deliberate artistry' in the history of the sonnet sequence in England.[3] Drayton has been the subject of an interesting essay by William H. Moore,[4] who contests the view that *Poly-Olbion* owes nothing to any previous writer, cites several works bearing a strong, though limited, resemblance to Drayton's own, and suggests that Drayton's book forms part of a wide and complex movement. Several articles on Donne have been concerned to place him in the context of Renaissance thought. Janel M. Mueller, in a discussion of the *Devotions upon Emergent Occasions* as representative of the syncretic spirit characteristic of English theology,[5] has stressed the meditative nature of the work, Rosalie Beck[6] has demonstrated that the reversal of Sacrobosco's system in *Goodfriday, 1613. Riding Westward* was current, and Thomas F. Merrill[7] has argued that Donne's attitude to the sermon is essentially Puritan rather than Anglican.[8] Fresh biographical information has appeared in the form of a new manuscript of Donne's poems[9] and essays both supporting and hotly disputing Lady Mary Clive's statement that Donne and Ann More married in January 1601/2.[10] Finally, before turning from Shakespeare's contemporaries to his stage, the fact that scholarly attention has been given to the work of a number of seventeenth-century prose writers must be celebrated. Launcelot Andrewes' *Preces Privatae* has been hailed[11] as one of the outstanding achievements of the devotional literature of the period, and a study has been made[12] of the work of eight writers (Donne, Bunyan, Lilburne, Burton, Baxter, Browne, Milton and Traherne) struggling, the author suggests, to find a significant meaning for their sense of self in terms of their own (Puritan or Anglican) tradition.

Of those works concerned with the history of the pre-Shakespearian stage, pride of place must go to *The English Drama 1485–1585* by F. P. Wilson, edited by G. K. Hunter.[13] Of Professor Hunter's contribution, the chronological table and extensive bibliography, I intend to say nothing except that the latter probably forms the most valuable part of the book as far as the scholar is concerned. Of the text, however, certain criticisms must be made.

[1] 'Samuel Daniel (1563–1619), Sa Vie—Son Oeuvre', *Études Anglaises*, XXIX (Didier, 1968).

[2] Lloyd Goldman, 'Samuel Daniel's *Delia* and the Emblem Tradition', *Journal of English and Germanic Philology*, LXVII (1968), 49–63.

[3] C. F. Williamson, 'The Design of Daniel's *Delia*', *The Review of English Studies*, XIX (1968), 251–60.

[4] 'Sources of Drayton's Conception of *Poly-Olbion*', *Studies in Philology*, LXV (1968), 783–803.

[5] 'The Exegesis of Experience: Dean Donne's *Devotions upon Emergent Occasions*', *Journal of English and Germanic Philology*, LXVII (1968), 1–19.

[6] 'A Precedent for Donne's Imagery in *Goodfriday, 1613. Riding Westward*', *The Review of English Studies*, XIX (1968), 166–9.

[7] 'John Donne and the Word of God', *Neuphilologische Mitteilungen*, LXIX (1968), 597–616.

[8] Also worthy of note are René Graziani's suggestion ('John Donne's *The Extasie* and Ecstasy', *The Review of English Studies*, XIX (1968), 121–36) that the Renaissance recognized a specialized use of the word ecstasy, exemplified in Donne's *The Extasie*, and Arthur F. Marotti's explication of lines 37–8 of *Loves Progress* by reference to comparable examples of Renaissance bawdry in *Romeo and Juliet* and *Bartholomew Fair* ('Donne's *Loves Progress*, ll. 37–8, and Renaissance Bawdry', *English Language Notes*, VI (1968–9), 24–5).

[9] Alan MacColl, 'A New Manuscript of Donne's Poems', *The Review of English Studies*, XIX (1968), 293–5.

[10] Edward Le Comte, 'The Date of Donne's Marriage', *Études Anglaises*, XXI (1968), 168–9; W. Milgate, 'The Date of Donne's Marriage. A Reply', *ibid.*, XXII (1969), 66–7.

[11] Elizabeth McCutcheon, 'Lancelot Andrewes' *Preces Privatae*: a Journey through Time', *Studies in Philology*, LXV (1968), 223–41.

[12] Joan Webber, *The Eloquent 'I'. Style and Self in Seventeenth-Century Prose* (University of Wisconsin Press, 1968).

[13] *The Oxford History of English Literature*, Vol. IV, Part I (Clarendon Press, Oxford, 1969).

Divisions both into chapters and within chapters sometimes seem arbitrary (for example, the Prodigal Son plays are included in a chapter entitled 'The Sacred Drama' rather than in 'The Late Tudor Morality Play' because 'the characters are non-allegorical'—but, as Professor Wilson himself admits, 'how easily do some of them dissolve into allegory'. Conversely, is not much of the allegorical drama sacred? More importantly, the coarseness of the comedy of the period is continually emphasized (cf. 'coarse as the play is, it still gives pleasure on the stage to anyone willing to spend an evening with our rude forefathers') but the function of this 'coarse' humour, within the morality play for example, is seen only in terms of 'light relief'. Equally dated is the tendency to see the drama not in its own right but in terms of the 'great age' which it heralded, a practice which, I am happy to say, has long been on the decline. In all, however, the book provides a readable, reliable and erudite guide to the drama of the period. Also concerned with the Tudor stage and Shakespeare's relationship with its traditions is David Bevington's interesting and well-documented book *Tudor Drama and Politics*.[1] Taking a wide definition of his subject to include all that relates to decision-making in government as well as those aspects of social and economic conditions which relate to the legal system, the author discusses the various types of political interest with which sixteenth-century drama is concerned. Four other items remain to be mentioned before turning to studies concerned with specific plays or aspects of them. A. Bartoshevich has produced an essay on pre-Shakespearian comedy[2] which adds little to our knowledge of the subject; Roderick Robertson[3] has provided us with a most interesting account of dramatic productions in Oxford during the Tudor period; John R. Elliott, Jr,[4] in a fascinating study of the dramatic uses of the Abraham and Isaac story, has demonstrated the radical differences between the medieval (basically comic) and Renaissance (incipiently tragic) treatments of the subject, emphasizing that 'in no sense does the medieval drama in this instance merely pave the way for the emergence of more artistic and sophisticated forms in the sixteenth century'; and Steven C. Young[5] has provided us with a full checklist of Tudor and Stuart Induction plays.

Contributions have been made to our understanding of a large number of plays by Shakespeare's predecessors. Edgar T. Schell[6] has suggested that *The Castle of Perseverence* is primarily a 'life pilgrimage' analogous with Deguileville's *Le Pelerinage de la Vie Humaine* rather than a dramatization of the psychomachia (the reviewer, while granting the presence of the journey motif, could not accept that it is the dominant element); D. C. Baker and J. L. Murphy[7] have argued that the *Burial and Resurrection* manuscript never formed part of Digby MS. 133 as Furnivall supposed; David G. Canzler[8] has discussed the printing of the Quarto editions of the *Play of the Wether*; Robert Carl Johnson[9]

[1] Harvard University Press, Cambridge Mass., 1968.

[2] 'The Comedy of Shakespeare's Predecessors', *Shekspirovski Cbornik*, ed. A. A. Anikst (Moscow, 1967).

[3] 'Oxford Theatre in Tudor Times', *Educational Theatre Journal*, XXI (1969), 41–50.

[4] 'The Sacrifice of Isaac as Comedy and Tragedy', *Studies in Philology*, LXVI (1969), 36–59.

[5] 'A Check List of Tudor and Stuart Induction Plays', *Philological Quarterly*, XLVIII (1969), 131–4.

[6] 'On the Imitation of Life's Pilgrimage in *The Castle of Perseverance*', *Journal of English and Germanic Philology*, LXVII (1968), 235–48.

[7] 'The Bodleian MS. *E.Mus.* 160 *Burial* and *Resurrection* and the Digby Plays', *The Review of English Studies*, XIX (1968), 290–3.

[8] 'Quarto Editions of *Play of the Wether*', *The Papers of the Bibliographical Society of America*, LXII (1968), 313–9.

[9] 'The Third Quarto of *Cambises*', *Notes and Queries*, CCXIII (1968), 247, and 'Press Variants in *Cambises*', *ibid.*, 246–7.

has considered the relationship between the three Quartos of *Cambises* and proposed fresh readings for lines 1042 and 1048–9 of the play; Rainer Pineas[1] has demonstrated the sophistication of the polemical techniques employed in *The Pedlers Prophecie*; John W. Velz and Carl P. Daw, Jr,[2] have urged that *Wyt and Science* should be assigned a more prominent place in the history of the English stage as an important link between medieval drama and Romantic comedy; T. N. S. Lennam[3] has given us an account of the life of Francis Merbury, generally accepted as the author of *The Marriage Between Wit and Wisdom*; Herbert R. Coursen, Jr,[4] has maintained that the motivating force behind *The Spanish Tragedy* is the dynastic ambition of the House of Castile (this transforms *The Spanish Tragedy* into a highly unified action, but unfortunately involves an unpardonably cavalier attitude to the text); and George M. Logan[5] has complicated the controversy over whether *The Misfortunes of Arthur* is to be regarded as traditional English history play or Senecan pastiche by pointing out that Lucan contributed more lines to the play than Seneca. An even larger body of material has appeared on Shakespeare's contemporaries. N. W. Bawcutt[6] has shown that the source for the blowing-up of Selim-Calymath's soldiers (*Jew of Malta*, Act V) may have been either Foxe's *Acts and Monuments* or Lonicerus' *Chronicorum Turcorum*; Frederick Burwick[7] has demonstrated Marlowe's ability to combine the 'contrived sophistries of dialectic enquiry with the spontaneous outburst of passion' in *Doctor Faustus*; Norman Gelber[8] has unravelled the 'thematic ambiguity' of Greene's *Orlando Furioso* (but did a problem exist?); Michael R. Best[9] has suggested that *Summer's Last Will and Testament* originated as a short entertainment by Lyly subsequently expanded by Nashe, and that it is best regarded 'as an exercise [by Nashe] in practical dramatic criticism'; G. K. Hunter has written an admirably succinct introduction to the work of Lyly and Peele for the Writers and Their Work series,[10] and Henry G. Lesnick[11] has defended the structural integrity of *The Arraignment of Paris*.

On the far side of the Elizabethan–Jacobean boundary Jonson rises clad in a multitude of stars of varying degrees of brilliance. Two general studies have been made of the entire corpus of his plays, one[12] arguing that his work is concerned with the conversion of things as they are into things as they should be with 'vision in the framework and judgment in the specific content', the other[13] contending (somewhat dubiously) that his dramatic works, with the exception of the single 'genuine Aristophanic drama' *Bartholomew Fair*, are the record of his failure to adapt the features of Old Comedy to the Elizabethan–Jacobean

1 'Polemical Technique in *The Pedlers Prophecie*', *English Language Notes*, VI (1968–9), 90–4.

2 'Tradition and Originality in *Wyt and Science*', *Studies in Philology*, LXV (1968), 631–46.

3 'Francis Merbury, 1555–1611', *ibid.*, 207–22.

4 'The Unity of *The Spanish Tragedy*', *ibid.*, 768–82.

5 'Hughes's Use of Lucan in *The Misfortunes of Arthur*', *The Review of English Studies*, XX (1969), 22–32.

6 'Marlowe's *Jew of Malta* and Foxe's *Acts and Monuments*', *Notes and Queries*, CCXIII (1968), 250.

7 'Marlowe's *Doctor Faustus*: Two Manners, the Argumentative and the Passionate', *Neuphilologische Mitteilungen*, LXX (1969), 121–45.

8 'Robert Greene's *Orlando Furioso*: A Study of Thematic Ambiguity', *The Modern Language Review*, LXIV (1969), 264–6.

9 'Nashe, Lyly, and *Summer's Last Will and Testament*', *Philological Quarterly*, XLVIII (1969), 1–11.

10 *Lyly and Peele* (Longmans, Green, 1968).

11 'The Structural Significance of Myth and Flattery in Peele's *Arraignment of Paris*', *Studies in Philology*, LXV (1968), 163–70.

12 Gabriele Bernhard Jackson, *Vision and Judgment in Ben Jonson's Drama* (Yale University Press, 1968).

13 Coburn Gum, *The Aristophanic Comedies of Ben Jonson* (Mouton, The Hague, 1969).

stage. Two writers have been concerned with the 'Renaissance' quality of his work—G. A. E. Parfitt[1] maintaining that his thought is Elizabethan rather than classical, but that he is individual in his emphasis on social rather than religious values, and Gayle Edward Wilson[2] discussing the extensive use made of the Bible and the concept of the Great Chain of Being in *Penshurst* (thus refuting, by implication, Parfitt's view that Penshurst is not seen as dependent on God's grace and help). On individual plays, Barbara N. Lindsay[3] has analyzed the three levels upon which *Sejanus* operates; William Empson,[4] in a typically lively essay, has urged us to take a more 'jovial' attitude to *Volpone*; Harriett Hawkins,[5] clearly one of that 'moralizing school' of critics of whom Empson disapproves, has demonstrated the relationship between folly and incurable disease throughout the same play and suggested that the 'perpetuall' nature of the punishments stresses the incurable folly of the protagonists; C. J. Gianakaris,[6] in a less cogently argued essay, has seen the central value of *Volpone* to be 'sound, reasonable conduct' with the audience rejecting the central character only when he begins to act irrationally (but is he ever rational?); L. A. Beaurline[7] has discussed the impulse towards 'controlled completeness' in Jonson's work as exemplified in the structure of *The Alchemist*; William Blissett,[8] also concerned with *The Alchemist*, has sought, rather unconvincingly, to see a morality play structure underlying the action; and Irena Janicka[9] has traced elements of various medieval forms of entertainment in the masques. Last but not least one must record a dissertation upon the Jonsonian tortoise.[10]

Various aspects of Chapman's work have received scholarly scrutiny, including his choice of material,[11] the ownership of *Bussy D'Ambois*,[12] whether the *Banquet of Sense* is concerned with the ascent or descent of the Platonic ladder,[13] and the possibility that the epigraph to the same poem may guide us towards an ironic reading of it.[14] Two writers have been concerned with Middleton's handling of his plots. Ruby Chatterji[15] has considered the relationship between the main and subsidiary actions of *Michaelmas Term* and found each to be concerned with a temptation/fall sequence (a further example of the increasing tendency to see a morality play basis beneath the non-allegorical products of the Elizabethan–Jacobean stage), while David M. Holmes[16] has

1 'Ethical Thought and Ben Jonson's Poetry', *Studies in English Literature 1500–1900*, IX (1969), 123–34.

2 'Jonson's Use of the Bible and the Great Chain of Being in *To Penshurst*', *Studies in English Literature 1500–1900*, VIII (1968), 77–89.

3 'The Structure of Tragedy in *Sejanus*', *English Studies*, Anglo-American Supplement (1969), xliv–l.

4 '*Volpone*', *The Hudson Review*, XXI (1968), 651–66.

5 'Folly, Incurable Disease, and *Volpone*', *Studies in English Literature 1500–1900*, VIII (1968), 335–48.

6 'Identifying Ethical Values in *Volpone*', *The Huntington Library Quarterly*, XXXII (1968–9), 45–57.

7 'Ben Jonson and the Illusion of Completeness', *PMLA*, LXXXIV (1969), 51–9.

8 'The Venter Tripartite in *The Alchemist*', *Studies in English Literature 1500–1900*, VIII (1968), 323–34.

9 'The Popular Background of Ben Jonson's Masques', *Shakespeare-Jahrbuch*, CV (1969), 183–208.

10 Ian Donaldson, 'Jonson's Tortoise', *The Review of English Studies*, XIX (1968), 162–6.

11 Robert K. Presson, 'Wrestling with This World: A View of George Chapman', *PMLA*, LXXXIV (1969), 44–50.

12 John Freehafer, 'The Contention For *Bussy D'Ambois*, 1622–41', *Theatre Notebook*, XXIII (1968–9), 61–9. Also on *Bussy D'Ambois* see N. W. Bawcutt, 'Chapman's "Friar Comolet"', *Notes and Queries*, CCXIII (1968), 250–2.

13 James Phares Myers, Jr, '"This Curious Frame": Chapman's *Ovid's Banquet of Sense*', *Studies in Philology*, LXV (1968), 192–206.

14 Raymond B. Waddington, 'Chapman and Persius: The Epigraph to *Ovids Banquet of Sence*', *The Review of English Studies*, XIX (1968), 158–62.

15 'Unity and Disparity in *Michaelmas Term*', *Studies in English Literature 1500–1900*, VIII (1968), 349–63.

16 'Thomas Middleton's *Blurt Master-Constable or, The Spaniard's Night-Walk*', *The Modern Language Review*, LXIV (1969), 1–10.

argued that the juxtaposition of complimentary plots in *Blurt, Master-Constable* is typical of the dramatist, as is the 'disenchanting realism' of the play. The records of The Merchant Taylors' Company have been re-examined by two scholars[1] in search of biographical information about John Webster (and, in one instance, Anthony Munday), and a massive two-volume study[2] of Webster's life and work has appeared. The question of Beaumont's share in *The Noble Gentleman* has been re-examined,[3] the biographies of Massinger's parents have been filled in,[4] and his non-dramatic poems edited.[5] Ford has been the subject of an important, if unequal, book by Mark Stavig,[6] who has taken issue with the traditional view of the dramatist as a purveyor of decadent and sensational plays for a jaded public. Stavig argues that Ford is a serious moralist, deeply concerned about order within society, and that he insists upon 'honesty, rationality, naturalness and simplicity as the values on which a meaningful life can be based'. Many individual points seem dubious (for example, it is hard to see the Friar in *'Tis Pity* as 'the symbol of true religion') but the book at least makes the reader consider the plays from a fresh angle. The chronology of Ford's plays has been the subject of an article by Tucker Orbison,[7] who suggests that the dating of *The Queen* can be narrowed to *c.* 1624–33 (as against Schoenbaum's *c.* 1621–42), and a source has been pointed out[8] for the characterization of John a Water in *Perkin Warbeck*. In the remoter regions of Elizabethan drama, *The Italian Night Piece* of the Stationers' Register and *The Italian Night Masque* to which Wotton refers have been identified with *Luminalia* and *Aglaura* respectively;[9] further evidence has been advanced to support the view that *The Captives* is by Heywood and that the sole surviving manuscript is an authorial copy;[10] the motives for the publication of *Pedantius* in 1630–1, fifty years after the play was composed, have been scrutinized;[11] and the sources of Sir Ralph Freeman's *Imperiale* and 'J.S.'s' *Andromana* have been examined.[12] The relevance of the term 'decadent' with reference to the products of the late Renaissance stage has been considered in an interesting study by Robert Weimann[13] relating drama before and after the turn of the century to the society for which each catered. Weimann argues that the typical Elizabethan play is a 'gallimaufry' directed towards a heterogenous audience, while the

[1] R. G. Howarth, 'Two Notes on John Webster', *The Modern Language Review*, LXIII (1968), 785–9, and Charles R. Forker, 'Two Notes on John Webster and Anthony Munday: Unpublished Entries in The Records of the Merchant Taylors', *English Language Notes*, VI (1968–9), 26–34.

[2] Fernand Lagarde, *John Webster*, Association des Publications de la Faculté des Lettres et Sciences Humaines de Toulouse, Vol. 7 (Toulouse, 1968).

[3] R. F. Willson, Jr, 'Francis Beaumont and *The Noble Gentleman*', *English Studies*, XLIX (1968), 523–9.

[4] Donald S. Lawless, 'The Parents of Philip Massinger', *Notes and Queries*, CCXIII (1968), 256–8.

[5] Donald S. Lawless, *The Poems of Philip Massinger, with Critical Notes*, Ball State Monograph No. 13 (Ball State University, Muncie, Indiana, 1968).

[6] *John Ford and the Traditional Moral Order* (University of Wisconsin Press, 1968).

[7] 'The Date of *The Queen*', *Notes and Queries*, CCXIII (1968), 255–6.

[8] Michael Neill, 'Ford and Gainsford: An Unnoticed Borrowing', *ibid.*, 253–5.

[9] John Freehafer, '*The Italian Night Piece* and Suckling's *Aglaura*', *Journal of English and Germanic Philology*, LXVII (1968), 249–65.

[10] Anthony Low, 'Thomas Heywood's Authorship of *The Captives*', *Notes and Queries*, CCXIII (1968), 252–3.

[11] J. Biller, 'Gabriel Harvey and the Publication of *Pedantius*', *ibid.*, 249–50.

[12] Kenneth Richards, 'The Sources of Sir Ralph Freeman's *Imperiale*', *Studia Neophilologia*, XL (1968), 185–96. Michael C. Andrews, 'The Sources of *Andromana*', *The Review of English Studies*, XIX (1968), 295–300.

[13] 'Le déclin de la scène "indivisible" élisabethaine: Beaumont, Fletcher et Heywood', *Dramaturgie et Société*, Colloques Internationaux du Centre National de la Recherche Scientifique (Paris, 1968), 815–27.

so-called 'decline' of Renaissance drama reflects a division of interests and consequent specialization analogous to the divisions taking place within church and state. Finally, three items from the penumbra of semi-dramatic material remain to be noted. David M. Bergeron[1] has cast considerable light on the Christmas family, the chief artificers of Stuart civic pageantry; Jean Knowlton[2] has assigned forty of the masques in B.M. Additional MS. 10444 to the Jacobean period (which supports other evidence that this is a Jacobean, not a Jacobean-Caroline, collection), and S. Musgrove[3] has demonstrated that (contrary to general opinion) string puppets were common (in Scotland, at least) before the Restoration.

The most important of the year's contributions to our knowledge of the Elizabethan stage have undoubtedly been two articles[4] on the significance of the Fludd engravings. Frances A. Yates, clarifying her original suggestion that the engravings represent the Globe in order to refute Shapiro's Blackfriars contention, has produced a reconstruction of the Globe based on the Fludd drawings. Though the author's objections to Shapiro's theory are sound, her own reconstruction takes such liberties with the original that virtually only the five doors of the memory system remain common to both. Opposed to both Frances Yates and Shapiro is Herbert Berry, who has argued convincingly that the engravers were not careful in their treatment of architectural details (and hence that their drawing cannot be regarded as a reliable reflection of any playhouse), that Fludd conceived his idea in a continental theatre and therefore probably had a continental theatre in mind, and that the work, being directed to a non-English audience, was not likely to employ an English playhouse as an example. Clearly we haven't heard the last of this issue. Two other interesting articles have appeared on aspects of Renaissance dramatic productions: William A. Ringler, Jr's 'The Number of Actors in Shakespeare's Early Plays', a new article published in *The Seventeenth-Century Stage*,[5] and Kenneth R. Richards' 'Changeable Scenery for Plays on the Caroline Stage'.[6] The former examines the character groupings in two of Shakespeare's early comedies, *Love's Labour's Lost* and *A Midsummer Night's Dream*, in order to establish how many actors took part in each and which parts were doubled. The results are startling; for example, it is suggested that the mechanicals in the latter play doubled with the fairies, who were hence distinguished not by their 'diminutive beauty' but their 'bulky grotesquerie'. The second article argues that there are no good grounds for believing that changeable painted scenery was used prior to the Restoration on other than 'special occasions' before 'exclusive audiences' in 'private and aristocratic venues'. Various minor points on Elizabethan stages, staging and stage history have been made. Ernest Schanzer[7] has discussed the sources and reliability of our information regarding the sign and motto of the Globe; A. L. Soens[8] has described the stage business implied in *Lear* III, iv, 62–5; Dieter Mehl[9] has considered

1 'The Christmas Family: Artificers in English Civic Pageantry', *ELH*, XXXV (1968), 354–64.

2 'Dating the Masque Dances in British Museum Additional MS. 10444', *The British Museum Quarterly*, XXXII no. 3–4 (Spring 1968), 99–102.

3 'A Seventeenth-Century Reference to String Puppets', *Notes and Queries*, CCXIII (1968), 262.

4 Frances A. Yates, 'The Stage in Robert Fludd's Memory System', *Shakespeare Studies*, III (1967), 138–66, and Herbert Berry, 'Dr. Fludd's Engravings and Their Beholders', *ibid.*, 11–21.

5 Ed. Gerald Eades Bentley (University of Chicago Press, 1968), pp. 110–34.

6 *Theatre Notebook*, XXIII (1968–9), 6–20.

7 'Hercules and his load', *The Review of English Studies*, XIX (1968), 51–3.

8 '*King Lear* III, iv, 62–65: A Fencing Pun and Staging', *English Language Notes*, VI (1968–9), 19–24.

9 'Emblematik im englischen Drama der Shakespearezeit', *Anglia*, LXXXVII (1969), 126–46.

the use of emblems, verbal and physical, on the Elizabethan stage; and J. M. Nosworthy[1] has made a minute contribution to our understanding of Henslowe's pawn accounts. Finally a general survey of 'Popular Entertainment in Seventeenth Century Scotland'[2] (gloomy reading) must be mentioned before turning to the chequered history of Shakespearian productions 1611–1969.

First mention in this section must undoubtedly go to Dennis Bartholomeusz's *Macbeth and the Players*.[3] In order to test 'the proposition that players achieve special insights into a text, insights not normally available to critics and scholars', the author has traced the history of *Macbeth* on the stage, from its first recorded performance in 1611 up to Olivier's appearance in the title role. All kinds of evidence—contemporary accounts, pictures, playbills, etc.—are used to aid the process of reconstruction, and the result makes entertaining and instructive reading (cf. Marvin Rosenberg's *The Masks of Othello*). One could wish that the reader were warned about the dubious nature of some kinds of evidence, e.g. Simon Forman's account of the 1611 *Macbeth*, but the study does nevertheless provide a useful corrective to the 'Shakespeare in the closet' type of approach. The acting texts of *Hamlet* have also been the subject of a thought-provoking historical study. Taking the scripts used for notable productions between 1676 and 1963, Claris Glick[4] has analyzed the type of material omitted and interpolated, the comparative length of performances and the gradual growth of a sense of respect for the original text. A statistical table demonstrates how much (or, more accurately, how little) Shakespearian material our ancestors heard during individual performances. Cornmarket Press, too, have contributed to our understanding of the forms in which the plays appeared on the seventeenth- and eighteenth-century stage with their series of facsimiles (published 1969) of Shakespearian adaptations from the Restoration to the death of Garrick. Included is the fascinating *Dramatic Character Plates For Bell's Edition of Shakespeare's Plays 1775–6*, which depicts leading actors and actresses of the day in what seem to us startlingly incongruous costumes. A number of studies of individual plays, players and playhouses have appeared. Maximillian E. Novak[5] has considered the authorship of the musical adaptation of the Dryden–Davenant version of *The Tempest*; Benjamin Blom have reprinted George Saunders' treatise on the ideal theatre (1790) which includes an account of a number of London playhouses existing *c.* 1790;[6] David Rostron[7] has examined the prompt books for Kemble's productions of *Coriolanus* and *Julius Caesar*; Richard Foulkes[8] has discussed Samuel Phelps' production of *A Midsummer Night's Dream* in 1853 and argued that 'certainly not before, and probably not since has *A Midsummer Night's Dream* received such a fine and appropriate staging'; and *Shakespeare-Jahrbuch*, CV (1969)[9] have printed Jenny Marx's reactions to London productions of the 1870s, including Irving's *Richard III*. Transmutations and interpretations of the corpus overseas including the Marquis d'Argens' translation

[1] 'Dornackes and Colysenes in Henslowe's Diary', *Notes and Queries*, CCXIII (1968), 247–8.

[2] Terence Tobin, *Theatre Notebook*, XXIII (1968–9), 46–54.

[3] Cambridge University Press, 1969.

[4] '*Hamlet* in the English Theater—Acting Texts, 1676–1963', *Shakespeare Quarterly*, XX (1969), 17–35.

[5] 'Elkannah Settle's Attacks on Thomas Shadwell and the Authorship of the "Operatic Tempest"', *Notes and Queries*, CCXIII (1968), 263–5.

[6] *A Treatise on Theatres* (New York, 1968).

[7] 'John Philip Kemble's *Coriolanus* And *Julius Caesar*. An Examination Of The Prompt Copies', *Theatre Notebook*, XXIII (1968–69), 26–34.

[8] 'Samuel Phelps's *A Midsummer Night's Dream*, Sadler's Wells—October 8th, 1853', *ibid.*, 55–60.

[9] 'Jenny Marx als Theaterkritikerin', 54–69.

of *Hamlet*,[1] the Herwegh *Lear* in Dresden,[2] *Hamlet* in the nineteenth-century Russian theatre,[3] Shakespeare in the Russian provinces before the Revolution,[4] the 1912 Craig–Stanislavsky *Hamlet*,[5] the 1940–3 *Hamlet* in Moscow,[6] and the translations of Küchelbekker[7] have all been recorded, while a fascinating account[8] has been published of the growth of the Gielgud–Burton *Hamlet* (New York, 1964), assembled from tape recordings made during rehearsals. Surveys of contemporary productions in Britain,[9] the USA,[10] Canada[11] and Germany[12] have appeared, and the contemporary scene has been surveyed.[13] Finally two contrasting styles of acting, one, post-Gielgud, concerned with the 'total emotional flow of a speech', the other, post-Olivier, with 'naturalism', have been defined and discussed.[14]

Shakespearian plays on film have received an unusually large share of critical attention. Robert Hamilton Ball[15] has written a most interesting account of the history of Shakespeare on the silent film screen between 1899 and 1925, Russian[16] and German[17] reactions to recent Shakespearian productions have been noted, and the difficulties attendant upon accommodating music to screenplay have been considered.[18]

This year has produced a number of major contributions to the documentation and study of Shakespearian criticism. Outstanding in this field is John W. Velz's *Shakespeare and the Classical Tradition*,[19] 'an attempt to gather, classify, summarize, and appraise' the material which has appeared on Shakespeare's classical learning since 1660. This Herculean task (made more difficult by the author's wide definition

[1] Hans Mattauch, 'Der französische *Hamlet* des Marquis d'Argens (1744)', *Deutsche Shakespeare-Gesellschaft West Jahrbuch* (1968), 179–92.

[2] Ursula Püschel, 'Gesichtspunkte für die Wahl der Herwegh-Übersetzung bei der Inszenierung von *König Lear* in Dresden', *Shakespeare-Jahrbuch*, CV (1969), 70–88.

[3] B. Eikhenbaum, 'A Contribution to the History of *Hamlet* in Russia', *Shekspirovski Cbornik*, ed. A. A. Anikst (Moscow, 1967).

[4] Sophia Nels, 'Shakespearean Performances of the Provincial Tragedians', *ibid.*

[5] Kaoru Osanai, 'Gordon Craig's Production of *Hamlet* at the Moscow Art Theatre', translated by Andrew T. Tsubaki, *Educational Theatre Journal*, XX (1968), 588–93.

[6] V. I. Nemirovich-Danchenko, 'From a Shorthand Report of Talks and Rehearsals of *Hamlet* in 1940–43', *Shekspirovski Cbornik*, ed. A. A. Anikst (Moscow, 1967).

[7] Yu. Levin, 'W. K. Küchelbekker as Translator of Shakespeare', *ibid.*

[8] Richard L. Sterne, *John Gielgud Directs Richard Burton in 'Hamlet'* (Heinemann, 1968).

[9] Robert Speaight, 'Shakespeare in Britain', *Shakespeare Quarterly*, XIX (1968), 367–75.

[10] See Bernard Beckerman, 'Stratford (Connecticut) Revisited 1968', *ibid.*, 377–80; Mildred C. Kuner, 'The New York Shakespeare Festival, 1968', *ibid.*, 385–6; Lynne K. Horobetz, 'The Washington Shakespeare Summer Festival, 1968', *ibid.*, 391–2.

[11] See Arnold Edinborough, 'Stratford, Ontario —1968', *ibid.*, 381–4; Robert Ornstein, 'The Great Lakes Shakespeare Festival', *ibid.*, 387–9.

[12] See Karl Brinkmann, 'Bühnenbericht 1967', *Deutsche Shakespeare-Gesellschaft West Jahrbuch* (1968), 207–16; Armin-Gerd Kuckhoff, 'Shakespeare auf den Bühnen der DDR im Jahre 1967', *Shakespeare-Jahrbuch*, CV (1969), 209–20; Armin-Gerd Kuckhoff, 'Shakespeare auf den Bühnen der Bundesrepublik Deutschlands und Westberlins im Jahre 1967', *ibid.*, 221–7; Anthony Vivis, 'Shakespeare without the shadows' (review of Peter Palitzsch's *The Wars of the Roses*, Württemburg State Theatre), *Gambit*, III (no. 10), 96–9.

[13] Robert Weimann, 'Shakespeare Pe Scena Contemporană', *Studii Şi Cercetări De Istoria Artei Seria Teatru-Muzică-Cinematografie*, XV (1968), 101–5.

[14] Gareth Lloyd Evans, 'Shakespeare and the Actors: Notes towards Interpretations', *Shakespeare Survey 21* (1968), 115–25.

[15] *Shakespeare On Silent Film* (George Allen and Unwin, 1968).

[16] 'Shakespeare on the Stage and Screen', *Shekspirovski Cbornik*, ed. A. A. Anikst (Moscow, 1967).

[17] Karl Brinkmann, 'Filmbericht', *Deutsche Shakespeare-Gesellschaft West Jahrbuch* (1968), 217–18.

[18] Charles Hurtgen, 'The Operatic Character of Background Music in Film Adaptations of Shakespeare', *Shakespeare Quarterly*, XX (1969), 53–64.

[19] University of Minnesota Press, Minneapolis, 1968.

of his field) is accomplished with remarkable thoroughness. The book covers bibliographies, general works, the plays (divided into sections rather than dealt with chronologically), the poems, and modern editions of classical material available to Shakespeare. Material in English, French and German is included, omissions are remarkably few (the most regrettable being the decision to exclude introductions to modern editions) and there is considerable cross-referencing between entries. All-in-all the book provides an invaluable handbook to the subject and should help to prevent duplication of research. Two surveys of the history of Shakespeare criticism deserve mention. Arthur M. Eastman's *A Short History of Shakespearean Criticism*[1] is misleadingly entitled since it devotes only 16½ pages to the first 150 years of Shakespearian scholarship (excluding Johnson who has a section to himself), while the nineteenth and twentieth centuries are dealt with in minute detail. An interesting book, in spite of a tendency to equate quantity with importance and to slip between the two stools of tracing movements and discussing specific works. Wertzman's 'Shakespeare Through the Ages'[2] argues that two distinct attitudes (Shakespeare as contemporary/Shakespeare as alien) dominate the history of Shakespearian criticism.

Most important among the year's contributions to the study of individual Shakespearian critics is *Johnson on Shakespeare*,[3] volumes VII and VIII of the Yale edition of Johnson's works. This immaculately produced edition includes all the longer pieces (the *Preface*, *Miscellaneous Observations on the Tragedy of Macbeth*, etc.) together with the notes on individual plays (relevant passages of text are included to make the force of the notes apparent). An introduction by Bertrand Bronson traces the history of Johnson's interest in an edition of Shakespeare and takes issue with the view that the long delay in the appearance of the work was the result of indolence. For students of Shakespeare and Johnson alike, this edition, to borrow Bronson's words on the *Preface*, 'is not to be superseded, and it is indispensable'. Scholars have contributed to our knowledge of the life and work of a number of other important Shakespearian critics. George B. Bryan[4] has discussed the theatrical education and critical attitudes of John Quincey Adams; J. R. de J. Jackson[5] has attempted to 'explain' some of Coleridge's 'mildly eccentric' critical views (the reviewer did not find Coleridge's views particularly eccentric); H. Kornilova[6] has discussed the work of Nicolai Ilyich Storozhenko, the founding father of Russian Shakespearian scholarship; and Charles Haywood,[7] in an entertaining article, has shown how Shaw's comments on the incidental music to Shakespearian productions throw light both on the musical tastes of his age and the perceptiveness of the critic.

The pervasive influence of the canon has, as usual, been richly documented. Scholars have pointed out the element of Shakespearian burlesque in *The Seven Champions of Christendom*,[8] the influence of *King Lear* on *Herod*

[1] Random House, New York, 1968.

[2] *Shekspirovski Cbornik*, ed. A. A. Anikst (Moscow, 1967).

[3] Ed. Arthur Sherbo, with an introduction by Bertrand H. Bronson (Yale University Press, 1968).

[4] 'Pilgrim at the Shrine of a Saint: John Quincey Adams on Shakespeare', *Educational Theatre Journal*, XX (1968), 516–23.

[5] 'Free Will in Coleridge's Shakespeare', *University of Toronto Quarterly*, XXXVIII (1968–9), 34–50.

[6] 'The First Russian Shakespearean Scholar', *Shekspirovski Cbornik*, ed. A. A. Anikst (Moscow, 1967).

[7] 'George Bernard Shaw on Incidental Music in the Shakespearean Theater', *Shakespeare-Jahrbuch* CV (1969), 168–82.

[8] John Freehafer, 'Shakespeare's *Tempest* and *The Seven Champions*', *Studies in Philology*, LXVI (1969), 87–103.

and Antipater,[1] the occurrence of a number of unrecorded Shakespearian allusions in miscellany editions of 1621 and 1630,[2] the presence of an echo of Sonnet 66 in *All For Love*,[3] the nature of the relationship between Verdi's *Otello* and *Othello*,[4] the un-Shakespearian mood of Delacroix's illustrations of the same play,[5] the ghost of *Hamlet* at work in Valéry's *Cimetière Marin*,[6] the similarities between the experience of King Lear and Father Sergius,[7] the effect of the plays on Chekhov,[8] Marx[9] and Gorki,[10] the impact of the songs on Housman,[11] and *Measure for Measure* on Pushkin,[12] the social implications (one shuddered to read them!) of contemporary Shakespearian parody,[13] and the Elizabethan origins of modern American non-heroic tragedy.[14] And finally one must note that the long shadow of the dramatist has extended as far as an 'American Tribal Love-Rock Musical'[15] before (reverently) closing the pages of Shakespeare's life, times and stage for this year.

[1] Leah Scragg, 'Shakespearian Influence in *Herod and Antipater*', *Notes and Queries*, CCXIII (1968), 258–62.

[2] Roland M. Frye, 'Five Shakespeare Allusions: 1621–1630', *Shakespeare Quarterly*, XX (1969), 81–3.

[3] H. Neville Davies, 'Shakespeare's Sonnet LXVI Echoed in *All for Love*', *Notes and Queries*, CCXIII (1968), 262–3.

[4] George Hauger, '*Othello* and *Otello*', *Music and Letters*, L (1969), 76–85, and Winton Dean, 'Verdi's *Otello*: a Shakespearian Masterpiece', *Shakespeare Survey 21* (1968), 87–96.

[5] Christina Merchant, 'Delacroix's Tragedy of Desdemona', *Shakespeare Survey 21* (1968), 79–86.

[6] Maria Teresa Maiorana, 'L'ombre de *Hamlet* dans *Le Cimetière Marin*', *Revue de Littérature Comparée*, XLII (1968), 346–65.

[7] John Bayley, '*King Lear* and *Father Sergius*: A Parallel', *Forum for Modern Language Studies*, IV (1968), 64–9.

[8] M. Smolkin, 'Shakespeare in the Life and Works of Chekhov', *Shekspirovski Cbornik*, ed. A. A. Anikst (Moscow, 1967).

[9] Johanna Rudolph, 'Karl Marx und Shakespeare', *Shakespeare-Jahrbuch*, CV (1969), 25–53.

[10] Wilfried Adling, 'Gorki und Shakespeare. Zur Shakespeare-Rezeption im dramatischen Spätwerk Maxim Gorkis', *ibid.*, 89–103.

[11] J. N. Wysong, 'The Influence of Shakespeare's Songs on the Poetry of A. E. Housman', *Shakespeare Quarterly*, XIX (1968), 333–9.

[12] Dmitrij M. Urnow, 'Puschkin und Shakespeares *Mass für Mass*', *Shakespeare-Jahrbuch*, CV (1969), 140–57.

[13] Clive Barker, 'Contemporary Shakespearean Parody in British Theatre', *ibid.*, 104–20.

[14] Samuel L. Macey, 'Nonheroic Tragedy: A Pedigree for American Tragic Drama', *Comparative Literature Studies*, VI (1969), 1–19.

[15] *Hair*, by Gerome Ragni and James Rado, produced by Michael Butler (London producer: James Verner).

3. TEXTUAL STUDIES

reviewed by Richard Proudfoot

The need for a new Shakespeare concordance, more complete and more accurate than John Bartlett's *New and Complete Concordance* of 1894, may not have been acute but it existed and it was inevitable that the aid of computers would be enlisted in compiling such a concordance. Not one but two computer-generated concordances are now in course of publication. The first volumes of Marvin Spevack's modern-spelling concordance, based on the forthcoming *Riverside Shakespeare* under the textual editorship of G. Blakemore Evans, were reviewed last year. The year 1969 has seen the publication of five sections of T. H. Howard-Hill's old-spelling concordance, based on the text of the First Folio and of selected Quartos.[1] His *Oxford Shakespeare Concordances* are intimately related to Dr Alice Walker's *Oxford Shakespeare* and use the early text of each play which she has chosen as her copy-text. Fears that the two concordances may render each other redundant are to some extent mitigated by the two editors' widely differing aims and methods: Spevack's promises to be a useful work of general reference, Howard-Hill's is essentially a tool for minute study of Shakespeare's language and text which preserves the linguistic and typographical details of the early texts.

The brief general introduction to the *Oxford Concordances* is supplemented by the editor's paper on 'The Oxford Old-Spelling Shakespeare Concordances' in *Studies in Bibliography*,[2] to which users of the concordances are referred for 'an account of the principles and methods by which the concordances were edited'. Howard-Hill faces squarely the question which will be in the minds of many users of the concordances, and expresses his own sympathy with the view that 'to use a computer just to produce a concordance seems an indefensible waste of time and resources'. He himself sees the concordances as only basic working tools and concedes the unsophisticated nature of any concordance as a tool for editors. The publication of the concordances is intended to be no more than the starting-point for a further and fuller study of the influence of scribes and compositors in the transmission of Shakespeare's text. It is for this reason and in the absence of any definitive edited text which could become the basis for a definitive concordance that he has chosen to concord the texts of the First Folio and of the good Quartos. These texts have been transferred to magnetic tape with a minimum of 'pre-editing' (carefully described in the article) and the production of the concordances is only one of many possible uses of the tapes.

Of Bartlett, until last year his only serious competitor, Howard-Hill justly writes that his 'omissions as well as his dependence on an obsolete modern-spelling edition [the Globe] renders his concordance practically useless for the detailed orthographical study which might lead to a better understanding of Shakespeare's text and language'. His own desiderata are 'the fullest possible array of information for the reader and at the same time ... a coherent text' and he states his intention to include all of the linguistic material, to be faithful to his chosen texts and to present his material so that reference from the concordances to the text and cross-reference within the concordances shall be as easy as possible.

The first five concordances may appropriately be considered in terms of this three-fold intention. All five are based on the First Folio and include all verbal material in it except head titles, running titles and catchwords. Stage directions are included, also speech prefixes and the 'Names of the Actors' attached to four of the plays, all of which are omitted from the Spevack volumes. It is the editor's realistic expectation that errors and omissions will be found, but a spot-check on arbitrarily selected pages and passages has revealed none and the comparison of some sections with Bartlett shows how often his record was incomplete, although it also raises admiration for the accuracy with which he carried out his task unaided by computers. On pages each of which contains some forty to fifty entries the average number of entries not also in Bartlett is in the region of from five to seven. Many of these are occurrences of common words of which Bartlett only claimed to record selected uses, others come from stage directions or from groups of words, such as the Latin of William's

[1] *Oxford Shakespeare Concordances*, edited by Dr T. H. Howard-Hill: *The Tempest; The Two Gentlemen of Verona; The Merry Wives of Windsor; Measure for Measure; The Comedy of Errors* (Oxford, 1969).

[2] XXII (1969), 143–64.

lesson in *Merry Wives*, Act IV, scene i, which he elected to omit. Very common words, specified in the introductions, are recorded only by numerical totals of instances, others by line reference only without quotation of context.

The fidelity of the concordances to their basic texts is likely, paradoxically, to lessen their appeal to all but the most serious investigators, although it greatly increases their utility for the textual and linguistic studies they are designed to further. Editorial interference has been limited to the exclusion of any accidental feature of the text which could not be translated for use on the computer, e.g. irregularities of spacing, the expansion (with note) of abbreviations and the correction of undoubted misprints, unless these produce feasible verbal forms, e.g. 'gold' for 'cold'. All corrections which are not merely mechanical are listed in the introductions. Asterisks are used throughout to designate all type-lines in the original text, whether in prose or verse, which fill the printer's measure and which are accordingly the most likely lines to include spellings introduced by compositors for justification.

The third of Howard-Hill's intentions is less consistently attained, at least on the evidence of the present volumes. Here he has to pay the penalty for using a method of compiling his concordances unprecedented in its speed and accuracy but correspondingly inflexible in some of its procedures. The persevering user will not have too much trouble with the adoption of through line numbering, geared to that of the *Shakespeare Quarto Facsimiles* and of the Norton facsimile of the First Folio—once firmly established, this system need never be altered—but the necessity of adopting complete type-lines as units leads to the printing of some very awkward and unhelpful contexts. For instance, Bartlett's context for 'regress' at *Merry Wives*, II, i, 226, is 'Thou shalt have egress and regress;—said I well?', which provides a useful stylistic setting for the use of the word and especially a link with 'egress' that is not afforded by Howard-Hill's entry:

REGRESSE—*I

*regresse, (said I well?) and thy name shall be *Broome*. It 748.

More disturbing, because more potentially productive of error, is the practice of listing all orthographic forms as separate entries, thus placing some variant spellings far apart and regularly producing such sequences of entry as RECEIUD, RECEIUE, RECEIUED, and that of including homographs of different etymology, semantic value or grammatical function under a single heading, so that in *Two Gentlemen of Verona* 'tide' and 'tied' are both listed under TIDE. Cross references are indeed given from the modern spelling where a given word occurs only in an unfamiliar earlier form, but such cross references are not invariably supplied from an entry under one frequent spelling to entries of all other spellings of the same word. Such cross references would seem to be indispensable if the practical difficulties of programming forbid the listing of various old spellings under a single heading in modern spelling. A few examples, again from *Merry Wives*, will illustrate some of the problems. No cross reference is given between WELCH (p. 267) and WELSH (pp. 269–70); MAKE-A-THETURD is also entered under its components, excepting THE but including A, while 'quoth'a' is not recorded under A; a modern-spelling entry (or the nearest the computer can get to one in upper case) RAGGD, for 'ragg'd', directs the reader to 'rag'd', where the relevant entry is listed under RAGD-HORNES, but there is no equivalent entry pointing to RAMD, 'ramm'd'. It is to be hoped that the editor will find ways of eliminating even such minor discrepancies from later volumes in a series which, once complete, should never need to be superseded.

So long as he is dealing with plays which

survive in a single substantive text, Howard-Hill's concordances will be of great utility to editors and to textual and linguistic scholars. Doubts arise, however, about the treatment of plays extant in collateral substantive texts, and we must hope both that it will prove feasible to record the variant readings of the rejected text, especially for *Troilus and Cressida*, *Othello*, *Hamlet*, *Richard III* and *King Lear*, and that the Clarendon Press will go on to complete the project in the manner envisaged by the editor in an earlier published statement:

> In the same way that the concordances should assist Dr. Walker in the Clarendon Old-spelling edition, as the volumes of her edition are published, the texts on magnetic tape will be amended with the readings adopted in her edition, and the Clarendon Press will publish a one-volume old-spelling concordance; this concordance will incorporate variant readings.[1]

Presumably the Oxford concordance to *Richard III* will be based on the text of the Folio, the orthodox choice as copy-text at least since D. L. Patrick argued at length, in *The Textual History of 'Richard III'*, that the Quarto text is reported. Among recent defenders of the Quarto, none has given more detailed attention to the question than Kristian Smidt, who now follows his monograph of 1964[2] with a handsome type facsimile edition of the Quarto and Folio texts of *Richard III* in parallel.[3] Like the concordances, this book is principally a tool for future editors: its intention is to provide a fuller and more accurate account of the transmission of the text of *Richard III* through the eight Quartos between 1597 and 1634 and the First Folio than has hitherto been available.

In a short introduction, Smidt describes his aims and reveals his view of the Quarto text, whose variants he thinks deserve more serious consideration than they have received from editors who consider it to be reported. He disclaims any intention of entering into the controversy about the identity of the Quarto used as copy for the Folio (not unexpectedly in view of his own earlier statement in favour of manuscript copy for the Folio, 'supported by Q3 and Q6'). He then describes his methods for presenting the two texts in parallel while preserving the page layout of the Quarto and as much as possible of the typographic character of the Folio. In view of the very many major discrepancies between the texts, an elaborate set of symbols and cross references has been devised to enable the reader to see at once the nature and extent of the differences. This system is efficient, though sometimes obtrusive to little end, as for instance at III, i, 1 in the Quarto text, where the introduction of a blank line from the Folio separates the two halves of a turned-over line, stranding '(ber.' two lines above 'cham-'. The introduction ends with a census of copies of the six Quartos published before the Folio, describing the condition of each copy and listing substantive press variants in each edition. A surprising feature of the descriptions of the Quartos is the use of very imprecise collational formulæ and the lack of reference to Greg's *Bibliography*. Even more surprisingly, the editor says nothing of the printing of the texts he is editing, although the division of the first Quarto between two printing houses and of the Folio text between two compositors is surely of interest and importance to users of such an edition.

The collations of the Quartos are both fuller and more accurate in detail than those of the Old Cambridge edition, but the exclusion of certain categories of variant, listed on pages 12–13, reduces their usefulness for close study of the history of the text. The rationale of the exclusions is hard to determine: it bears some

1 *Shakespeare Newsletter*, XVII (1967), 33–4.

2 *Iniurious Impostors and 'Richard III'* (Norwegian Universities Press, 1964).

3 William Shakespeare, *The Tragedy of King Richard the Third. Parallel Texts of the First Quarto and the First Folio with Variants of the Early Quartos*, edited by Kristian Smidt (Oslo; New York, 1969).

relation to a distinction between substantive and accidental variants, but the inclusion of, for instance, spelling variants in proper names, when other spelling variants are excluded unless they are associated with substantive variation, falls outside this pattern. Exigencies of space may have made some exclusions necessary, but they materially restrict the range of utility of the lists and one is left wondering why so meticulous a preservation of typographical detail as is given for the recorded variants should be of interest to readers assumed to have no interest in variants consisting only of similar details. Happily, no such reservations need be made about the parallel texts themselves which make the different characters of the Quarto and the Folio more easily and directly comparable than hitherto.

The reprinting of the New Arden Shakespeare for publication in paperback continues. This year's reprints are of *Titus Andronicus*, edited by J. C. Maxwell (1968), the three parts of *Henry VI*, edited by A. S. Cairncross, *The Poems*, edited by F. T. Prince, *Timon of Athens*, edited by H. J. Oliver and *Pericles*, edited by F. D. Hoeniger (all 1969). *Titus*, which has been reset to incorporate earlier additions, and *Pericles*, of which this is the first reprint, contain a few new corrections and additions.

The latest New Arden volume is Clifford Leech's edition of *The Two Gentlemen of Verona*,[1] a play whose fortunes have been various in the sixty-three years since R. W. Bond's Old Arden edition, but which remains among the least applauded of Shakespeare's works. In 1969 its star is in the ascendant, with two new editions,[2] two professional stage productions, in Regent's Park and at Stratford, and a single-volume concordance.

Professor Leech's edition is on the scale we have come to expect of the New Arden series, very fully annotated and with a substantial and stimulating introduction. His view of the text is complicated and involves a lengthy discussion of the play's internal inconsistencies, in which he finds evidence of stratification of composition, holding, in particular, that 'the case for seeing the Launce-section of the play as a result of second thoughts seems considerable'. The case is closely argued and may carry conviction if one accepts the basic postulate that the inconsistencies in *The Two Gentlemen* are so glaring as to constitute a special case among Shakespeare's plays. Leech is the first to admit the possibility of alternative explanations of the details which he has listed and gives ample space to the dissenting voice of his general editor, Dr Harold Brooks, who finds it easier to account for Shakespeare's inconsistencies of locality and of title for Silvia's father (now Emperor, now Duke of Milan) by reference to his known narrative sources and associative habits of mind. The editors are agreed on one essential point, that the copy for the Folio was a transcript from Shakespeare's 'foul papers'.

A full discussion of sources extends to the wider association of the play with 'love and friendship' literature and with narrative romance. The stage history affords evidence and prepares the ground for Leech's handling of Valentine's renunciation of Silvia as a crux of criticism and interpretation. His own view of the final scene is consonant with his general contention that 'the play... has its own degree of complexity'. He finds this complexity partly in Shakespeare's discreet but pervasive burlesquing of dramatic and romantic convention, arguing ably for subtlety in the dénouement where many critics have found bathos or artistic ineptitude. Willingly though one would welcome a vindication of the ending of *The Two Gentlemen*, two reservations remain. The first arises from Leech's own account of the

[1] London, 1969.

[2] Also *The Two Gentlemen Of Verona*, edited by Norman Saunders (Harmondsworth, 1968).

composition and transmission of the text: can we imagine Shakespeare, in one and the same play, as careless of consistency of detail to an unparallelled extent and at the same time as exercising the 'careful and, within its limits, subtle dramaturgy' posited to claim the final scene as a successful exercise in detached sophistication? The second is more fundamental: the weakness of the final scene is a verbal and imaginative weakness; that it is perfunctory rather than sophisticated is argued by the flatness and conventionality of its key speeches, especially those of Proteus. Wishing to vindicate *The Two Gentlemen*, Leech has perhaps tended to argue for an overall artistic achievement comparable with its seminal nature and outstanding interest as a document of Shakespeare's apprenticeship in comedy. A play need not be successful to be seminal, although this seems to be implied by the sentence, 'If it were as poor a thing as has been commonly thought, he would have been less likely to take so many hints from it in the eight years or so subsequent to its writing'. At least it might be objected, on the evidence of his later avoidance of the 'love and friendship' conflict, that Shakespeare was aware of some unresolved difficulties in the play.

By contrast, and within the narrower limits imposed by the layout of the New Penguin Shakespeare, Norman Saunders presents a more conventional estimate of *The Two Gentlemen*, laying stress upon its early date and experimental nature. His treatment of the sources is flawed by several inaccuracies of fact: *Felix and Philiomena* was acted in 1585, not 1595, and Antony Mundy's Huntingdon plays were written too late to have been among Shakespeare's sources. A contrast between Proteus, deceived by appearances, and Valentine, concerned with the essence, though tactfully developed, seems too neat and certainly disregards the extent to which the overall impression of the two gentlemen is of Proteus' cleverness and perceptiveness and of Valentine's stupidity and blindness to what lies beneath his nose. The final scene is defused by adducing historical considerations to reduce the shock of Valentine's behaviour. Saunders is at his best on the relation between the main plot and the comic scenes, which 'do not simply satirize and belittle the love and friendship codes subscribed to in the main plot but ... are the method whereby the characters in the central love situation are shown in terms of a reality which exists even though they ignore it'.

Less convincing is his account of the Folio text as a shortened version of the play. Of the many features of the text listed as evidence of abridgement only two, Proteus' enigmatic reference to Silvia's 'picture' at II, iv, 207, and perhaps the baldness and rapidity of the final action, cannot be more plausibly accounted for by invoking 'foul papers' behind the copy for the Folio. Both Arden and Penguin texts necessarily stick close to the Folio, differing from each other most often in the placing of additional stage directions and also occasionally in the lining of verse. Of the two editors, Leech is generally the more conservative in accidentals as well as in substantive readings, although he rightly accepts Marshall's 'wind' at III, ii, 49, where Saunders retains the Folio's 'weed', on the very good grounds that 'A regular feature of this play is the taking up of a word from one speech to another'.

By contrast with other recent New Penguins, Saunders' list of 'Further Reading' may seem hardly selective enough for the guidance of the general or undergraduate reader. Editors of forthcoming volumes will be able to simplify their task at this point by referring their readers to Stanley Wells' *Shakespeare: A Reading Guide*[1] for standard works both on general Shakespearian topics and on particular plays or groups of plays.

[1] The English Association (London, 1969).

The swing away from critical positions until recently orthodox is apparent in the introductions to the other three new volumes in the New Penguin Shakespeare.[1] J. M. Nosworthy discusses *Measure for Measure* squarely in terms of comic traditions, though allowing that 'no single term seems adequately to cover all that it achieves'; Stanley Wells presents *Richard II* as a stage-play in its own right rather than as a piece in the 'grand design' of Shakespeare's histories; and Ernest Schanzer firmly anchors *The Winter's Tale* to human character and motive with some patent distrust for those critical approaches which pin their faith on the uncovering of an 'inner meaning' in it. Specialists may wish to question some details. Is *Woodstock* certainly of earlier date than *Richard II*? Is it helpful to speak of the Duke as the 'hero' of *Measure for Measure*? Are there substantial grounds for referring to *The Winter's Tale* as 'what may be Shakespeare's last play written without a collaborator'? But the general reader will be well supplied with relevant information by each of these essays and will be led towards each play as an acting text.

Textually, *Measure for Measure* offers more problems than the other plays. The state of the Folio text is explained by Nosworthy as resulting from setting by four compositors from a transcript, probably by Ralph Crane, of 'an untidy, and possibly imperfected, Shakespearian draft which had suffered a measure of deterioration'. He is accordingly readier to emend than some editors of the play and has a number of new suggestions, not all in notoriously difficult passages. A few of these result from his stated principle, that 'metrically defective lines may readily be attributed to Crane or the compositors, but, under no circumstances, to Shakespeare'. Sometimes, for instance at I, i, 50; II, ii, 3 and V, i, 256, the metrical adjustments seem unnecessary and the rearrangement of II, iv, 112–13, so that line 112 ends 'is', rather than 'mercy', only apparently increases the smoothness of that line and creates a problem of stress in line 113 which the Folio arrangement avoids. But these are details, and elsewhere the editor's determination to print a text that makes sense has led to interesting or convincing emendations. The reinstatement of 'God' for 'Heaven' is thoroughly carried out and yields a certain improvement in 'God in my mouth, As if I did but only chew His name'; 'an' for 'and' at I, ii, 171, 'then' for 'them' at II, i, 196, and 'or' for 'for' at IV, iii, 8, are seemingly trivial alterations or restorations all of which remove slight rubs and yield satisfactory sense. Nosworthy's suggestions for the major cruxes, 'brakes of Ice', II, i, 39, and 'prenzie', III, i, 97 and 100, are, respectively, 'brakes of office', a phrase which he sees as indicating that Escalus is speaking of the Duke rather than of Angelo, and 'precise' for the first 'prenzie', which is familiar, 'precious' for the second, which is not, and which is offered more tentatively in the awareness that it is a less likely source of the compositorial misreading. Unlike the other New Penguin editors, Nosworthy does not list emendations which he has not accepted, thereby concealing the frequency with which he has restored the readings of the Folio in passages usually emended: these include, 'mortality', I, ii, 133; 'weeds', I, iii, 20; 'yond generation', IV, iii, 87 and 'reliver', IV, iv, 5, all of which are discussed in the commentary.

The theatrical orientation of Wells' *Richard II*, clear in his introduction, is maintained in the commentary, which also contains a useful scene-by-scene account of Shakespeare's handling of his chronicle sources. His conservative editing is justified by his view of the text: the first Quarto of 1597 'seems to have been

[1] *Measure for Measure*, edited by J. M. Nosworthy; *Richard II*, edited by Stanley Wells; *The Winter's Tale*, edited by Ernest Schanzer (Harmondsworth, 1969).

printed from [Shakespeare's] own manuscript, and with an unusually high standard of accuracy', but the Folio is the best source for stage directions and necessarily the basic text for IV, i, 154–319, the abdication scene, omitted from all the Elizabethan Quartos, and printed in a poor memorial text in those of 1608 and 1615. The collation lists, though accurate, are not presented with total consistency of layout, and a note explaining that the absence of a siglum at the right of the bracket in the first list indicates that the reading is that of all early editions not otherwise specified would save the reader a moment's confusion.

The reassertion of rational norms in the face of tortuous subtlety or mystical enthusiasm which marks Schanzer's introduction to *The Winter's Tale* is likewise apparent in his commentary, which gives short shrift to the wilder fancies of the hunters after ambiguity, if only by exclusion. Perhaps he runs the risk of omitting to indicate the full ironic force of some lines, especially in the speeches of Leontes in the early acts. The meaning of 'All's true that is mistrusted', II, i, 48, is not exhausted by the gloss 'all one's suspicions prove to be true': by this point in the play we are aware that Leontes' mistrust is tantamount to evidence of 'truth', in the sense of honesty or fidelity, especially in Hermione, but also in Polixenes and Camillo, to whom the line relates more directly. The Folio text is accepted as a good one, printed from copy that 'seems to have been a transcript made by Ralph Crane', and Schanzer's handling of it combines trust in it with the confidence to depart from it when he finds good reason to do so, which he does in some forty places. Like some other editors for the series, he is prepared to extend the principle of modernization to verbal forms, reading 'its' for 'it' in two places, as well as removing misprints and certainly erroneous readings.

It is to be regretted that the three New Penguins with songs in them do not all follow the earlier practice of printing the earliest musical setting in an appendix. Schanzer does include F. W. Sternfeld's transcriptions of the surviving seventeenth-century settings for three of the six songs in *The Winter's Tale*, but John Wilson's setting of 'Take, O take those lips away', published in 1652, is not included in Nosworthy's *Measure for Measure*, perhaps on the grounds that it could not have been the version used in the original production, while Saunders' omission of a setting for 'Who is Silvia?' is presumably explained by the lack of any known setting earlier than 1727.

The problems of presenting Shakespeare attractively and intelligibly to readers without a specialist interest are sensibly tackled by the New Penguins, whose editors manage to be selective and decisive while generally avoiding the risks of dogmatism and of oversimplification of issues. The ever-increasing problem of mere comprehension is reflected in a volume of a comparable new American series, Maurice Charney's edition of *Julius Caesar*.[1] As the author of a study of the style of Shakespeare's Roman plays, Charney is particularly well-equipped to elucidate what is not, in any case, a very obscure text for readers unfamiliar with the idiom of the sixteenth century and his comments on the Roman style of *Julius Caesar* will have an interest for more experienced readers.

In his introduction, he considers the play's political and historical themes, stressing connections with the English histories and drawing attention to the complexity of the issues and the multiplicity of the characters' responses to them. His brief section on *Julius Caesar* as a revenge tragedy is less convincing, if only because of the vagueness of the label, which encourages such general comments as 'Only in revenge tragedy can the dead win so decisively over the living'. Problems of staging

1 *The Tragedy of Julius Caesar*, edited by Maurice Charney (Indianapolis; New York, 1969).

occupy a large section of the introduction and appendices contain lengthy excerpts from North's Plutarch, an account of Shakespeare's English, illustrated from the play, and a brief stage-history, including photographs from stage and film productions.

The text sticks close to the Folio, which is sensible, but conservatism is carried too far, especially in a popular edition, when mislinings of verse and misspellings of characters' names are preserved on 'the unequivocal evidence of the Folio'. '*Murellus*' may be Shakespeare's version of the name Marullus, and a case could be made for retaining it, but the sporadic incidence of the forms '*Antonio*', '*Octavio*', '*Flavio*' and '*Claudio*' is more likely to be explained by the compositors' shortage of ligatured italic *us* types, as described by Charlton Hinman,[1] than as Shakespeare's usage of 'colloquial variants of the more formal Latin nominatives': such forms should probably still be regularized as '*Antonius*', etc. The usual problems of modernization arise: is 'wafter' really more current than 'wafture', or 'a clock' than 'o'clock'? The commentary, which avoids problems of interpretation, is full and informative and is conveniently located on the text page.

No article in volume XXII of *Studies in Bibliography* is devoted exclusively to the text of Shakespeare, but there are two papers of very different scope and aims which have an important bearing on Shakespearian studies. T. H. Howard-Hill's account of the Oxford concordances has already been discussed above. D. F. McKenzie's extended essay which opens the volume, 'Printers of the Mind: Some Notes on Bibliographical Theories and Printing-House Practices',[2] follows from his history of *The Cambridge University Press, 1696–1712*.[3] In the preface to the earlier work, McKenzie stressed the wider implications of his detailed account of the work of the Cambridge University Press during its first sixteen years:

> its basic demonstration that the organization of work on any one book is meaningful only in relation to the work of the printing house as a whole suggests that the context of much bibliographical analysis needs to be somewhat wider than it has been.

The present essay discusses the nature of bibliographical analysis and comments on some recent examples in the light of documentary evidence for the practices of early printing houses. McKenzie's broad plea is for the replacement of inductive by deductive method in analytical bibliography, on the grounds that 'any general laws derived by the inductive method remain highly vulnerable to fresh evidence. Where the known particulars are few,' as is the case with early printing-house conditions, 'this risk will be greatest'.

Using documentary evidence relating both to the Cambridge University Press and to the Bowyers' printing house between 1730 and 1739, he calls in question fundamental assumptions about 'normal' conditions which underlie much recent work in bibliographical analysis. Topics handled in the central section of the essay include the use of compositors' measures, running titles and skeleton formes as evidence about the process of printing a given book; composition by formes in folio and quarto printing; proof-correction, and press figures. In each instance press records are used to challenge the neatness and logical simplicity of conclusions inductively derived from particular categories of evidence. Most important, and in McKenzie's opinion as relevant to the late sixteenth and early seventeenth centuries as to the period from which he draws his detailed evidence, is his demonstration that

> both at Cambridge and in the Bowyers' shop, books were produced concurrently. This meant not only that several books were in production at the same time but that each workman, whether at press or case, was often engaged on several books more or less at once.

[1] *The Printing and Proof-Reading of the First Folio of Shakespeare* (Oxford, 1963), II, 173–4.

[2] Pp. 1–76.

[3] Cambridge, 1966.

This fact is used to call in question, for example, prevalent assumptions about the relation of composition to press-work, and consequently to cast doubt on all analyses of printing which depend on a simple and consistent relation between them. Several Shakespearian examples are used. In particular, Hinman's conclusions about the printing of the First Folio are held up to a scrutiny whose main textual implications lie in McKenzie's vindication of the thoroughness and accuracy of Jaggard's correction of proofs. He points out that the surviving evidence for proof-correction in the Folio is limited almost exclusively to stop-press correction, the third of the processes of correction as described by Moxon and other early writers, which was mainly a final check to remove typographical blemishes. Hinman's 'full record of the press variants' should rather be described as 'a full record of the *surviving* press variants', and Jaggard should be freed from the imputation of having taken little care to correct the text of Shakespeare's plays 'whether with or without benefit of some kind of printed proof'.[1] The full implications of McKenzie's argument will not be quickly exhausted and debate is likely to continue about many of his specific contentions, but no bibliographer engaged in the analysis of early printed texts can afford to ignore this article.

While McKenzie calls bibliographers to a stocktaking, Ernest Leisi issues an exhortation to philologists in an address delivered to the Deutsche Shakespeare-Gesellschaft West at Bochum on 23 April 1967.[2] Surveying the history of the editing of Shakespeare, he draws attention both to cautionary examples of lack of rigour and of historical method and to selected achievements of philologists in retrieving the authentic sense of Shakespeare's lines. Neither his position nor his choice of examples is unfamiliar, but his emphasis on the insidious dangers of seemingly easy words in Shakespeare whose sense today is not what it was three and a half centuries ago can never be untimely. He makes a particularly telling point about the misinterpretation of the word 'closet' in *Hamlet* as 'bed-chamber', whose theatrical consequence—the prominent presence of Gertrude's bed on stage in III, iv—has lent specious support to the depth-psychologizing of Hamlet's relationship with his mother.

In a paper which ill-health prevented him from delivering to the International Shakespeare Conference at Stratford-upon-Avon in September 1968, the late Professor Peter Alexander makes a last contribution to the controversy about the endings of *The Taming of the Shrew* and *The Taming of a Shrew*.[3] With characteristic incisiveness he argues for the authenticity of the last appearance of Christopher Sly in *A Shrew*, rejecting Richard Hosley's contention that it is the invention of a reporter rather than Shakespeare's original ending for his play, with which he effects a final transition from play to reality. He concludes:

> Shakespeare, some time before the closing of the theaters in 1592, wrote *The Shrew* for Pembroke's men. He had then at his disposal a company of considerable size that would allow the tinker and his aristocratic attendants to sit and watch the Shrew piece. The Quarto is a piracy that reports however imperfectly the conclusion that was originally played in these pre-1592 years. Later the Sly business was cut down as too demanding in personnel.

J. W. R. Meadowcroft[4] argues that most modern editors of *Merry Wives* have had insufficient grounds for following Capell's conflation of the Quarto and the Folio at I, iv,

[1] Hinman, *Printing and Proof-Reading of the First Folio*, I, 288, n. 2.

[2] 'Vom Dienst des Philologen an Shakespeares Wort', *Deutsche Shakespeare-Gesellschaft West Jahrbuch* (1968), 13–27.

[3] 'The Original Ending of *The Taming of the Shrew*', *Shakespeare Quarterly*, XX (1969), 111–16.

[4] 'The Physiognomy of Master Abraham Slender', *Notes and Queries*, N.S. XVI (1969), 134–5.

22, 'a little whey-face', in preference to the Folio's 'a little wee-face'. *OED* cites a further early seventeenth-century use of 'wee' and the context does not support the assumption that Peter Simple wishes to denigrate the courage of his master, Abraham Slender. John W. Velz[1] draws attention to fifteen sophisticated readings in *Julius Caesar* in the 1909 Methuen facsimile of the Second Folio and lists press variants in two formes of the same play. Adam A. Mendilow[2] proposes to repunctuate *The Winter's Tale*, IV, iv, 131–2, reading 'Not like a Coarse: or if not: to be buried,/But quicke, and in mine armes.' for the Folio's 'Not like a Coarse: or if: . . .'. Although this change slightly improves the logic of the passage, his claim that 'The passage now takes on new poetic qualities' seems exaggerated. J. C. Arens[3] describes what may be 'the oldest printed translation of a work of Shakespeare'. 'De vyerighe liefde vande Godinne Venus, tot den Jonghelingh Adonis', published at The Hague in 1621, contains a version of lines 1–810 of *Venus and Adonis* in Dutch alexandrines by an unnamed 'amateur of Rhetorica', followed by two poems by I. W. vander Niss, not based on Shakespeare, on the despair of Venus and the death of Adonis. 'The unnamed translator understood the English text tolerably well.'

[1] 'The Text of *Julius Caesar* in the Second Folio: Two Notes', *Shakespeare Quarterly*, XX (1969), 95–8.

[2] 'Two Notes on Shakespeare: A. Perdita's Living Corpse', *Studies in the Drama*, edited by Arieh Sachs, *Scripta Hierosolymitana*, XIX (Jerusalem, 1967), 262–5.

[3] 'Shakespeare's *Venus and Adonis* (1–810): A Dutch Translation Printed in 1621', *Neophilologus*, LII (1968), 421–30.

INDEX

INDEX

INDEX

INDEX